AMERICA'S

SCENIC DRIVES

TRAVEL GUIDE
& ATLAS

Published by:
Roundabout Publications
2767 S. Parker Rd., Suite 240
Aurora, CO 80014

Please Note

Every effort has been made to make this book as complete and as accurate as possible. However, there may be mistakes both typographical and in content. Therefore, this text should be used as a general guide to the scenic drives covered. Although we regret any inconvenience caused by inaccurate information, the author and Roundabout Publications shall have neither liability nor responsibility to any person or entity with respect to any loss or damage caused, or alleged to be caused, directly or indirectly by the information contained in this book.

Library of Congress Catalog Card Number: 97-65806

ISBN: 1-885464-28-2

Publisher's Cataloging in Publication
(Prepared by Quality Books Inc.)

Herow, William C.
   America's scenic drives: travel guide & atlas / William C. Herow
   p. cm.
   Includes index.
   LCCN: 97-65806
   ISBN: 1-885464-28-2

   1. Scenic byways—United States—Guidebooks. 2. Scenic byways—United States—Atlases. 3. Automobile travel—United States—Guidebooks. 4. Automobile travel—United States—Atlases. I. Title

E158.H47 1997   917.304'929
                                                                        QBI97-40375

TABLE OF CONTENTS

Colorado

Connecticut

Florida

Georgia

Idaho

INTRODUCTION

America's Best

America is linked by a vast network of roads, nearly 4 million miles of roads. And most of those roads are not four lanes of concrete carrying fast moving vehicles. They're roads that twist and turn, conforming to the curves dictated by the river that flows beside it. They're roads that cut a path through canyons and dense forests. They are roads that take you across mountain tops, to fishing holes, and small towns.

This book describes some of those roads. These scenic drives can take you through that canyon or forest, only to find that there are many other side roads inviting you to drive on them. You can ride on a mountain top, and see other mountain tops tempting you to "discover" them too. And there are plenty of these roads that lead to a great fishing hole or a secluded spot for a picnic. In other words, the scenic drives described in this book are among the best America has to offer.

Whatever your pleasure, however you decide to move, by car, motorcycle, or recreational vehicle, this book is your guide to the scenic drives of America. Get off the interstate and take some time to explore and experience the America we are proud to call home!

About The Scenic Drives

On January 28, 1985, President Ronald Reagan established the President's Commission on Americans Outdoors. The Commission was to review public and private outdoor recreational opportunities and make recommendations to ensure the future availability of outdoor recreation for the American people.

The results of the study found that 43% of American adults identified driving for pleasure as a favorite leisure pursuit, second only to walking. In response to these findings, several scenic byway programs were born.

National Forest Scenic Byways

In 1988 the U.S. Forest Service (USFS) began designating routes as *National Forest Scenic Byways*. The Forest Service administers more than 190 million acres of public lands in 156 forests across the country. The officially designated byways represent the very best scenic routes from over 100,000 miles of roads that run through the national forests.

The recreational opportunities found along these byways are numerous. Developed recreation areas and campgrounds are located along most of the routes. Camping may also be permitted anywhere within the national forest for those interested in a more primitive setting. Many of the national forests also have areas designated for off-road vehicle use, mountain biking, hunting, hiking, horseback riding, boating, fishing, and backpacking.

BLM Back Country Byways

The Bureau of Land Management manages more than 270 million acres of public lands, over 40% of all federal land. Their *Back Country Byways* program, born in 1989, provides a unique opportunity for traveling the more remote areas and back roads of America.

Recreational opportunities found along these routes are in the form of primitive camping, bicycling, four-wheeling, fishing in lakes and rivers, or simply enjoying an afternoon picnic and the solitude. Many of the byways provide developed campgrounds, however, camping is permitted nearly anywhere on BLM administered lands.

Since many of the Back Country Byways travel through remote countryside, it is always a good idea to be prepared for your journey. Carry plenty of water for you and for your vehicle's radiator. Be sure to start each trip with enough gasoline to drive the entire route. It is also a good idea to have a spare tire, jack, shovel, blanket, and tools for emergency road repairs.

Many of these byways become impassable during winter or after periods of heavy rainfall, so it's a good idea to inquire about the current road conditions and any possible limitations for your type of vehicle before attempting to travel the route.

The Back Country Byways have been classified into four types for determining the level of difficulty, road surface, and type of vehicle required to travel them. Listed below are descriptions of each classification.

Type I - Roads that are paved or have an all-weather surface and have grades that are negotiable by a normal touring car. These roads are usually narrow, slow speed, secondary roads.

Type II - These roads require a high-clearance type vehicle such as a truck or four-wheel drive. These roads are usually unpaved but may have some type of surfacing. Grades, curves, and road surface are such that they can be negotiated with a two-wheel drive high-clearance vehicle without undue difficulty.

Type III - These are roads that require a four-wheel drive vehicle or other specialized vehicle such as a dirt bike or all-terrain vehicle (ATV). These roads are usually not surfaced, but are managed to provide for safety considerations and resource protection needs. They have grades, tread surfaces, and other characteristics that require specialized vehicles to negotiate.

Type IV - These are trails managed specifically to accommodate dirt bikes, mountain bikes, snowmobiles, or all-terrain vehicles. These are usually single track trails.

National Scenic Byways & All-American Roads

The National Scenic Byways Program was established under the Intermodal Surface Transportation Efficiency Act of 1991 (ISTEA). The Scenic Byways Advisory Committee, working with the Federal Highway Administration, recommended that the program designate a system of National Scenic Byways and All American Roads.

National Scenic Byways are chosen by the Secretary of Transportation for their scenic, historic, natural, cultural, recreational, or archaeological qualities. *All-American Roads* are also chosen for the same qualities but are considered to be the "best of the best." These scenic byways represent the finest examples of scenic drives in America, making them "destinations unto themselves." In 1996, the first 20 byways were designated.

National Parkways

The National Park Service has designated four routes as *National Parkways*. Initial efforts for funding *Parkways* began as early as 1930. Today, these ribbons of land flanking the designated roadways offer an opportunity for a leisurely drive through areas of scenic and historical interest.

About This Book

This book will provide you with a wealth of information on traveling America's best scenic drives. Understanding how to use the information presented will help you fully reap the benefits that this information provides.

The name for each scenic byway is given at the top of the page with a map of the route directly beneath its name. A location map in the right corner shows the general location of the byway within the state. The legend along the side and bottom of the map provides information on the icons used. Details for each scenic drive is divided into five headings for easy reference. The following is a brief description of each heading.

Route Location: This provides the general location of the route, usually in perspective to a major city and indicates the scenic drive's starting and ending points.

Roads Traveled: This section details the length, name, number and type of surface for the roads followed. This section may also warn you of any vehicle limitations such as length or type of vehicle. The agency who has officially designated the byway is also provided.

Travel Season: Most often the scenic drives are open year-round, however, this section provides information on possible road closures due to adverse weather conditions.

Description: This section provides a brief overview of the attractions and recreational opportunities that travelers will encounter along or near the route. Keep in mind this is not a complete listing of all the opportunities available. The opportunities are many and the information on them is free from the sources provided.

Nearby Routes: This simply informs you of any other scenic byways described in this book that are near the one you are traveling, usually within 50 miles. The page number follows the byway's name.

A sidebar with the heading *Local Information* is also provided for each scenic byway. Here you will find a list of addresses and phone numbers to contact for a free brochure or more information on each scenic drive. The list of local information also includes the address and phone number for state parks, national parks, and chambers of commerce. The chambers of commerce are excellent sources of information for the communities that the byway travels through or is near.

Lodging Directory

This special feature of *America's Scenic Drives* refers to the **Lodging Directory** located at the end of the book. It will assist you in locating the lodging opportunities available along and near the scenic byway. For more information please refer to page 430.

Helpful Tips

As you drive these scenic byways of America, you may occasionally come across sites of interest that seem to beg for closer examination. Many buildings or other attractions, however, may be located on private property. Please respect the rights of landowners and obtain their permission to enter their property before inspecting any sites of interest to you.

Many of the scenic drives will take you to sites of historic or archaeological significance, such as ancient Indian pictographs. It is better to enjoy the site and leave it undisturbed so that others may enjoy it. Take only pictures and leave only footprints!

When you find yourself on a scenic byway that is a one-lane mountain pass road, remember the rule of courtesy that gives the right of way to uphill traffic. And always use caution when approaching blind turns and be prepared for another vehicle around the bend.

Abbreviations Used Throughout This Book

BLM	Bureau of Land Management
CR	County Road
FDR	Forest Development Road
NBS	National Battlefield Site
NF	National Forest
NM	National Monument
NP	National Park
NRA	National Recreation Area
NRS	National Recreation Site
NRT	National Recreation Trail
NST	National Scenic Trail
NWR	National Wildlife Refuge
RA	Recreation Area
SH	State Highway
SHA	State Historic Area
SHM	State Historic Monument
SHP	State Historic Park
SHS	State Historic Site
SP	State Park
SRA	State Recreation Area
SRS	State Recreation Site

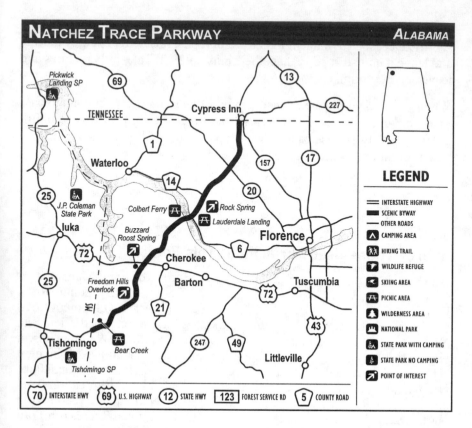

This historic route generally follows the old Indian trace, or trail, between Nashville, Tennessee and Natchez, Mississippi. By 1810, the trace was an important wilderness road and the most heavily traveled pass/trail in the Old Southwest.

Tennessee section see page 334 / Mississippi portion see page 199

Route Location

The Natchez Trace Parkway is a 445-mile drive between Natchez, Mississippi and Nashville, Tennessee. This portion of the Natchez Trace Parkway cuts across the northwestern corner of Alabama.

Roads Traveled

The Natchez Trace Parkway is a two-lane paved route that is suitable for all types of vehicles. This portion in Alabama is about 33 miles in length. The byway is designated a National Parkway by the National Park Service and an All-American Road by the Federal Highway Administration.

Travel Season

The route is open year-round.

Description

Once trekked by Indians and trampled into a rough road by traders, trappers, and missionaries, the Natchez Trace Parkway is now a scenic 445 mile road traveling from Natchez, Mississippi to Nashville, Tennessee. In the late 1700s and early 1800s, "Kaintucks," as the river merchants were called, would float downriver on flatboats loaded with their merchandise to be sold in New Orleans. Since there wasn't any practical way to return by river, the boats were dismantled and the lumber sold. The Natchez Trace would be the only pathway home. At that time, the Trace was a dangerous path to take. Travelers waded through swamps and swam streams and fended off attacks by wild animals and poisonous snakes, not to mention keeping an eye open for murderous bandits and Indian attacks. The terrain of the trace was rough, too. A broken leg of a lone traveler would often mean certain death. The dangers of the route earned the Trace the nickname "Devil's Backbone." Modern-day travelers don't have these dangers to face as they travel this historic route. Now you can safely travel the route in the comfort of your own vehicle.

Through the Alabama portion of the Natchez Trace, visitors are given the opportunity for relaxing recreational activities. Bear Creek, near the Mississippi state line, provides picnic facilities and access to the creek for canoe enthusiasts. Colbert Ferry, on the banks of the Tennessee River, has a picnic area, restrooms, telephone, and boat ramp. A ranger station is also located here, where George Colbert once operated a stand and ferry. Mr. Colbert is reported to have once charged Andrew Jackson $75,000 to ferry his army across the river. Lauderdale Landing is also a nice spot for a picnic.

If you have no time for a picnic, be sure to stop at the Freedom Hills Overlook where a steep ¼-mile trail leads you to the highest point of the parkway in Alabama. Also worth stopping for is the Buzzard Roost Spring area where an exhibit tells the story of Levi Colbert, a Chickasaw chief who owned a nearby stand. A short trail here leads to the spring. A nature trail follows Colbert Creek at the Rock Spring area, milepost 330, and will take about 20 minutes to complete.

Local Information

National Park Service
Natchez Trace Parkway
RR 1, NT- 143
Tupelo, MS 38801
Phone: 601-842-1572

Shoals Chamber of Commerce
201 S. Court St., 5th Floor
Florence, AL 35631
Phone: 205-764-4661

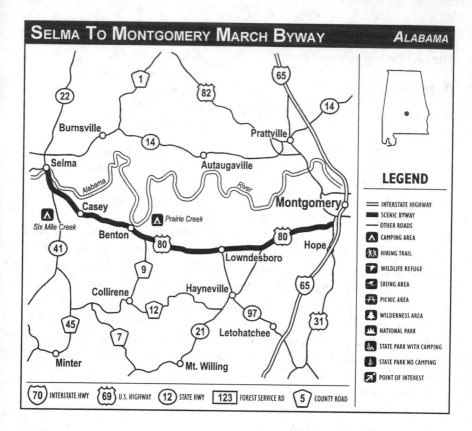

Route Location

This scenic byway is located in central Alabama and travels between the cities of Selma and Montgomery.

Roads Traveled

The 43-mile byway follows U.S. Highway 80, a four-lane divided highway suitable for travel by all types of vehicles. The route is designated an All-American Road by the Federal Highway Administration.

Travel Season

U.S. Highway 80 is open year-round.

Description

The Selma To Montgomery March Byway is more than a scenic drive, it celebrates one of the major historic events in 20th century American history. The Selma to Montgomery march represents two fundamental ideals of the

American people—democratic equality and nonviolent protest. It is also recognized as a catalyst for passage of the Voting Rights Act of 1965.

On March 7, 1965, more than 500 African-Americans determined to march arrived at Brown Chapel A.M.E. Church in Selma. Early that afternoon, the marchers left the church. When they reached the Edmund Pettus Bridge, the

Local Information

Selma - Dallas County C of C
513 Lauderdale St.
Selma, AL 36702
Phone: 334-875-7241

Montgomery Area C of C
41 Commerce St.
Montgomery, Al 36101
Phone: 334-834-5200

marchers could see state troopers waiting on the other side. The troopers blocked the road, just outside the city limits of Selma. The commander of the troopers declared that the march was unlawful and ordered the marchers to disperse. When they did not move, the troopers began to move toward the marchers and pushed them back with their billy clubs. Then suddenly, the troopers attacked by firing tear gas and striking marchers with their clubs. The two hospitals in Selma that admitted blacks reported 65 injuries from the attack. Footage of the attack was broadcast that evening on network television, outraging much of the Nation. Dr. Martin Luther King, Jr. urged clergy nationwide to come to Selma to join in a minister's march the following Tuesday.

On Tuesday, March 10, 1965, King and the group of ministers marched only to the site of the attack. When the ministers reached the line of troopers, they offered prayers and then turned around.

At about 1:15 p.m. on Sunday, March 21, about 3,000 marchers once again began the march to Montgomery. This time they had the protection of the National Guard. It was in Lowndes County that the march size was reduced to 300 and the road narrowed to two lanes. It was also in Lowndes that Stokely Carmichael began to speak to the African-Americans about registering to vote. On March 25, the marchers arrived at the state capitol in Montgomery where a platform had been erected for King and others to speak. The largest civil rights march ever to take place in the South had finally reached its destination.

Recreational opportunities are limited directly along the scenic byway, however, camping facilities can be found at Six Mile Creek on Dannelly Reservoir, and at Prairie Creek Park on Woodruff Lake. These Corps of Engineers projects also provide opportunities for water-related recreation.

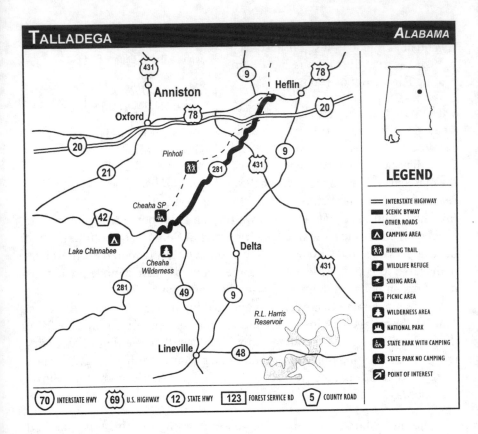

Route Location

The byway is located in east-central Alabama, approximately 70 miles east of Birmingham. The northern access starts just west of Heflin off U.S. Highway 78 and travels south through the Talladega National Forest to Cheaha State Park.

Roads Traveled

The Talladega scenic drive follows Alabama State Highway 281 which is a two-lane paved road suitable for all vehicles. The byway is approximately 23 miles in length. The route has been designated a National Forest Scenic Byway.

Travel Season

The Talladega scenic byway is open year-round.

Description

This scenic drive travels through the woodlands of the Talladega National Forest, offering spectacular views of the surrounding Appalachian Mountains. Travelers reach the highest point in Alabama, Cheaha Mountain at 2,407 feet above sea level, at the byway's end in Cheaha State Park. The state park offers opportunities for hiking, boating, swimming, fishing and camping.

Those that enjoy hiking or horseback riding will find several access points to the Pinhoti National Recreation Trail. The Cheaha Wilderness, situated south of the state park, also offers hiking, backpacking, and horseback riding opportunities in addition to hunting, fishing, and camping. Motorized vehicles and bicycles are prohibited in the wilderness area.

Local Information

National Forests In Alabama
2950 Chestnut St.
Montgomery, AL 36107
Phone: 334-832-4470

Cheaha State Park
Rt.1 - Box 77-H
Delta, AL 36258
Phone: 205-488-5111

Cleburne County Chamber of Commerce
P.O. Box 413
Heflin, AL 36264
Phone: 205-463-2222

Calhoun County Chamber of Commerce
1330 Quintard
Anniston, AL 36202
Phone: 205-237-3536

Clay County Chamber of Commerce
P.O. Box 85
Lineville, AL 36266
Phone: 205-396-2828

Talladega National Forest offers the visitor many developed recreation areas. There are two areas within the national forest that have been designated for off-road vehicle use, the Ivory Mountain and the Kentuck Mountain Off-Road Vehicle Areas. Coleman Lake, Lake Chinnabee, and Pine Glen Recreation Areas provide opportunities for camping, picnicking, fishing, hiking, and hunting.

Wildlife is abundant in this area. Careful observers may catch glimpses of white-tailed deer prancing through the forest. The bald eagle can also sometimes be seen soaring gracefully overhead. Other forms of wildlife inhabiting the region include bobwhite quail, gray and fox squirrel, turkey, rabbit, opossum, and various waterfowl.

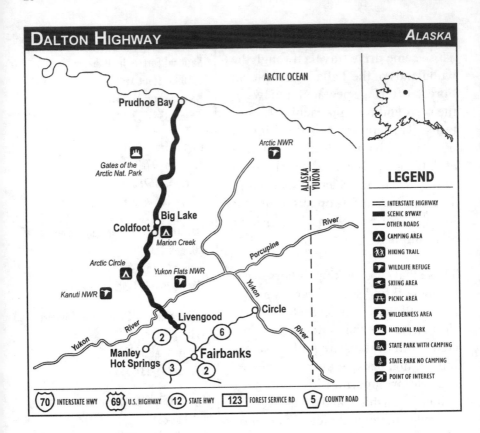

Route Location

The Dalton Highway is located in north-central Alaska, approximately 80 miles northwest of Fairbanks. The southern access starts in Livengood off State Highway 2 and travels north to Prudhoe Bay on the coast of the Arctic Ocean.

Roads Traveled

As its name implies, this scenic byway follows the Dalton Highway which is a rough, two-lane, gravel-surfaced road. The byway is approximately 417 miles in length and is suitable for travel by all types of vehicles. At times, the road can be very dusty or slippery, depending on the weather.

Travel Season

The route is generally open year-round although winter driving conditions can be hazardous and delays are possible.

Description

The Dalton Highway travels through some of the most remote and spectacular land in Alaska. It parallels the Trans-Alaska Pipeline from Livengood to the Arctic Ocean and is the only highway in Alaska where you can cross the Arctic Circle.

The Yukon River is crossed near the byway's southern end. This river is the fifth largest in North America, beginning in Canada and flowing 1,900 miles to the Bering Sea. The bridge spanning the river is 2,290 feet long and has a grade of six percent.

Coldfoot is an historic mining camp that was originally named Slate Creek for the creek that flows into the Koyukuk River. The name was later changed when early gold prospectors reached this point and got cold feet as winter set in and left the country. Old mining cabins located here are on private property, please respect them.

Most of the land along the route is undeveloped and offers a wealth of unusual and seldom-seen wildlife. Muskoxen may be seen from the highway north of the Brooks Range, the northernmost extension of the Rocky Mountains. Alaska natives call these animals "oomingmak," which means "the animal with skin like a beard."

Gasoline, food, a telephone, lodging, tire repair, and emergency towing are available at the Yukon River crossing area and in Coldfoot. Please note that there are no other services available between these two areas, a distance of 119 miles.

Nearby Routes

Richardson Highway, page 24

Local Information

BLM - Arctic District
1150 University Ave.
Fairbanks, AK 99709
Phone: 907-474-2300

Big Lake Chamber of Commerce
P.O. Box 520067
Big Lake, AK 99652
Phone: 907-892-6109

Greater Fairbanks C of C
546 9th Ave., #100
Fairbanks, AK 99701
Phone: 907-452-1105

Gates of the Arctic National Park
P.O. Box 74680
Fairbanks, AK 99707
Phone: 907-456-0281

Arctic, Kanuti & Yukon Flats NWR
P.O. Box 20
Fairbanks, AK 99701

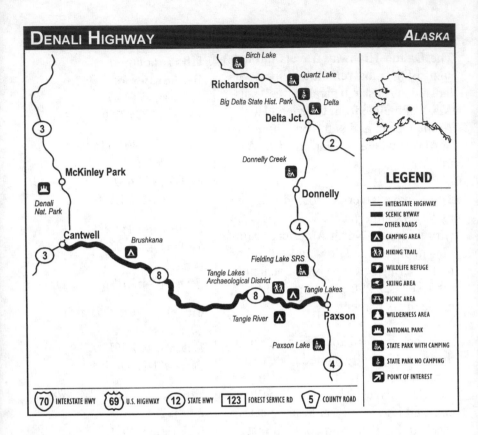

Route Location

Denali Highway is located in central Alaska, about 150 miles south of Fairbanks. The eastern access starts in Paxson off Alaska State Highway 4 and travels west to Cantwell near the entrance to Denali National Park and Preserve.

Roads Traveled

The 135-mile route follows Alaska State Highway 8 and is suitable for all vehicles. The first 21 miles west of Paxson travel over a paved surface with the remaining 114 miles traveling over a gravel-surfaced road. Currently, this highway is not an officially designated scenic byway.

Travel Season

Denali Highway is generally open from around late May to early October and then closed by heavy winter snows.

Description

The Denali Highway is the highest road in Alaska as it crosses the Maclaren summit at 4,086 feet. Traveling this route offers views of a variety of wildlife, spectacular scenery, and a glimpse into Alaska's past.

Wildlife inhabiting this area includes caribou, moose, bears, ptarmigan, and trumpeter swans. Lake trout and grayling can be found in the many lakes and streams along the highway. Salmon are only found in the upper Gulkana River near Paxson.

Spectacular views of Mt. McKinley to the west, the Wrangell Mountains to the east, and the many peaks of the Alaska Range to the north are all offered along this route.

Recreational opportunities exist in the 455,000 acre Tangle Lakes Archaeological District. Numerous trails in this area provided hiking, mountain biking, and off-road vehicle use opportunities. There are two campgrounds in this area, the Tangle Lakes and Tangle River campgrounds. Tangle Lakes Campground has fourteen campsites, a waterpump, toilets, boat ramp, and picnic area. The Tangle River Campground offers seven campsites, a boat ramp, and restrooms. Another campground with seventeen campsites is located at milepost 104.3, near the byway's western terminus. The campground also offers water, toilets, picnic tables, firepits, and trails.

The entrance to Denali National Park is located approximately 25 miles north of Cantwell. Visitors to the park are permitted to drive their own vehicle for only the first 14 miles of the roadway into the park. Shuttle buses operate throughout the day that will take you deeper into the park. Denali National Park has seven campgrounds with a total of 291 sites.

Local Information

BLM - Glennallen District Office
P.O. Box 147
Glennallen, AK 99588
Phone: 907-822-3217

Delta Junction Chamber of Commerce
P.O. Box 987
Delta Junction, AK 99737
Phone: 907-895-5068

Greater Copper Valley C of C
P.O. Box 469
Glennallen, AK 99588
Phone: 907-822-5555

Denali National Park & Preserve
P.O. Box 9
McKinley Park, AK 99755
Phone: 907-683-2294

Fielding Lake State Rec. Site
Alaska State Parks-Northern Region
3700 Airport Way
Fairbanks, AK 99709
Phone: 907-451-2695

Nearby Routes

Richardson Highway, page 24

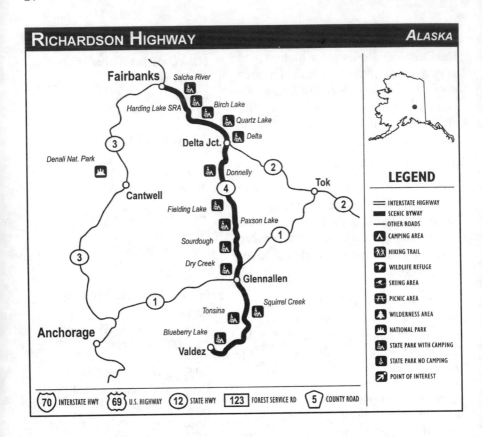

Route Location

The Richardson Highway is located in central Alaska with the northern access starting in Fairbanks. The byway travels south to the town of Valdez situated on the Prince William Sound.

Roads Traveled

Richardson Highway follows Alaska State Highways 2 and 4 which are two-lane paved roads suitable for all vehicles. The route is approximately 365 miles long. At the present time, this highway has not been officially designated as a scenic byway.

Travel Season

The route is open year-round although winter driving conditions can be hazardous and delays are possible.

Description

The Richardson Highway was the first road in Alaska and the original north-south route from Valdez to the Klondike gold fields.

Portions of the route travel alongside the 13,200,000-acre Wrangell-Saint Elias National Park and Preserve. Several mountain ranges converge here; the park includes 9 of the 16 highest peaks in the United States. Activities consist of backpacking, hiking, camping, hunting, and fishing.

The Sourdough Roadhouse, located just south of Paxson, was built in 1903 and is the oldest roadhouse still operating in its original structure. The building was placed on the National Register of Historic Places in 1974.

Recreational opportunities are found all along the route at several state recreation areas. The Big Delta and Harding Lake State Recreation Areas offer camping, picnicking, hiking, and fishing opportunities as does the Paxson Lake Recreation Site. A portion of the scenic drive travels alongside the Delta National Wild and Scenic River which offers rafting and floating opportunities.

Local Information

Greater Fairbanks C of C
546 9th Ave.
Fairbanks, AK 99701
Phone: 907-452-1105

Delta Junction Chamber of Commerce
P.O. Box 987
Delta Junction, AK 99737
Phone: 907-895-5068

Greater Copper Valley C of C
P.O. Box 469
Glennallen, AK 99588
Phone: 907-822-5555

Valdez Chamber of Commerce
P.O. Box 512
Valdez, AK 99686
Phone: 907-835-2330

BLM - Glennallen District Office
P.O. Box 147
Glennallen, AK 99588
Phone: 907-822-3217

Alaska Public Lands Information Center
250 Cushman St., Suite 1A
Fairbanks, AK 99701
Phone: 907-451-7352

Nearby Routes

Dalton Highway, page 21 / Denali Highway, page 22

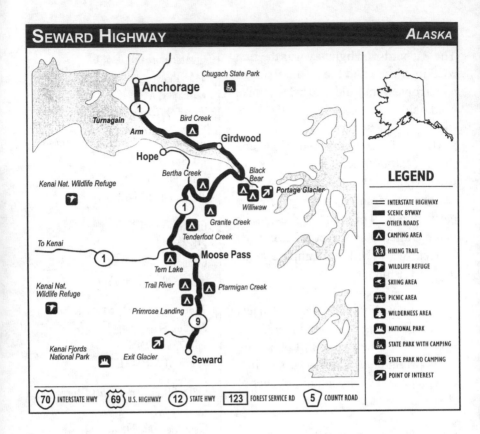

Route Location

Seward Highway is located in south-central Alaska on the Cook Inlet.
The byway begins in the city of Anchorage and travels south through
the Chugach National Forest to the community of Seward.

Roads Traveled

The byway follows Alaska State Highways 1 and 9 which are two-lane
paved roads suitable for travel by all types of vehicles although some
sections are narrow and winding. The 127-mile route has been designated a National Forest Scenic Byway.

Travel Season

The route is open year-round although winter driving conditions may be
hazardous. Snow avalanches can temporarily close sections of the highway.

Description

The Seward Highway ties Alaska's metropolitan center with the port of Seward on Resurrection Bay. From Anchorage the byway follows along the shores of Turnagain Arm as it travels through the Chugach State Park. After passing through Girdwood, the byway enters the beautiful scenery of the Chugach National Forest.

The byway offers spectacular scenery and a variety of wildlife all along its 127 miles. Beluga whales are occasionally seen rolling at the surface of the Turnagain Arm as they chase salmon and searun smelt. Dall sheep can sometimes be spotted as they scale the rugged mountainsides. Bald eagles, moose, bear, mountain goat, and a variety of birds also inhabit this region of Alaska.

Tracks of the Alaska Railroad are visible along the Turnagain Arm. This railroad was completed in 1923 and linked the port of Seward to the gold fields. The Alaska Railroad operates several scenic train rides from May through September.

Local Information

Chugach National Forest
3301 C Street
Anchorage, AK 99503
Phone: 907-271-2500

Anchorage Chamber of Commerce
441 W. 5th Ave., #300
Anchorage, AK 99501
Phone: 907-272-7588

Seward Chamber of Commerce
P.O. Box 749
Seward, AK 99664
Phone: 907-224-8051

Kenai Chamber of Commerce
402 Overland
Kenai, AK 99611
Phone: 907-283-7989

Chugach State Park
P.O. Box 107001
Anchorage, AK 99510
Phone: 907-345-5014

Alaska Railroad Corporation
Passenger Services
P.O. Box 107500
Anchorage, AK 99510
Phone: 800-544-0552

The byway provides the visitor with the opportunity to view glaciers closeup. Portage Glacier lies at the end of Turnagain Arm and is Alaska's most visited recreation site. Exit Glacier, outside of Seward in the Kenai Fjords National Park, is also a great place to experience a glacier first-hand.

LODGING DIRECTORY

The Taroka Inn Motel - Seward, page 455 — Hotel / Motel

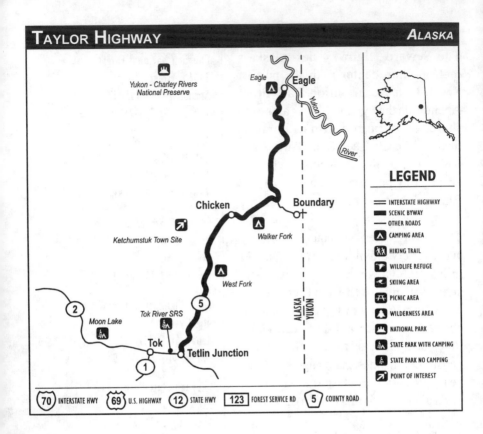

Route Location

The Taylor Highway scenic drive is located in east-central Alaska, approximately 200 miles southeast of Fairbanks. The southern access starts in Tetlin Junction off Alaska State Highway 2 (Alaska Highway) and travels northeast to the town of Eagle near the boundary of the Yukon Charley Rivers National Preserve.

Roads Traveled

The 160-mile route follows Alaska State Highway 5 over a two-lane gravel road that is suitable for all vehicles. The road ends in Eagle so you will need to retrace the route back to Tetlin Junction or the junction of State Highway 5 with the Top Of The World Highway which leads to Boundary.

Travel Season

The entire route is closed in the winter from heavy snows.

Description

The Taylor Highway climbs to over 3,500 feet in elevation three times as it crosses Mount Fairplay, Polly Summit, and American Summit. This area is known as the Fortymile River region and is the site of Alaska's earliest gold mining activity. The Fortymile Mining District became the richest gold mining area in the Yukon valley.

Located about 5 miles north of Tetlin Junction is a short ½-mile trail that leads to Four Mile Lake. Fishermen will find excellent opportunities for catching rainbow trout in the lake.

Those interested in four-wheeling into the backcountry will find the Taylor Creek all-terrain vehicle trail rewarding. This trail will take you to the Taylor and Ketchumstuk Mountains. The abandoned village of Ketchumstuk can also be reached from the trail.

There are three recreation sites found along the route that have been developed by the Bureau of Land Management. Walker Fork Campground, east of Chicken, has 20 campsites, drinking water, and restrooms. West Fork Campground lies next to the Dennison Branch of the Fortymile River and offers 25 campsites, some that can accommodate large recreational vehicles. A hand-pumped well supplies drinking water at this campground. The restrooms here are accessible to the handicapped. The Eagle recreation site has 16 campsites, restrooms, and drinking water. All of the recreation sites are open from May through September.

In the village of Eagle, the byways northern terminus, is historic Fort Egbert. The U.S. Army built Fort Egbert in 1899. The BLM has restored five buildings and daily tours are given during the summer.

Local Information

BLM - Steese-White Mountains D.O.
1150 University Ave.
Fairbanks, AK 99709
Phone: 907-474-2350

BLM - Tok Field Office
P.O. Box 309
Tok, AK 99780
Phone: 907-883-5121

Tok Chamber of Commerce
P.O. Box 389
Tok, AK 99780
Phone: 907-883-5887

Yukon-Charley Rivers National Preserve
P.O. Box 167
Eagle, AK 99738
Phone: 907-547-2233

Tok River State Recreation Site
Moon Lake State Recreation Site
Alaska State Parks-Northern Region
3700 Airport Way
Fairbanks, AK 99709
Phone: 907-451-2695

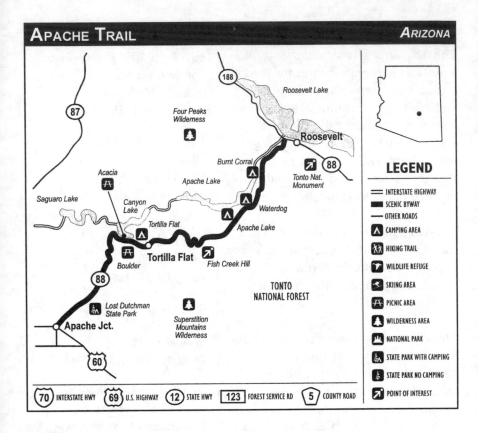

Route Location

Located in central Arizona, east of Phoenix with the southwestern access starting in Apache Junction off U.S. Highway 60/89. The scenic drive travels northeast to the town of Roosevelt on Theodore Roosevelt Lake.

Roads Traveled

The 46-mile route follows Arizona State Highway 88 to the junction with Arizona State Highway 188. The route travels over dirt and paved roads with numerous sharp curves and an occasional narrow stretch of road. The portion of the route from Tortilla Flat to Roosevelt, especially over Fish Creek Hill, are not recommended for vehicles pulling trailers. Thirty-eight miles of this route are designated a National Forest Scenic Byway.

Travel Season

Generally open year-round although portions of the route are subject to temporary closure due to heavy rains.

Description

The Apache Trail winds through some of the most awe-inspiring country in Arizona as it travels across the Tonto National Forest. The scenic drive is bound on the north by the Canyon, Apache, and Roosevelt Lakes, and on the south by the rugged Superstition Mountains. At Fish Creek Hill, perhaps the most impressive part of the Apache Trail, the road is primarily one-way and drops 1,000 feet in elevation over a 15 to 17 percent grade. The views of the Walls of Fish Creek Gorge are simply fantastic from this area.

The Tonto National Forest covers nearly three million acres of rugged, scenic landscapes ranging from cactus-studded desert to pine-covered mountains. Seven wilderness areas encompassing 589,000 acres are found within the boundary of the national forest. Two wilderness areas are located adjacent to the byway, Four Peaks Wilderness and Superstition Wilderness. Hiking trails may be accessed along the drive that lead you deep into the Superstition Wilderness.

The Forest Service has developed several recreation sites along or not far off the byway. There are two areas along the byway that provide picnic facilities, Acacia and Boulder recreation sites. A swimming beach is also found at the Acacia recreation area. The Tortilla Flat Camp ground has 77 campsites suitable for recreational vehicles. Running water and a dump station are also provided.

The state of Arizona has developed the Lost Dutchman State Park that provides 35 campsites, day use areas, and several nature trails.

Local Information

Tonto National Forest
2324 E. McDowell Rd.
Phoenix, AZ 85006
Phone: 602-225-5262

Apache Jct. Chamber of Commerce
P.O. Box 1747
Apache Junction, AZ 85217
Phone: 800-252-3141

Greater Globe - Miami C of C
1360 N. Broad St.
Globe, AZ 85502
Phone: 800-804-5623

Superior Chamber of Commerce
151 Main St.
Superior, AZ 85273
Phone: 520-689-2441

Lost Dutchman State Park
6109 N. Apache Trail
Apache Junction, AZ 85219
Phone: 602-982-4485

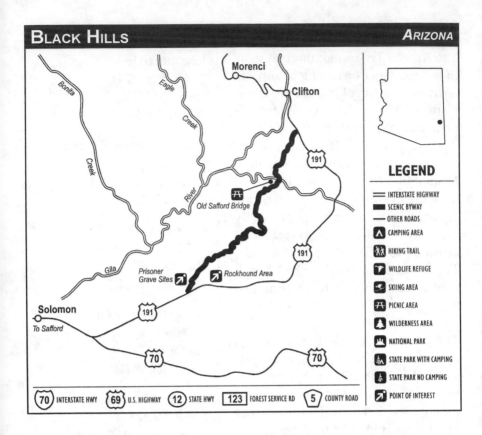

Route Location

The Black Hills Back Country Byway is located in southeastern Arizona, east of Safford near the New Mexico border. The northeastern access starts south of Clifton off U.S. Highway 191 (milepost 160) and travels southwest back to U.S. Highway 191 (milepost 139) near U.S. Highway 70.

Roads Traveled

The 21-mile route travels the Old Safford-Clifton Road over an unpaved surface along a narrow and winding road. Do not attempt this route if you have a travel trailer or any vehicle more than 20 feet long. Motorhomes and trailers can be left at parking areas on each end of the route. The route has been designated a BLM Type II Back Country Byway.

Travel Season

Open year-round, although sections may become impassable during and after heavy rains.

Description

The Black Hills Back Country Byway passes through the historical territory of the Chiricahua and Western Apache, who arrived in southeastern Arizona around 1600. Some Apaches used the area as a local travel route and hideout prior to the surrender of Geronimo in 1886. In 1540, Coronado passed through the area as he led Spanish conquistadors in search of gold and the Seven Cities of Cibola.

Each end of the byway begins in a desert shrub plant community traveling higher through bands of desert grassland and even higher up into stands of juniper, pinyon pine, and oaks. The Gila Box Riparian National Conservation Area preserves 21,000 acres of scenic desert canyons surrounding perennial rivers and creeks. The byway crosses this conservation area near the Old Safford Bridge.

The Old Safford Bridge was originally designed as a steel structure but was constructed of concrete due to limits on the use of steel during World War I. The bridge was completed in 1918 and is on the National Register of Historic Places. Picnic areas at each end of the bridge serve as launch points for those interested in floating the Gila River.

Recreation along the byway is plentiful. Many primitive side roads provide opportunities for four-wheeling and a challenging ride for the experience mountain biker. Rock collectors will be interested in visiting the Black Hills Rockhound Area. Fishermen will find catfish in the waters of the Gila River. In early spring, snowmelt enables rafts, kayaks, and canoes to float through the Gila Box to Bonita Creek, 19 miles downstream.

Near the byway's western end are rock piles marking prisoner grave sites. This road was built by prisoners between 1914 and 1920. One of the prisoners was killed by a guard while attempting to escape in 1916.

Nearby Routes

Coronado Trail, page 34

Local Information

BLM - Safford District Office
711 14th Ave.
Safford, AZ 85546
Phone: 520-428-4040

Graham County Chamber of Commerce
1111 Thatcher Blvd.
Safford, AZ 85546
Phone: 520-428-2511

Greenlee County Chamber of Commerce
P.O. Box 1237
Clifton, AZ 85533
Phone: 520-865-3313

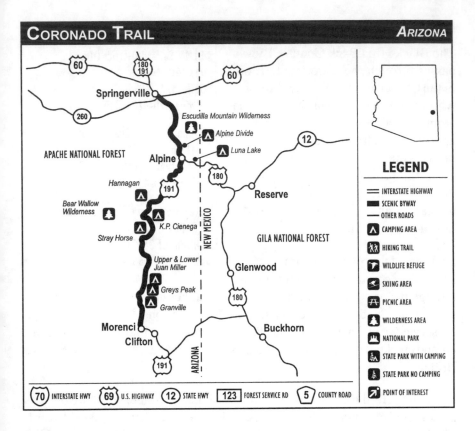

Route Location

Located in east-central Arizona, northeast of Safford. The southern access starts in the town of Morenci and parallels the Arizona-New Mexico border as it travels north to Springerville.

Roads Traveled

The 123-mile route follows U.S. Highways 180 and 191 which are two-lane paved roads. There are sharp curves and steep drop-offs along several sections of narrow road with no guardrails. The route is not recommended for vehicles towing a trailer or motorhomes over 20 feet long. The entire route has been designated a National Forest Scenic Byway.

Travel Season

The route is generally open year-round with the exception of possible temporary closure during the winter for snow removal.

Description

The Coronado Trail travels through steep canyons and across high, rolling mountains with spectacular views of the surrounding lakes and meadows. The route crosses the Apache-Sitgreaves National Forests, which have the largest stand of ponderosa pines in the nation.

There are two wilderness areas adjacent to the byway, the 5,200-acre Escudilla Wilderness and 11,080-acre Bear Wallow Wilderness. Numerous trails found along the byway provide access to these wilderness areas. The areas provide excellent opportunities for hiking, backpacking, and horseback riding.

Local Information

Apache-Sitgreaves National Forests
309 S. Mountain Ave. Hwy. 180
Springerville, AZ 85938
Phone: 520-333-4301

Greenlee County Chamber of Commerce
P.O. Box 1237
Clifton, AZ 85533
Phone: 520-865-3313

Round Valley Chamber of Commerce
318 E. Main St.
Springerville, AZ 85938
Phone: 520-333-2123

Alpine Chamber of Commerce
P.O. Box 410
Alpine, AZ 85920
Phone: 520-339-4330

Several national forest campgrounds along the byway provide just the right spot for spending the night under the stars. Luna Lake Campground, located east of Alpine off U.S. Highway 180, has 50 campsites. Other campgrounds along the byway are smaller, offering a more secluded setting. A three-mile hiking trail at K.P. Cienega Campground will take you to a scenic waterfall on the K.P. Creek. If you're interested in camping spots away from the crowds, try some of the logging roads in the area. They will lead you to beautiful meadows and streams where you will likely be by yourself. The Forest Service permits such dispersed camping on national forest lands.

Nearby Routes

Black Hills, page 32 / White Mountain Scenic Highway, page 46

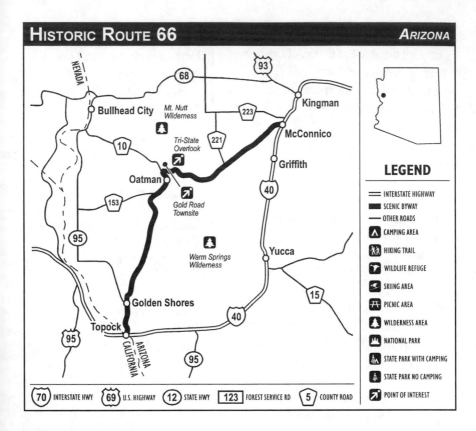

Route Location

Historic Route 66 is located in west-central Arizona, just south of Kingman.
The northeastern access starts in McConnico off Interstate 40 and travels
southwest to the town of Topock, returning to Interstate 40 near the Cali-
fornia-Arizona state line.

Roads Traveled

The 48-mile route travels on a paved, two-lane road suitable for most vehicles. There are sharp curves along this route and it is not recommended for
vehicles over 40 feet long. Forty-two miles of the route are designated a
BLM Type I Back Country Byway.

Travel Season

The entire route is open year-round.

Description

The Black Mountains section of historic Route 66 is preserved here along this scenic drive. There are famous sites to be discovered or revisited, including the Sitgreaves Pass tri-state overlook which provides a spectacular view into the states of California, Nevada, and Arizona. Also found along this back country byway is the vintage Cool Springs Gas Station which was in operation during the 1930s. All that remains today of the stone structure is located on private property, please take only pictures.

Building foundations, rock formations, and mine shafts are all that remain of the once bustling gold mining community of the Gold Road Townsite. In its heyday, thousands of people inhabited the area. The former townsite is privately owned, please respect the owners rights!

Local Information

BLM - Barstow Resource Area
150 Coolwater Lane
Barstow, CA 92311
Phone: 619-256-3591

Kingman Area Chamber of Commerce
P.O. Box 1150
Kingman, AZ 86402
Phone: 520-753-6106

Oatman - Goldroad C of C
P.O. Box 423
Oatman, AZ 86433
Phone: 520-768-4603

Bullhead Area Chamber of Commerce
1251 Hwy. 95
Bullhead City, AZ 86429
Phone: 520-754-4121

Oatman was first settled in the late 1880s and once claimed a bustling population of 8,000. Oatman is famous for the honeymoon hideaway of Clark Gable and Carole Lombard, the Oatman Hotel which is now a museum. Wild burros also freely wander through the streets of Oatman.

Mount Nutt Wilderness lies to the north of the byway and Warm Springs Wilderness to the south. These wilderness areas provide opportunities for hiking, backpacking, and horseback riding. Camping is permitted anywhere within the wilderness boundaries. A number of unmaintained, unmarked sideroads along the byway provide access points to the areas. There are no maintained trails; travel is cross-country.

Nearby Routes

Hualapai Mountains, page 38 / Parker Dam Road, page 42 / East Mojave National Scenic Area, page 75

Lodging Directory

Kingman KOA - Kingman, page 440 — Campground / RV Park
Travelodge - Kingman, page 440 — Hotel / Motel

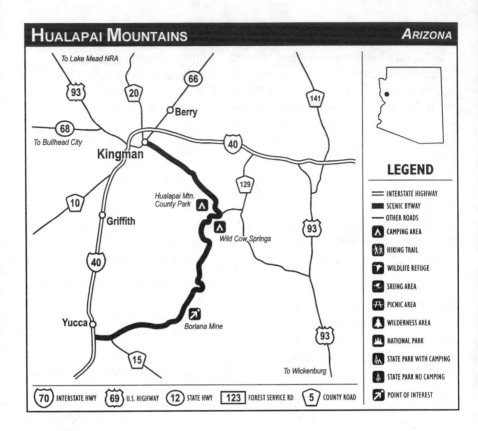

Route Location

Hualapai Mountains Back Country Byway is located in western Arizona, near Kingman. The byway's northern access is from the corner of Stockton Hill Road and Andy Devine Avenue in Kingman. The byway may also be accessed from the south off Interstate 40 near Yucca.

Roads Traveled

Travelling from the northern access point, the route is divided into four road type segments. The first segment is the Hualapai Mountain Road, 13 miles of paved two-lane road suitable for passenger cars. The next segment of road is mostly one-lane with an unpaved surface that can be negotiated by passenger cars when the road is dry and free of ice. This segment is approximately 4 miles in length. The third segment is 21 miles of unpaved single-lane that requires high-clearance or 4-wheel-drive vehicles. The final segment is 12 miles of unimproved two-lane dirt road that is suitable for passenger cars from the Boriana Mine to its terminus at Interstate 40. The entire 50-mile route is designated a Type I and II Back Country Byway.

Travel Season

Portions of the route are closed during various times of the year due to rain and snow. Inquire locally about the current road conditions before traveling the entire route.

Local Information

BLM - Kingman Resource Area
2475 Beverly Ave.
Kingman, AZ 86401
Phone: 520-757-3161

Kingman Area Chamber of Commerce
333 W. Andy Devine Ave.
Kingman, AZ 86402
Phone: 520-753-6106

Description

The Hualapai Mountains Back Country Byway traverses a varied landscape from the open Mojave Desert near Kingman up through steep foothills covered in pinyon pine and juniper to an oak and ponderosa pine forest. Travelers begin at 3,500 feet in elevation and climb to 6,500 feet in the Hualapai Mountains. Descending from the crest, travelers are given breathtaking views of pinyon and juniper woodland extending into the desert vegetation below.

Wildlife observation opportunities are bountiful as the area is home to more than 80 species of birds, including hawks, owls, whippoorwills, and hummingbirds. Mule deer and elk also share the countryside with coyotes and bobcats, among other wildlife. This area also once provided habitat for the Hualapai Mexican vole.

Recreation along the byway is provided in the form of hiking, backpacking, off-road vehicle pursuits, and camping. The very popular 2,320-acre Hualapai Mountain County Park offers emergency first aid, campgrounds, water, hiking trails, rental cabins, and picnicking facilities. A smaller, less developed campground is operated by the BLM, the Wild Cow Springs Recreation Site. This site is only partially developed but provides camping and restroom facilities, grills, fire pits, and picnic tables. No potable water is available.

Nearby Routes

Historic Route 66, page 36 / Parker Dam Road, page 42

LODGING DIRECTORY

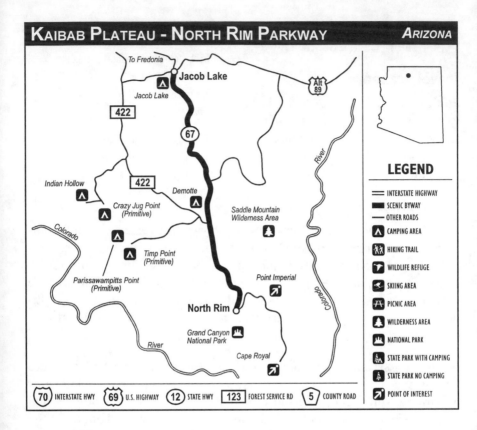

KAIBAB PLATEAU - NORTH RIM PARKWAY   *ARIZONA*

Route Location

The Kaibab Plateau - North Rim Parkway scenic drive is located in north-central Arizona about 35 miles south of the Utah-Arizona border, south of Fredonia. The northern access is in Jacob Lake off U.S. Highway Alternate 89 and travels south to North Rim in the Grand Canyon National Park.

Roads Traveled

The 44-mile route follows Arizona State Highway 67 which is a paved, two-lane road suitable for all vehicles. The route ends in North Rim where you will need to retrace the route back to Jacob Lake. The entire route is designated a National Forest Scenic Byway.

Travel Season

Due to heavy winter snow cover, this route is normally closed from mid to late November through mid-May.

Description

This scenic byway crosses the high-elevation plateau known as the Kaibab Plateau through dense forests of pine, fir, and aspen. The Piute Indians call this high plateau "the mountain lying down" or "Kaibab." The byway ends on the North Rim of the magnificent Grand Canyon National Park.

The Kaibab National Forest offers many recreational activities throughout its 650,000 acres. There are two wilderness areas within the forest, Saddle Mountain Wilderness to the west and Kanab Creek Wilderness in the southeast. Both areas offer excellent opportunities for hiking the remote countryside.

Local Information

Kaibab National Forest
800 S. 6th St.
Williams, AZ 86046
Phone: 520-635-2681

Fredonia Chamber of Commerce
P.O. Box 547
Fredonia, AZ 86022
Phone: 520-643-7241

Page - Lake Powell C of C
P.O. Box 727
Page, AZ 86040
Phone: 520-645-2741

Grand Canyon National Park
P.O. Box 129
Grand Canyon, AZ 86023
Phone: 520-638-7888

There are three developed campgrounds for picnicking or camping on the Kaibab National Forest. Jacob Lake Campground sits at an elevation of 7,900 feet and has 53 campsites with tables, cooking grills, and water. Demotte Campground offers 20 campsites; Indian Hollow Campground has 3 camping sites. Camping is not restricted to the developed campgrounds. Those who prefer solitude and privacy may camp anywhere within the forest boundaries, with some restrictions. Some of the more popular and most accessible primitive camping areas are shown on the map.

Although Arizona State Highway 67 is closed during the winter, the national forest remains open to winter sport enthusiasts. The snowpacked national forest roads provide excellent opportunities for snowmobiling or cross-country skiing.

The diversity of wildlife inhabiting the Kaibab National Forest provides enjoyment for the photographer, bird-watcher, and nature lover. Mule deer and wild turkey are among the many species of wildlife found in this part of Arizona.

Route Location

Located in southeastern California and west-central Arizona on the banks of the Colorado River. On the California side, the byway travels between Earp and Parker Dam. Earp is on California Highway 62 about 50 miles north of Blythe. The Arizona side travels between Parker and Lake Havasu City. Lake Havasu City is approximately 60 miles south of Kingman.

Roads Traveled

The California side of the byway is the officially designated portion. As its name implies, the scenic drive follows the Parker Dam Road which is a two-lane paved road that is safe for travel by all types of vehicles. The Arizona side also follows a two-lane pave road, Arizona Highway 95. Eleven miles of this 55-mile route is designated a Type I Back Country Byway.

Travel Season

The route is open year-round.

Description

Parker Dam Road travels along the banks of the cool Colorado River through an area commonly referred to as the Parker Strip. The byway passes through the wide river valley with views of the surrounding mountains. Hiking trails found along the byway take you into the mountains that offer beautiful panoramic views.

Many recreational opportunities can be found along this back country byway. Anglers will find bass, bluegill, and catfish in the waters of the Colorado River and Lake Havasu. Off-road vehicle driving enthusiasts will find satisfaction on the many desert trails of the Copper Basin Dunes and Crossroads Off-Road Vehicle Areas. There are many public and privately-owned campgrounds along the route. Facilities vary but most offer trailer hookups, drinking water, picnic areas, gasoline, food, marinas, and swimming areas. Golf courses may also be available in some areas. On the Arizona side are two state parks, Buckskin Mountain and Lake Havasu, that provide developed camping facilities. Some of the campgrounds at the parks are accessed only by boat.

Local Information

BLM - Havasu Resource Area
3189 Sweetwater Ave.
Lake Havasu City, AZ 86403
Phone: 520-505-1200

Lake Havasu Area C of C
1930 Mesquite Ave., #3
Lake Havasu City, AZ 86403
Phone: 520-855-4115

Parker Area Chamber of Commerce
1217 California Ave.
Parker, AZ 85344
Phone: 520-669-2174

Lake Havasu State Park
P.O. Box 1990
Lake Havasu City, AZ 86405
Phone: 520-855-1223

Buckskin Mountain State Park
54751 Hwy. 95
Parker, AZ 85344
Phone: 520-667-3231

On the Arizona side of the Colorado River in Lake Havasu City is the famous bridge that once spanned the Thames River in London, England. The London Bridge, built in 1825, was put up for sale in 1967 after engineers discovered the structure was slowly sinking into the river and could no longer handle busy city traffic. Robert McCulloch purchased the bridge for $2,460,000, dismantled it block by block, and had it shipped to California. From there, it was trucked to its present location and reassembled over a three-year period. It now stretches across the water to Lake Havasu's largest island. An English Tudor village is located on the east end of the bridge.

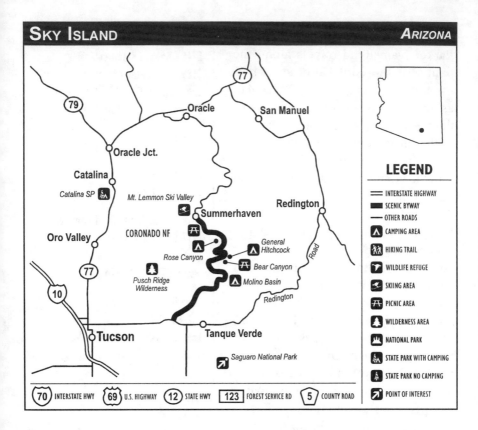

Route Location

The Sky Island Scenic Byway is located in southern Arizona. The byway's southern access begins near the eastern city limits of Tucson. Sky Island can be reached from I-10 by following Grant Road east to the Catalina Highway.

Roads Traveled

The 30-mile scenic byway follows Catalina Highway through the Coronado National Forest. Catalina Highway is also known as General Hitchcock Highway or Mount Lemmon Highway. The byway officially terminates near the village of Summerhaven. The route is a winding two-lane paved road with turns becoming more severe as the road increases in elevation. The scenic drive is designated a National Forest Scenic Byway.

Travel Season

The route is generally open year-round.

Description

The Santa Catalina Mountains rise from the Sonoran desert at 2,500 feet to a mixed conifer forest over 9,000 feet in elevation. The highway, originally constructed by prison labor, travels alongside the Pusch Ridge Wilderness. Travelers begin their journey in the Sonoran desert scrub, dotted with mesquite and palo verde trees in the low lying areas and majestic saguaros and other cacti braced upon the steep rocky mountainside and canyon walls. As you climb up into the mountains, the desert gives way to oak and cypress trees. Further into the mountains, you enter into a forest of juniper, mixed conifers, and ponderosa pine.

Nearly three miles from the forest boundary, visitors reach the first vista point, Babat Duag, Tohono O'odham for "frog mountain." From here you can gaze upon the Tucson Basin and the many other mountain ranges that rise sharply above the desert floor. This vista point is popular with visitors in the evening who want to watch the sun set behind the Tucson Mountains.

Local Information

Coronado National Forest
Federal Building
300 West Congress
Tucson, AZ 85701
Phone: 520-670-4552

Tucson Metropolitan C of C
P.O. Box 991
Tucson, AZ 85702
Phone: 520-792-2250

SMOR Chamber of Commerce
P.O. Box 1886
Oracle, AZ 85623
Phone: 520-896-9322

Catalina State Park
P.O. Box 36986
Tucson, AZ 85740
Phone: 520-628-5798

Saguaro National Park
3693 S. Old Spanish Trail
Tucson, AZ 85730
Phone: 520-296-8576

Mt. Lemmon Ski Valley
P.O. Box 612
Mt. Lemmon, AZ 85619
Phone: 520-576-1321

The national forest has several developed areas for camping and picnicking. The first campground you come to is Molino Basin. There are nearly 50 sites here for pitching a tent or parking your RV. The Arizona Trail can also be accessed from this area. General Hitchcock campground is nestled in the oak woodlands of the upper reaches of Bear Canyon and offers 13 camping spots. Rose Canyon is a popular spot offering 74 campsites and a 7-acre lake that is stocked with trout. In addition to the camping opportunities, there are several developed picnic areas or pullouts for finding a shade tree and enjoying lunch.

The Sky Island terminates near the village of Summerhaven where visitors can eat, shop, or stretch their legs before going back down.

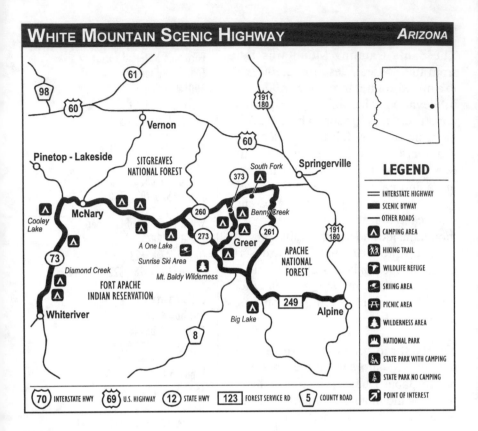

WHITE MOUNTAIN SCENIC HIGHWAY   ARIZONA

LEGEND

- ══ INTERSTATE HIGHWAY
- ▬ SCENIC BYWAY
- — OTHER ROADS
- 🅰 CAMPING AREA
- 🚶 HIKING TRAIL
- 🦌 WILDLIFE REFUGE
- ⛷ SKIING AREA
- 🌲 PICNIC AREA
- 🌲 WILDERNESS AREA
- 🏔 NATIONAL PARK
- 🏕 STATE PARK WITH CAMPING
- 🌲 STATE PARK NO CAMPING
- 🚩 POINT OF INTEREST

70 INTERSTATE HWY   69 U.S. HIGHWAY   12 STATE HWY   123 FOREST SERVICE RD   5 COUNTY ROAD

Route Location

The White Mountains Scenic Highway is located in east-central Arizona, approximately 170 miles east of Phoenix. The southwestern access starts in Whiteriver on the Fort Apache Indian Reservation and travels north to McNary, then east to the junction of U.S. Hwy. 180/191 north of Alpine.

Roads Traveled

The 123-mile route follows Arizona Highways 73, 260, 261, 273, and 373 and Forest Service Roads 87 and 249. These series of connecting roads travel over a combination of two-lane paved and gravel-surfaced roads suitable for all vehicles. The route is designated a National Forest Scenic Byway.

Travel Season

Arizona routes 73 and 260 are open year-round. The remaining portions of the route are subject to closure due to winter snows.

Description

The scenic drive crosses the Apache-Sitgreaves National Forest and Fort Apache Indian Reservation, through forests of pinyons, junipers, and ponderosa pine. A tribal permit is required for all recreational activities on the reservation. Permits are available in Whiteriver at the tribal Game and Fish Office.

The byway provides access to several lakes and streams that offer excellent opportunities for catching trout. Some of the lakes are too shallow for fish survival, but are deep enough for canoes or rowboats. Due to their small size, most lakes have restrictions on horsepower for boat motors.

Local Information

Apache-Sitgreaves National Forest
309 S. Mountain Ave. Hwy. 180
Springerville, AZ 85938
Phone: 520-333-4301

Alpine Chamber of Commerce
P.O. Box 410
Alpine, AZ 85920
Phone: 520-339-4330

Pinetop - Lakeside C of C
592 W. White Mountain Blvd.
Lakeside, AZ 85929
Phone: 520-367-4290

Round Valley Chamber of Commerce
318 E. Main St.
Springerville, AZ 85938
Phone: 520-333-2123

Camping opportunities are plentiful along the byway. The national forest has developed several campgrounds with varying facilities. Big Lake has several developed campgrounds offering nearly 250 campsites for tents or recreational vehicles. Several other smaller campgrounds provide a more secluded setting.

Hiking opportunities range from short nature walks to longer back country hikes. Within the boundary of the forest, there are over 800 miles of trails. Two trails form a 28-mile loop between Greer and Mt. Baldy. Each trail is 14 miles long and half of each is in the 7,000-acre Mt. Baldy Wilderness. The portions of the trails within the wilderness are heavily used while those between Greer and the wilderness are less crowded. The summit of Mt. Baldy lies within the indian reservation; this area should not be entered without first contacting the tribal headquarters in Whiteriver.

Nearby Routes

Coronado Trail, page 34

Lodging Directory

Bonanza Motel - Pinetop, page 461 —— Hotel / Motel
White Mountain Lodge - Greer, page 461 —— Bed & Breakfast / Inns & Cabin / Cottage / Guest Ranch

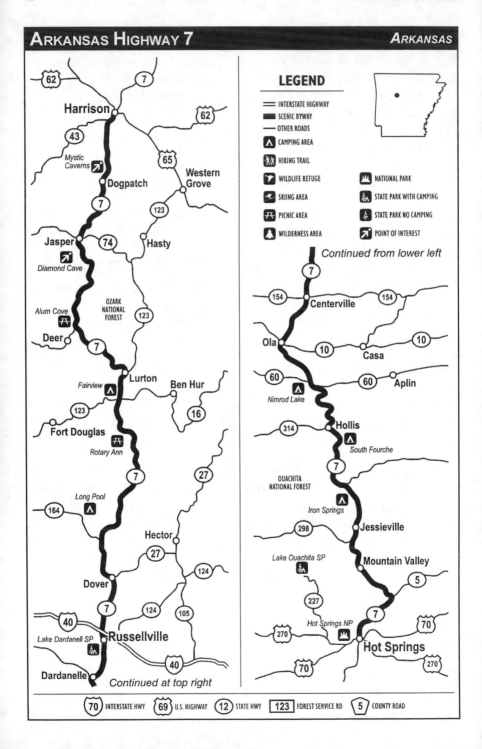

ARKANSAS HIGHWAY 7   ARKANSAS

LEGEND

═══ INTERSTATE HIGHWAY
▬ SCENIC BYWAY
— OTHER ROADS
🅰 CAMPING AREA
🚶 HIKING TRAIL
🦌 WILDLIFE REFUGE   🏛 NATIONAL PARK
⛷ SKIING AREA   🏕 STATE PARK WITH CAMPING
🧺 PICNIC AREA   🌲 STATE PARK NO CAMPING
🌲 WILDERNESS AREA   ➚ POINT OF INTEREST

62 7
Harrison
62
43
Mystic Caverns Dogpatch
65
Western Grove
7
123
Jasper 74 Hasty
Diamond Cave
OZARK NATIONAL FOREST
Alum Cove 123
Deer 7
Fairview Lurton Ben Hur
123 16
Fort Douglas
Rotary Ann
7 27
Long Pool
164
Hector
Dover 27 124
7 124 105
40
Lake Dardanell SP Russellville
40
Dardanelle *Continued at top right*

Continued from lower left
7
154 Centerville 154
Ola 10 10
60 Casa
Nimrod Lake 60 Aplin
314 Hollis
South Fourche
7
OUACHITA NATIONAL FOREST
Iron Springs
298 Jessieville
Lake Ouachita SP Mountain Valley
227 5
7
Hot Springs NP 70
270 Hot Springs
70 270

70 INTERSTATE HWY   69 U.S. HIGHWAY   12 STATE HWY   123 FOREST SERVICE RD   5 COUNTY ROAD

Route Location

The Arkansas Highway 7 scenic by-way cuts across western Arkansas. The byway crosses two national forests as it travels between Harrison in the north to Hot Springs in the south.

Roads Traveled

The 160-mile scenic drive follows State Highway 7 which is a two-lane paved route suitable for travel by all types of vehicles. The portions traveling through the national forests have been designated National Forest Scenic Byways. In the north, the route travels through the Ozark National Forest for 36 miles. The scenic drive crosses the Ouachita National Forest in the south for 24 miles.

Travel Season

The entire route is generally open year-round.

Description

From Harrison, the Arkansas Highway 7 scenic byway travels south through the Ozark National Forest, winding its way through the Ozark Mountains. The byway then descends into the Arkansas River Valley before climbing into the Ouachita Mountains of the Ouachita National Forest.

The byway cuts through the Buffalo National River just south of Dogpatch. The Buffalo National River offers nearly 150 miles of free-

Local Information

Ozark - St. Francis National Forest
605 W. Main St.
Russelville, AR 72801
Phone: 501-968-7354

Harrison Chamber of Commerce
621 E. Rush
Harrison, AR 72602
Phone: 800-880-6265

Russellville Chamber of Commerce
708 W. Main
Russellville, AR 72801
Phone: 501-968-2530

Dardanelle Chamber of Commerce
510 N. 2nd St.
Dardanelle, AR 72834
Phone: 501-229-3328

Greater Hot Springs C of C
659 Ouachita
Hot Springs, AR 71902
Phone: 501-321-1700

Hot Springs National Park
P.O. Box 1860
Hot Springs, AR 71902
Phone: 501-623-1433

Lake Ouachita State Park
5451 Mountain Pine Road
Mountain Pine, AR 71956
Phone: 501-767-9366

Mt. Nebo State Park
Route 3 - Box 374
Dardanelle, AR 72834
Phone: 501-229-3655

flowing river for canoeing or rafting. There are outfitters that will provide you with all the necessary items to enjoy a float down this scenic river of white water, long stretches of calm water, and rock bluffs reaching high above the river.

Local Information

Lake Dardanelle State Park
2428 Marina Road
Russellville, AR 72801
Phone: 501-967-5516

The Ozark National Forest covers more than a million acres of hardwood forests and gently rolling mountains. There are numerous public campgrounds that offer campsites for tents or recreational vehicles. You'll also find many areas for enjoying a picnic. Hiking trails are plentiful through the national forest. The 160-mile Ozark Highlands National Recreation Trail passes through the forest and its wilderness areas. In the Alum Cove picnic area is a short one-mile trail that leads to the Alum Cove Natural Bridge. This 130-foot natural bridge was carved out of the solid rock by a small stream.

The southern portion of the route passes through the Ouachita National Forest. Like the Ozark National Forest, there are numerous camping and picnicking areas throughout. Hundreds of miles of trails lie within the forest, including the 192-mile Ouachita National Recreation Trail. Two camping areas along Arkansas Highway 7 offer a wooded setting next to a meandering stream. Iron Springs has 13 campsites and South Fourche has 7 campsites. Both areas also have picnic facilities, drinking water, and sanitary facilities.

Lying between the national forests are two Corps of Engineers projects, Lake Dardanelle and Nimrod Lake. On the byway's southern end is Lake Ouachita, another Corps project. The Corps of Engineers has developed several public use areas that provide camping facilities for tents and recreational vehicles as well as numerous picnic areas. The lakes also offer opportunities for swimming, fishing, and boating. In addition to the public use areas, Arkansas has developed state parks around each lake.

Nearby Routes

Mount Magazine, page 51 / Ozark Highlands, page 53

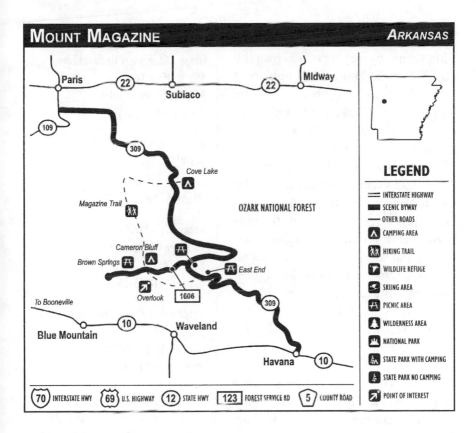

Route Location

The Mount Magazine scenic byway is located in west-central Arkansas, approximately 40 miles east of Fort Smith. The northern access starts south of Paris off Arkansas State Highway 109 and travels southeast to Havana, ending at the junction with Arkansas State Highway 10.

Roads Traveled

The Mount Magazine byway is a 30 mile route following Arkansas State Highway 309 and Forest Service Road 1606. The entire route travels over two-lane paved roads that are suitable for all vehicles. Twenty-three miles of this route are officially designated a National Forest Scenic Byway.

Travel Season

The route is generally open year-round.

Description

This scenic byway travels across the Ozark National Forest through areas of small farms and forests of short-leaf pine, red oak, white oak, and hickory. The byway winds its way through the forest to the top of Mt. Magazine, the highest point in Arkansas at 2,753 feet above sea level. The overlook from the top of the mountain offers sweeping vistas of the timber-covered mountains, rugged rock bluffs, and sparkling mountain lakes. Mt. Magazine is not only the highest point in Arkansas, but is considered the highest mountain between the Rocky Mountains and the Appalachian Mountains.

Local Information

Ozark - St. Francis National Forest
605 W. Main St.
Russelville, AR 72801
Phone: 501-968-2354

North Logan County C of C
301 W. Walnut
Paris, AR 72855
Phone: 501-963-2244

Booneville Chamber of Commerce
96 W. 2nd & Bennett
Booneville, AR 72927
Phone: 501-675-2666

Dardanelle Chamber of Commerce
510 N. 2nd St.
Dardanelle, AR 72834
Phone: 501-229-3328

The Mt. Magazine recreation area consists of the Cameron Bluff Campground and Brown Springs picnic area. The campground offers 16 campsites, chemical toilets, and drinking water. A hiking trail is located here that goes to Cove Lake, a 160-acre mountain lake offering boating, swimming, and fishing. The Cove Lake recreation area also has 29 camping spots for tents or recreational vehicles, drinking water, restrooms, and shower facilities.

Nearby Routes

Arkansas Highway 7, page 48
Ozark Highlands, page 53
Pig Trail, page 55

Route Location

The Ozark Highlands byway is located in northwestern Arkansas, about 60 miles east of Fort Smith. The southern access starts just east of Clarksville off U.S. Highway 64 and travels north to the Ozark National Forest boundary, just beyond Mossville.

Roads Traveled

The scenic byway follows Arkansas State Highway 21 which is a two-lane paved road that is safe for travel by all types of vehicles. The byway is approximately 45 miles long. Thirty-five miles of the route are officially designated a National Forest Scenic Byway.

Travel Season

The entire route is open year-round.

Description

The Ozark Highlands scenic drive cuts across the Boston Mountains as it winds through the Ozark National Forest. Blanketing the byway are large stands of hardwood forest, primarily oak and hickory, with scattered areas of native shortleaf pine. Scenic vistas along the route provide outstanding views of the tree-covered mountains.

Lying near the byway's northern end is the 10,500-acre Upper Buffalo Wilderness with the headwaters of the Buffalo River running through the heart of the area. This wilderness area provides solitude and excellent back country hiking and camping opportunities.

Local Information

Ozark - St. Francis National Forest
605 W. Main St.
Russelville, AR 72801
Phone: 501-968-2354

Huntsville Chamber of Commerce
P.O. Box 950
Huntsville, AR 72740
Phone: 501-738-6000

Johnson County Chamber of Commerce
P.O. Box 396
Clarksville, AR 72830
Phone: 501-754-2340

Harrison Chamber of Commerce
621 E. Rush
Harrison, AR 72602
Phone: 501-741-2659

For those interested in a more "civilized" setting, the national forest has developed several campgrounds within the forest. The Ozone recreation area is located just off the byway and offers eight camping units suitable for tents or recreational vehicles. The park also has drinking water, chemical toilets, and picnic tables. This area was originally the site of a Civilian Conservation Corps camp during the late 1930s and early 1940s. There are several other developed camping areas throughout the forest that are shown on the map.

The Ozark Highlands Trail may be accessed from the Ozark recreation area. This 160-mile trail cuts across the national forest from west to east.

Wildlife is abundant in this area. Keep your eyes on the lookout for mule deer and wild turkey. Black bear also inhabit the region. Occasionally bald eagles and golden eagles are also seen.

Nearby Routes

Arkansas Highway 7, page 48 / Mount Magazine, page 51 / Pig Trail, page 55

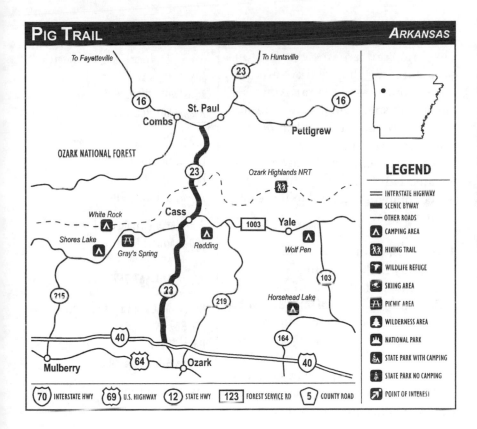

Route Location

The Pig Trail is located approximately 30 miles east of Fort Smith in northwestern Arkansas. The byway's southern terminus can be reached from Interstate 40, just north of Ozark. The route then travels north through the Ozark National Forest to its northern terminus at the junction of Arkansas State Highway 6, south of St. Paul.

Roads Traveled

The 28-mile byway follows Arkansas State Highway 23, a two-lane paved road suitable for all types of vehicles. The U.S. Forest Service has designated 19 miles of this route as a National Forest Scenic Byway.

Travel Season

The entire route is usually open year-round.

Description

The Pig Trail crosses the Boston Mountains of the Ozark National Forest showcasing rural America along with spectacular views of timber-covered mountains, clear mountain streams and rivers, isolated farms and ranches, and seasonal waterfalls. Fall brings beautiful colors of red, orange, and gold to these ancient mountains.

The closest campground found along the byway is the Redding recreation site, located 3 miles east of the route. This camping area offers 27 units suitable for tents or recreational vehicles, restrooms, drinking water, shower facilities, and picnic tables. There are other campgrounds located within the forest if you're willing to venture off the byway. These other camping areas are shown on the map.

Local Information

Ozark - St. Francis National Forest
605 W. Main St.
Russellville, AR 72801
Phone: 501-968-2354

Fayetteville Chamber of Commerce
123 W. Mountain St.
Fayetteville, AR 72702
Phone: 501-521-1710

Ozark Area Chamber of Commerce
300-A Airport Road
Ozark, AR 72949
Phone: 501-667-2525

Huntsville Chamber of Commerce
P.O. Box 950
Huntsville, AR 72740
Phone: 501-738-6000

There are four wilderness areas within the boundaries of the national forest, lying to the east of this route (see Ozark Highlands and Arkansas Highway 7 scenic byways). These wilderness areas provide excellent opportunities for back county hiking and enjoying the sounds associated with secluded areas. The Ozark Highlands Trail, a National Recreation Trail, crosses this route toward the byway's northern end.

The Redding recreation area is adjacent to the Mulberry River, a meandering mountain stream. The river is popular with the fishermen as well as canoe enthusiasts. Canoe rentals are available from several outfitters in the area.

Nearby Routes

Mount Magazine, page 51 / Ozark Highlands, page 53

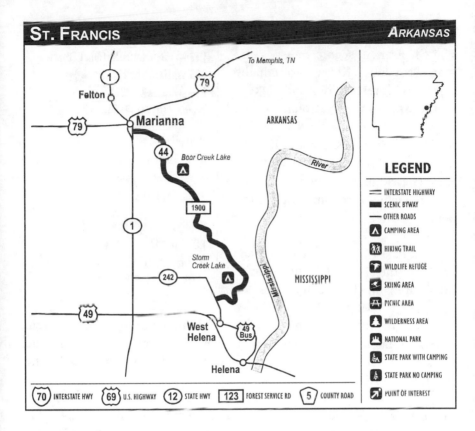

Route Location

The St. Francis scenic drive is located in east-central Arkansas, approximately 57 miles southwest of Memphis, Tennessee. The northern access starts in Marianna and travels south to the junction of Arkansas State Highway 242 north of West Helena, near the Arkansas-Mississippi border.

Roads Traveled

The 23-mile byway follows Arkansas State Highway 44 and Forest Service Road 1900. The route travels on a combination of paved and gravel roads that are suitable for all vehicles. Twenty miles of this route are officially designated a National Forest Scenic Byway.

Travel Season

The entire route is open year-round although the gravel portion can become slippery after heavy rains.

Description

The St. Francis scenic byway rides atop Crowley's Ridge through the hardwood forests of oak and hickory of the St. Francis National Forest. Crowley's Ridge runs north and south for 200 miles from southern Missouri down to the Mississippi River at Helena. The ridge rises more than 200 feet above the surrounding delta farm lands.

Legend has it that a tribe of Indians known as the "Mound Builders" lived in this area long before the American Indian. The "Mound Builders" were the ancestors of the Indians found by white men moving into this area. The tribal name comes from their custom of burying the dead with the tools considered necessary for existence in another world. Some of the mounds can still be found in the area.

There are two developed recreation areas found along the byway. Bear Creek Lake is located near the byway's northern end. This 625-acre lake offers boating, swimming, and fishing opportunities. The lake is stocked with bass, crappie, and bluegill. Two campgrounds are located on the lake offering a total of 41 campsites that can accommodate tents or recreational vehicles, however no hookups are provided. The developed picnic area, Beaver Point, offers 17 picnic tables.

The other developed camping area is located near the southern end of the byway. The 420-acre Storm Creek Lake offers boating and fishing for bass, crappie, or bluegill. A swimming beach is also found here with shower facilities. The campground here has 18 sites for tents and recreational vehicles; no hookups are provided.

Local Information

Ozark - St. Francis National Forest
605 W. Main St.
Russelville, AR 72801
Phone: 501-968-2354

Marianna - Lee County C of C
67 W. Main St.
Marianna, AR 72360
Phone: 501-295-2469

Phillips County Chamber of Commerce
P.O. Box 447
Helena, AR 72342
Phone: 501-338-8327

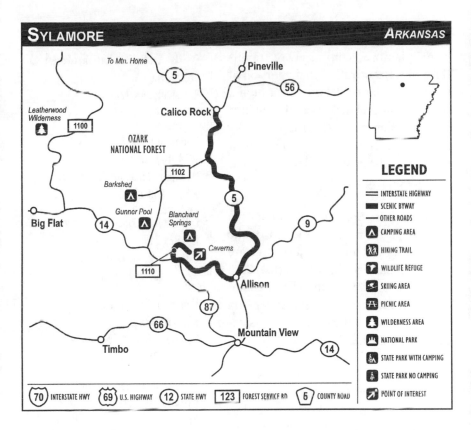

Route Location

The Sylamore scenic byway is located in north-central Arkansas, about 25 miles southeast of Mountain Home. The northern access starts just south of Calico Rock and travels south to Allison and then west to Blanchard Springs Caverns.

Roads Traveled

The 26-mile route follows Arkansas State Highways 5 and 14 and Forest Service Road 1110 to Blanchard Springs Caverns. The entire route travels on two-lane paved roads suitable for all vehicles. All 26 miles have been designated a National Forest Scenic Byway.

Travel Season

The entire route is usually open year-round.

Description

The Sylamore scenic byway travels through a beautifully scenic portion of the Ozark National Forest, through a forest of oak and hickory with stands of shortleaf pine, and across rugged, rocky outcrops. Portions of the byway follow the banks of the White River, popular for canoeing and fishing.

The Blanchard Springs Recreation Area is perhaps the main attraction of the byway. Within this recreation area are the Blanchard Springs Caverns. Cavern tours depart from the visitor center daily throughout the year except on some holidays. One guided tour is accessible to the handicapped.

Also found in the recreation area is a 32-site campground on the bank of the North Sylamore Creek. Picnic tables, drinking water, restrooms, and a sanitary dump station are provided. The day use area has 32 picnic tables, restrooms, and a swimming area with bathhouses and showers. The North Sylamore Trail can be accessed in this area. During the summer months, evening programs about the many facets of the national forest are presented at the Shelter Cave Amphitheater.

Local Information

Ozark - St. Francis National Forest
605 W. Main St.
Russelville, AR 72801
Phone: 501-968-2354

Mountain Home Area C of C
1023 Hwy. 62 E.
Mountain Home, AR 72653
Phone: 800-822-3536

Calico Rock / Pineville Trade Area
P.O. Box 245
Calico Rock, AR 72519
Phone: 501-297-8868

Mountain View Area C of C
P.O. Box 133
Mountain View, AR 72560
Phone: 501-269-8068

Blanchard Springs Caverns
USDA Forest Service
P.O. Box 1279
Mountain View, AR 72560
Phone: 501-757-2211.
Reservations are recommended during the summer.

Wildlife observers should be on the lookout for white-tailed deer and wild turkey. Birdwatchers can look for more than 150 species of birds, including bluejays, robins, cardinals, warblers, and finches. During the winter months, bald eagles can occasionally be seen soaring overhead.

The Leatherwood Wilderness lies to the west of the byway. This area offers seclusion in a hardwood forest setting. The area also provides opportunities for back country camping and hiking.

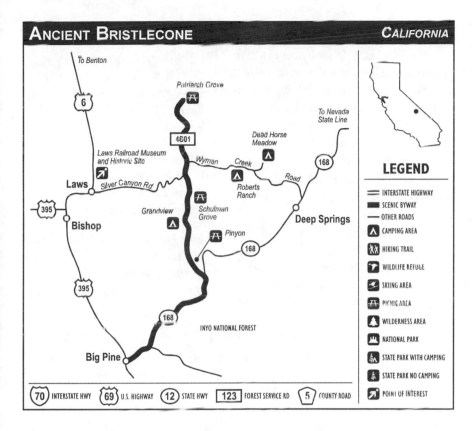

Route Location

Located in east-central California, south of Bishop near the Nevada state line. The scenic byway begins in Big Pine off U.S. Highway 395 and travels northeast to the road's end at Patriarch Grove on the Inyo National Forest.

Roads Traveled

The 36-mile route follows California State Highway 168 and Forest Service Road 4S01, also known as the White Mountain Road. The route travels over a paved surface to Schulman Grove and then on a graded dirt road to Patriarch Grove. Because of the grade and tight curves, motorhomes or vehicles pulling trailers are not recommended beyond the paved section. Travelers will need to retrace the route back to State Highway 168. The entire route is designated a National Forest Scenic Byway.

Travel Season

Open year-round although sections may be closed in the winter months.

Description

The Ancient Bristlecone scenic drive begins at an elevation around 8,000 feet and climbs through the White Mountains to a height of 11,200 feet at Patriarch Grove. The byway crosses the Inyo National Forest providing occasional views of the Great Basin desert to the east and the mountain peaks of the Sierra Nevada Range to the west.

The Ancient Bristlecone Pine Forest, situated within the national forest, provides the visitor the opportunity to view the oldest-known living trees on Earth, the Bristlecone Pine. These trees were discovered by Dr. Edmund Schulman, a scientist from the University of Arizona. Schulman traveled throughout the southwest in search of old trees that would provide a sensitive record of climatic conditions. His investigations led him to the White Mountains and the discovery of the Bristlecone Pine.

There are two self-guided nature trails at Schulman Grove, named in memory of this dedicated scientist, that provide an up-close look at these ancient trees. The oldest living tree, the 4,700 year-old Methuselah tree, grows along the Methuselah Trail. A trek along the Discovery Walk will take you to the first tree dated at over 4,000 years by Dr. Schulman, the Pine Alpha. There is a visitor center and picnic facilities at Schulman Grove.

Further up the scenic byway is Patriarch Grove. This area also offers picnic facilities and a nature trail. The self-guide trail here leads to the Patriarch Tree, the largest Bristlecone Pine in the world.

Local Information

Inyo National Forest
White Mountain Ranger District
798 N. Main St.
Bishop, CA 93514
Phone: 760-873-2525

Bishop Chamber of Commerce
690 N. Main St.
Bishop, CA 93514
Phone: 760-873-8405

Laws Railroad Museum & Historical Site
P.O. Box 363
Bishop, CA 93514
Phone: 760-873-5950

Nearby Routes

Owens Valley To Death Valley, page 90 / Saline Valley, page 98

Lodging Directory

Super 8 Motel High Sierra Lodge - Bishop, page 431 — Hotel / Motel

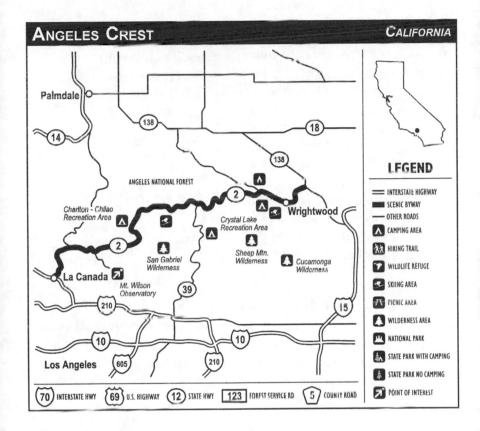

Route Location

Angeles Crest is located in southwestern California, northeast of Los Angeles. The western access starts in the town of La Canada off Interstate 210 and travels east to the junction of California State Highway 138, northeast of Wrightwood.

Roads Traveled

The 70-mile scenic byway follows California State Highway 2 which is a two-lane paved road suitable for all vehicles. The sixty-four miles of this route within the forest boundary are designated a National Forest Scenic Byway.

Travel Season

Most of the route is open year-round except for a small segment closed by winter snows from late December through early April.

Description

The Angeles Crest scenic byway crosses the San Gabriel Mountains of the Angeles National Forest, traveling alongside the San Gabriel and Sheep Mountain Wilderness areas. The scenic byway offers an escape from the hustle and bustle of the city of Los Angeles. The byway offers outstanding panoramic vistas of Los Angeles, the San Fernando and San Gabriel Valleys and, on clear days, Santa Catalina Island.

The Angeles National Forest offers numerous recreational activities. During the winter months, the byway provides access to several ski and snowplay areas. The warmer months brings those interested in camping or hiking. There are several campgrounds and picnic areas located along the byway as are many hiking trails ranging from short nature trails to longer, more strenuous hiking.

The two wilderness areas adjacent to the byway provide excellent opportunities for back country hiking. The many hiking trails accessible along the route lead to secluded areas with scenic vistas or walk-in-only camping and picnicking sites. The Pacific Crest National Scenic Trail may also be accessed along the byway.

A short side trip off the byway on Mount Wilson Forest Road will lead you to the world-famous, 100-inch telescope at Mount Wilson Observatory. The observatory is open to the public for touring on weekends.

Opportunities for viewing wildlife are also plentiful along the byway. Nelson bighorn sheep are often seen. Other wildlife found here includes deer, black bears, coyotes, mountain lions, badgers, and raccoons.

Local Information

Angeles National Forest
30800 Bouquet Canyon Rd.
Santa Clarita, CA 91350
Phone: 805-296-9710

Wrightwood Chamber of Commerce
P.O. Box 416
Wrightwood, CA 92397
Phone: 619-249-4320

La Canada Flintridge C of C
4529 Angeles Crest Hwy. #102
La Canada Flintridge, CA 91011
Phone: 818-790-4289

Nearby Routes

Rim Of The World, page 96

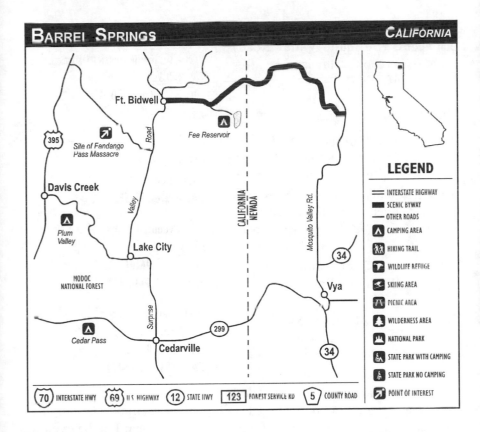

Route Location

The Barrel Springs Back Country Byway is located in the northeastern corner of California, approximately 50 miles northeast of Alturas. The byway begins in Fort Bidwell and travels east into Nevada ending at the intersection with Mosquito Valley Road.

Roads Traveled

The 25-mile route follows the Barrel Springs Road which is a single-lane gravel-surfaced road that can safely be driven in a two-wheel drive, high-clearance vehicle. Note that the route travels across remote country where other vehicles may not pass through for one or two days at a time, so be prepared for any road emergencies. Twenty miles of this scenic drive are officially designated a BLM Type II Back Country Byway.

Travel Season

The route is generally open from May through mid-November and then closed due to heavy winter snows. The eastern access (Mosquito Valley Road) may also become impassable after heavy rains.

Description

The Barrel Springs Back Country Byway winds through a maze of rocky rims and rolling hills covered with sagebrush and juniper. The byway offers wide open vistas of the Great Basin Plateau country in the shadow of the Warner Mountains to the west. The byway offers scenic views of many shallow desert lakes.

Excellent opportunities exist for observing wildlife common to the Great Basin. Mule deer and pronghorn antelope are usually encountered along the drive. Golden eagles, red-tailed hawks, and prairie falcons are birds of prey that are often seen. Coyotes may also be seen occasionally, but are more often heard in the evening serenading the moon.

Not far off of the byway is Fee Reservoir. This small desert lake is stocked with trout in the spring and early summer months. Visitors will also find a primitive campground here. Other camping opportunities can be found in Modoc National Forest to the west of the byway.

Nearby Routes

Lakeview To Steens, page 296

Local Information

BLM - Susanville District Office
705 Hall St.
Susanville, CA 96130
Phone: 916-257-5381

Modoc National Forest
441 N. Main St.
Alturas, CA 96101
Phone: 916-233-5811

Modoc County Chamber of Commerce
522 S. Main St.
Alturas, CA 96101
Phone: 916-233-4434

Lake County Chamber of Commerce
126 North E St.
Lakeview, OR 97630
Phone: 541-947-6040

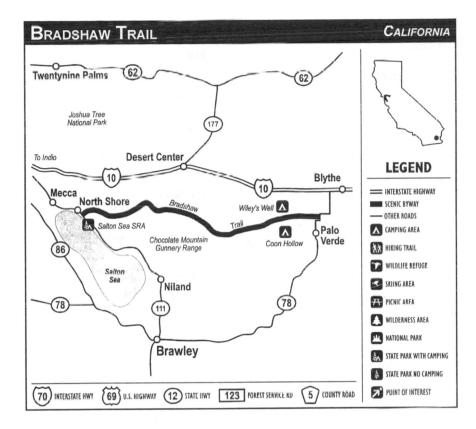

Route Location

The Bradshaw Trail is located in southeastern California, west of Blythe near the Arizona state line. The byway's eastern terminus is located at the intersection of California State Highway 78, south of Blythe. The byway then travels west to State Highway 111, ending just south of North Shore.

Roads Traveled

The 70-mile route follows the Bradshaw Trail Road which is a county maintained graded dirt road. The route travels across remote country and requires a four-wheel drive vehicle or other specialized vehicle such as a dirt bike or all-terrain vehicle. The entire route is officially designated a BLM Type III Back Country Byway.

Travel Season

The route is generally open year-round with possible temporary closures at

Travel Season

The route is generally open from mid-May through mid-November. Snow closes the route during the winter months. Travelers should be advised that heavy rains may also cause the road to become impassable.

Description

The Buckhorn Back Country Byway travels across the primitive expanses of the Great Basin Plateau through sagebrush-covered hills and stands of aspen, mountain mahogany, and juniper.

Local Information

BLM - Susanville District Office
705 Hall St.
Susanville, CA 96130
Phone: 916-257-5381

Lassen County Chamber of Commerce
84 N. Lassen St.
Susanville, CA 96130
Phone: 916-257-4323

Modoc County Chamber of Commerce
522 S. Main St.
Alturas, CA 96101
Phone: 916-233-4434

The Buckhorn byway provides excellent opportunities for viewing wildlife. Small herds of wild horses can occasionally be seen roaming the open range. More commonly seen, however, are pronghorn antelope and mule deer. Coyotes also inhabit this area, but are most likely heard rather than seen. Two intermittent dry lakes along the byway provide habitat for ducks, geese and other wild birds during the spring.

There are no developed campgrounds along the byway, however, the BLM permits overnight camping on BLM-administered lands. To the north of the byway is the Modoc National Forest. Camping and picnicking facilities may be found within the forest.

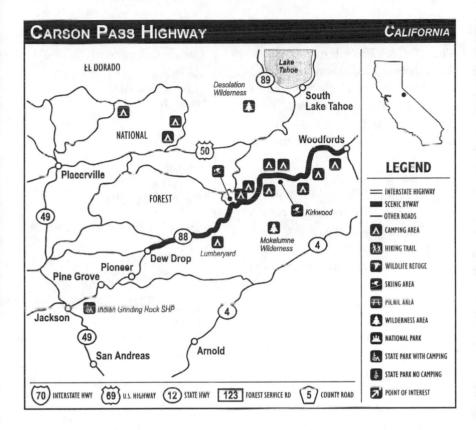

CARSON PASS HIGHWAY — CALIFORNIA

LEGEND

- ═══ INTERSTATE HIGHWAY
- ▬ SCENIC BYWAY
- ─── OTHER ROADS
- CAMPING AREA
- HIKING TRAIL
- WILDLIFE REFUGE
- SKIING AREA
- PICNIC AREA
- WILDERNESS AREA
- NATIONAL PARK
- STATE PARK WITH CAMPING
- STATE PARK NO CAMPING
- POINT OF INTEREST

(70) INTERSTATE HWY   (69) U.S. HIGHWAY   (12) STATE HWY   [123] FOREST SERVICE RD   (5) COUNTY ROAD

Route Location

The Carson Pass Highway is located in east-central California, approximately 60 miles east of Sacramento. The byway's southwestern access is in the town of Dewdrop, north of Pioneer. The byway travels northeast to Woodfords near the Nevada border.

Roads Traveled

Carson Pass Highway follows California State Highway 88 which is a two-lane paved road suitable for all types of vehicles. The byway is approximately 58 miles long and is designated a National Forest Scenic Byway.

Travel Season

The route is open year-round except for occasional closures in the winter for snow and ice removal.

Description

The Carson Pass Highway travels through the Eldorado and Toiyabe National Forests, winds through the western slope of the Sierra Nevada, reaches the summit at Carson Pass, and ends up on the eastern slope of the Sierra Nevada. The road travels through rugged volcanic skylines, lush green meadows, mountain lakes surrounded by timber-covered slopes, and rock valleys. This highway was one of the first trans-Sierra routes into California and was first explored in 1844 by John C. Fremont and mountain man Christopher "Kit" Carson.

Recreational opportunities are numerous along the byway. Beautiful lakes found along the byway offer boating and fishing. There are numerous camping and picnicking areas adjacent to the byway. Winter brings recreation in the form of cross-country skiing, downhill skiing, snowmobiling, and sledding.

Those interested in hiking will find the Pacific Crest National Scenic Trail crossing the route. The Mokelumne Wilderness also provides hiking and backpacking opportunities.

Local Information

Eldorado National Forest
100 Forni Rd.
Placerville, CA 95667
Phone: 916-622-5061

Toiyabe National Forest
Carson Ranger District
1536 Carson St.
Carson City, NV 89720
Phone: 702-882-2766

Amador County Chamber of Commerce
125 Peek St.
Jackson, CA 95642
Phone: 800-649-4988

Alpine County Chamber of Commerce
P.O. Box 265
Markleeville, CA 96120
Phone: 916-694-2475

El Dorado County Chamber of Commerce
542 Main St.
Placerville, CA 95667
Phone: 800-457-6279

Calaveras County Chamber of Commerce
P.O. Box 115
San Andreas, CA 95249
Phone: 209-754-4009

Indian Grinding Rock SHP
14881 Pine Grove-Volcano Rd.
Pine Grove, CA 95665
Phone: 209-296-7488

Nearby Routes

Fort Churchill To Wellington, page 229 / Eastshore Drive, page 226

LODGING DIRECTORY

Druid House Bed & Breakfast - Pine Grove, page 434 — Bed & Breakfast / Inns

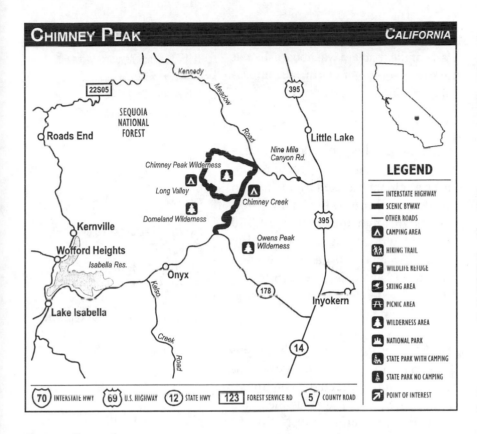

Route Location

The Chimney Peak Back Country Byway is situated in the southern
Sierra Mountains in south-central California. The route is approximately
60 miles northwest of Bakersfield, off State Highway 178. This is the
best point to begin the scenic drive.

Roads Traveled

Chimney Peak is a 38½ mile, Type II Back Country Byway designated
by the Bureau of Land Management. Beginning from State Highway
178, the route follows Canebrake Road north to Kennedy Meadows Road
and then circles Chimney Peak on Long Valley Loop Road back to its
junction with Canebrake Road. The road is mostly a narrow, slow speed,
secondary road. High-clearance vehicles are recommended on this route,
however, normal passenger cars can usually travel the route by using
extra care in some places.

Travel Season

Parts of the road are washboard-like at times and some sections may be impassible in winter and early spring.

Description

The Chimney Peak back country byway offers a unique opportunity to drive a seldom traveled route through the Sierra Mountains. The route passes through more than 50,000 acres of wilderness in a transition zone between the Mojave Desert and the Sierra Nevadas. The remoteness of this route lends a feeling of the rugged old west.

The byway is surrounded by the Owens Peak Wilderness, Chimney Peak Wilderness, and Domeland Wilderness. Trails can be accessed along the route, including the Pacific Crest National Scenic Trail, that will lead you into the wilderness areas. Wildlife inhabiting this area includes black bear, bobcat, mountain lion, and mule deer.

Those interested in camping will find two campgrounds along the route. Chimney Creek Campground offers 36 sites, all with picnic tables and fire rings. Pit toilets are available. No water or trash receptacles are provided. Be sure to bring your own drinking water and take out all trash, including food scraps. Bears do inhabit this area of California!

The second campground is the Long Valley Campground. This campground provides eleven campsites with picnic tables and fire rings. Pit toilets are provided but there is no water or trash facilities. A primitive trail here leads to the scenic South Fork Kern River.

Local Information

BLM - Caliente Resource Area
3801 Pegasus Drive
Bakersfield, CA 93308
Phone: 805-391-6000

Sequoia National Forest
900 W. Grand Ave.
Porterville, CA 93257
Phone: 209-784-1500

Inyokern Chamber of Commerce
P.O. Box 232
Inyokern, CA 93527
Phone: 760-377-4712

Lake Isabella Chamber of Commerce
P.O. Box 567
Lake Isabella, CA 93240
Phone: 760-379-5236

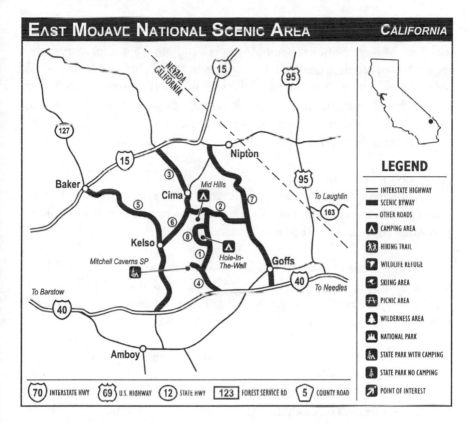

①	Black Canyon Road	⑤	Kelbaker Road
②	Cedar Canyon Road	⑥	Kelso-Cima Road
③	Cima Road	⑦	Lanfair-Ivenpah Road
④	Essex Road	⑧	Wild Horse Canyon

Route Location

The following eight scenic drives are all located in southeastern California, east of Barstow between Interstates 15 and 40, near the Nevada border. All of the routes travel through the East Mojave National Scenic Area. All eight routes are interconnecting, giving you the option to choose those you wish to explore.

Travel Season

All of the routes are open year-round except after severe thunderstorms which can make the routes impassable due to flash flooding.

Description

The East Mojave National Scenic Area is a unique 1.5 million acre desert region full of scenic, historic, and natural wonders. Table Mountain is a flat topped mesa visible from many of the scenic drives as are the Providence Mountains. The scenic drives travel through pinyon-juniper woodlands, sage-covered hills, cactus gardens, and colorful volcanic Cinder Cones and Lava Beds while offering outstanding views of the surrounding mountains.

A variety of recreational opportunities are available in the East Mojave National Scenic Area. Camping is offered in two developed campgrounds, the Mid Hills and Hole-In-The-Wall, as well as primitive camping which is permitted anywhere on BLM administered lands.

Old mining roads in the New York, Castle, Clark, and Providence Mountains provide plenty of opportunities for hiking and mountain biking. Several developed trails can be found in the Piute Range, Providence Mountains, and between the two developed campgrounds.

There are two off-road vehicle trails crossing the region, the Mojave Road and the East Mojave Heritage Trail. The Mojave Road is a 130-mile historic Native American trade route, later developed into a wagon trail, and crosses east to west through the heart of the national scenic area. The East Mojave Heritage Trail is a 700-mile loop beginning and ending in Needles, with much of this trail passing through the East Mojave region.

Listed below are descriptions and conditions of the roads travelled for each scenic byway.

① Black Canyon Road

This scenic drive is a 20-mile route that travels over a graded dirt road suitable for all vehicles as long as caution is used on the occasional rough or sandy segments. The entire route is designated a BLM Type I Back Country Byway.

② Cedar Canyon Road

This is a 25-mile long route that travels over a graded dirt road suitable for all vehicles as long as caution is used on the occasional rough or sandy segments. The byway is designated a BLM Type I Back Country Byway.

③ Cima Road

This 17-mile route travels over a paved road suitable for all vehicles. The entire route has been designated a BLM Type I Back Country Byway.

④ Essex Road

The 16-mile route travels over a paved road suitable for all types of vehicles and is designated a BLM Type I Back Country Byway.

⑤ Kelbaker Road

All but 5 miles of this 60-mile route travel over a paved road. The route is suitable for all vehicles. The entire route has been designated a BLM Type I Back Country Byway.

⑥ Kelso-Cima Road

The 20-mile route travels over a paved road suitable for all vehicles and has been designated a BLM Type I Back Country Byway.

⑦ Lanfair-Ivenpah Road

This 55-mile route travels over a combination of paved and graded dirt road suitable for all vehicles. The entire route has been designated a BLM Type I Back Country Byway.

Local Information

BLM - Needles Resource Area
101 W. Spikes Rd.
Needles, CA 92363
Phone: 760-326-3896

BLM - California Desert District Office
6221 Box Springs Blvd.
Riverside, CA 92507
Phone: 909-697-5200

Barstow Area Chamber of Commerce
P.O. Box 698
Barstow, CA 92312
Phone: 760-256-8617

Needles Area Chamber of Commerce
100 G St.
Needles, CA 92363
Phone: 760-326-2050

Laughlin Chamber of Commerce
1725 Casino Dr.
Laughlin, NV 89028
Phone: 800-227-5245

Mitchell Caverns Natural Preserve
Essex Rd.
Essex, CA 92332
Phone: 805-942-0662

⑧ Wild Horse Canyon

This is a 12-mile route traveling over a dirt road that can be safely driven in a two-wheel drive, high-clearance vehicle. The entire route is designated a BLM Type II Back Country Byway.

Nearby Routes

Historic Route 66, page 36 / Red Rock Canyon, page 239

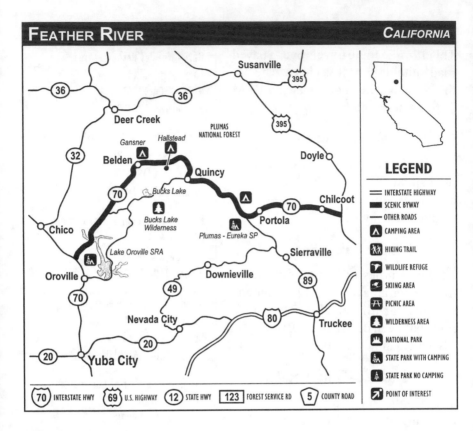

Route Location

Feather River is located in northeastern California, about 65 miles north of Sacramento. The western access is north of Oroville on California State Highway 70. The scenic byway travels north to Belden and then east to the byway's intersection with U.S. Highway 395, near the Nevada border.

Roads Traveled

The 130-mile route follows California State Highway 70 which is a two-lane paved road safe for travel by all types of vehicles. The entire route has been designated a National Forest Scenic Byway.

Travel Season

The byway is generally open year-round although winter driving conditions can be hazardous.

Description

This Feather River National Forest Scenic Byway follows a route that is the dividing line between the Sierra Nevada and Cascade Mountain Ranges. The byway provides the lowest pass route through the Sierras. The byway crosses the Plumas National Forest through steep canyon walls covered in places with moss and ferns, past large rock outcrops, and waterfalls.

For those interested in experiencing remote countryside, the Bucks Lake Wilderness area offers such opportunities for backpacking, secluded picnicking, hiking, and horseback riding. The Pacific Crest National Scenic Trail may also be accessed from the byway as it crosses the route in Belden.

The national forest provides several developed recreation areas adjacent to the byway that offer camping and picnicking facilities for tents and recreational vehicles. Other camping areas may be found within the national forest if you're willing to venture off the byway.

Local Information

Plumas National Forest
159 Lawrence St.
Quincy, CA 95971
Phone: 916-283-2050

Eastern Plumas Chamber of Commerce
P.O. Box 1379
Portola, CA 96122
Phone: 916-832-5444

Quincy Main Street C of C
522 Lawrence St.
Quincy, CA 95971
Phone: 916-283-0188

Oroville Area Chamber of Commerce
P.O. Box 3829
Oroville, CA 95965
Phone: 800-655-GOLD

Plumas-Eureka State Park & Museum
310 Johnsville Rd.
Blairsden, CA 96130
Phone: 916-836-2380

Lake Oroville State Recreation Area
400 Glen Dr.
Oroville, CA 95966
Phone: 916-538-2200

The Lake Oroville State Recreation Area offers over 200 sites for tents and recreational vehicles; hookups are available at many of the campsites. The 15,500-acre lake offers excellent boating, skiing, swimming, and fishing. Plumas-Eureka State Park has 67 campsites suitable for tents or RVs.

Nearby Routes

Lassen, page 86 / Yuba Donner, page 114

LODGING DIRECTORY

Bucks Lakeshore Resort - Bucks Lake, page 438 — Campground / RV Park & Resort
The Feather Bed - Quincy, page 438 — Bed & Breakfast / Inns

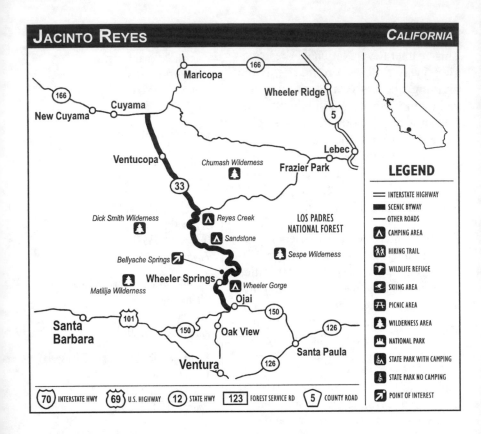

Route Location

Jacinto Reyes is located in southwestern California, approximately 15 miles north of Ventura. The byway's southern terminus begins just west of Ojai on California State Highway 150. The northern end of the byway is east of Cuyama on California Highway 166.

Roads Traveled

The scenic byway follows California State Highway 33 which is a two-lane paved road suitable for all vehicles. The byway is approximately 56 miles long. Thirty-seven miles of the byway are officially designated a National Forest Scenic Byway.

Travel Season

The entire route is generally open year-round.

Description

Traveling across the Los Padres National Forest, the byway begins nearly at sea level, winds upward through the coastal mountains to an elevation of 5,020 feet, and then makes a dramatic descent into the Cuyama Valley. Views of the Pacific Ocean and the distant Channel Islands are possible at times.

There are four wilderness areas that surround the scenic drive; Sespe, Dick Smith, Matilija, and Chumash Wildernesses. These areas provide outstanding opportunities for hiking, backpacking, and horseback riding in a secluded, wild setting.

A 31½-mile segment of Sespe Creek, which a portion of the byway follows, has been designated a Wild and Scenic River. This area offers fishing, swimming, camping, and hiking. The creek runs through the beautiful Sespe Gorge, a popular spot for rock climbing.

Local Information

Los Padres National Forest
6144 Calle Real
Goleta, CA 93117
Phone: 805-683-6711

Ojai Valley Chamber of Commerce
P.O. Box 1134
Ojai, CA 93024
Phone: 805-646-8126

Santa Barbara County C of C
P.O. Box 299
Santa Barbara, CA 93102
Phone: 805-965-3023

Greater Ventura Chamber of Commerce
785 S. Seaward Ave.
Ventura, CA 93001
Phone: 805-648-2875

Santa Paula Chamber of Commerce
P.O. Box 1
Santa Paula, CA 93061
Phone: 805-525-5561

An interesting spot worth visiting is Bellyache Springs. Contrary to its name, the spring produces water of exceptional quality. Visitors are also treated to a cascading waterfall at this site.

Those interested in staying overnight or longer will find several national forest campgrounds along the byway. Facilities vary but most provide restrooms, picnic tables, and fire rings.

Lodging Directory

Capri Motel - Ojai, page 441   — Hotel / Motel

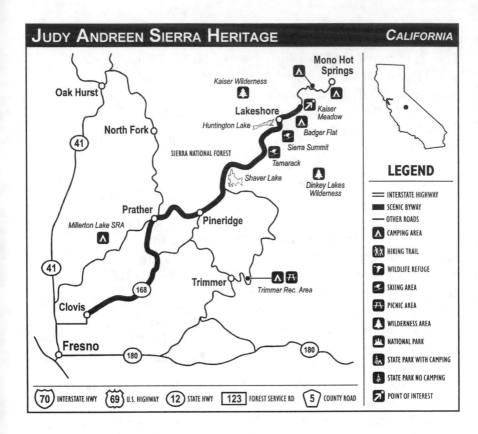

Route Location

Located in east-central California, northeast of Fresno. The byway begins in Clovis on California State Highway 168 and travels northeast to Kaiser Meadow, near Mono Hot Springs.

Roads Traveled

The 70-mile route follows California State Highway 168 to Huntington Lake and then Forest Route 80 to Kaiser Meadow. State Highway 168 is a two-lane paved road suitable for all vehicles. Forest Route 80 is primarily a two-lane paved route, however, the last mile to Kaiser Meadow becomes a one-lane paved route that is suitable only for passenger vehicles. Judy Andreen Sierra Heritage is a National Forest Scenic Byway.

Travel Season

The byway is open year-round from Clovis to Huntington Lake. During the

winter months, the portion from Huntington Lake to Kaiser Meadow is
closed due to snow.

Description

The Judy Andreen Sierra Heritage
scenic byway begins in Clovis at an
elevation of about 500 feet and winds
upward through the Sierra Nevada
Mountains to about 9,500 feet. The
byway crosses the Sierra National
Forest through oak, ponderosa pine,
and mixed conifer forests. A beautiful display of wildflowers are offered
in the foothills in spring and in the
mountains during summer months.

Recreational opportunities are plentiful within the national forest and
along the byway. Shaver Lake offers
developed camping areas and excel-

Local Information

Sierra National Forest
1600 Tollhouse Rd.
Clovis, CA 93611
Phone: 209-297-0706

Fresno Chamber of Commerce
2331 Fresno St.
Fresno, CA 93716
Phone: 209-495-4800

Clovis District Chamber of Commerce
325 Pollasky Ave.
Clovis, CA 93612
Phone: 209-299-7273

Millerton Lake State Recreation Area
5290 Millerton
Friant, CA 93626
Phone: 209-822-2332

lent trout fishing. Further up the byway is Huntington Lake. This lake
is rated one of the top sailing lakes in California; several sailboat races
are held throughout the summer months. Huntington Lake also offers
several campgrounds surrounding the lake with excellent fishing spots.

The byway offers spectacular views into the wilderness areas surrounding the route. Hiking trails can be found along the byway that provide
access to the mountainous wilderness areas. The White Bark Vista near
Kaiser Meadow has a gentle half-mile nature trail offering sweeping
views of the Sierra Nevada Mountains.

Nearby Routes

Kings Canyon, page 84 / Sierra Vista, page 100

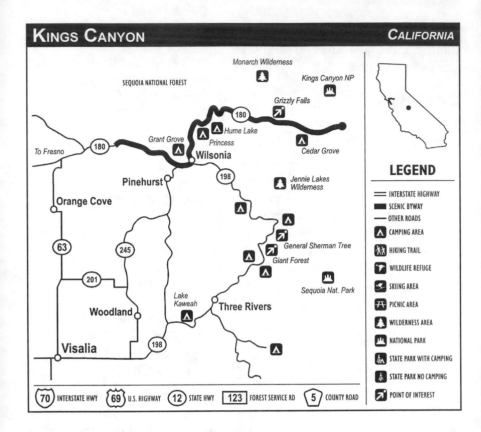

Route Location

The byway is located in central California, approximately 35 miles east of Fresno. The byway officially begins at the Sequoia National Forest boundary and travels east into the Kings Canyon National Park.

Roads Traveled

The 50-mile route follows California State Highway 180 which is a two-lane paved road suitable for all vehicles. The road ends in the national park where you will need to retrace the route back to the junction of California State Highways 180 and 198. The entire route has been designated a National Forest Scenic Byway.

Travel Season

The byway is generally open from mid-April through early November then the eastern section is closed from heavy winter snows.

Description

Dramatic changes in vegetation, wild-life, and geology are experienced along this byway as one climbs 4,000 feet through the western foothills of the Sierra Nevada Mountains, descends 3,700 feet into Kings Canyon, and then climbs again 2,000 feet to the beautiful Zumwalt Meadows. The eastern 20 miles of this byway follow alongside the South Fork of the Kings River, a National Wild and Scenic River. Within these 20 miles are 13 miles dividing the rugged Monarch Wilderness.

Kings Canyon is one of North America's deepest canyons. Kings Canyon reaches a depth of 8,200 feet from river level up to the Spanish Mountain's peak. At the eastern end of this byway you can stand in the valley and stare up at canyon walls rising nearly a mile above the river's level.

Just as impressive as the canyon are the giant sequoia trees that grow here, on the western slope of the Sierra Nevada Mountains. These trees can reach heights of 311 feet with branches 8 feet in diameter and bases 40 feet in width.

Local Information

Sequoia National Forest
900 W. Grand Ave.
Porterville, CA 93257
Phone: 209-784-1500

Fresno Chamber of Commerce
2331 Fresno St.
Fresno, CA 93716
Phone: 209-495-4800

Visalia Chamber of Commerce
720 W. Mineral King
Visalia, CA 93291
Phone: 209-734-5876

Orange Cove Chamber of Commerce
490 Park Blvd.
Orange Cove, CA 93646
Phone: 209-626-7934

Kings Canyon National Park
83918 Grant Grove
Kings Canyon Nat'l. Park, CA 93633
Phone: 209-335-2856

Sequoia National Park
47050 Generals Hwy.
Sequoia Nat'l. Park, CA 93262
Phone: 209-565-3341

There are many recreation areas along the byway and within the national forest and national parks. Many hiking and nature trails can be accessed along the route. In the Grant Grove recreation area, nature trails take you among the giant sequoias and to the huge General Grant Tree. Most of these recreation areas also provide camping and picnicking facilities.

Nearby Routes

Judy Andreen Sierra Heritage, page 82

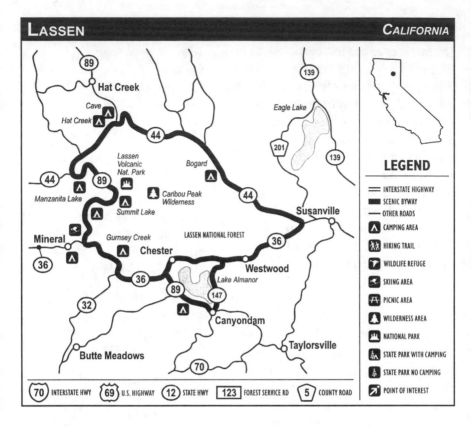

Route Location

The Lassen scenic byway is located in northeastern California, about 40 miles east of Redding. The byway forms a loop drive within the Lassen National Forest and a side trip traveling around Lake Almanor and through Canyondam.

Roads Traveled

The byway follows California State Highways 36, 44, 89, and 147 which are all two-lane paved roads suitable for all vehicles. The byway is approximately 172 miles in length. The route is officially designated a National Forest Scenic Byway.

Travel Season

The scenic byway is generally open year-round with temporary closures possible during the winter months.

Description

The Lassen National Forest Scenic By-way travels through this region of California known as the Crossroads. It is within this area that the peaks of the Sierra Nevada and Cascade Mountains meet and blend together with the sagebrush of the Great Basin.

For 30 miles the byway passes through the active Lassen Volcanic National Park. In May of 1914 Lassen Peak burst into eruption, beginning a 7-year cycle of sporadic outbursts. Before the eruption of Mount Saint Helens in 1980, Lassen Peak was the most recent volcanic outburst in the lower 48 states. This portion of the byway can provide interesting insight into the workings of active volcanoes.

The rest of the scenic drive crosses the beautiful Lassen National Forest. Scattered along the byway and throughout the national forest are developed recreation areas that provide camping and picnicking facilities.

Lake Almanor lies along the byway's southern portion and offers excellent fishing for Chinook salmon, rainbow and brown trout, and smallmouth bass. In addition to fishing, the lake is also popular for swimming, boating, and waterskiing. Several campgrounds and picnic areas surround the lake.

There are many hiking trails both in the national park and national forest. Hikers, backpackers, and horseback riders will find over 460 miles of trails within the national forest alone. The trails range from wide, easy-walking trails to more rugged and steep trails requiring more endurance. The Pacific Crest National Scenic Trail also crosses the scenic byway.

Local Information

Lassen National Forest
7288 Humboldt Rd.
Forest Ranch, CA 95942
Phone: 916-873-0580

Chester - Lake Almanor C of C
529 Main St.
Chester, CA 96020
Phone: 916-258-2426

Westwood Area Chamber of Commerce
P.O. Box 1235
Westwood, CA 96137
Phone: 916-256-2456

Lassen County Chamber of Commerce
84 N. Lassen St.
Susanville, CA 96130
Phone: 916-257-4323

Lassen Volcanic National Park
P.O. Box 100
Mineral, CA 96063
Phone: 916-595-4444

Nearby Routes

Feather River, page 78 / Trinity River, page 112

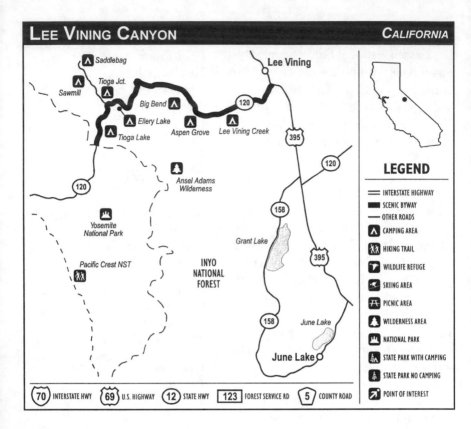

Route Location

Lee Vining Canyon is located in east-central California between Mono Lake and Yosemite National Park. The byway begins just south of Lee Vining and travels west through the Inyo National Forest to the Tioga Pass Entrance of Yosemite National Park. This road continues on through the national park as the Tioga - Big Oak Flat scenic byway.

Roads Traveled

The byway follows California State Highway 120 which is a two-lane paved road safe for travel by all types of vehicles. The 12-mile route is officially designated a National Forest Scenic Byway.

Travel Season

The route is normally open from Memorial Day through early November then closed by heavy snows during the winter.

Description

The Lee Vining Canyon byway is the highest vehicle crossing in the Sierra Nevada Range, climbing 3,200 feet to an elevation of 9,945 feet at Tioga Pass. As the byway travels through the rugged canyon and across the high Sierra Nevada Mountains, spectacular views of mountain meadows and jagged peaks reward the scenic byway traveler. Following alongside the byway are the cool waters of Lee Vining Creek. In autumn, large stands of aspen paint the canyon with colors of gold. Wildlife observers will want to be looking for bighorn sheep.

Those interested in camping will find six national forest campgrounds adjacent to the byway. These six campgrounds provide a total of 80 campsites, most having drinking water and restrooms. Two campgrounds operated by Mono County provide over 150 campsites. Approximately 10 miles south of the byway on June Lake Loop there are over 600 camping units available.

For those interested in primitive camping, the Ansel Adams Wilderness provides just that. Hiking trails accessed from the byway lead deep into the wilderness area where there are plenty of places one can pitch a tent and enjoy the seclusion.

Local Information

Inyo National Forest
White Mountain Ranger District
798 N. Main St.
Bishop, CA 93514
Phone: 760-873-2525

Lee Vining Chamber of Commerce
P.O. Box 130
Lee Vining, CA 93541
Phone: 760-647-6629

Mariposa County Chamber of Commerce
5158 Hwy. 140
Mariposa, CA 95338
Phone: 209-966-2456

Yosemite National Park
P.O. Box 577
Yosemite National Park, CA 95389
Phone: 209-372-0200

Nearby Routes

Tioga - Big Oak Flat, page 108

LODGING DIRECTORY

Whispering Pines - June Lake, page 443 — Hotel / Motel

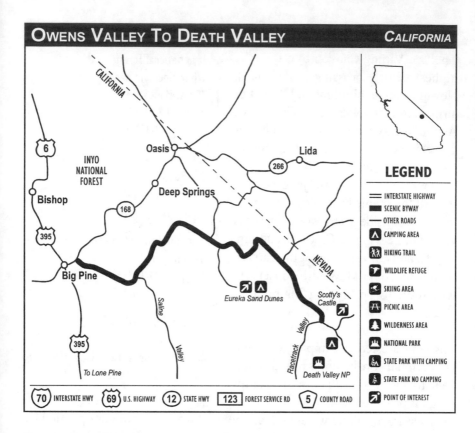

Route Location

Located in east-central California, south of Bishop, near the Nevada border. The byway's western access begins east of Big Pine off State Highway 168. The scenic byway heads east to the northern entrance of Death Valley National Park.

Roads Traveled

The 63-mile byway follows the Big Pine Death Valley Road which is a county maintained road. The first 32 miles are paved with the remaining 31 miles traveling over a graded dirt surface. You can safely drive this route in a two-wheel drive, high-clearance vehicle. The entire route has been designated a BLM Type II Back Country Byway.

Travel Season

The route is generally open year-round, but is subject to closure at times of heavy rainfall or winter snowfall.

Description

The Owens Valley To Death Valley byway begins east of Big Pine with excellent views of the Sierra Nevada Mountains and travels east through narrow canyons, badlands, high plateaus, and vast desert valleys. The byway traveler will pass through joshua tree and pinyon-juniper woodlands and sage-covered hills. The 700 foot high Eureka Sand Dunes, situated 10 miles south of the byway, can be seen from the byway. Camping and day use facilities can be found at the foot of the dunes.

There are five wilderness study areas, covering over 570,000 acres of land, that line the byway from end to end. These areas lend to excellent hiking, backpacking, and wildlife viewing opportunities.

Death Valley National Park contains the lowest point in the western hemisphere. Attractions found in the north unit of Death Valley National Park are Scotty's Castle and Ubehebe Crater. Guided tours of Scotty's Castle are offered throughout the year. The valley received its name in the winter of 1849 after the death of several gold seekers who attempted a shortcut through this area to the goldfields of California.

Local Information

BLM - Ridgecrest Resource Area
300 S. Richmond Rd.
Ridgecrest, CA 93555
Phone: 760-375-7125

Inyo National Forest
873 N. Main St.
Bishop, CA 93514
Phone: 760-873-5841

Bishop Chamber of Commerce
690 N. Main St.
Bishop, CA 93514
Phone: 760-873-8405

Lone Pine Chamber of Commerce
P.O. Box 749
Lone Pine, CA 93545
Phone: 760-876-4444

Death Valley National Park
P.O. Box 579
Death Valley, CA 92328
Phone: 760-786-2331

Nearby Routes

Ancient Bristlecone, page 61 / Saline Valley, page 98

LODGING DIRECTORY

Super 8 Motel High Sierra Lodge - Bishop, page 447 — Hotel / Motel

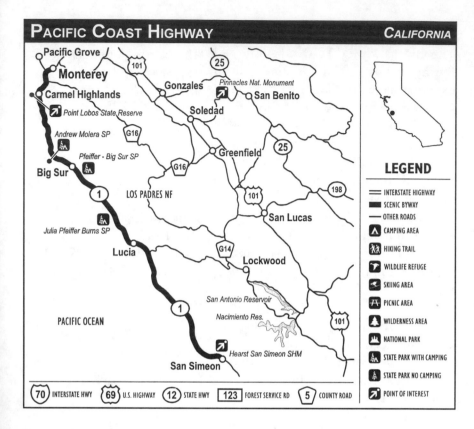

Route Location

The Pacific Coast Highway travels alongside the rugged coastline of the Pacific Ocean in west-central California. The highway travels between Monterey and San Simeon offering views of the ocean to the west and Los Padres National Forest to the east.

Roads Traveled

California Highway 1 is the route followed along this 95-mile scenic drive. The route is a two-lane paved road that is suitable for all types of vehicles. Seventy-two miles of the drive have been designated an All-American Road by the Federal Highway Administration.

Travel Season

The entire route is generally open year-round, however, slides caused by storms can periodically close the road during winter. During the summer months, fog can sometimes bring about hazardous driving conditions.

Description

The Pacific Coast Highway rides atop the rugged cliffs of California's scenic coastline, offering spectacular views of the vast ocean as waves crash upon the rocky shores. Miles of state parklands along the shore allow visitors to walk the beaches and watch playful sea otters or migrating gray whales in the winter months. On the northern end of the scenic drive is the Point Lobos State Reserve. This area holds one of the few remaining native Monterey cypress tree groves and offers observation platforms and walking trails. Several state parks are also found along the route that provide opportunities for pitching a tent or parking your recreational vehicle.

To the east of the scenic drive, if you can steer your eyes away from the west, lies the Los Padres National Forest. Found within the forest is the Ventana Wilderness which offers opportunities for hiking and horseback riding. The national forest also offers numerous campsites and picnic areas nestled among towering trees.

Also of interest is the Hearst Castle, officially named the Hearst San Simeon State Historical Monument. Publishing tycoon William Hearst built this magnificent estate that he called "The Enchanted Hill in the 1920s. The estate houses 165 rooms, exquisite pools, a vast collection of art and antiques, terraces and walkways, and acres of gardens. Hearst Castle is open for tours year-round and reservations are recommended.

Local Information

Los Padres National Forest
6144 Calle Real
Goleta, CA 93117
Phone: 805-683-6711

Monterey Peninsula C of C
P.O. Box 1591
Monterey, CA 93942
Phone: 408-649-1770

Pacific Grove Chamber of Commerce
P.O. Box 167
Pacific Grove, CA 93950
Phone: 408-373-3304

Seaside - Sand City C of C
505 Broadway Ave.
Seaside, CA 93955
Phone: 408-394-6501

San Simeon Chamber of Commerce
P.O. Box 1
San Simeon, CA 93452
Phone: 805-927-3500

Pfeiffer - Big Sur State Park
MAF Big Sur Station 1
Big Sur, CA 93920
Phone: 408-667-2315

Andrew Molera State Park
Phone: 408-667-2315

Julia Pfeiffer Burns State Park
Phone: 408-667-2315

LODGING DIRECTORY

The Martine Inn - Pacific Grove, page 447 — Bed & Breakfast / Inns

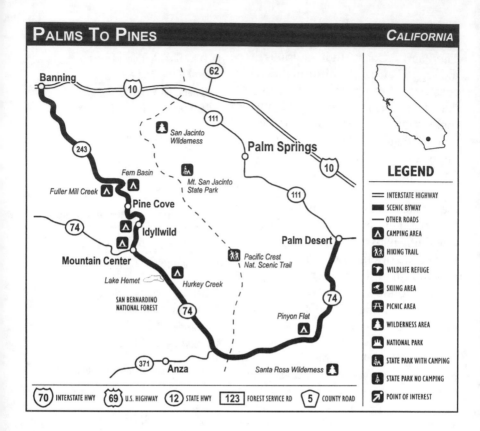

Route Location

Located in southern California near Palm Springs. The byway forms an open loop as it travels between Banning off I-10 and the town of Palm Desert on California State Highway 111.

Roads Traveled

Palms To Pines follows California State Highways 74 and 243 which are two-lane paved roads safe for travel by all types of vehicles. The 67-mile byway is designated a National Forest Scenic Byway.

Travel Season

The route is generally open year-round.

Description

The scenic byway winds through the San Jacinto Mountains of the San Bernardino National Forest. This mountain range is isolated from other southern California mountain ranges by the Sonoran Desert, Banning Pass, and the Coachella and San Jacinto Valley. The mountains provide a drastic contrast to the surrounding desert landscape.

The byway offers access to many recreational activities including wilderness exploration, hunting, rock climbing, and off-road vehicle use. Wildlife observers will find bald eagles nesting along the shores of Lake Hemet during the winter. Bighorn sheep may also be spotted along the rocky mountainsides.

Over 150 miles of trails to be explored are found within this area of the national forest. The Pacific Crest National Scenic Trail crosses the byway. Hiking, backpacking, and horseback riding are popular activities in the two wilderness areas. Trailheads into the San Jacinto Wilderness can be found near Idyllwild.

The national forest has developed several campgrounds along the byway. Camping and picnicking facilities are also available in the Mt. San Jacinto State Park.

Local Information

San Bernardino National Forest
1824 S. Commercenter Cir.
San Bernardino, CA 92408
Phone: 909-383-5588

Palm Desert Chamber of Commerce
72-990 Hwy. 111
Palm Desert, CA 92260
Phone: 800-873-2428

Idyllwild Chamber of Commerce
54274 N. Circle Dr.
Idyllwild, CA 92349
Phone: 909-659-3259

Banning Chamber of Commerce
123 E. Ramsey St.
Banning, CA 92220
Phone: 909-849-4695

Palm Springs Chamber of Commerce
190 W. Amado Rd.
Palm Springs, CA 92262
Phone: 760-325-1577

Mt. San Jacinto State Park
25905 Hwy. 243
Idyllwild, CA 92549
Phone: 909-659-2607

Nearby Routes

Bradshaw Trail, page 67 / Rim Of The World, page 96

LODGING DIRECTORY

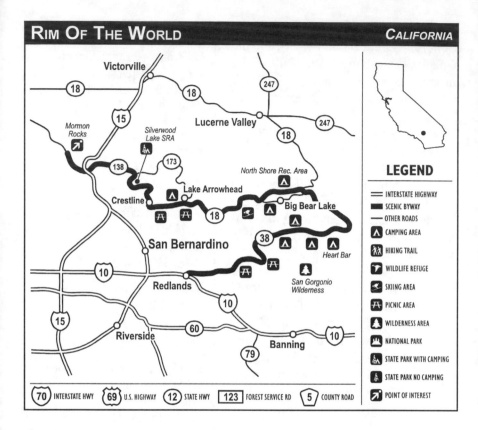

Route Location

The Rim Of The World scenic byway begins at the Mormon Rocks Fire Station on State Highway 138, just west of Interstate 15. The byway travels southeast along the shores of Silverwood Lake and Big Bear Lake before turning west to end in Redlands. The byway is located in southwestern California on the San Bernardino National Forest.

Roads Traveled

Rim Of The World follows a series of California State Highways which are two-lane paved roads. The highways followed are SH 138, SH 18, and SH 38 and are suitable for all types of vehicles. All but 13 miles of the 115-mile byway are designated a National Forest Scenic Byway.

Travel Season

The entire route is usually open year-round.

Description

Rim Of The World offers some of the most naturally beautiful scenery in southern California. Sweeping views of the San Bernardino Mountains reward the traveler of this scenic drive. The byway follows some of the routes taken by travelers of the past. Native Americans, Mormon pioneers, and miners all came through this area with different destinations in mind.

The San Bernardino National Forest offers nearly unlimited recreational opportunities. The San Gorgonio Wilderness is nearly 57,000 acres of granite ridges, subalpine meadows, and placid lakes. Excellent hiking and backpacking opportunities may be found here.

Numerous camping and picnicking areas developed by the Forest Service are all along the byway. Some of the more secluded camping areas can be reached by taking a short drive off the byway. The North Shore Recreation Area along the banks of Big Bear Lake offers a 130-site campground, visitor center, and a 3-mile walking and bicycling trail.

The Silverwood Lake SRA is located on the shores of Silverwood Lake. The 100-acre lake is popular for swimming, fishing, and boating. The park has developed campsites, picnic facilities, and miles of paved trails.

Local Information

San Bernardino National Forest
1824 S. Commercenter Cir.
San Bernardino, CA 92408
Phone: 909-383-5588

Crestline Resorts Chamber of Commerce
P.O. Box 926
Crestline, CA 92325
Phone: 909-338-2706

Lake Arrowhead Chamber of Commerce
28200 Hwy. 189, Bldg. F-290
Lake Arrowhead, CA 92352
Phone: 909-337-3715

Running Springs Area C of C
P.O. Box 96
Running Springs, CA 92382
Phone: 909-867-2411

Big Bear Chamber of Commerce
630 Bartlett Rd.
Big Bear Lake, CA 92315
Phone: 909-866-4608

Redlands Chamber of Commerce
1 E. Redlands Blvd.
Redlands, CA 92373
Phone: 909-793-2546

Silverwood Lake State Recreation Area
14651 Cedar Cir.
Hesperia, CA 92345
Phone: 760-389-2303

Nearby Routes

Angeles Crest, page 63 / Palms To Pines, page 94

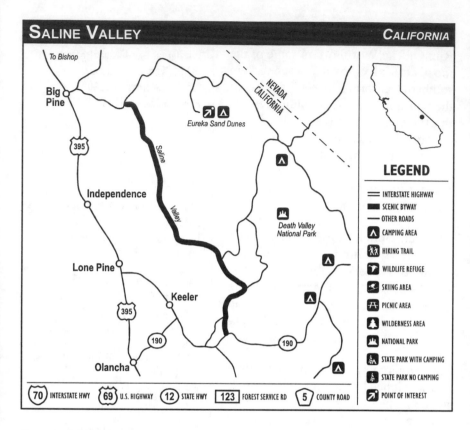

Route Location

Located in east-central California, near the Nevada border. The southern access starts southeast of Keeler off California State Highway 190 and travels north to the junction of the Owens Valley To Death Valley scenic drive, east of Big Pine.

Roads Traveled

The 82-mile route follows the Saline Valley Road which is mostly a county maintained graded dirt road. Ten miles of the byway are paved. The route can safely be traveled in a two-wheel drive, high-clearance vehicle. The entire route has been designated a BLM Type II Back Country Byway.

Travel Season

The byway is normally open year-round, but may occasionally close due to heavy summer rains or winter snowfall.

Description

The Saline Valley Back Country By-way offers sweeping vistas of the Panamint and Saline Valleys as it travels through this remote desert region. Views of the Inyo Mountains dominate the landscape as they reach heights of 10,000 feet above the valley floor

Remnants of the Saline Valley Salt Works and Tram are visible along the byway. This once was the steepest tramway in the United States operating between 1911 and 1913, and is now listed on the National Register of Historic Places. The tramway rises from 1,100 feet in the Saline Valley floor to 8,500 feet at the Inyo Crest. It then drops to 3,600 feet at Swansea in the Owens Valley.

Saline Valley Warm Springs is a BLM special management area providing warm spring bathing and camping opportunities. The area is located off a spur road six miles east of the Saline Valley Road.

Death Valley National Park lies to the east of the byway. Side roads provide access to this area where the lowest point in the western hemisphere resides.

Local Information

BLM California Desert Information Ctr.
831 Barstow Rd.
Barstow, CA 92311
Phone: 760-256-8617

Inyo National Forest
873 N. Main St.
Bishop, CA 93514
Phone: 760-873-5841

Bishop Chamber of Commerce
690 N. Main St.
Bishop, CA 93514
Phone: 760-873-8405

Lone Pine Chamber of Commerce
126 S. Main St.
Lone Pine, CA 93545
Phone: 760-876-4444

Death Valley National Park
P.O. Box 579
Death Valley, CA 92328
Phone: 760-786-2331

Nearby Routes

Ancient Bristlecone, page 61 / Owens Valley To Death Valley, page 90

LODGING DIRECTORY

Super 8 Motel High Sierra Lodge - Bishop, page 452 — Hotel / Motel

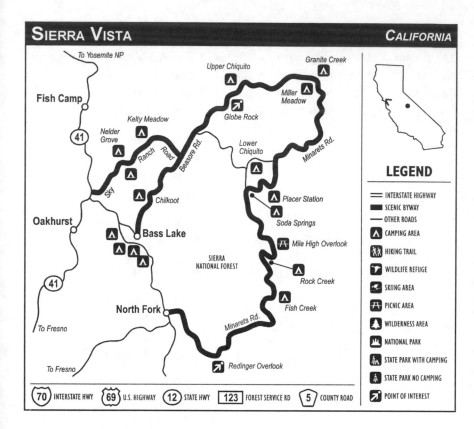

Route Location

The Sierra Vista scenic byway is located in east-central California, between Yosemite National Park and Kings Canyon National Park. The byway forms an open loop between Bass Lake and North Fork, with a side
trip off the main byway ending at the junction with California State Hwy. 41.

Roads Traveled

Beginning in North Fork, the byway follows Minarets Road northeasterly to
Beasore Road. The byway then follows Beasore Road south to Bass Lake.
The side road that is also a part of the byway follows Sky Ranch Road to
State Highway 41. Minarets Road is a two-lane paved road from North
Fork to Beasore Road. From this point, the first 8 miles of Beasore Road
has a graded dirt surface; expect to travel at slow speeds on this portion.
The rest of this road to Bass Lake is paved. The entire byway is safe for
travel by all types of vehicles. The 100-mile byway has been officially des-
ignated a National Forest Scenic Byway.

Travel Season

The route is generally open from mid-May through mid-November and then is closed by winter snows.

Description

The Sierra Vista scenic byway begins at an elevation of 3,000 feet and climbs to more than 7,000 feet as it crosses the Sierra National Forest. Several scenic overlooks along the byway provide sweeping views of the surrounding Sierra Nevada Mountains. The Redinger Overlook provides an excellent view of Redinger Lake and the San Joaquin River. The Mile High Overlook offers spectacular views of the Minarets, Mount Ritter, and Mammoth Mountain as well as views of Mammoth Pool Reservoir and the San Joaquin River.

Those interested in camping overnight or longer will find plenty of camp-grounds available. All campgrounds operate on a first-come, first-served basis as no reservations are accepted. The Forest Service also permits camping nearly anywhere on national forest land. Nelder Grove is popular with campers. Here you'll find over 100 giant sequoias intermingled with pine, fir, and incense cedar. The Shadow of the Giants National Recreation Trail here is a one-mile, self-guided trail along the banks of Nelder Creek. Another point of interest found in this area is what's known as "Granddad and the Grandkids." A single, isolated mature sequoia tree has one large branch outstretched over several younger sequoias growing beneath.

Local Information

Sierra National Forest
1600 Tollhouse Rd.
Clovis, CA 93611
Phone: 209-297-0706

Eastern Madera County C of C
49074 Civic Cir.
Oakhurst, CA 93644
Phone: 209-683-7766

North Fork Chamber of Commerce
P.O. Box 426
North Fork, CA 93643
Phone: 209-877-2410

Bass Lake Chamber of Commerce
P.O. Box 126
Bass Lake, CA 93604
Phone: 209-642-3676

Yosemite National Park
P.O. Box 577
Yosemite National Park, CA 95389
Phone: 209-372-0200

Nearby Routes

Judy Andreen Sierra Heritage, page 82 / Tioga - Big Oak Flat, page 108

Lodging Directory

High Sierra RV - Oakhurst, page 456 — Campground / RV Park
Shilo Inn Oakhurst / Yosemite - Oakhurst, page 456 — Hotel / Motel

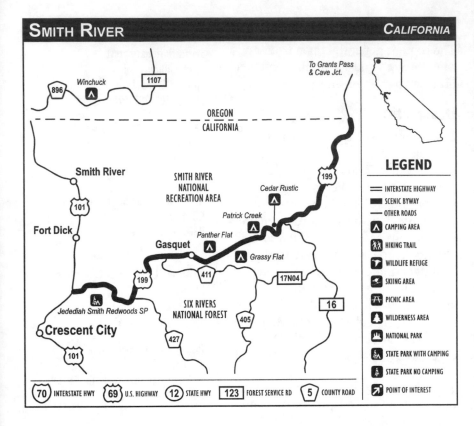

Route Location

The Smith River scenic byway is located in the northwest corner of California, beginning just north of Crescent City off U.S. Highway 101. The byway then travels northeast, ending at the Oregon state line.

Roads Traveled

The byway follows U.S. Highway 199 for 39 miles. U.S. Highway 199 is a two-lane paved route that is safe for all types of vehicles. Thirty-three miles of this route are designated a National Forest Scenic Byway.

Travel Season

The route is usually open year-round although poor driving conditions may exist during the winter months.

Description

The Smith River scenic byway travels through dense forests of mixed conifer as it crosses the Six Rivers National Forest and the Smith River National Recreation Area. Following alongside the byway for most of its 39 miles is the Middle Fork of the Smith River, popular with rafting enthusiasts as well as fishermen. Several access points to the river are provided along the byway. The Smith River is the only undammed river system in California and is designated a Wild and Scenic River.

The byway passes through the river canyon of rugged rock outcrops with the river below forming pools of calm, gently flowing water while other times swiftly flowing and crashing into rocks standing above river level. Otters, ducks, osprey, kingfishers, and occasional bald eagles can be seen along the river. Oftentimes you'll see fishermen on the banks of the river trying their luck at the Chinook salmon or steelhead found in the river.

Numerous trails within the forest and recreation area range from just over a ½ mile to more than 15 miles. These trails provide excellent opportunities for hiking, backpacking, or horseback riding into the beautiful country.

Local Information

Six Rivers National Forest
1330 Bayshore Way
Eureka, CA 95501
Phone: 707-442-1721

Crescent City-Del Norte County C of C
1001 Front St.
Crescent City, CA 95531
Phone: 800-343-8300

Illinois Valley Chamber of Commerce
P.O. Box 312
Cave Junction, OR 97523
Phone: 503-592-3326

Jedediah Smith Redwoods State Park
1440 US Hwy. 199
Crescent City, CA 95351
Phone: 707-458-3310

Redwood National Park
1111 Second St.
Crescent City, CA 95531
Phone: 707-464-6101

Smith River National Recreation Area
1375 Elk Valley Rd.
Crescent City, CA 95531
Phone: 707-458-3310

Several national forest campgrounds provide the weary traveler just the right spot for staying overnight or longer. Located at the western end of this byway is the Jedediah Smith Redwoods State Park. Here you can pitch your tent or park your recreational vehicle in the shade of the giant redwoods.

Nearby Routes

State Of Jefferson, page 104 / Galice - Hellgate, page 290 / Rouge Umpqua - North Umpqua River, page 312

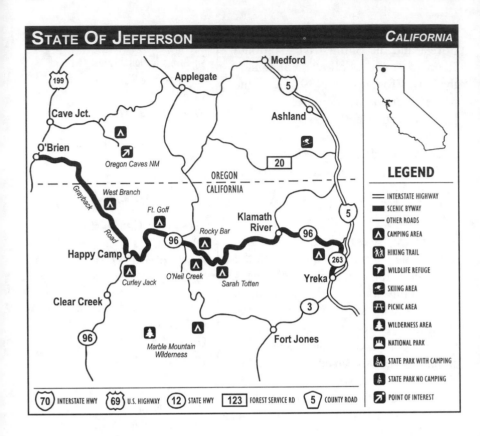

Route Location

This byway is located in the northwestern corner of California near the Oregon border. The southeastern access is located in the town of Yreka off Interstate 5. The byway travels northwest, eventually crossing the Oregon state line, and ends at the junction of U.S. Highway 199 south of Cave Junction, Oregon.

Roads Traveled

The State Of Jefferson is a 108-mile scenic byway that follows California State Highways 263 and 96 and Forest Service Road 40S07, also called the Grayback Road. All of the roads travel over a two-lane paved surface suitable for all vehicles. The byway is officially designated a National Forest Scenic Byway.

Travel Season

Open year-round with possible closures for snow removal in the winter.

Description

This scenic byway has a particularly interesting footnote in history. On Thursday, November 27, 1941, the State of Jefferson "seceded" from California and Oregon to form the 49th state of the Union. Several counties in northern California and southern Oregon proclaimed their independence to protest the lack of good roads and other basic services. Armed miners displaying the seal of the State of Jefferson stopped traffic at the "border" on U.S. Hwy. 99 (now Hwy. 263) to distribute the "Proclamation of Independence" which declared an intent to "secede each Thursday until further notice." The movement for secession, however, was stopped abruptly by the attack on Pearl Harbor. Nowadays the scenic byway traveler is free to cross this beautiful territory known as the Klamath National Forest.

Local Information

Klamath National Forest
1312 Fairlane Rd.
Yreka, CA 96097
Phone: 916-842-6131

Yreka Chamber of Commerce
117 W. Miner St.
Yreka, CA 96097
Phone: 916-842-1649

Northern Klamath River C of C
P.O. Box 25
Klamath River, CA 96050
Phone: 916-496-3325

Illinois Valley Chamber of Commerce
P.O. Box 312
Cave Junction, OR 97523
Phone: 503-592-3326

Ashland Chamber of Commerce
P.O. Box 1360
Ashland, OR 97520
Phone: 541-482-3486

Much of the byway follows alongside the meandering Klamath River, a designated National Wild and Scenic River. The waters of the river are home to steelhead and Chinook salmon, which fishermen may wish to spend some time trying to pull from the river. Rafting, canoeing, kayaking, and tubing are also popular activities offered by the river. Several campgrounds can be found along the banks of the river.

Wildlife observers will need to be on the lookout for a variety of wildlife inhabiting this area. Deer, otters, geese, ducks, osprey and bear inhabit this region of California. Occasionally bald eagles have been spotted riding on the wind currents up above.

Nearby Routes

Smith River, page 102 / Trinity Heritage, page 110 / Galice - Hellgate, page 290 / Rogue Umpqua - North Umpqua River, page 312

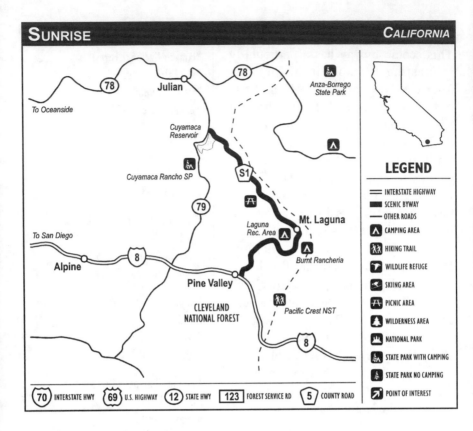

Route Location

The Sunrise scenic byway is located in southwestern California, approximately 45 miles east of San Diego. The southern terminus of the byway is about one mile east of Pine Valley off Interstate 8. The byway then travels north through the Cleveland National Forest and ends at the junction with California State Highway 79, south of Julian.

Roads Traveled

The 24-mile scenic byway follows County Road S1 which is a two-lane paved road suitable for all vehicles. The entire length of the route is officially designated a National Forest Scenic Byway.

Travel Season

The Sunrise byway is generally open year-round except for temporary closures in the winter for snow removal.

Description

The Sunrise scenic drive crosses the Cleveland National Forest, adjacent to the Anza Borrego Desert State Park. Views along the drive are of mountain meadows, pine and oak forests, and breathtaking views of the Anza Borrego Desert State Park from 6,000 feet above.

Wildlife observers will want to be on the lookout for the many species found in the area including blacktail deer, coyotes, and red-tailed hawks. Numerous other birds and small mammals inhabit this region of California and, to the patient observer, may be seen along the byway.

Recreational opportunities are not in short supply along this scenic byway. The Pacific Crest National Scenic Trail and the Noble Canyon National Recreation Trail may be accessed from the route. The nearby Cuyamaca Rancho State Park offers hundreds of miles of hiking and nature trails. The state park also offers developed camping and picnicking facilities.

The national forest also offers recreational areas along the byway that provide camping and picnicking opportunities. The two campgrounds found along the byway have a total of more than 200 campsites from which to choose from for an overnight stay.

The visitor center located in Mount Laguna offers wildlife exhibits and information on the scenic drive and surrounding area. The center is open on weekends during the summer. A nature trail is also located here.

Local Information

Cleveland National Forest
10845 Rancho Bernardo Rd.
San Diego, CA 92127
Phone: 619-673-6180

Julian Chamber of Commerce
P.O. Box 413
Julian, CA 92036
Phone: 760-765-1857

Alpine Chamber of Commerce
2157 Alpine Blvd.
Alpine, CA 91903
Phone: 619-445-2722

Greater San Diego C of C
402 W. Broadway, #1000
San Diego, CA 92101
Phone: 619-232-0124

Cuyamaca Rancho State Park
State Route 79
Julian, CA 92036
Phone: 760-765-0755

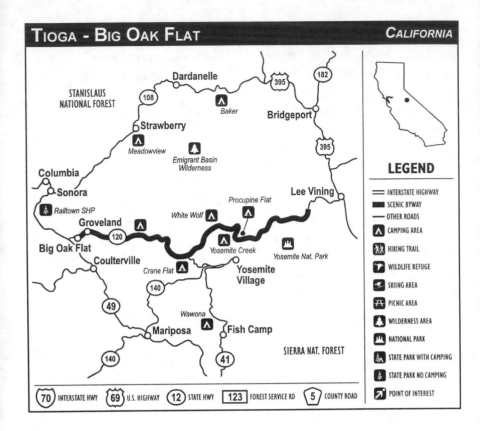

Route Location

Located in east-central California, the byway's western end is located in the community of Big Oak Flat. The eastern terminus is officially located at the Tioga Pass entrance of Yellowstone National Park. Travelers may wish to continue driving east to Lee Vining; this portion is another scenic drive known as the Lee Vining Canyon scenic byway.

Roads Traveled

The byway follows California State Hwy. 120 (Big Oak Flat Road and Tioga Pass Road within the national park), a two-lane paved route suitable for all vehicles. The byway is 80 miles in length with 64 miles designated as a National Scenic Byway by the Federal Highway Administration.

Travel Season

Portions of the byway are usually open year-round. Tioga Pass Road within the national park is closed during the winter.

Description

Travelers of this scenic byway begin their journey in the town of Big Oak Flat, just west of the entrance to the Stanislaus National Forest. The national forest encompasses about 850,000 acres of mountainous land on the western slopes of the Sierra Nevada Mountains. The first 16 miles of this byway will take you through this beautiful countryside before entering Yosemite National Park.

Yosemite National Park is one of the crown jewels of the National Park System. The park was established in 1890 to preserve a portion of the Sierra Nevada Mountains that stretch along California's eastern flank. The byway offers spectacular views of these mountains along with meadows and valleys covered with wildflowers. Most of the surrounding land is undisturbed by man, in fact, nearly 95% of the park has been designated as wilderness. And many miles of the rivers that flow within the park are protected under the designation of National Wild and Scenic Rivers.

Recreational opportunities are abundant within the park. Birdwatchers will delight in the more than 200 species of birds inhabiting this area. Other wildlife inhabiting the area includes black bear, mule deer, and mountain lion. Numerous campgrounds within the park provide a total of over 800 campsites. Fishermen will find the rivers flowing through the park filled with cutthroat, steelhead, and golden trout, among many other species.

Local Information

Stanislaus National Forest
19777 Greenley Road
Sonora, CA 95370
Phone: 209-532-3671

Sierra National Forest
1600 Tollhouse Road
Clovis, CA 93611
Phone: 209-297-0706

Yosemite National Park
P.O. Box 577
Yosemite NP, CA 95389
Phone: 209-372-0200

Lee Vining Chamber of Commerce
P.O. Box 130
Lee Vining, CA 93541
Phone: 760-647-6629

Coulterville Chamber of Commerce
P.O. Box 333
Coulterville, CA 95311
Phone: 209-878-3074

Nearby Routes

Lee Vining Canyon, page 88 / Sierra Vista, page 100

LODGING DIRECTORY

Marble Quarry RV Park - Columbia, page 459 — Campground / RV Park
The Groveland Hotel - Groveland, page 459 — Historic Country Inn

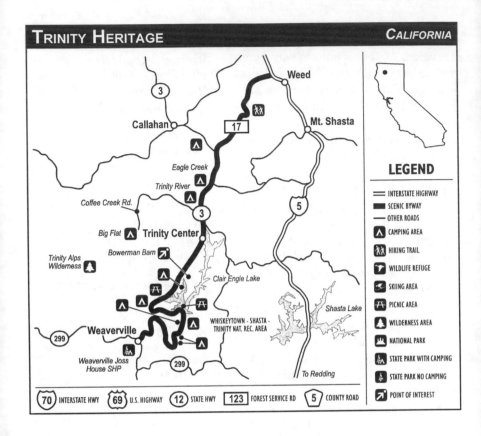

Route Location

Trinity Heritage scenic drive is located in northwestern California, approximately 45 miles northwest of Redding. The byway begins in Weaverville and travels northeast, ending at the junction with I-5 north of Weed.

Roads Traveled

The 120-mile route follows California State Highway 3 and Forest Service Road 17. The roads followed are two-lane paved roads suitable for all types of vehicles. The byway is designated a National Forest Scenic Byway.

Travel Season

The route from Weaverville to Forest Service Road 17 is open year-round with the remaining section closed by winter snows from around late November through the end of May.

Description

The Trinity Heritage scenic byway climbs over 4,000 feet in elevation as it crosses the Shasta-Trinity National Forests. Several scenic vistas provide spectacular views of the surrounding mountains, including Mount Shasta. Much of the byway follows along the shores of 16,000-acre Clair Engle Lake. The lake's shoreline is rugged and densely forested with hundreds of hidden coves.

Much of the byway parallels the beautiful 517,500-acre Trinity Alps Wilderness. This is an excellent area for exploring the back country of the Salmon Mountains. Coffee Creek Road provides access to the heart of this wilderness. At the road's end is a 5-unit campground. In the spring you can see large herds of deer feeding among the meadows here. Thousands of miners lived along Coffee Creek and its tributaries during the Gold Rush and evidence of their activity is visible from the road.

A short side trip will lead you to the Bowerman Barn. This barn is one of the last of its kind, with a foundation of hand-laid stone, mortise and tenon framework, and whipsawn pine boards attached with hand-forged square nails.

Local Information

Shasta - Trinity National Forests
2400 Washington Ave.
Redding, CA 96001
Phone: 916-246-5222

Trinity County Chamber of Commerce
317 Main St.
Weaverville, CA 96093
Phone: 916-623-6101

Yreka Chamber of Commerce
117 W. Miner St.
Yreka, CA 96097
Phone: 916-842-1649

Weed Chamber of Commerce
34 Main St.
Weed, CA 96094
Phone: 916-938-4624

Mount Shasta Chamber of Commerce
P.O. Box 273
Mount Shasta, CA 96067
Phone: 916-926-6212

Weaverville Joss House SHP
Main & Oregon Streets
Weaverville, CA 96093
Phone: 916-623-5284

Whiskeytown-Shasta-Trinity NRA
P.O. Box 188
Whiskeytown, CA 96095
Phone: 916-241-6584

Clair Engle Lake lies within the Trinity Unit of the Whiskeytown-Shasta-Trinity NRA. This recreation area offers numerous developed camping and picnicking areas. You aren't limited to camping in the developed areas, however, as dispersed camping is permitted nearly anywhere along the lake. Several camping areas are also found within the national forest.

Nearby Routes
State Of Jefferson, page 104 / Trinity River, page 112

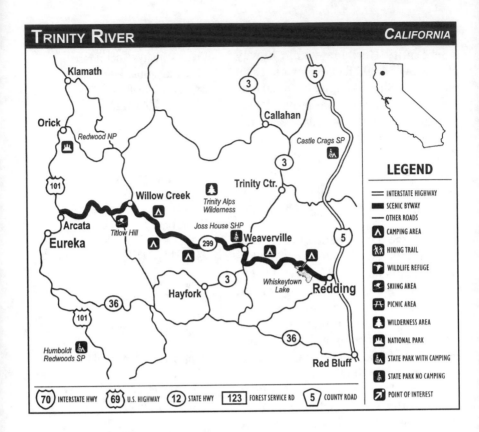

Route Location

The Trinity River scenic byway travels east-west between Interstate 5 and U.S. Highway 101 in northwestern California. The byway's eastern access is near Redding off Interstate 5 and its western terminus is near Arcata at the junction with U.S. Highway 101.

Roads Traveled

The byway is approximately 140 miles in length and follows California State Highway 299. The highway is a two-lane paved road that is safe for travel by all types of vehicles. The Forest Service has designated all of this scenic drive as a National Forest Scenic Byway.

Travel Season

The entire route is generally open year-round although winter driving conditions may be hazardous.

Description

The Trinity River scenic byway crosses the Shasta-Trinity National Forests with a small portion running through the Six Rivers National Forest. The byway travels through the spectacular mountain scenery of the Trinity Alps and winds alongside the crystal waters flowing through the Trinity River gorge.

The scenic drive provides access to California's largest wilderness area, the Trinity Alps Wilderness, which is over 500,000 acres of pristine wilderness in which you can hike, backpack, camp, fish, and ride horseback. More than 60 alpine lakes within the wilderness invite the fisherman, photographer, or wildlife observer.

Whiskeytown Lake lies adjacent to the byway near the eastern terminus. This unit of the Whiskeytown-Shasta-Trinity National Recreation Area is administered by the National Park Service. Lake fishing is good either from the shore or from a boat. Species found in the lake include rainbow and brown trout, largemouth and smallmouth bass, spotted bass, and kokanee. The recreation area provides camping facilities for tents and recreational vehicles. Camping is also permitted nearly anywhere within the recreation area.

Local Information

Shasta - Trinity National Forests
2400 Washington Ave.
Redding, CA 96001
Phone: 916-246-5222

Greater Redding Chamber of Commerce
747 Auditorium Dr.
Redding, CA 96001
Phone: 916-225-4433

Arcata Chamber of Commerce
1062 G St.
Arcata, CA 95521
Phone: 707-822-3619

Greater Eureka Chamber of Commerce
2112 Broadway
Eureka, CA 95501
Phone: 707-442-3738

Willow Creek Chamber of Commerce
P.O. Box 704
Willow Creek, CA 95573
Phone: 916-629-2178

Trinity County Chamber of Commerce
317 Main St.
Weaverville, CA 96093
Phone: 916-623-6101

Weaverville Joss House SHP
Main & Oregon Streets
Weaverville, CA 96093
Phone: 916-623-5284

Whiskeytown-Shasta-Trinity NRA
P.O. Box 188
Whiskeytown, CA 96095
Phone: 916-241-6584

Nearby Routes

Lassen, page 86 / Trinity Heritage, page 110

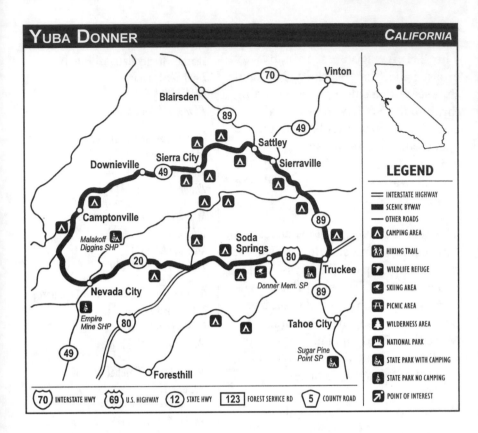

Route Location

The Yuba Donner scenic byway is located in northeastern California, approximately 80 miles northeast of Sacramento, near the Nevada border. The byway forms a loop drive through the Tahoe National Forest. The southeastern access starts on I-80 near Truckee.

Roads Traveled

The byway follows California State Highways 20, 49, and 89 and Interstate 80. All of the roads are two-lane paved routes that are suitable for all vehicles. The 170-mile byway is officially designated a National Forest Scenic Byway.

Travel Season

Generally, the entire byway is open year-round, however, winter driving conditions may be hazardous.

Description

The byway travels through the foothills and mountains of the Northern Sierra Nevada as it passes through the Tahoe National Forest. It climbs through miles of forests and valleys with meandering rivers and streams. This area is also rich with gold mining history and emigrant and transportation history, including Native American trade routes, and the campsites of the ill-fated Donner Party.

The Donner Party was actually comprised of two families, the Donners and the Reeds who left Illinois in 1846 and headed for California under the leadership of George Donner. After difficulty crossing the Great Salt Lake in Utah, they were trapped by heavy snows in the Sierra Nevada Mountains in November. They were forced to camp for the winter at a small lake, now named Donner Lake. They suffered tremendous hardships, and members of the group resorted to cannibalism in order to survive. Forty-seven of the original 87-member party were eventually brought into California by rescue parties over what is now known as Donner Pass.

Local Information

Tahoe National Forest
631 Coyote St.
Nevada City, CA 95959
Phone: 916-265-4531

Truckee - Donner C of C
12036 Donner Pass Rd.
Truckee, CA 96161
Phone: 916-587-2757

Nevada City Chamber of Commerce
132 Main St.
Nevada City, CA 95959
Phone: 916-265-2692

Donner Memorial State Park
P.O. Box 9210
Truckee, CA 95737
Phone: 916-582-7892

Malakoff Diggins State Historic Park
23579 N. Bloomfield Rd.
Nevada City, CA 95959
Phone: 916-265-2740

Empire Mine State Historic Park
10791 E. Empire St.
Grass Valley, CA 95975
Phone: 916-273-8522

The national forest offers a large number of developed campgrounds with a variety of settings from foothills to high mountain elevations located along the banks of rivers or the shores of lakes. There are also many places to pull off the byway and enjoy a picnic or photograph the surrounding wilderness. Camping areas may also be found at the state parks.

Nearby Routes

Feather River, page 78 / Eastshore Drive, page 226

LODGING DIRECTORY

Coachland RV Park - Truckee, page 463 — Campground / RV Park

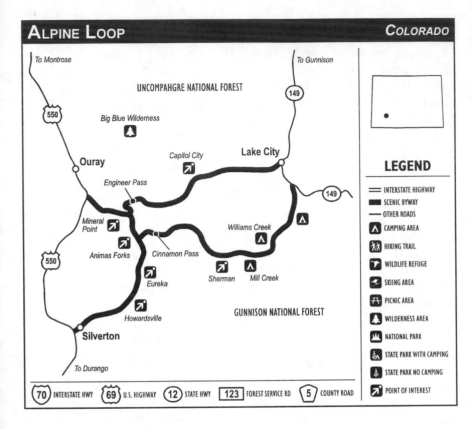

Route Location

The Alpine Loop is located in southwestern Colorado, about 100 miles southeast of Grand Junction. The byway forms an open loop drive between Lake City on the east and the towns of Ouray and Silverton to the west. The byway can be reached from any of these communities.

Roads Traveled

From south of Ouray, the route follows Mineral Creek Road to Engineer Pass. From the south near Silverton, the byway follows Animas River Road to Cinnamon Pass. On the east, the northern portion of the byway follows Henson Creek Road to Engineer Pass and the southern segment follows the Lake Fork of the Gunnison River Road to Cinnamon Pass. The old mining roads are marked with "Alpine Loop" signs. About two-thirds of the route travels over paved and dirt roads that are suitable for two-wheel drive vehicles. A four-wheel drive vehicle is needed to travel the entire route. The 65-mile byway is designated a BLM Type III Back Country Byway.

Travel Season

Roads are generally open from late June through October. Heavy snow closes the route for the remainder of the year.

Description

The roads of the Alpine Loop were originally constructed by prospectors in the late 1800s enabling them to transport ore and supplies by mule-drawn wagons. Today, most of the mines are closed but the roads remain.

The scenic drive winds through the beautiful San Juan Mountains to elevations as high as 12,800 feet, crossing Engineer and Cinnamon passes. Spectacular views of rugged, snow-capped mountain peaks, many over 14,000 feet, are offered from these two mountain passes. Meadows of dazzling wildflowers, ghost towns, and deep blue lakes are also among the scenic views from this back country route.

Numerous side roads tempt the four-wheeler to explore the back country. Mountain bikers also find these roads challenging. Four-wheel drive vehicles may be rented in the local communities.

Local Information

BLM - Gunnison Resource Area
216 N. Colorado Ave.
Gunnison, CO 81230
Phone: 970-641-0471

Uncompahgre National Forest
Ouray Ranger District
2505 S. Townsend
Montrose, CO 81401
Phone: 970-249-3711

Gunnison National Forest
216 N. Colorado St.
Gunnison, CO 81230
Phone: 970-641-0471

Silverton Chamber of Commerce
P.O. Box 565
Silverton, CO 81433
Phone: 800-752-4494

Ouray Chamber Resort Association
1222 N. Main St.
Ouray, CO 81427
Phone: 800-228-1876

Lake City / Hinsdale County C of C
306 N. Silver St.
Lake City, CO 81235
Phone: 800-569-1874

Numerous hiking trails can be accessed from the byway including five that lead to peaks over 14,000 feet high. Visitors will find opportunities for photographing and exploring the many structures of ghost towns from the 1800s. Fishermen will find the lakes, rivers, and streams of the byway teaming with rainbow, brook, and cutthroat trout. There are three campgrounds along the byway for those interested in prolonging their stay.

Nearby Routes

San Juan Skyway, page 134 / Silver Thread Highway, page 137

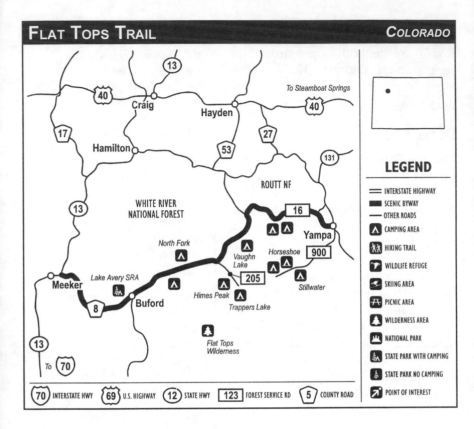

Route Location

The Flat Tops Trail crosses the White River and Routt National Forests between Meeker and Yampa. The byway is located in northwestern Colorado approximately 102 miles northeast of Grand Junction.

Roads Traveled

The 82-mile route follows County Road 8 and Forest Service Road 16 over a combination of paved and gravel-surfaced roads that are safe for travel by most vehicles. The byway is officially designated a National Forest Scenic Byway.

Travel Season

The Flat Tops Trail receives from 2 to 10 feet of snow in the winter and is not maintained for automobile use. The route is open, however, for snowmobile and cross-country ski use.

Description

The Flat Tops Trail passes through sage-covered rolling hills, hay meadows, and working ranches as it makes its way through the national forests. The byway offers views of sheer escarpments and deep canyons, forests of lodgepole pine, spruce, fir, and aspen mingled with grassland parks and meadows.

A side trip down FDR 205 will take you to Trappers Lake, known as the "Cradle of Wilderness" due to the efforts of Arthur H. Carhart. In 1919 his recommendations stopped further con struction of roads and homes around the lake. The concept to protect areas such as this from development was the start of the wilderness movement, which ultimately led to the Wilderness Act of 1964. Four campgrounds located here provide a total of 56 units for tents and recreational vehicles.

The byway continues to climb east of FDR 205 to cross Ripple Creek Pass at an elevation of 10,343. Here you pass from the White River National Forest into the Routt National Forest. Vaughn Lake lies just ahead with rainbow and brown trout fishing opportunities as well as camping and picnicking.

The byway continues east on FDR 16 for several miles before ending in Yampa. South of Yampa on FDR 900 are several lakes and camping areas for those wishing to extend their stay.

Local Information

Routt National Forest
Yampa Ranger District
P.O. Box 7
Yampa, CO 80483
Phone: 970-638-4516

White River National Forest
P.O. Box 948
Glenwood Springs, CO 81602
Phone: 970-945-2521

Meeker Chamber of Commerce
P.O. Box 869
Meeker, CO 81641
Phone: 970-878-5510

Greater Craig Area C of C
360 E. Victory Way
Craig, CO 81625
Phone: 970-824-5689

Hayden Chamber of Commerce
P.O. Box 517
Hayden, CO 81639
Phone: 970-276-3737

Lake Avery State Recreation Area
Colorado State Parks
1313 Sherman St., #618
Denver, CO 80203
Phone: 303-866-3437

LODGING DIRECTORY

Buford Hunting & Fishing Lodge - Buford, page 438 —— Cabin / Cottage / Guest Ranch & Campground / RV Park

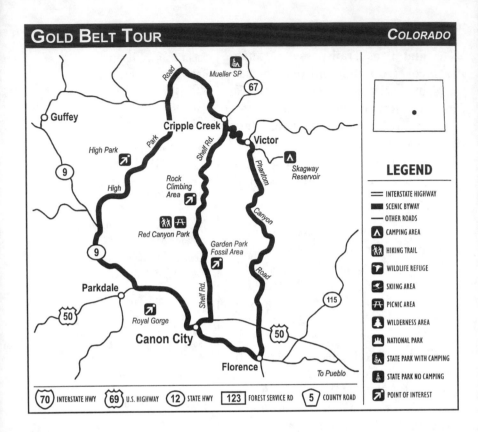

Route Location

Situated along the Front Range in central Colorado about one hour's drive from either Colorado Springs or Pueblo, the Gold Belt Tour follows a series of roads between Cañon City and historic Cripple Creek. From the north, the byway can be reached from Colorado Springs by taking U.S. Highway 24 west to SH 67, then south to Cripple Creek. The southern end of the byway is off U.S. Highway 50 in Cañon City.

Roads Traveled

The 122-mile loop follows Phantom Canyon, Shelf, and High Park Roads. All are unpaved, but are accessible by normal passenger cars during dry weather. Phantom Canyon Road and the upper portion of Shelf Road should not be traveled by motorhomes or vehicles pulling trailers since these routes are confined by canyon walls and narrow in many places to one lane. The byway is designated a BLM Type I and II Back Country Byway.

Travel Season

The roads followed are generally open year-round although heavy snows may temporarily close portions of the route.

Description

This back country byway gets its name from the historic Florence and Cripple Creek Railroad, "The Gold Belt Line." This route linked the Cripple Creek District gold camps with the towns of Florence and Cañon City during the gold mining boom of the late 1890s.

The Gold Belt Tour traverses three different routes, each with their own unique characteristics. The Phantom Canyon route, named for its distinctive rock formations, follows the old railroad grade. Just to the west is the Shelf Road, so named for the narrow "shelf" on which it rides, high above the streambed. High Park Road travels through more open landscape with wide vistas. This road provides an alternate route to the narrow confines of the other two roads.

Red Canyon Park is a 500-acre park containing unusual eroded red rock formations with some spires up to 100 feet high. Facilities found here include picnic sites, restrooms, and hiking trails. To the north of this park is the Shelf Road Rock Climbing Area. Climbers come from around the world to scale these limestone walls. The climbs are short but difficult with limited handholds and many overhangs. The back roads here provide opportunities for four-wheeling or mountain biking.

A side trip off Phantom Canyon Road will lead to the 84-acre Skagway Reservoir. This lake is popular for trout fishing, camping, and picnicking. Other camping facilities are found in the Mueller State Park, north of Cripple Creek on State Highway 67. The state park has 90 campsites, many with electrical hookups.

Local Information

BLM - Royal Gorge Resource Area
3170 E. Main St.
Canon City, CO 81215
Phone: 719-275-0631

Florence Chamber of Commerce
117 S. Pikes Peak Ave.
Florence, CO 81226
Phone: 719-784-3544

Canon City Chamber of Commerce
403 Royal Gorge Blvd.
Canon City, CO 81215
Phone: 719-275-2331

Cripple Creek Chamber of Commerce
P.O. Box 650
Cripple Creek, CO 80813
Phone: 800-526-8777

Mueller State Park
P.O. Box 49
Divide, CO 80814
Phone: 719-687-2366

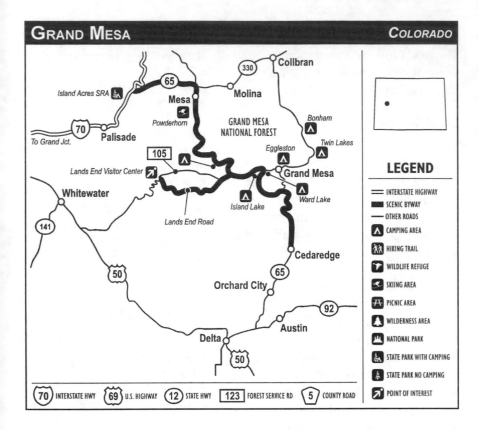

Route Location

Located in west-central Colorado approximately 22 miles east of Grand Junction. The byway can be accessed in the north from I-70 at Exit 49. The southern portion of the route begins in Cedaredge on Colorado Highway 65.

Roads Traveled

The 63-mile byway follows Colorado Hwy. 65 and Forest Development Road 100, also known as the Lands End Road. Colorado Hwy. 65 is a two-lane paved route that is suitable for all vehicles. Lands End Road is a maintained gravel road that is suitable for most passenger cars and recreational vehicles. Inquire locally as to the current road conditions before attempting this portion of the route. The route is designated a National Scenic Byway.

Travel Season

Lands End Road is closed during winter months, however, the rest of the scenic drive generally remains open year-round.

Description

From the exit off I-70, you begin in the canyon of Plateau Creek with sandstone walls rising 400 to 1,000 feet above the highway. The byway continues climbing from the town of Mesa to an elevation of around 11,000 feet. It is here that you've reached the top of the Grand Mesa, the world's largest flat-top mountain. The panoramic views from the top of the mesa are astounding. In a short drive you've traveled from the pinyon-juniper desert canyon to a cool, evergreen forest.

Excellent outdoor opportunities abound along the drive. Over 300 streamfed lakes are scattered across the Mesa teaming with rainbow, cutthroat, and brook trout. Several national forest campgrounds provide the perfect spot for pitching a tent or settling in your RV. Facilities offered at the campgrounds include picnic tables, water, fire rings, and pit toilets, but no hookups or dump stations. During the winter months, this area becomes a haven for cross-country and downhill skiers as well as snowmobilers. There are also plenty of opportunities during the warmer months for hiking, backpacking, mountain biking, and horseback riding. Wildlife is abundant in this part of Colorado and includes such species as mule deer, elk, coyotes, mountain lions, and bear.

Local Information

Grand Mesa - Uncompahgre & Gunnison National Forests
2250 Highway 50
Delta, CO 81416
Phone: 970-874-7691

Delta Area Chamber of Commerce
301 Main Street
Delta, CO 81416
Phone: 970-874-8616

Plateau Valley Chamber of Commerce
P.O. Box 143
Collbran, CO 81624
Phone: 970-487-3402

Palisade Chamber of Commerce
P.O. Box 729
Palisade, CO 81526
Phone: 970-464-7458

Grand Junction Area C of C
360 Grand Avenue
Grand Junction, CO 81501
Phone: 970-242-3214

Powderhorn Ski Resort
P.O. Box 370
Mesa, CO 81643
Phone: 970-242-5637

Island Acres State Recreation Area
Colorado State Parks
1313 Sherman St., #618
Denver, CO 80203
Phone: 303-866-3437

Pioneer Town in Cedaredge offers travelers the chance to turn back the clock. Authentic stores and the Cedaredge Town Jail, along with period clothes and memorabilia from the past 100 years, create a realistic old-west atmosphere.

Nearby Routes

Unaweep - Tebeguache, page 141

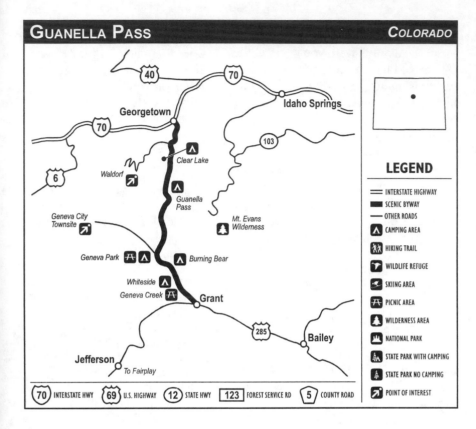

Route Location

Located in central Colorado, about 45 miles west of Denver. The byway is accessed from the north in Georgetown. The southern terminus of the byway is in Grant on U.S. Highway 285.

Roads Traveled

The 22 mile route follows the Guanella Pass Road. The first 10 miles from Georgetown are paved with the remaining segment to Grant being a gravel-surfaced road. This route is not recommended for large recreational vehicles or vehicles pulling trailers. The byway has been designated a National Forest Scenic Byway.

Travel Season

Guanella Pass is maintained year-round except for days following heavy snowfall. Caution should be exercised while traveling this route in the winter months.

Description

From an elevation of 8,500 feet in Grant, the Guanella Pass byway climbs through Geneva Creek Canyon, passing Scott Gomer Creek Falls, into the large mountain meadow of Geneva Park. This park is surrounded by mountain peaks exceeding 13,000 feet.

Just beyond Geneva Park is a side trip worth taking. This rough road (recommended only for high-clearance vehicles or experienced mountain bikers) will lead to the townsite of Geneva City. This side road is popular with mountain bikers, be on the lookout for them. The townsite is situated in the basin above timberline at the head of Geneva Creek. Here, historic cabins and mills dot the landscape. It is recommended that visitors park at timberline and hike a short distance to the townsite. The remnants of this town are on private property, please take only pictures.

The summit of Guanella Pass provides panoramic views of the surrounding mountains. The summit is a popular area for hikers, climbers, and cross-country skiers. The Scott Gomer trail provides hiking access into the 73,000-acre Mount Evans Wilderness.

Once beyond the summit of Guanella Pass, the byway begins its descent into Georgetown. The meandering waters of South Clear Creek will flow beside the byway for the remainder of the journey into Georgetown.

Gold mining lured prospectors to Georgetown in 1859, but silver became the town's claim to fame. Georgetown was known as the "Silver Queen" and once boasted of over 5,000 residents during the 1880s. In 1966 the Department of the Interior designated the Georgetown Silver Plume Mining District a National Historic Landmark. There are over 200 Victorian structures built during the silver mining boom days of the late 1800s found in the old part of town.

Local Information

Arapahoe and Roosevelt N.F.
240 W. Prospect Rd.
Fort Collins, CO 80526
Phone: 970-498-1100

Georgetown Chamber of Commerce
P.O. Box 444
Georgetown, CO 80444
Phone: 303-569-2888

Idaho Springs Chamber of Commerce
P.O. Box 97
Idaho Springs, CO 80452
Phone: 303-567-0607

Nearby Routes

Mount Evans, page 130 / Peak To Peak, page 132

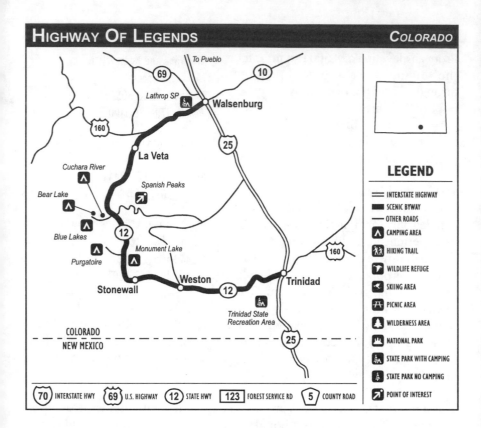

Route Location

The Highway of Legends scenic byway is located in southern Colorado near the New Mexico state line about 50 miles south of Pueblo. The byway forms an open loop, beginning in Walsenburg near Lathrop State Park and ending in Trinidad. The scenic drive travels through the San Isabel National Forest.

Roads Traveled

The byway follows U.S. Highway 160 and Colorado State Highway 12. Both highways are two-lane paved roads suitable for all vehicles. This officially designated National Forest Scenic Byway is approximately 82 miles long.

Travel Season

The entire route is usually open year-round.

Description

The Highway Of Legends offers excellent views of the Sangre de Cristo ("Blood of Christ") mountains, the Spanish Peaks, and a variety of unique geological formations. These mountains were named by Spanish explorers for their colorful alpen glow at sunrise and sunset. Some of the more interesting rock formations you'll pass include the magnificent Stonewall, Dakota Wall, the Devil's Stairsteps, and the Profile Rock.

Sitting quietly among the pine forest near the midpoint of this byway is Monument Lake, one of many high altitude lakes along the drive. In the center of the lake is a rock formation jutting 15 feet above the surface of the water. This is the "monument" for which the lake is named. It is a natural rock formation said to represent two Indian chiefs. Camping and picnicking facilities may be found here.

Further north of Monument Lake lies the San Isabel National Forest. A short side trip off the byway (FDR 413) will take you along the Cuchara River to Blue Lake and Bear Lake. Blue Lake is known for its beautiful blue color and shores covered with spruce trees. Beyond Blue Lake lies pristine Bear Lake. Camping facilities with a total of 30 sites are found at both lakes. This area also offers many nature and hiking trails.

Trinidad and Lathrop State Parks also offer camping and picnicking facilities. A total of 160 camping sites, many with electrical hookups, are available in the parks.

Nearby Routes

Los Caminos Antiguos, page 128

Local Information

Pike and San Isabel National Forests
1920 Valley Dr.
Pueblo, CO 81008
Phone: 719-545-8737

Huerfano County Chamber of Commerce
400 Main St.
Walsenburg, CO 81089
Phone: 719-738-1065

Trinidad - Las Animas County C of C
309 Nevada Ave.
Trinidad, CO 81082
Phone: 719-846-9285

LaVeta / Cuchara Chamber of Commerce
P.O. Box 32
LaVeta, CO 81055
Phone: 719-742-3676

Trinidad State Recreation Area
Rt. 3, Box 360
Trinidad, CO 81082
Phone: 719-846-6951

Lathrop State Park
70 County Rd. 502
Walsenburg, CO 81089
Phone: 719-738-2376

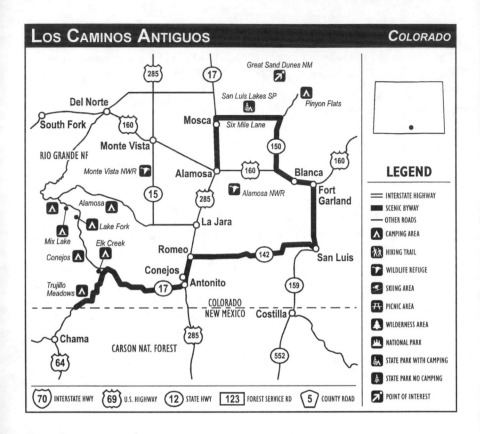

Route Location

The Los Caminos Antiguos scenic drive is located in south-central Colorado about 120 miles southwest of Pueblo. The byway begins in the city of Alamosa, travels by the Great Sand Dunes National Monument, and then southward to the Colorado-New Mexico border.

Roads Traveled

The 152-mile scenic drive follows Colorado Highways 17, 142, 150, and 159, and U.S. Highways 160 and 285. A short portion of the route also follows Six Mile Lane between SH 17 and SH 150. All of the roads are two-lane paved routes that are safe for travel by all types of vehicles. The byway is designated a Type I Back Country Byway by the BLM and a Scenic and Historic Byway by the state of Colorado.

Travel Season

All of the roads followed are generally open year-round.

Description

This byway explores the rich heritage of Colorado's San Luis Valley and its blend of distinctive cultures. The byway passes through Fort Garland, site of an 1858 fort that is now run as a state museum; San Luis, Colorado's oldest community, founded in 1851; and Conejos which is home to the oldest church in Colorado, Our Lady of Guadalupe.

The Great Sand Dunes NM is one of the main attractions along the route. The sand dunes, with the rugged Sangre de Cristo Mountains as a backdrop, seem out of place here. These dunes rise nearly 700 feet above the valley floor, making these the tallest sand dunes in North America. The dunes cover approximately 55 square miles. The Pinyon Flats Campground is located here and is open year-round.

Near the southern end of this drive is the town of Antonito where you can catch an authentic narrow-gauge steam train. The train ride takes you through the Rio Grande National Forest, crossing the Colorado-New Mexico state line several times. After your train ride, continue your scenic tour on State Highway 17 through the national forest, crossing LaManga Pass and Cumbres Pass before entering into New Mexico.

Nearby Routes

Highway Of Legends, page 126
Silver Thread Highway, page 137
Enchanted Circle, page 245
Wild Rivers, page 261

Local Information

BLM - San Luis Resource Area
1921 State Street
Alamosa, CO 81101
Phone: 719-589-4975

Rio Grande National Forest
1803 W. Highway 160
Monte Vista, CO 81144
Phone: 719-852-5941

Carson National Forest
P.O. Box 558
Taos, NM 87571
Phone: 505-758-6200

Alamosa County Chamber of Commerce
Cole Park
Alamosa, CO 81101
Phone: 719-376-5443

Costilla County Chamber of Commerce
P.O. Box 9
San Luis, CO 81152
Phone: 719-672-3355

Antonito Chamber of Commerce
P.O. Box 427
Antonito, CO 81120
Phone: 719-376-5443

Great Sand Dunes National Monument
11500 Highway 150
Mosca, CO 81146
Phone: 719-378-2312

San Luis Lakes State Park
Colorado State Parks
1313 Sherman St., #618
Denver, CO 80203
Phone: 303-866-3437

Cumbres & Toltec Scenic Railroad
P.O. Box 668
Antonito, CO 81120
Phone: 719-376-5483

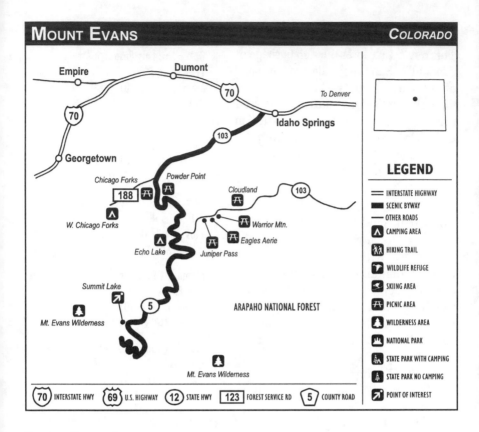

Route Location

The Mount Evans scenic drive is approximately 30 miles west of Denver in central Colorado. The byway begins near Idaho Springs and travels south through Arapaho National Forest to the summit of Mount Evans.

Roads Traveled

The 28-mile byway follows Colorado State Highways 103 and 5 which are two-lane paved roads. Highway 103 is well suited for all vehicles including those with small trailers (25 feet or less). Highway 5 is not recommended for large RVs or vehicles pulling trailers. The route is designated a National Forest Scenic Byway.

Travel Season

Colorado State Highway 103 is usually open year-round with possible temporary closures in the winter for snow removal. Highway 5 is usu-

ally open from Memorial Day
through Labor Day.

Description

Traveling through the Arapaho National Forest, the Mount Evans scenic byway rises almost 7,000 feet in
elevation to 14,150 feet above sea
level, making this the highest paved
automobile road in North America.
The view from the summit of Mount
Evans is incredible as you are provided a 360 degree view of over 100
miles of Rocky Mountain peaks as
well as the plains to the east.

The scenic byway takes you into the
heart of the Mount Evans Wilderness.
Trailheads found along the byway
provide access to the wilderness for
those interested in hiking or backpacking.

Local Information

Arapahoe and Roosevelt N.F.
240 W. Prospect Rd.
Fort Collins, CO 80526
Phone: 970-498-1100

Arapahoe National Forest
Clear Creek Ranger District
101 Chicago Creek
Idaho Springs, CO 80452
Phone: 303-567-2901

Idaho Springs Chamber of Commerce
P.O. Box 97
Idaho Springs, CO 80452
Phone: 303-567-0607

Georgetown Chamber of Commerce
P.O. Box 444
Georgetown, CO 80444
Phone: 303-569-2888

As you climb up the byway you'll pass two scenic alpine lakes, both
teaming with trout. Echo Lake and Summit Lake offer park areas managed by the city of Denver. A campground is located at Echo Lake offering a total of 16 campsites for those interested in prolonging their
stay. Another campground with 11 campsites is but a short drive off the
byway on Forest Development Road 188.

A visitor center is located at the start of the byway in Idaho Springs, just off
Interstate 70. The center provides educational and interpretive exhibits, nature and historical literature, guidebooks and reference books, and a self
guide tape tour of the Mount Evans scenic drive.

Nearby Routes

Guanella Pass, page 124 / Peak To Peak, page 132

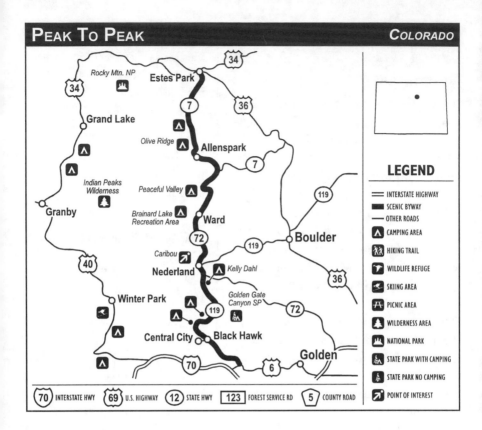

Route Location

The Peak To Peak scenic drive is located in north-central Colorado, approximately 30 miles west of Denver. The byway's northern terminus is in Estes Park. The route travels south through Roosevelt National Forest and ends at the intersection with U.S. Highway 6, south of Blackhawk.

Roads Traveled

The byway follows a series of state-maintained roads; Colorado State Highways 7, 72, and 119. All are two-lane paved roads suitable for travel by all types of vehicles. All but 5 miles of the 60-mile byway are designated a National Forest Scenic Byway.

Travel Season

The roads traveled are usually open all year long with possible delays during the winter for snow removal.

Description

Views of the snow-capped Continental Divide and high mountain valleys are offered to travelers along this route. Relics from the late 1800s mining boom days are scattered throughout the area. Central City and Blackhawk are two examples of the history of the area. These communities were established in the late 1800s as mining towns and are now historical districts with much of that period's architecture preserved. Today, within these structures of historical architecture, one will find casino-style gambling establishments.

Just a short drive west of Nederland takes you to the ghost town of Caribou. The mines here produced an estimated 8 million dollars worth of silver, making it one of Colorado's greatest silver mines. Silver bricks from Caribou were laid in a sidewalk in Central City for a visit by Ulysses S. Grant in 1872. When the bottom fell out of the silver market in 1893, Caribou was left to become a ghost town.

In the charming mountain village of Estes Park you'll find the historic Stanley Hotel, built in 1909 by F.O. Stanley. Mr. Stanley would transport guests from the Lyons rail station in Stanley Steamers along the very roads now known as the Peak To Peak scenic byway.

Local Information

Arapahoe and Roosevelt N.F.
240 W. Prospect Rd.
Fort Collins, CO 80526
Phone: 303-498-1100

Estes Park Chamber of Commerce
500 Big Thompson Hwy.
Estes Park, CO 80517
Phone: 000-44-ESTES

Nederland Chamber of Commerce
P.O. Box 85
Nederland, CO 80466
Phone: 800-221-0044

Gilpin County Chamber of Commerce
P.O. Box 343
Black Hawk, CO 80422
Phone: 303-582-5077

Rocky Mountain National Park
Estes Park, CO 80517
Phone: 970-586-1206

Golden Gate Canyon State Park
3873 Hwy. 46
Golden, CO 80403
Phone: 303-592-1502

Nearby Routes

Guanella Pass, page 124 / Mount Evans, page 130 / Trail Ridge & Beaver Meadow Roads, page 139

LODGING DIRECTORY

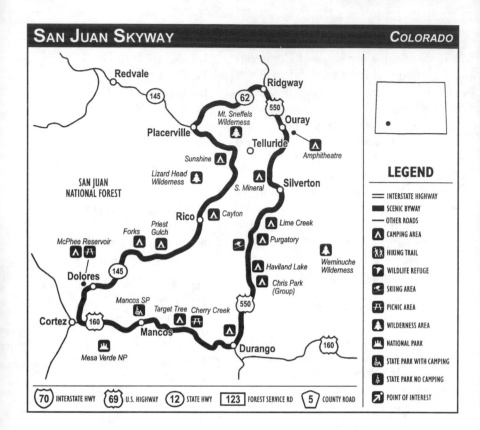

Route Location

The beautiful San Juan Skyway is located in the southwestern corner of Colorado near the New Mexico and Utah borders. The southeastern access starts in Durango and forms a loop drive through Cortez, Placerville, Ridgway, Ouray, Silverton, and then back to Durango.

Roads Traveled

The 236-mile route follows U.S. Highway 160 and 550 and Colorado State Highways 145 and 62. All of the roads are two-lane paved roads suitable for all types of vehicles. The byway is designated a National Forest Scenic Byway and All-American Road by the Federal Highway Administration.

Travel Season

The entire route is generally open year-round although winter driving conditions can be hazardous and sections may temporarily close for snow removal.

Description

The San Juan Skyway scenic drive passes through millions of acres of the San Juan and Uncompahgre National Forests, offering views of cascading waterfalls in spring, fields of wildflowers ablaze with color in summer, mountain sides glistening a brilliant gold in autumn, and a wintery wonderland. The historic toll road, "Million Dollar Highway," is traveled across along this route, winding through the Red Mountains, along the sheer sides of the Uncompahgre Gorge, and through tunnels above scenic waterfalls.

There are three wilderness areas accessed along the byway. These areas provide excellent opportunities for hiking, backpacking, or horseback riding in the wild San Juan Mountains. Numerous other trails found all along the byway range from short, gentle walking trails to more rigorous hiking trails leading deep into the national forests.

Campgrounds are in no short supply along this byway. Whether you're searching for a highly developed campsite with the amenities of home or a small, secluded spot to pitch a tent, you're sure to find what you're looking for. Many camping areas are situated along streams or lakeshores offering excellent opportunities for trout fishing.

Local Information

San Juan National Forest
701 Camino del Rio, Room 301
Durango, CO 81301
Phone: 970-247-4874

Grand Mesa-Uncompahgre &
Gunnison National Forests
2250 Hwy. 50
Delta, CO 81416
Phone: 970-874-7691

Durango Area Chamber Resort Assn.
111 S. Camino del Rio
Durango, CO 81302
Phone: 970-247-0312

Cortez Area Chamber of Commerce
928 E. Main St.
Cortez, CO 81321
Phone: 970-565-3414

Dolores River Valley C of C
P.O. Box 602
Dolores, CO 81323
Phone: 970-882-4018

Rico Chamber of Commerce
P.O. Box 176
Rico, CO 81332
Phone: 970-967-2861

Telluride Chamber Resort Association
P.O. Box 653
Telluride, CO 81435
Phone: 970-728-4431

Ridgway Area Chamber of Commerce
P.O. Box 378
Ridgway, CO 81432
Phone: 800-220-4959

The town of Cortez is located south of
Dolores and is known as the "Archeo-
logical Center of the United States." To
the east of Cortez is the Mesa Verde
National Park, showcasing the cliff
dwellings once inhabited by the
Anasazi Indians. Guided tours, a museum, camping, and lodging are available here. To the southwest is the famous Four Corners Monument where
you can stand in four states at once.

Durango was founded in 1880 and
served the once booming mining in-
dustry. Many restored historic land-
marks line the streets of downtown.
Also found here is the historic Durango
and Silverton Narrow-Gauge Railroad.
Visitors can ride the train, from May
through October, for a unique sight-
seeing trip through the rugged mountains. The station is located downtown
at the south end of Main.

The town of Telluride is a Victorian mining town founded in the late 1800s
and is now an international ski resort. Butch Cassidy's first bank robbery
took place here. Located in the area are four-wheel drive roads that lead to
other historic mining towns within the forest.

Local Information

Ouray Chamber Resort Association
1222 N. Main St.
Ouray, CO 81427
Phone: 800-228-1876

Silverton Chamber of Commerce
P.O. Box 565
Silverton, CO 81433
Phone: 800-752-4494

Mancos State Park
County Rd. 42
Durango, CO 81301
Phone: 970-883-2208

Durango & Silverton Narrow-Gauge RR
479 Main Ave.
Durango, CO 81301
Phone: 970-247-2733

Nearby Routes

Alpine Loop, page 116 / Unaweep - Tebeguache, page 141

Lodging Directory

A B & B on Maple Street - Cortez, page 453 — Bed & Breakfast / Inns
Anasazi Motor Inn - Cortez, page 453 — Hotel / Motel
Kelly Place - Cortez, page 453 — Bed & Breakfast / Inns & Cabin / Cottage / Guest Ranch
Purgatory Village Hotel - Durango, page 453 — Hotel / Motel & Resort
River House B & B - Durango, page 453 — Bed & Breakfast / Inns
Riversbend Bed & Breakfast - Mancos, page 454 — Bed & Breakfast / Inns
Tomahawk Lodge - Cortez, page 454 — Hotel / Motel

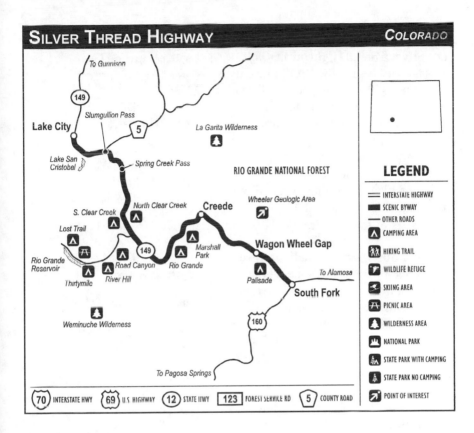

SILVER THREAD HIGHWAY — COLORADO

To Gunnison

149

Slumgullion Pass

Lake City

5

La Garita Wilderness

Lake San Cristobal

Spring Creek Pass

RIO GRANDE NATIONAL FOREST

North Clear Creek   Creede

Wheeler Geologic Area

S. Clear Creek

Lost Trail

Marshall Park

149   Wagon Wheel Gap

Rio Grande Reservoir   Road Canyon   Rio Grande

To Alamosa

Thirtymile   River Hill   Palisade

South Fork

Weminuche Wilderness

160

To Pagosa Springs

LEGEND

— INTERSTATE HIGHWAY
— SCENIC BYWAY
— OTHER ROADS
CAMPING AREA
HIKING TRAIL
WILDLIFE REFUGE
SKIING AREA
PICNIC AREA
WILDERNESS AREA
NATIONAL PARK
STATE PARK WITH CAMPING
STATE PARK NO CAMPING
POINT OF INTEREST

70 INTERSTATE HWY   69 U.S. HIGHWAY   12 STATE HWY   123 FOREST SERVICE RD   5 COUNTY ROAD

Route Location

The Silver Thread scenic byway is approximately 50 miles northwest of Alamosa in southwestern Colorado. The southern terminus is in South Fork on U.S. Highway 160. The byway travels northeast through Creede to the northern terminus in Lake City.

Roads Traveled

The Silver Thread scenic byway follows Colorado State Highway 149 which is a two-lane paved road suitable for all types of vehicles. The entire 75-mile route has been designated a National Forest Scenic Byway.

Travel Season

The state highway is open year-round. Travelers may encounter temporary road closure for snow removal during the winter.

Description

The Silver Thread Highway has been a passageway from Creede to Lake City since the 1870s. It was once a toll road and stage route for the miners. Traveling through the Gunnison and Rio Grande National Forests, this scenic route offers spectacular views of the San Juan Mountains, cascading waterfalls, and historic mining towns. Flowing alongside much of the byway are the waters of the Rio Grande River.

Wildlife observers will delight in seeing Rocky Mountain Sheep grazing along the highway. In fall, winter, and early spring, elk are commonly seen as they descend to the lower elevations for winter range. Other wildlife found in the area includes mule deer, coyotes, porcupines, and bears.

Those interested in extending their stay along this byway will find numerous national forest campgrounds. Campground facilities vary from the primitive to the more developed. Many of the camping areas are situated on the banks of the Rio Grande River. Near the North Clear Creek Campground is a scenic overlook providing views of the beautiful North Clear Creek Falls.

Rio Grande Reservoir and Colorado's second largest natural lake, San Cristobal, offer excellent opportunities for fishing. Campgrounds are located nearby. Hiking trails near the area will lead you deep into the national forest and its wilderness areas.

Local Information

Rio Grande National Forest
Creede Ranger District
P.O. Box 270
Creede, CO 81130
Phone: 719-658-2556

San Juan National Forest
701 Camino del Rio - Room 301
Durango, CO 81301
Phone: 970-247-4874

South Fork Chamber of Commerce
P.O. Box 577
South Fork, CO 81154
Phone: 719-873-5512

Creede - Mineral County C of C
P.O. Box 580
Creede, CO 81130
Phone: 800-327-2102

Lake City / Hinsdale County C of C
306 N. Silver St.
Lake City, CO 81235
Phone: 800-569-1874

Nearby Routes

Alpine Loop, page 116 / Los Caminos Antiguos, page 128

Lodging Directory

Foothills Lodge - South Fork, page 456 — Cabin / Cottage / Guest Ranch

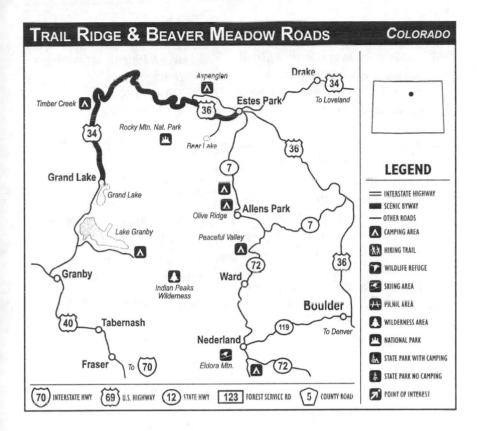

TRAIL RIDGE & BEAVER MEADOW ROADS — COLORADO

Route Location

This scenic byway is located in north-central Colorado about 30 miles east of Loveland. The route begins in Estes Park at the junction of U.S. Highways 34 and 36 and travels west and south to the city of Grand Lake.

Roads Traveled

The 53-mile scenic byway follows U.S. Highway 36 for approximately 5 miles from Estes Park and then U.S. Highway 34 for 48 miles to Grand Lake. The entire route is made up of two-lane paved roads that are suitable for all types of vehicles. This scenic byway is designated as an All American Road by the Federal Highway Administration.

Travel Season

Heavy snows and high winds keep Trail Ridge Road impassable during the winter months. The road generally opens around Memorial Day and closes mid-October.

Description

Trail Ridge & Beaver Meadow Roads take the visitor to the "top of the world" as it reaches 12,183 feet above sea level, higher than any other continuous paved highway in the United States. In fact, Trail Ridge Road stays above treeline, the alpine tundra, for eleven beautiful miles. The view from this point is truly spectacular. Views to the north, south, east, and west extend into Wyoming and three national forests adjacent to Rocky Mountain National Park. The Alpine Visitor Center, located at Fall River Pass, provides exhibits explaining the life of the alpine tundra. This is also a good place to stop for a snack or two before continuing on.

Local Information

Arapahoe & Roosevelt National Forest
240 W. Prospect Road
Fort Collins, CO 80526
Phone: 970-498-1100

Estes Park Chamber of Commerce
P.O. Box 3050
Estes Park, CO 80517
Phone: 970-586-4431

Grand Lake Area Chamber of Commerce
P.O. Box 57
Grand Lake, CO 80447
Phone: 970-627-3402

Rocky Mountain National Park
Estes Park, CO 80517
Phone: 970-586-1206

Rocky Mountain National Park was born in 1915, several years after Enos Mills, a naturalist, writer, and conservationist, began campaigning in 1909 for preservation of this pristine area. In addition to the rugged and majestic mountain scenery, Rocky Mountain National Park offers plenty of opportunities for horseback riding, camping, fishing, hiking, skiing, and snowmobiling. A side trip worth taking is the 10-mile road to Bear Lake. This little alpine lake offers a ½-mile, wheelchair accessible trail that surrounds the lake. This area, however, is heavily used and is often congested. You can expect parking lots to be full between 10:00 a.m. and 3:00 p.m. on summer days.

Nearby Routes

Peak To Peak, page 132

Lodging Directory

Romantic RiverSong Inn - Estes Park, page 460 — Bed & Breakfast / Inns
The Baldpate Inn - Estes Park, page 460 — Bed & Breakfast / Inns
Victoria Cottages - Grand Lake, page 460 — Cabin / Cottage / Guest Ranch
Woodlands on Fall River - Estes Park, page 460 — Hotel / Motel

UNAWEEP / TEBEGUACHE   COLORADO

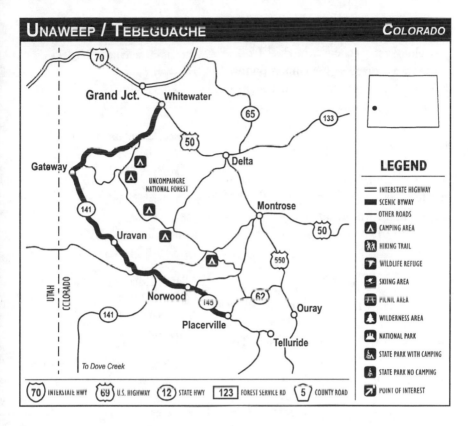

LEGEND

▬▬▬ INTERSTATE HIGHWAY
▬ SCENIC BYWAY
— OTHER ROADS
🅰 CAMPING AREA
🏃 HIKING TRAIL
🦌 WILDLIFE REFUGE
🎿 SKIING AREA
🍴 PICNIC AREA
🌲 WILDERNESS AREA
🏛 NATIONAL PARK
🏕 STATE PARK WITH CAMPING
🌲 STATE PARK NO CAMPING
🔁 POINT OF INTEREST

70 INTERSTATE HWY   69 U.S. HIGHWAY   12 STATE HWY   123 FOREST SERVICE RD   5 COUNTY ROAD

Route Location

The northern access to the Unaweep / Tebeguache scenic byway is but 10 miles south of Grand Junction in western Colorado. The traveler can begin their journey in Whitewater and travel south around the Uncompahgre National Forest to the byway's end in Placerville.

Roads Traveled

The 133-mile scenic byway follows Colorado State Highways 141 and 145 which are two-lane paved roads safe for travel by all types of vehicles. The entire route has been designated a BLM Type 1 Back Country Byway.

Travel Season

During the winter months, delays are possible for snow removal, otherwise the byway is usually open all year long.

Description

The Unaweep / Tebeguache Back Country Byway circles the Uncompahgre National Forest, traveling through 1,200-foot granite walls rising above lush green fields. This area was once the home of the Ute Indians and a hideout for Butch Cassidy. Ancient structures built by Native American hunters and gatherers, petroglyphs, geological formations, and waterfalls are some of the highlights of the byway.

A variety of wildlife inhabits this region of Colorado including black bear, mountain lion, bobcat, coyotes, and various rodents and reptiles. The large meadows and south-facing canyon slopes provide winter habitat for mule deer and elk. Wild turkeys and pheasants may also be spotted in the meadows. During the winter months, the watchful eye may catch glimpses of bald eagles perched in the cottonwood trees along West Creek or the Dolores and San Miguel rivers.

Abandoned mines and mills quietly testify to the mining history of this area. Attached to the sheer canyon walls above the Dolores River are portions of the Hanging Flume, which was built in the late 1800s to carry water from the San Miguel River to placer mines in the canyon.

The many side roads found along the byway lead into the Uncompahgre National Forest and offer challenges to four-wheel drive and mountain bike enthusiasts. The national forest also has several developed camping areas available.

Local Information

Uncompahgre National Forest
2250 Hwy. 50
Delta, CO 81416
Phone: 970-874-7691

Norwood Chamber of Commerce
P.O. Box 116
Norwood, CO 81423

Grand Junction Area C of C
360 Grand Ave.
Grand Junction, CO 81501
Phone: 970-242-3214

Telluride Chamber Resort Association
P.O. Box 653
Telluride, CO 81435
Phone: 800-525-3455

BLM-Uncompahgre Basin Resource Area
2505 S. Townsend Ave.
Montrose, CO 81401
Phone: 970-249-6047

Nearby Routes

San Juan Skyway, page 134 / Grand Mesa, page 122

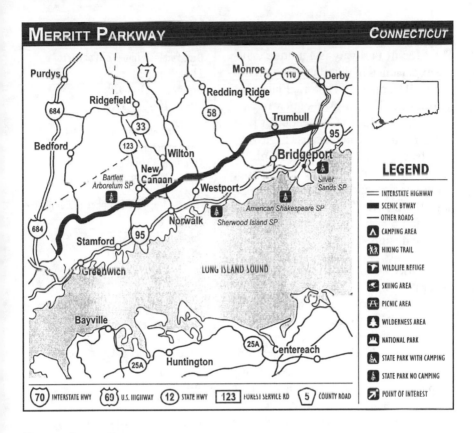

Route Location

Located in Connecticut's southwest corner, the Merritt Parkway travels between the New York state line and the Housatonic River, just northeast of Bridgeport.

Roads Traveled

The Merritt Parkway is also known as Connecticut State Highway 15 which is a four-lane divided highway suitable for most types of vehicles. Connecticut regulations, however, restrict the use of Merritt Parkway to "non-commercial motor vehicles which do not exceed 7,500 pounds, 24 feet in length, 8 feet in height, and 7 feet 6 inches in width." The scenic byway is 38 miles in length and is designated a National Scenic Byway by the Federal Highway Administration.

Travel Season

The Merritt Parkway is generally open all year.

Description

The Merritt Parkway is a unique driving experience in that it is listed on the National Register of Historic Places for its bridges. The 38-mile parkway was built in the 1930s as Connecticut's first divided-lane, limited access highway. The tree-lined corridor is a unique achievement in highway landscape, bridge design and engineering. Originally there were 72 bridges constructed, of which 69 remain, and no two were alike in design.

The Parkway is the culmination of a generation of experiments in combining the talents of engineers and landscape architects to create parkways that served recreational purposes, were scenic, and provided safe transportation. The planners of the parkway's landscape, A. Earl Wood and Weld Thayer Chase, gave priority to fitting the road into the natural surroundings. The spring brings brilliant displays from the flowering trees and shrubs, while autumn brings its own display of magnificent colors.

The Barlett Arboretum is a facility operated by the University of Connecticut. Here you can enjoy a wide variety of plants indigenous to New England. Walking trails invite inspection of swamps, woodlands, and cultivated gardens. The Sherwood Island State Park offers wide sandy beaches on the Long Island Sound, waterside picnic areas, and fishing jetties.

Local Information

Greenwich Chamber of Commerce
21 W. Putnam Avenue
Greenwich, CT 06830
Phone: 203-869-3500

Stamford Chamber of Commerce
One Landmark Sq.
Stamford, CT 06901
Phone: 203-359-4761

Greater Norwalk Chamber of Commerce
P.O. Box 668
Norwalk, CT 06852
Phone: 203-866-2521

Bridgeport Reg. Bus. Cncl.
P.O. Box 999
Bridgeport, CT 06601
Phone: 203-335-3800

Wilton Chamber of Commerce
P.O. Box 7094
Wilton, CT 06897
Phone: 203-762-0567

New Canaan Chamber of Commerce
111 Elm Street
New Canaan, CT 06840
Phone: 203-966-2004

Bartlett State Park
151 Brookdale Rd.
Stamford, CT 06903
Phone: 203-322-6971

Sherwood Island State Park
Westport, CT 06436
Phone: 203-226-6983

American Shakespeare State Park
1850 Elm St.
Stratford, CT 06497
Phone: 203-381-9518

LODGING DIRECTORY

Roger Sherman Inn - New Canaan, page 443 — Bed & Breakfast / Inns

STATE ROUTE 169   CONNECTICUT

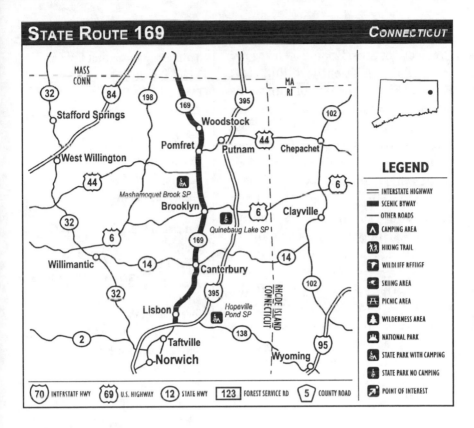

Route Location

This scenic drive along State Route 169 is located in eastern Connecticut with its southern terminus being a few miles north of Norwich. The byway travels north from Interstate 395 in the south to the Massachusetts state line north of N. Woodstock.

Roads Traveled

As its name implies, this byway travels on Connecticut State Highway 169 which is a two-lane paved route that is safe for travel by all types of vehicles. The scenic route is approximately 34 miles in length and is designated by the Federal Highway Administration as a National Scenic Byway. The route has also been designated as a Connecticut State Scenic Byway.

Travel Season

Connecticut State Route 169 is generally open year-round.

Description

Connecticut State Route 169 takes the traveler through gently rolling New England hills covered with corn stalks and apple orchards. Small farms dot the countryside; their livestock pastures enclosed with stone fences and grain elevators standing proudly. Fall strikes this area ablaze with brilliant colors of orange, red, and gold. Each town you pass through seems to proudly display its various architectural styles, teaming with history.

In Canterbury, you'll discover the Prudence Crandall House, New England's first school for black women. The museum, listed as a National Historic Landmark, features changing exhibits, period furnishings, a research library, and gift shop. In Woodstock is the Roseland Cottage, circa 1846. This was built by publisher Henry Bowen for use as a summer home. Listed as a National Historic Landmark, the landscape has the original 1850 boxwood parterre garden.

Local Information

Northeastern Connecticut C of C
3 Central Street
Danielson, CT 06239
Phone: 203-774-8001

Eastern Connecticut C of C
35 Main Street
Norwich, CT 06360
Phone: 203-887-1647

Mashamoquet Brook State Park
Route 45
Pomfret Center, CT 06259
Phone: 860-928-6121

Quienebaug Lake State Park
Hopeville Pond State Park
Bureau of Outdoor Recreation
CT Dept. of Environmental Protection
79 Elm Street
Hartford, CT 06106
Phone: 860-424-3200

For those interested in extending their stay in the area , the 916-acre Mashamoquet Brook State Park offers 55 campsites for tents and recreational vehicles. The park also offers opportunities for fishing, swimming, hiking, and picnicking.

Hopeville Pond State Park is located to the east of the byway's southern terminus. This 554-acre park also offers camping and picnicking facilities. There are 82 campsites available, many with electrical hookups. You can also enjoy hiking, swimming, fishing, and boating.

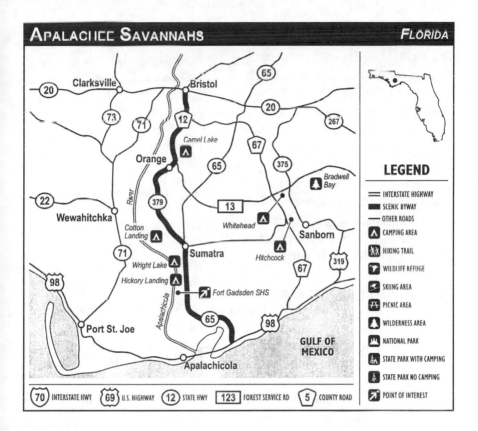

Route Location

The byway is located in northwestern Florida, about 45 miles west of Tallahassee. The byway's northern access begins in Bristol on Florida Highway 20 and travels south through the Apalachicola National Forest to U.S. Highway 98, east of Apalachicola.

Roads Traveled

The Apalachee Savannahs byway is about 60 miles long and follows County Road 12 and State Highways 379 and 65. The roads are two-lane paved roads that are safe for all types of vehicles. Thirty-two miles of the route are designated a National Forest Scenic Byway.

Travel Season

All of the roads followed are open year-round.

Description

The Apalachee Savannahs scenic byway traverses the Apalachicola National Forest through the landscape of gentle slopes, longleaf pine flats, savannahs, cypress bogs, and numerous sloughs and creeks. Over one hundred species of wildflowers grow among the grasses and sedges of the savannahs, offering a beautiful display of seasonal color. Flowing alongside much of the byway is the meandering Apalachicola River.

Recreational opportunities are abundant along this byway. The Florida National Scenic Trail crosses the national forest and can be accessed from the byway. The trail passes through the 23,432-acre Bradwell Bay Wilderness, mainly a large fresh water swamp with several hundred acres of pine, mixed hardwoods, and titi.

Local Information

National Forests In Florida
325 John Knox Rd. Suite 200S
Tallahassee, FL 32303
Phone: 904-942-9300

Liberty County Chamber of Commerce
P.O. Box 523
Bristol, FL 32321
Phone: 904-643-2359

Apalachicola Bay C of C
84 Market St.
Apalachicola, FL 32320
Phone: 904-653-9419

Fort Gadsen State Historical Site
P.O. Box 157
Sumatra, FL 32335
Phone: 904-670-8988

Several developed recreation areas are located along the byway. Camel Lake offers 10 campsites situated next to a small natural lake. Access to the Florida National Scenic Trail is provided. Cotton Landing is a smaller recreation area with only four campsites available. Wright Lake has a 21-unit campground set in a wooded area along the shores of the lake. The Hickory Landing Recreation Area provides 10 camping units and access to the Apalachicola River for boating and fishing.

Fishing, hiking, and picnicking are among the attractions of Fort Gadsden State Historic Site. This site also offers interpretive exhibits depicting the history of the fort and its role in Florida's history.

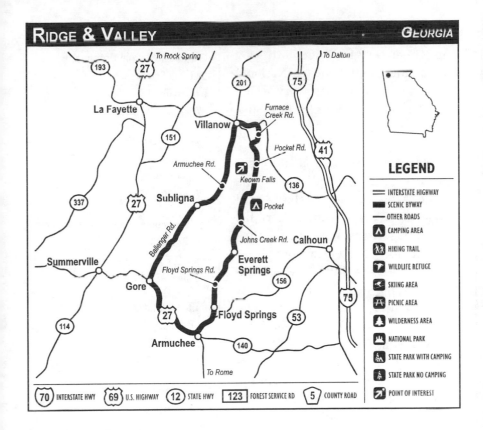

Route Location

The Ridge & Valley scenic byway is located in the northwest corner of Georgia, approximately 75 miles northwest of Atlanta. The scenic route forms a loop drive between Villanow in the north and Armuchee in the south.

Roads Traveled

The 47-mile route follows U.S. Highway 27, Georgia State Highways 136 and 156 and the Armuchee, Thomas Ballenger, Floyd Springs, Johns Creek, Pocket, and Furnace Creek Roads. All of the roads are two-lane paved roads suitable for all vehicles. The entire route has been designated a National Forest Scenic Byway.

Travel Season

The roads followed are generally open year-round.

Description

The Ridge & Valley scenic byway crosses the Chattahoochee National Forest offering excellent scenery of long parallel ridges with broad valleys situated in between.

Two beautiful waterfalls are the highlight of the 218-acre Keown Falls Scenic Area. A short walking trail will lead you to the scenic waterfalls. Picnic facilities have been constructed for your enjoyment. Near this area is the John's Mountain Overlook, the site of an old fire tower that has since been removed. The spectacular view from the platform looks west as far as Lookout Mountain in Alabama and Tennessee. A 3-mile walking trail departs from the overlook, goes to Keown Falls, and returns to the overlook.

Wildlife observers will delight in the many species found in this region of Georgia. White-tailed deer and wild turkey are among some of the wildlife commonly seen.

Local Information

Chattahoochee and Oconee N. F.
508 Oak St. NW
Gainesville, GA 30501
Phone: 404-536-0541

Chattooga County C of C
P.O. Box 217
Summerville, GA 30747
Phone: 706-857-4033

Walker County Chamber of Commerce
P.O. Box 430
Rock Spring, GA 30739
Phone: 706-375-7702

Dalton - Whitfield C of C
524 Holiday Ave.
Dalton, GA 30720
Phone: 706-278-7373

Greater Rome Chamber of Commerce
One Riverside Pkwy.
Rome, GA 30161
Phone: 706-291-7663

Those interested in prolonging their stay will find camping and picnicking facilities at the Pocket Recreation Area. This area was once the site of a Civilian Conservation Corps encampment utilized from 1938 to 1942. A 3-mile loop trail here will take you deep into the wooded countryside. The campground offers 27 campsites, restrooms, and drinking water.

There are two privately owned lakes along the byway that are open to the public, Lake Marvin and Lake Arrowhead. These lakes offer good warm water fishing opportunities in beautiful woodland settings.

RUSSELL - BRASSTOWN   GEORGIA

Route Location

The Russell - Brasstown scenic drive is located in northeastern Georgia, about 90 miles north of Atlanta. The southeastern access is located near Helen off Georgia State Highway 75 and travels northwest, forming a loop drive back to Helen.

Roads Traveled

The byway follows Georgia State Highways 75, 180, and 348 which are all two-lane paved roads suitable for all vehicles. The 38-mile route has been designated a National Forest Scenic Byway.

Travel Season

The byway is generally open year-round with occasional temporary closures for winter snow removal.

Description

The Russell - Brasstown scenic byway crosses the Chattahoochee National Forest winding through forested hills, mountains, and valleys. The headwaters of the Chattahoochee River are completely encircled by the byway.

Brasstown Bald is Georgia's highest mountain and is adjacent to the byway. The view from the 4,784-foot high mountain is spectacular. The visitor center here offers slide programs and interpretive exhibits. Picnicking facilities along with restrooms and drinking water are available. A short ¼-mile walking trail from the parking lot leads to the summit.

Of interest to hikers and backpackers is the Appalachian National Scenic Trail which crosses the byway. Several wilderness areas also provide opportunities for hiking and backpacking in a secluded, primitive setting.

Local Information

Chattahoochee and Oconee N. F.
508 Oak St. NW
Gainsville, GA 30501
Phone: 404-536-0541

Helen Chamber of Commerce
P.O. Box 192
Helen, GA 30545
Phone: 706-878-3677

Blairsville / Union County C of C
385 Blue Ridge Hwy.
Blairsville, GA 30512
Phone: 706-745-5789

Unicoi State Park
P.O. Box 849
Helen, GA 30545
Phone: 706-878-2201

Vogel State Park
7485 Vogel State Park Rd.
Blairsville, GA 30512
Phone: 706-745-2628

A short side trip off the byway worth taking is Georgia State Highway 356 to the Anna Ruby Falls Scenic Area. In this 1,600-acre area, twin waterfalls merge to form Smith Creek. It is necessary to walk a ½-mile trail to reach the falls. Five scenic waterfalls can be seen within the 170-acre High Shoals Scenic Area. A one-mile hiking trail will take you to the waterfalls.

Andrews Cove is the only developed national forest campground along the byway. The campground is situated on Andrews Creek and has 11 units available to campers. Restrooms and drinking water are also provided.

Nearby Routes

Oscar Wigington, page 324 / Ocoee, page 337

BEAR LAKE - CARIBOU   *IDAHO*

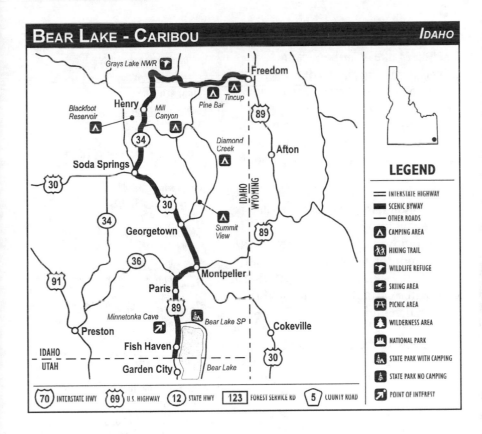

Route Location

The Bear Lake - Caribou scenic drive is located in southeastern Idaho, about 55 miles east of Pocatello. The northeastern access is located on the Wyoming border, in the town of Freedom off U.S. Highway 89. The byway then travels southwest to the Utah border, south of Fish Haven.

Roads Traveled

The 115-mile scenic byway follows Idaho State Highway 34 and U.S. Highways 30 and 89. All of the roads are two-lane paved roads suitable for all vehicles. Approximately 57 miles of this route are officially designated a National Forest Scenic Byway. The route is also a state scenic byway.

Travel Season

The route is generally open year-round although heavy winter snows can temporarily close the roads for snow removal.

Description

The Bear Lake - Caribou scenic byway travels along the shores of Bear Lake, across rolling farm lands, open livestock ranges, and through forested canyons. The northern portion runs through the Caribou National Forest with scenic vistas of the Caribou Mountains to the north.

Bear Lake stretches for 20 miles from north to south in Idaho and Utah and is 8 miles wide. The lake offers excellent rainbow and cutthroat trout fishing in addition to swimming and sailing. Bear Lake State Park offers 40 campsites suitable for tents and recreational vehicles.

To the west of the byway near its southern terminus is the Minnetonka Cave. The cave was accidentally discovered by a grouse hunter more than 50 years ago. The cave is a ½-mile long cavern with nine chambers. Tours operate from mid-June through Labor Day. The national forest has developed three campgrounds near the cave.

The northern portion of the byway crosses the Caribou National Forest, alongside Blackfoot Reservoir and Grays Lake National Wildlife Refuge. Blackfoot Reservoir is popular for fishing and boating. Grays Lake National Wildlife Refuge is an excellent place to see the largest concentration of sandhill crains in the United States during the summer.

Local Information

Caribou National Forest
Federal Building, Suite 294
250 S. 4th Ave.
Pocatello, ID 83201
Phone: 208-236-6700

Soda Springs Chamber of Commerce
P.O. Box 697
Soda Springs, ID 83276
Phone: 208-547-3044

Star Valley Chamber of Commerce
P.O. Box 1097
Afton, WY 83110
Phone: 800-426-8833

Greater Bear Lake Valley C of C
P.O. Box 265
Montpelier, ID 83254
Phone: 208-847-3717

Bear Lake Chamber of Commerce
P.O. Box 55
Garden City, UT 84028
Phone: 801-946-2901

Bear Lake State Park
181 S. Main
Paris, ID 83261
Phone: 208-945-2790

Nearby Routes

Teton, page 142 / Logan Canyon Highway, page 361

Lodging Directory

Three Sisters Motel - Montpelier, page 431 — Hotel / Motel

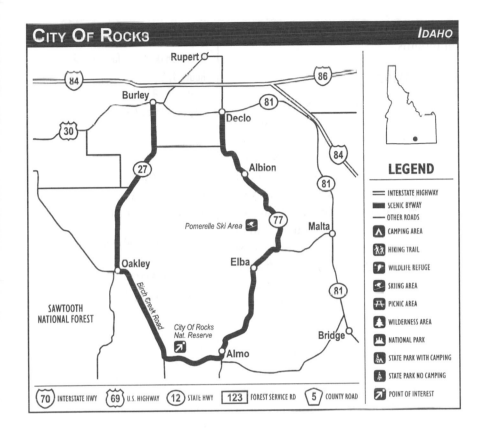

Route Location

The City of Rocks Back Country Byway is located in south-central Idaho approximately 75 miles southwest of Pocatello. Travelers can begin this scenic drive in either Burley or Declo, both towns being just south of I-84.

Roads Traveled

The 75-mile City of Rocks scenic drive follows Idaho State Highways 27 and 77 which are two-lane paved roads suitable for all vehicles. The portion of the route between Oakley and Almo is mostly a graded dirt road with the first few miles south of Oakley being paved. The road from Almo to its junction with State Highway 77 is also paved and suitable for all types of vehicles. Forty-nine miles of this route are officially designated by the BLM as a Type I Back Country Byway.

Travel Season

Most of the route is open year-round, however, the portion between Oakley

June due to heavy snowpack. The route is groomed, however, in the winter for use by snowmobilers.

Description

The Lewis & Clark Back Country Byway passes through stands of fir and pine trees, across mountain meadows, and rolling hills as it climbs the Bitterroot Range to the Continental Divide and Lemhi Pass. The byway offers magnificent views of the Bitterroot and Beaverhead Mountains and the Salmon and Lemhi Valleys.

Local Information

BLM - Salmon District Office
P.O. Box 430
Salmon, ID 83467
Phone: 208-756-5400

Salmon Valley Chamber of Commerce
200 Main St. #1
Salmon, ID 83467
Phone: 208-756-2100

President Thomas Jefferson commissioned the expedition to explore and map the vast new territory west of the Mississippi River acquired by the United States in the Louisiana Purchase of 1803. The Lewis & Clark expedition began in May of 1804 and crossed Lemhi Pass late in the summer of 1805. Here the expedition unfurled the flag of the United States for the first time west of the Rocky Mountains, laying claim to the Pacific Northwest. At the top of Lemhi Pass is a memorial to the one woman of the expedition who served as a guide and interpreter.

The byway passes the site of Fort Lemhi, built in 1855 by Mormon missionaries. The remote outpost once had over 100 inhabitants before being abandoned in 1858. The remains of the fort are on private property, obtain permission from the landowner before inspecting!

Agency Creek Campground is a small campground maintained by the BLM. There are four campsites available, all with picnic tables and fire rings. Pit toilets are provided. No drinking water or trash receptacles are provided.

Nearby Routes

Salmon River, page 165 / Big Sheep Creek, page 208

MESA FALLS   *IDAHO*

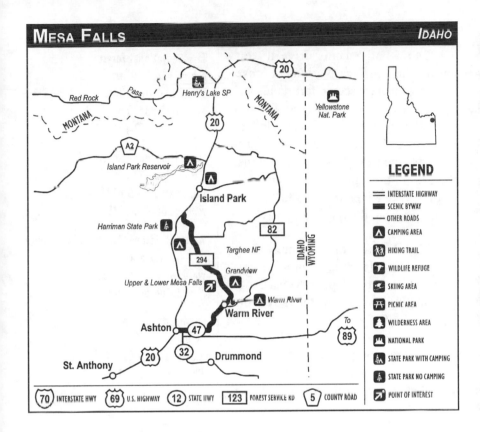

LEGEND

═══ INTERSTATE HIGHWAY
▬▬▬ SCENIC BYWAY
─── OTHER ROADS
🅰 CAMPING AREA
🚶 HIKING TRAIL
🦌 WILDLIFE REFUGE
⛷ SKIING AREA
🏕 PICNIC AREA
🌲 WILDERNESS AREA
🏛 NATIONAL PARK
🅰 STATE PARK WITH CAMPING
🅰 STATE PARK NO CAMPING
↗ POINT OF INTEREST

(70) INTERSTATE HWY   (69) U.S. HIGHWAY   (12) STATE HWY   [123] FOREST SERVICE RD   (5) COUNTY ROAD

Route Location

The byway is located in eastern Idaho, approximately 50 miles northeast of Idaho Falls near the Wyoming and Montana borders. The southern access is located in Ashton off U.S. Highway 20 and travels an open loop north back to the junction of Highway 20, near Harriman State Park.

Roads Traveled

The 28-mile route follows Idaho State Highway 47 and Forest Service Road 294. The byway travels over narrow two-lane paved roads suitable for all vehicles, although portions of the road can be rough. The entire route is designated a National Forest Scenic Byway and a state scenic byway.

Travel Season

The roads are generally open from mid-May through October, then portions are closed by heavy winter snows.

Description

The Mesa Falls scenic drive travels across the Targhee National Forest, winding through scenic farmlands before entering the Three Rivers Canyon and climbing to a mixed forest of lodgepole pine, Douglas-fir, and aspen. Views of the west slopes of the Tetons, the Mesa Falls, and the Henry's Fork of the Snake River are but a few of the highlights found along the byway.

The Mesa Falls are the last undisturbed major waterfalls of the Columbia River system, with the Upper Mesa Falls plummeting 100 feet and the lower falls dropping 70 feet. The Lower Mesa Falls were chosen as the site for a Civilian Conservation Corps project. CCC crews constructed a stone overlook that provides a panoramic view of both falls.

The Three Rivers area is a popular spot for camping, fishing, inner tubing, and hiking. The rails of the Yellowstone Railway, which once operated as a passenger railroad through Idaho to Yellowstone National Park, have been removed and it is now used for hiking, bicycling, cross-country skiing, and snowmobiling.

The national forest offers several developed campgrounds along the byway as well as throughout the national forest. The Warm River Campground is a popular spot that offers 12 units, drinking water, and restrooms. Henry's Lake State Park is located north of the byway and has 50 campsites. Other facilities found in the state park include drinking water, showers, and recreational vehicle hookups.

Nearby Routes

Teton, page 169

Local Information

Targhee National Forest
Ashton Ranger District
30 S. Yellowstone Hwy.
Ashton, ID 83420
Phone: 208-652-7442

South Fremont Chamber of Commerce
110 W. Main St.
Saint Anthony, ID 83445
Phone: 208-624-3775

West Yellowstone Chamber of Commerce
30 Yellowstone Ave.
West Yellowstone, MT 59758
Phone: 406-646-7701

Harriman State Park
HC 66
Island Park, ID 83429
Phone: 208-558-7368

Henry's Lake State Park
Island Park, ID 83429
Phone: 208-558-7532

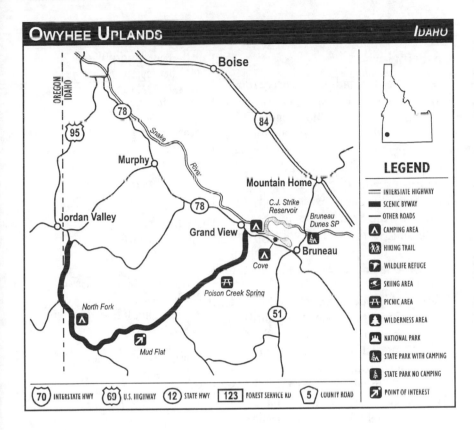

Route Location

The Owyhee Uplands Back Country Byway is situated in the southwestern corner of Idaho, about 75 miles south of Boise. The northeastern access is located in Grand View off Idaho State Highway 78. The byway travels southwest, forming an open loop drive that ends just south of U.S. Highway 95 near Jordan Valley, Oregon.

Roads Traveled

The 101-mile route follows the Deep Creek-Mud Flat Road which averages 1½ lanes in width of gravel-surfaced road with frequent opportunities for passing. There are short grades of 12% at plateau breaks, but the route can be driven safely in an automobile. The byway is officially designated a Type I Back Country Byway by the Bureau of Land Management.

Travel Season

The byway is generally open from June through September after which heavy winter snows can close the route.

Description

The Owyhee Uplands scenic drive travels across a remote area in Idaho with a small portion crossing into Oregon. This route travels through juniper and mountain mahogany woodlands, sheer-walled river canyons, mountain valleys, and sagebrush covered hills. To the south and west, the vast desert expanse is framed by the Santa Rosa and Steens Mountains. In the spring, wildflowers growing in the open fields add a splash of color to the desert landscape.

There is only one campground located directly along the byway, the primitive BLM-operated North Fork Campground. The BLM also maintains the Cove Campground, just a few miles south of the byway's eastern end. This campground offers 26 units for tents and recreational vehicles and also has drink-

Local Information

BLM - Boise District Office
3948 Development Ave.
Boise, ID 83705
Phone: 208-384-3300

Mountain Home Chamber of Commerce
P.O. Box 3
Mountain Home, ID 83647
Phone: 208-587-4334

Caldwell Chamber of Commerce
300 Frontage Rd.
Caldwell, ID 83606
Phone: 208-459-7493

Homedale Chamber of Commerce
P.O. Box 845
Homedale, ID 83628
Phone: 208-337-4611

Bruneau Dunes State Park
Star Route B - Box 41
Mountain Home, ID 83647
Phone: 208-366-7919

ing water, shower facilities, and restrooms. The Bureau of Land Management does permit dispersed camping nearly anywhere upon BLM land.

A few other camping areas may be found within the area. The Idaho Power Company maintains three parks near the C.J. Strike Reservoir's dam with a total of 50 campsites available, some being pull through sites. The reservoir offers abundant fishing and boating opportunities.

Further east of the byway is the Bruneau Dunes State Park. This 4,800-acre park encompasses sand dunes reaching heights of several hundred feet. There are also several lakes within the park that offer good fishing. The campground here has 48 sites, some with hookups, drinking water, shower facilities, flush toilets, and a dump station.

Nearby Routes

Ponderosa Pine, page 163 / Sawtooth, page 167 / Leslie Gulch - Succor Creek, page 298

PONDEROSA PINE   *IDAHO*

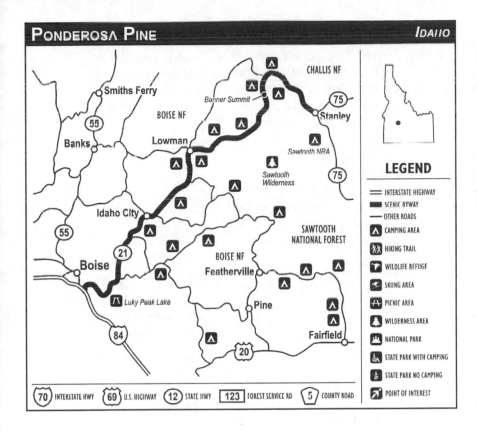

Route Location

The Ponderosa Pine scenic drive is located in west-central Idaho near Boise. The byway can be accessed from the south off Interstate 84. The scenic drive then travels north across the Boise National Forest to its end in Stanley with the junction of Idaho State Highway 75.

Roads Traveled

The 130-mile route follows Idaho State Highway 21 which is a two-lane paved road suitable for all types of vehicles. The road is narrow with some steep grades and passing lanes. The scenic drive is designated a National Forest Scenic Byway and a state scenic byway.

Travel Season

The entire route is generally open year-round although sections may temporarily close for snow removal. Severe avalanche conditions exist in the Banner Summit area and closures can be frequent.

Description

The Ponderosa Pine scenic byway winds through the Boise National Forest with a small portion through the Challis National Forest and Sawtooth National Recreation Area. The byway passes through dense forests of pine, across high mountain valleys, and along portions of the Boise River, Lucky Peak Lake, and the South Fork of the Payette River. Visitors to the byway are treated to spectacular views of the rugged Sawtooth Mountains.

Much of the Sawtooth Mountains are protected from development by the 217,000-acre Sawtooth Wilderness. This wilderness area provides excellent opportunities for hiking, backpacking, and horseback riding.

The Boise National Forest is rich with wildlife. In the higher elevations are mountain lions and black bears. Mule deer and elk may be seen grazing early in the morning or evening. Birdwatchers will want to be on the lookout for hummingbirds, larks, swallows, and many more species. Bald eagles, hawks, and falcons can also be seen flying overhead.

If you're interested in staying awhile, the national forest offers several camping areas directly along the byway. You can venture into the forest from the many side roads to find more camping and picnicking opportunities.

Local Information

Sawtooth National Forest
2647 Kimberly Rd. E
Twin Falls, ID 83301
Phone: 208-737-3200

Boise National Forest
1750 Front St.
Boise, ID 83702
Phone: 208-364-4100

Challis National Forest
HC63 - Box 1671
Challis, ID 83226
Phone: 208-879-2285

Boise Area Chamber of Commerce
300 N. 6th St.
Boise, ID 83701
Phone: 208-344-5515

Stanley - Sawtooth C of C
P.O. Box 8
Stanley, ID 83278
Phone: 208-774-3411

Nearby Routes

Owyhee Uplands, page 161 / Salmon River, page 165 / Sawtooth, page 167 / Leslie Gulch - Succor Creek, page 298

Lodging Directory

Shilo Inn - Boise Airport, page 450 — Hotel / Motel
Shilo Inn - Boise Riverside, page 451 — Hotel / Motel
Torrey's Burnt Creek Inn - Stanley, page 451 — Cabin / Cottage / Guest Ranch & Campground / RV Park

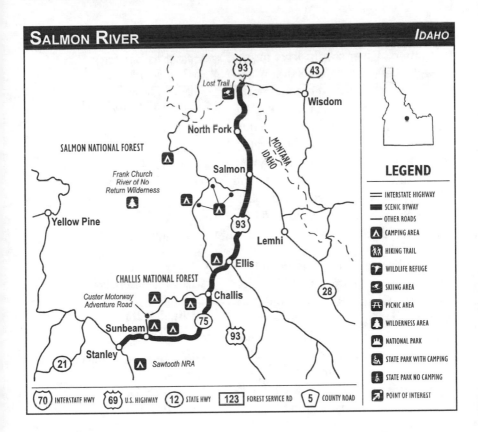

Route Location

The Salmon River scenic byway travels from the town of Stanley to Lost Trail Pass on the Idaho-Montana border. The byway is located in central Idaho, approximately 130 miles northwest of Boise.

Roads Traveled

The 161-mile scenic byway follows Idaho State Highway 75 and U.S. Highway 93. Both highways are two-lane paved roads safe for travel by all types of vehicles, however, there are no passing lanes and some tight curves dictating slow speeds. Eighty-three miles of this route are officially designated a National Forest Scenic Byway. The entire length of the byway is also designated a state scenic byway.

Travel Season

The roads followed are generally open year-round although extra caution should be excerised during the winter months.

Description

The Salmon River scenic drive passes through the Challis and Salmon National Forests and a portion of the Sawtooth National Recreation Area. Flowing alongside the byway for almost its entire length are the cool blue waters of the Salmon River. As the byway travels through forested canyons and valleys, spectacular vistas of the Bitterroot, Salmon River, Lemhi, and Lost River Mountains come into view.

The Challis and Salmon National Forests provide access to the 2.3 million acre Frank Church River of No Return Wilderness. There are more acres of roadless wilderness in this region than anywhere else in the lower 48 states. This vast wilderness area provides excellent fishing, hunting, hiking, backpacking, and horseback riding.

Local Information

Sawtooth National Forest
2647 Kimberly Rd. E
Twin Falls, ID 83301
Phone: 208-737-3200

Salmon National Forest
P.O. Box 729
Salmon, ID 83467
Phone: 208-756-2215

Challis National Forest
HC63 - Box 1671
Challis, ID 83226
Phone: 208-879-2285

Stanley - Sawtooth C of C
P.O. Box 8
Stanley, ID 83278
Phone: 208-774-3411

Salmon Valley Chamber of Commerce
200 Main St. #1
Salmon, ID 83467
Phone: 208-756-2100

Those less interested in the primitive back country experience of the wilderness area will find plenty of opportunities for pitching a tent or parking their RV in a developed campground. Numerous public campgrounds are located directly along or a short distance off the byway.

If you're driving this byway in a high-clearnce or four-wheel-drive vehicle, then you might consider taking a side trip known as the Custer Motorway Adventure Road. This side trip explores the historic Yankee Fork Mining District and will take you past ghost towns and abandoned mining sites of the late 1800s.

Nearby Routes

Lewis & Clark, page 157 / Ponderosa Pine, page 163 / Sawtooth, page 167

Lodging Directory

Torrey's Burnt Creek Inn - Stanley, page 452 — Cabin / Cottage / Guest Ranch & Campground / RV Park

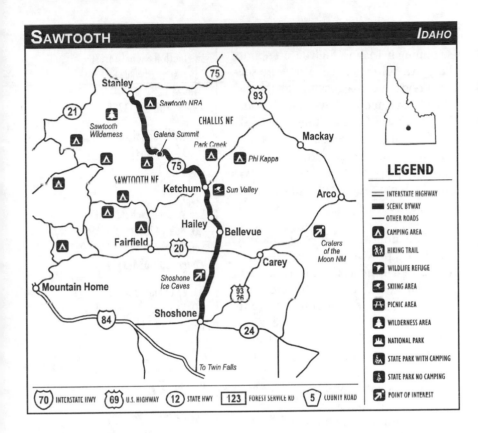

Route Location

The Sawtooth scenic byway begins in Shoshone, approximately 25 miles north of Twin Falls in central Idaho. The scenic drive then travels north through national forest land and the Sawtooth National Recreation Area to the byway's end in Stanley.

Roads Traveled

The 116-mile route follows Idaho State Highway 75 which is a two-lane paved road suitable for all types of vehicles. Sixty-one miles of the byway from Ketchum to Stanley are designated a National Forest Scenic Byway. The entire length of the scenic drive is a state scenic byway.

Travel Season

The entire route is open year-round although caution should be used during the winter months. Five to six percent grades are encountered from Galena Summit to Stanley.

Description

Beginning in Idaho's high desert region, the byway climbs north along the scenic Wood River, passes through the forested landscape of Sawtooth National Forest, crosses Galena Summit at 8,701 feet, and then descends to its end in Stanley. The overlook near Galena Summit provides panoramic views into the Sawtooth Mountains and wilderness area.

The Shoshone Ice Caves are natural lava tubes in which air currents have formed striking ice sculptures. The caves are located 90 feet below the earth's surface and maintain a year-round temperature below freezing. Guided tours of the ice caves are offered during the summer.

The visitor center for the 756,000-acre Sawtooth National Recreation Area is located north of Ketchum and is open year-round. Visitors will find information and exhibits here. This vast recreation area offers unlimited opportunities for camping, picnicking, hiking, backpacking, fishing, and bicycling.

Local Information

Sawtooth National Forest
2647 Kimberly Rd. E
Twin Falls, ID 83301
Phone: 208-737-3200

Challis National Forest
HC63 - Box 1671
Challis, ID 83226
Phone: 208-879-2285

Sun Valley-Ketchum C of C
P.O. Box 2420
Sun Valley, ID 83353
Phone: 800-634-3347

Hailey Chamber of Commerce
P.O. Box 100
Hailey, ID 83333
Phone: 208-788-2700

Shoshone Chamber of Commerce
P.O. Box 575
Shoshone, ID 83352
Phone: 208-886-2979

Stanley - Sawtooth C of C
P.O. Box 8
Stanley, ID 83278
Phone: 208-774-3411

The Sawtooth National Forest also offers opportunities for camping, picnicking, and hiking. Several public campgrounds have been developed along the byway as well as within the national forest.

Nearby Routes

Owyhee Uplands, page 161 / Ponderosa Pine, page 163 / Salmon River, page 165 / City Of Rocks, page 155

Lodging Directory

Torrey's Burnt Creek Inn - Stanley, page 455 — Cabin / Cottage / Guest Ranch & Campground / RV Park

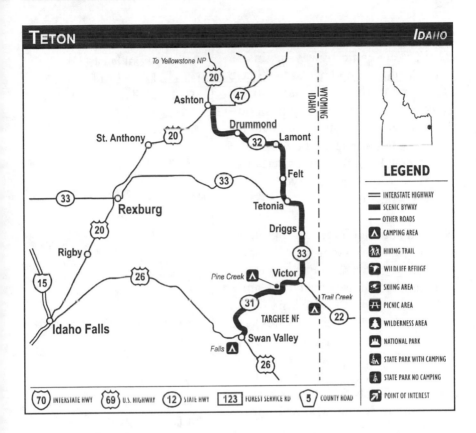

Route Location

This scenic drive is located in eastern Idaho, about 50 miles east of Idaho Falls near the Wyoming state line. The southern terminus is located in Swan Valley off U.S. Highway 26. The byway travels north to the junction of State Highway 47 near the town of Ashton.

Roads Traveled

The Teton scenic byway follows Idaho State Highways 31, 32, and 33 all of which are two-lane paved roads suitable for all vehicles. Pine Creek Pass has six percent grades and sharp curves requiring slow speeds. Twenty miles of this 68-mile byway are officially designated a National Forest Scenic Byway. The entire byway is also a state scenic byway.

Travel Season

The roads followed are usually open year-round although winter driving conditions may be hazardous.

Description

The Teton scenic byway begins in Swan Valley with views of the Snake River and Caribou Mountains to the south. The byway then begins climbing through the Targhee National Forest along Pine Creek to the 6,764-foot Pine Creek Pass. Spectacular views of the Teton Mountains in Wyoming can be seen from here.

Several national forest campgrounds can be found along or near this portion of the byway. Near the byway's southern terminus is the Falls Campground with 24 sites, drinking water, and pit toilets. Just beyond Pine Creek Pass is a small national forest campground. The Pine Creek Campground has 11 campsites with picnic tables, fire rings, toilets, and drinking water. About 6 miles southeast of Victor is another public campground named Trail Creek. There are 11 campsites available here.

Local Information

Targhee National Forest
Palisades Ranger District
3659 E. Ririe Hwy.
Idaho Falls, ID 83401
Phone: 208-523-1412

Greater Idaho Falls C of C
505 Lindsay Blvd.
Idaho Falls, ID 83405
Phone: 208-523-1010

Teton Valley Chamber of Commerce
P.O. Box 250
Driggs, ID 83422
Phone: 208-354-2500

South Fremont Chamber of Commerce
110 W. Main St.
Saint Anthony, ID 83445
Phone: 208-624-3775

Yellowstone National Park
P.O. Box 168
Yellowstone Nat'l. Park, WY 82190
Phone: 307-344-7381

A variety of wildlife inhabits the mountains and valleys of the national forest. Elk and mule deer may be seen grazing in the fields; the best time to view them is early in the morning or evening. Other wildlife includes black bear, coyotes, and moose. Hawks can often be seen gliding on the wind currents.

After traveling through the national forest, the byway continues north across rolling agricultural land through the communities of Victor, Driggs, and Tetonia. The byway ends near Ashton where the Mesa Falls scenic byway begins.

Nearby Routes

Bear Lake - Caribou, page 153 / Mesa Falls, page 159

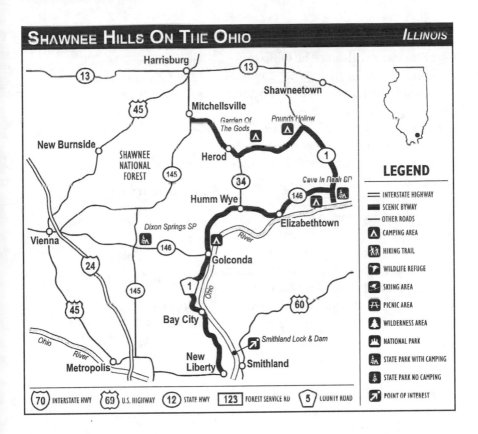

Route Location

The Shawnee Hills On The Ohio scenic byway is located in southern Illinois. The byway begins in Mitchellsville approximately 7 miles south of Harrisburg. The byway travels south following the banks of the Ohio River and ends in New Liberty.

Roads Traveled

The byway follows State Highway 34 from Mitchellsville to the intersection of Karbers Ridge Road, just south of Herod. The byway then follows Karbers Ridge Road to State Highway 1 which it then follows to the Cave In Rock State Park. Between the state park and Golconda, the byway follows State Highway 146. From Golconda to the byway's end, the road followed is County Road 1. All of the routes are two-lane paved roads safe for travel by all types of vehicles.

Travel Season

The byway is open all year, however, drive with extra care during the winter.

Description

The Shawnee Hills On The Ohio travels through the heart of the Shawnee National Forest, winding through gently rolling hills and ridgetops before descending to follow the Ohio River. The Shawnee National Forest preserves over 250,000 acres of hardwood forest, meandering streams, and placid lakes.

White-tailed deer can be found throughout the national forest and are most commonly seen along the forested creek bottoms. Alert wildlife observers may occasionally catch a glimpse of a wild turkey or two. Fishermen will find largemouth bass, bluegill, catfish, and crappie in the many creaks and lakes throughout the national forest.

A short distance off the byway will lead the traveler to the Garden of the Gods Recreation Area and Wilderness. Here there are 8 miles of trails that wind above and below the bluffs and sandstone rock formations. There is a campground here with 12 campsites, picnic area, and drinking water.

Cave In Rock State Park offers a campground with 48 sites for tents and recreational vehicles. Hookups are also available at many of the sites. A short hiking trail here leads to a cave that was once a pirate's den in the 1790s. The cave was also used as the headquarters for outlaws and gangs.

Near the end of the byway is the Smithland Lock & Dam, a facility operated by the Corps of Engineers. There is a picnic area here where you can enjoy a lunch while watching the locks in operation.

Nearby Routes

Ohio River Scenic Route, page 173

Local Information

Shawnee National Forest
901 S. Commercial St.
Harrisburg, IL 62946
Phone: 618-253-7114

Harrisburg Chamber of Commerce
325 E. Poplar St.
Harrisburg, IL 62946
Phone: 618-252-4192

Paducah Area Chamber of Commerce
417 S. 4th St.
Paducah, KY 42002
Phone: 502-443-1746

Cave In Rock State Park
P.O. Box 338
Cave-In-Rock, IL 62919
Phone: 618-289-4325

Dixon Springs State Park
RR 2
Golconda, IL 62938
Phone: 618-949-3394

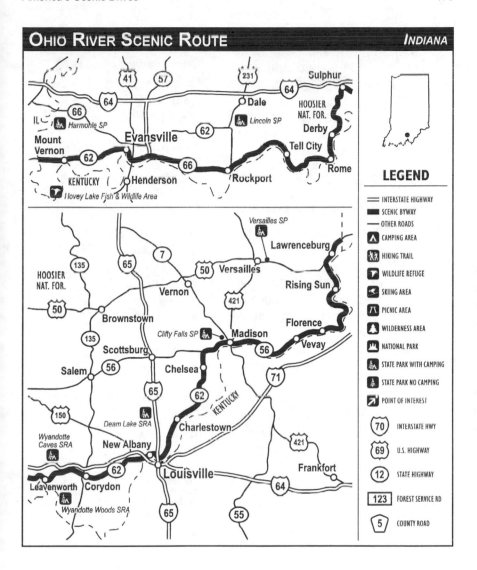

Route Location

The Ohio River Scenic Route crosses the entire state of Indiana from east to west in the southern portion of the state. The city of Lawrenceburg lies near the byway's eastern terminus on the Ohio state line. Mount Vernon is near the western terminus of the byway which is the Illinois state line.

Roads Traveled

The 302-mile route consists primarily of two-lane paved roads that are suitable for all types of vehicles. The primary routes followed are State Highways 56, 62, and 66. For detailed directions, please refer to the sidebar entitled "Following The Ohio River Scenic Route." The route has been designated a National Scenic Byway by the Federal Highway Administration.

Travel Season

The entire length of the route is generally open year-round.

Description

The Ohio River Scenic Route winds through southern Indiana's rolling hills, forests, and farmlands, at times clinging to the river's edge. As you travel this route, you'll pass through quaint towns with towering church spires, stately mansions, and historic buildings. You'll pass cypress swamps and travel atop rock outcrops peering over the Ohio River, and leisurely pass through dense hardwood forests. At times you'll be given sweeping views of the river, while other times you hardly know it's there. Below is just a small sample of the many attractions and scenery you will discover along this route.

Something you wouldn't expect to find in Indiana is a cypress swamp, complete with water lilies and rare birds. This makes for an interesting and enjoyable short side trip from the main route of the scenic drive. Just west of Mount Vernon in southwestern Indiana, you can take State Highway 69 south to the Hovey Lake State Fish & Wildlife Area, a 4,300-acre wetland. Here,

Local Information

Wayne - Hoosier National Forest
811 Constitution Ave.
Bedford, IN 47421
Phone: 812-275-5987

Mount Vernon Chamber of Commerce
405 E. Fourth St.
Mount Vernon, IN 47620
Phone: 812-838-3639

Metro Evansville Chamber of Commerce
100 NW Second St., #202
Evansville, IN 47708
Phone: 812-425-8147

Rockport Area Chamber of Commerce
P.O. Box 85
Rockport, IN 47635
Phone: 812-649-4626

Perry County Chamber of Commerce
P.O. Box 82
Tell City, IN 47586
Phone: 812-547-2385

Crawford County Chamber of Commerce
RR 1, Box 149
Leavenworth, IN 47137
Phone: 812-739-4458

Chamber of Commerce of Harrison Cnty.
310 N. Elm St.
Corydon, IN 47112
Phone: 812-738-2137

Southern Indiana Chamber of Commerce
4100 Charlestown Road
New Albany, IN 47150
Phone: 812-945-0266

you can do some fishing or enjoy a relaxing boat ride on the waters of Hovey
Lake. Next to the lake is the Twin
Swamps Nature Preserve, an excellent
example of a cypress swamp, in Indiana!

North of Rockport on State Hwy.162,
just east of U.S. 231, is Lincoln State
Park and the Lincoln Boyhood National
Memorial. It is on this farm that
Abraham Lincoln lived from 1816 to
1830. During this time, he grew from a
7-year-old boy to a 21-year-old man.
Log farm buildings are staffed by cos-
tumed interpreters during the summer
months. The visitor is invited to par-
ticipate in the daily chores that Abe and
his family would have performed including breaking flax, splitting wood,
or making butter.

The Ohio River Scenic Route passes
through portions of the 80,000-acre
Hoosier National Forest. The byway
travels along the Ohio River in the
forest's southern portion before turning
north, passing through stands of hardwoods, pine and cedar, springs, caves,
and sinkholes. Several recreation areas
are available throughout the national
forest that provide camping (no hookups available) and picnicking facilities.

Rock outcrops, forested hills, caves, and
scenic waterways can be found in the
most ruggedly scenic part of the byway,
the Harrison Crawford State Forest.
This state forest encompasses the Wyandotte Woods and Wyandotte Caves State
Recreation Areas. Visitors can tour the
caves here that were once used by prehistoric people for mining operations.

Local Information

Madison Area Chamber of Commerce
301 E. Main St.
Madison, IN 47250
Phone: 812-265-3135

Switzerland County Chamber of Commerce
P.O. Box 212
Vevay, IN 47043
Phone: 812-427-2670

Dearborn County Chamber of Commerce
P.O. Box 66
Lawrenceburg, IN 47025
Phone: 812-537-0814

Louisville Area Chamber of Commerce
600 W. Main St.
Louisville, KY 40202
Phone: 502-625-0000

Harmonie State Park
Route 1, Box 5A
New Harmony, IN 47631
Phone: 812-682-4821

Lincoln State Park
Box 216
Lincoln City, IN 47552
Phone: 812-937-4710

Wyandotte Caves State Recreation Area
RR 1, Box 85
Leavenworth, IN 47137
Phone: 812-738-2782

Wyandotte Woods State Recreation Area
7240 Old Forest Road
Corydon, IN 47112
Phone: 812-738-8232

Following the Ohio River Scenic Route

The following description is traveling the route from east to west.

Begin at the Indiana-Ohio border and follow U.S. 50 west to Oberting Road. Follow Oberting Road to the town of Greendale. In Greendale, turn left onto Ridge Avenue (State Highway 1), which will become Main Street in Lawrenceburg. In Lawrencburg, turn right (west) on U.S. 50 and follow to the town of Aurora. In Aurora, you will want to turn left onto George Street, then left on Second Street, and then south on State Highway 56.

Local Information

Deam Lake State Recreation Area
1217 Deam Lake Road
Borden, IN 47106
Phone: 812-246-5421

Clifty Falls State Park
1501 Green Road
Madison, IN 47250
Phone: 812-265-1331

Versailles State Park
Box 205, U.S. 50
Versailles, IN 47042
Phone: 812-689-6424

Continue traveling south on SH 56, through Rising Sun, until you reach the intersection with State Highway 156. State Highway 156 will rejoin State Highway 56 in Vevay. Continue traveling west on SH 56 to SH 62, just west of Hanover. Follow SH 62 until you reach the outskirts of Jeffersonville.

In Jeffersonville, you will want to turn left on Allison Lane, right onto Market Street, left on Walnut Street, right on Riverside Drive, right on Sherwood, left on South Clark Boulevard, right on Harrison Avenue, left on Randolph Avenue, then westward on SH 62 once again. State Highway 62 will become Spring Street when you enter New Albany.

In New Albany, State Highway 62 (Spring Street) will intersect with Vincennes Street; turn left and then right onto Main Street. Main Street will eventually turn into the Corydon Pike which, in turn, will end at the intersection with State Highway 62. Turn left onto State Highway 62.

Follow State Highway 62 westward until you reach the town of Sulpher and the intersection with State Highway 66. Turn left onto State Highway 66 and follow it until you reach State Highway 662 near Newburgh. Follow SH 662 west to Interstate 164. Follow I-164 west to Evansville. I-164 will become Veterans Memorial Drive and then Riverside Drive in Evansville. Follow this route until you reach the intersection with State Highway 62 (Lloyd Expressway) From here on out, you'll want to follow State Highway 62 west through Mt. Vernon to the Indiana-Illinois state line.

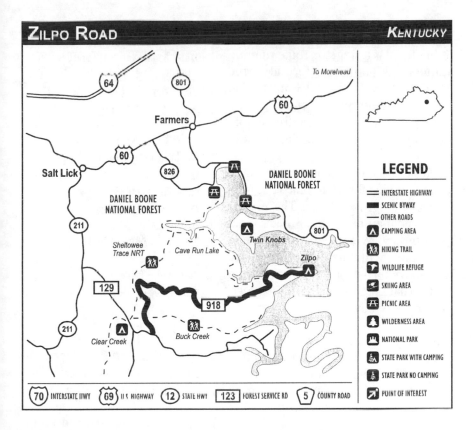

Route Location

The Zilpo Road scenic byway is situated in the forested hills of eastern Kentucky, approximately 60 miles east of Lexington. The byway begins at the intersection with Forest Development Road 129 and ends at the Zilpo Recreation Area on Cave Run Lake.

Roads Traveled

The 9-mile route follows Forest Service Road 918 which is a wide two-lane paved road suitable for all vehicles. The road dead ends in the Zilpo Recreation Area so travelers will need to retrace the route back to Kentucky State Highway 211. The byway is officially designated a National Forest Scenic Byway.

Travel Season

Forest Development Road 918 is normally open all year long.

Description

Zilpo Road is a ridgetop route running through the hardwood forests of the Daniel Boone National Forest. The road is a wide, gently curving road among trees that offer beautiful colors of orange, red, and gold during autumn.

Wildlife observers will want to stay alert and be looking for white-tailed deer foraging among the woods. The patient observer may also see an occasional wild turkey. Woodpeckers, owls, and whip-poor-wills make their presence known within the forest. Hawks, osprey, and the bald eagle can also be seen soaring on the wind currents.

Local Information

Daniel Boone National Forest
100 Vaught Rd.
Winchester, KY 40391
Phone: 606-745-3100

Daniel Boone National Forest
Morehead Ranger District
2375 KY 801 S.
Morehead, KY 40351
Phone: 606-784-6428

Morehead - Rowan County C of C
150 E 1st St.
Morehead, KY 40351
Phone: 606-784-6221

Cave Run Lake is perhaps the main attraction of this byway. It is a 7,390-acre lake constructed on the Licking River by the Corps of Engineers. The lake provides excellent fishing and boating opportunities. The Zilpo Recreation Area, to which the byway travels, is a 355-acre park offering 172 wooded campsites, some with hookups. Some of the facilities found here include restrooms with showers, a boat ramp, swimming beach, drinking water, walking trails, and two dump stations.

On the other side of the lake is the 700-acre Twin Knobs Recreation Area. Each of the 277 campsites found here will accommodate large recreational vehicles or tents. Restrooms with showers, a swimming beach, and walking trails are among the facilities offered. Weekly programs are offered at the amphitheater here.

A smaller, more primitive camping area is found near the beginning of the byway, the Clear Creek Campground. This campground has 21 units with picnic tables and chemical toilets.

The Zilpo Road scenic byway runs through the heart of the Pioneer Weapons Wildlife Management Area. This 7,480-acre area provides hunters the opportunity to experience hunting the way Daniel Boone did years ago. Hunting is limited to pioneer weapons such as the bow and arrow, cross bow, and black powder firearms.

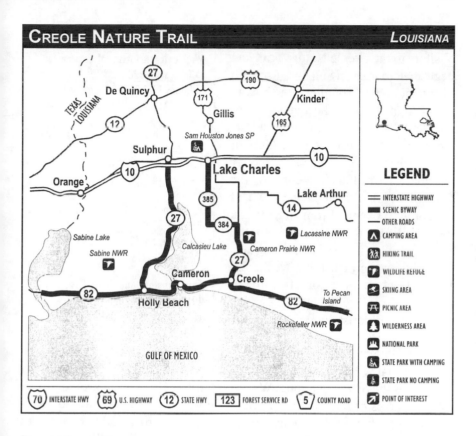

Route Location

The Creole Nature Trail is located in the Cajun country of Louisiana's southwest. The byway forms an open loop from Lake Charles to Sulphur. On the byway's southern portion, the route continues west to the Texas state line and east to the Vermilion parish line, near the Rockefeller National Wildlife Refuge.

Roads Traveled

The scenic drive follows State Highways 27, 82, 384, and 385. The two-lane roads are paved and suitable for travel by all types of vehicles. The 180-mile route has been designated a National Scenic Byway by the Federal Highway Administration.

Travel Season

The entire route is open year-round.

Description

Visitors to the Creole Nature Trail can begin their journey in Sulphur, just north of Interstate 10. From here, the byway travels south through the marshlands of southern Calcasieu and Cameron Parishes to Holly Beach on the Gulf of Mexico. From Holly Beach, the byway continues east along the coast of the Gulf of Mexico through the town of Cameron to Creole. From Creole, you can continue driving north to the byway's end in Lake Charles. You also have the option of driving west from Holly Beach to the Texas state line or east from Creole to the byway's end at the Vermilion parish line.

Local Information

West Calcasieu Assn. of Commerce
800 Picard Road
Sulphur, LA 70663
Phone: 318-527-7142

The Chamber / Southwest Louisiana
P.O. Box 3110
Lake Charles, LA 70602
Phone: 318-433-3632

Cameron Parish Chamber of Commerce
P.O. Box 590
Cameron, LA 70631
Phone: 318-775-5222

Sam Houston Jones State Park
101 Sutherland Road
Lake Charles, LA 70611
Phone: 318-855-2665

The Creole Nature Trail travels near four national wildlife refuges. The first encountered traveling south from Sulphur is the Sabine National Wildlife Refuge. This refuge provides over 124,000 acres of marshland for migrating waterfowl in addition to recreational opportunities for the byway traveler. A 1½-mile trail here provides excellent opportunities for viewing the wildlife, including alligators. Over 150 miles of canals, bayous, and waterways are open to the public for boating and fishing.

The Cameron Prairie National Wildlife Refuge plays host to ducks, geese, herons, egrets, and the endangered peregrine falcon. A boardwalk here overlooks the marsh. The Rockefeller and Lacassine NWR offer a total of nearly 117,000 acres of marshland. The Rockefeller NWR is open to the public from March 1 through December 1 for the purpose of sight-seeing and sport fishing. Lacassine NWR is primarily a freshwater marshland with a variety of wildlife inhabitants including alligator, coyote, mink, muskrat, and white-tailed deer.

Camping and picnicking facilities may be found in the Sam Houston Jones State Park in Lake Charles. The park offers 73 campsites, some with electrical hookups, suitable for tents and recreational vehicles. There are 12 cabins that are also available within the park.

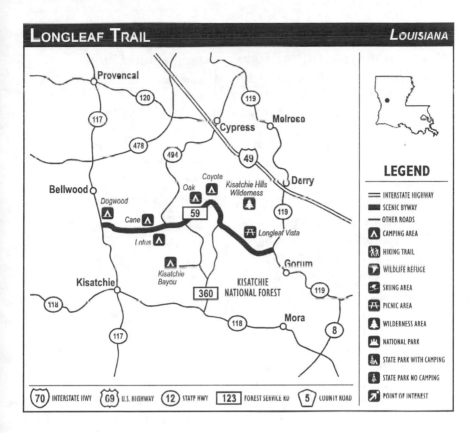

Route Location

The Longleaf Trail is located in west-central Louisiana, approximately 35 miles northwest of Alexandria. The byway begins about 5 miles south of Derry at the junction of State Highway 119 and travels west across the Kisatchie National Forest, ending at its junction with Louisiana Highway 117, just south of Bellwood.

Roads Traveled

The scenic byway follows Forest Service Road 59 which is a two-lane paved road safe for travel by all types of vehicles. The byway is about 17 miles long and is designated a National Forest Scenic Byway.

Travel Season

Forest Service Road 59 usually remains open all year long.

Description

The Longleaf Trail National Forest Scenic Byway travels across the Kisatchie National Forest through some of the most unique scenery in the state. The terrain along the byway is unusually rugged for Lousiana, with elevations ranging from 120 to 400 feet above sea level. The byway offers many scenic vistas of mesas, buttes, and sandstone outcrops set against the backdrop of longleaf pines. The trail was originally constructed as a single-lane road by the Civilian Conservation Corps around 1935.

Local Information

Kisatchie National Forest
2500 Shreveport Highway
Pineville, LA 71360
Phone: 318-473-7160

Greater Vernon Chamber of Commerce
P.O. Box 1228
Leesville, LA 71496
Phone: 318-238-0349

Natchitoches Area Chamber of Commerce
700 Front St.
Natchitoches, LA 71458
Phone: 318-352-4411

The Kisatchie Hills Wilderness lies next to the byway and is known locally as the "Little Grand Canyon" due to its steep slopes, rock outcrops, and mesas. Hiking and horseback riding trails lead you deep into this wilderness area. The Longleaf Vista Picnic Area is surrounded on three sides by this 8,700-acre wilderness area. A 1½-mile nature trail is located here as is a small visitor center. Restrooms and drinking water are also provided.

Wildlife observers will find white-tailed deer, foxes, oppossums, squirrels, raccoons, and coyotes inhabiting this area. The occasional roadrunner may also be spotted. Birdwatchers will delight in the many songbirds here.

Most of the camping areas found along the byway are primitive but do provide drinking water or restroom facilities. The Dogwood Campground is the most developed of the campgrounds along the byway. It offers 20 sites suitable for tents or recreational vehicles, drinking water, and flush toilets. Kisatchie Bayou has 17 walk-in sites and only 1 drive-in unit. Drinking water and vault toilets are also available here. There is no water available at the Coyote, Cane, and Oak Campgrounds.

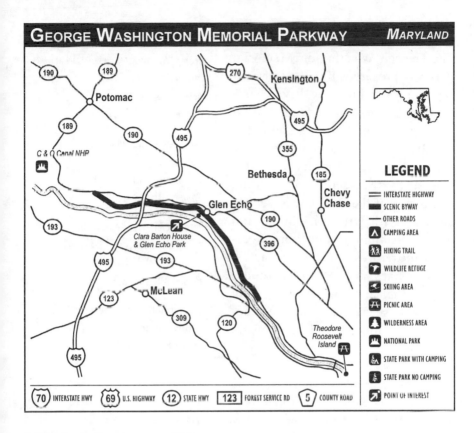

GEORGE WASHINGTON MEMORIAL PARKWAY — *MARYLAND*

LEGEND

- ═══ INTERSTATE HIGHWAY
- ▬ SCENIC BYWAY
- ─── OTHER ROADS
- 🅰 CAMPING AREA
- 🏃 HIKING TRAIL
- 🐾 WILDLIFE REFUGE
- ⛷ SKIING AREA
- 🎪 PICNIC AREA
- 🌲 WILDERNESS AREA
- 🏛 NATIONAL PARK
- 🏕 STATE PARK WITH CAMPING
- 🏕 STATE PARK NO CAMPING
- 📍 POINT OF INTEREST

(70) INTERSTATE HWY   (69) U.S. HIGHWAY   (12) STATE HWY   [123] FOREST SERVICE RD   (5) COUNTY ROAD   📍 POINT OF INTEREST

Virginia section see page 386

Route Location

The George Washington Memorial Parkway is located in northeastern Virginia and south-central Maryland. Portions of the scenic drive pass through Washington, D.C. This portion of the parkway is located just north of the District of Columbia.

Roads Traveled

The George Washington Memorial Parkway follows a four-lane divided highway named Clara Barton Parkway. The byway is approximately 6 miles in length and is safe for travel by all types of vehicles. The drive is designated a National Parkway by the National Park Service.

Travel Season

The route is open year-round.

Description

The George Washington Memorial Parkway preserves the natural scenery along the Potomac River, connecting historic sites from Mount Vernon, past the Nation's Capital, to the Great Falls of the Potomac. The many historic sites are complemented by the scenic countryside. The banks of the Potomac River are covered with willows, elders, and birches. Autumn brings vibrant colors to the parkway as the red maples, oaks, sumacs, and hickories proudly display their autumn attire. It is not unusual to see white-tailed deer, raccoon, wild turkey, and opossum in the area.

Local Information

George Washington Memorial Parkway
Turkey Run Park
McLean, VA 22101
Phone: 703-285-2598

Chesapeake and Ohio Canal NHP
P.O. Box 4
Sharpsburg, MD 21782
Phone: 301-739-4200

Potomac Chamber of Commerce
9812 Falls Road, #114-321
Potomac, MD 20854
Phone: 301-299-2170

Greater Bethesda - Chevy Chase C of C
7910 Woodmont Ave., #1204
Bethesda, MD 20814
Phone: 301-652-4900

The Clara Barton National Historic Site was the home of American Red Cross founder, Clara Barton, from 1897 to 1904. The 38-room house was designed by Clara and was first used as a Red Cross warehouse. Over 30 large closets in the building were used for storage of relief supplies. It was later modified for living quarters and offices in 1897. The building is furnished with original and period artifacts that provide interesting insights into the character of Clara Barton and the American Red Cross. Guided tours are given daily from 10:00 a.m. to 5:00 p.m.

Glen Echo Park is located adjacent to the Clara Barton National Historic Site. Glen Echo is now an arts and cultural center where classes are taught year-round by well-known artists and professionals. It was once an amusement park that served the Washington area until 1967. An antique, hand-carved and hand-painted Dentzel Carousel operates on summer weekends. The gallery offers monthly exhibitions of Glen Echo's artists.

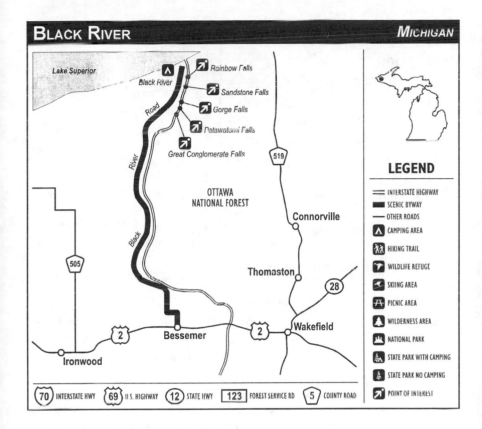

Route Location

The Black River scenic byway is located in the western corner of Michigan's Upper Peninsula, near the Wisconsin state line. The byway begins in the town of Bessemer, off U.S. Highway 2, and travels north across the Ottawa National Forest to the road's end on the shores of Lake Superior.

Roads Traveled

The 15-mile byway follows North Moore Street, Saint Johns Road, and the Black River Road (County Road 513). All of the two-lane roads are paved and safe for travel by all types of vehicles. It will be necessary for travelers to retrace the route back to U.S. Highway 2. Eleven miles are officially designated a National Forest Scenic Byway.

Travel Season

The entire route is open year-round although caution should be exercised during the winter months.

Description

The Black River scenic byway crosses the Ottawa National Forest alongside the meandering Black River through areas of old growth hemlock and hardwoods of the Black River Valley. The byway offers scenic views of the distant Porcupine Mountains. In autumn, the byway is bathed in colors of red, orange, and gold.

Near the byway's northern end are five cascading waterfalls on the Black River. Short hiking trails provide access to each of the falls. The difficulty level of the trails range from easy to strenuous as there may be a series of steps and steep grades. None of the trails are accessible to the handicapped.

Local Information

Ottawa National Forest
Bessemer Ranger District
500 North Moore St.
Bessemer, MI 49911
Phone: 906-667-0261

Bessemer Chamber of Commerce
Bessemer, MI 49911
Phone: 906-663-4913

Ironwood Area Chamber of Commerce
100 E. Aurora St.
Ironwood, MI 49938
Phone: 906-932-1122

The byway ends at the Black River Recreation Area, a popular spot throughout the year. The day use area provides picnic tables, restrooms, and drinking water. The campground here has 40 sites suitable for tents and recreational vehicles. The campground also offers drinking water, flush toilets, and a trailer dump station. A boat ramp on the Black River provides access to Lake Superior.

Those interested in hiking or backpacking will find access to the North Country National Scenic Trail. Much of the trail parallels the Black River. This hiking trail begins in New York, cuts through seven states, and ends in North Dakota where it links up with the Lewis & Clark National Historic Trail.

Nearby Routes

Great Divide Highway, page 404

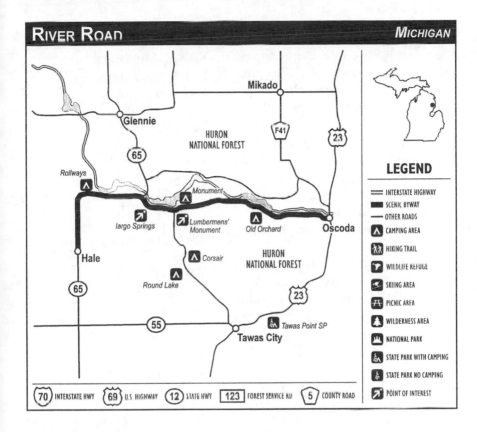

Route Location

This scenic byway is located in northeastern Michigan, approximately 90 miles north of Saginaw. The byway's eastern terminus is in Oscoda on U.S. Highway 23. The scenic route then heads west along the AuSable River and ends in the town of Hale on State Highway 65.

Roads Traveled

The byway follows River Road from its junction with U.S. Highway 23 in Oscoda west to the intersection with Michigan State Highway 65. It then follows SH 65 west and south into the community of Hale. The two-lane roads are paved and suitable for all types of vehicles. Twenty-two miles of this 30-mile route are designated a National Forest Scenic Byway.

Travel Season

The roads are generally open all year, however, extra caution should be exercised during the winter.

Description

The River Road scenic byway travels across the AuSable River Valley, following a portion of an early Indian trail along the AuSable River. The trail connected a Chippewa village at the mouth of the Riviere aux Sables (River of Sand) with the main north-south trails of interior Michigan. There are several platforms on the high banks above the river that provide panoramic views of the river and the surrounding forest.

Four dams constructed on the river have created thousands of acres of tree-lined lakes that offer excellent fishing and boating opportunities. Fishermen will find northern pike, bass, walleye, and muskie in the lakes.

Those interested in prolonging their stay here will find several campgrounds to choose from. The Old Orchard Park is a highly developed park on the banks of the AuSable River offering 500 campsites. Recreational vehicle hookups are available at 200 of the campsites. The park also has restrooms, showers, picnic areas, swimming beach, and drinking water. Rollways and Monument Campgrounds provide a total of 40 campsites with picnic tables, fire rings, drinking water, and restrooms. Two other national forest campgrounds are located a short distance off the byway that provide an additional 45 campsites to choose from.

Midway along the byway is the Lumbermens' Monument. This 9-foot bronze statue was erected in 1932 as a memorial to Michigan's logging era. A visitor center here has information on the monument and the surrounding area. Guided walks of the grounds are given.

Further west on the byway is the Iargo Springs Interpretive Site. The Chippewa once used this site for pow-wows with as many as 500 gathering at one time. They believed the springs held mystical or curative powers. An overlook here provides views of the AuSable River Valley.

Local Information

Huron-Manistee National Forest
Tawas Ranger District
326 Newman St.
East Tawas, MI 48730
Phone: 517-362-4477

Oscoda - Au Sable C of C
4440 N. US Hwy. 23
Oscoda, MI 48750
Phone: 517-739-7322

Hale Area Chamber of Commerce
P.O. Box 96
Hale, MI 48739
Phone: 517-728-3633

Tawas Area Chamber of Commerce
P.O. Box 608
Tawas City, MI 48764
Phone: 517-362-8643

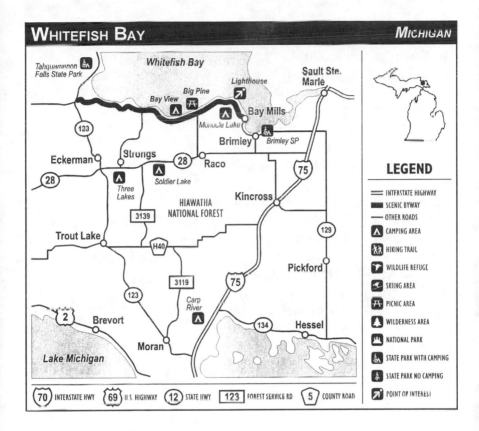

Route Location

The Whitefish Bay scenic drive is located on Michigan's Upper Peninsula in the east, about 15 miles west of Sault Ste. Marie. The byway begins in Bay Mills and travels west across the Hiawatha National Forest to its end at the intersection with Michigan State Highway 123.

Roads Traveled

The byway follows Forest Service Roads 3150 and 42 which are two-lane paved roads safe for travel by all types of vehicles. The 27-mile route has been designated a National Forest Scenic Byway.

Travel Season

The roads are usually open all year long, however, extra caution should be used when driving the byway during winter months.

Description

The Whitefish Bay scenic byway travels through the hardwood forests of Hiawatha National Forest often hugging the shores of Lake Superior. The byway passes miles of undisturbed beaches and sand dunes with several access roads to the beaches.

The panoramic views of Lake Superior and Canada at the Spectacle Lake Overlook are impressive and should not be missed. You may also wish to visit the Point Iroquois Lighthouse which is listed on the National Register of Historic Places. Visitors are welcome to climb to the top of the 65-foot lighthouse for a panoramic view of Lake Superior. A museum here tells the stories of the lightkeepers and their families through family album photographs, antiques, and artifacts.

There are two national forest campgrounds located along the byway, Monocle Lake and Bay View. Monocle Lake Campground has 39 campsites set among northern hardwood, aspen, red maple, and white birch. Fire rings and picnic tables are provided at each site. A boat ramp provides access to the lake. The Bay View Campground is situated on the shores of Lake Superior and has 24 campsites. Fire rings and picnic tables are also provided at each site. Other public campgrounds are scattered throughout the national forest.

Brimley State Park is to the east of the byway and is more developed than the national forest campgrounds. The park offers 270 sites for tents and recreational vehicles, many with electrical hookups. The park also has laundry facilities, restrooms with showers, and a swimming beach.

Local Information

Hiawatha National Forest
2727 N. Lincoln Rd.
Escanaba, MI 49829
Phone: 906-786-4062

Sault Area Chamber of Commerce
2581 I-75 Business Spur
Sault Sainte Marie, MI 49783
Phone: 800-647-2858

Upper Peninsula Travel & Rec. Assn.
P.O. Box 400
Iron Mountain, MI 49801
Phone: 906-774-5480

Tahquamenon Falls State Park
Park Headquarters
HC 48, Box 225
Paradise, MI 49768
Phone: 906-492-3415

Brimley State Park
RR 2 - Box 202
Brimley, MI 49715
Phone: 906-248-3422

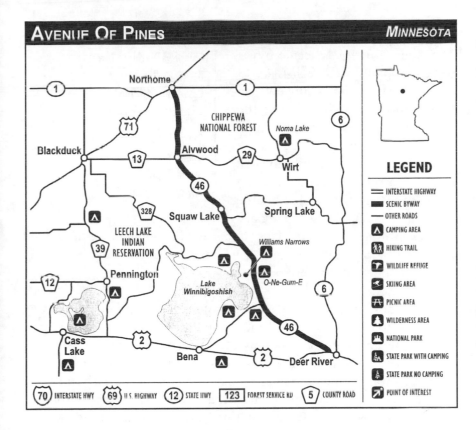

Route Location

The Avenue of Pines scenic byway is approximately 15 miles northwest of Grand Rapids in north-central Minnesota. The southern access is located just west of Deer River on U.S. Highway 2. The scenic route travels northwest to the junction of U.S. Highway 71 in the town of Northome.

Roads Traveled

The byway follows Minnesota State Highway 46 which is a two-lane paved road that is suitable for all types of vehicles. Thirty-nine miles of the 46-mile byway are officially designated a National Forest Scenic Byway.

Travel Season

State Highway 46 is normally open all year but delays may be possible during the winter for snow removal.

Description

The Avenue of Pines scenic byway travels through the Leech Lake Indian Reservation and Chippewa National Forest crossing low rolling hills covered with red and white pines and numerous lakes. The scenic byway passes Lake Winnibigoshish, Minnesota's fifth largest lake that offers excellent fishing and boating opportunities. Bald eagles may also be seen circling around the lake. Other wildlife inhabiting the region along the byway includes osprey, white-tailed deer, black bear, gray wolf, and numerous waterfowl.

Local Information

Chippewa National Forest
Route 3 - Box 244
Cass Lake, MN 56633
Phone: 218-335-2226

Grand Rapids Area C of C
One NW Third St.
Grand Rapids, MN 55744
Phone: 218-326-6619

The Cut Foot Sioux Visitor Center is located midway along the byway and offers tourists information and displays on the natural resources of the area. Films and presentations are given throughout the summer months. The Cut Foot Sioux National Recreation Trail is located near here. This trail follows the approximate location of the early fur trade routes and overland portages used by Indians. Also near the visitor center is the Cut Foot Sioux Ranger Station which was constructed in 1904. The original log cabin is listed as a National Historic Site.

The Chippewa National Forest was the first national forest established east of the Mississippi. It offers over 600,000 acres of land for a variety of recreational uses. Several national forest campgrounds have been developed along the byway, with more available throughout the forest. The large number of lakes and rivers provide excellent canoeing opportunities. Fishermen will find excellent fishing for muskie, walleye, northern pike, bass, and sunfish. Numerous trails cross the national forest providing opportunities for hiking, horseback riding, and bicycling.

Nearby Routes

Edge Of The Wilderness, page 193 / Scenic Highway, page 197

EDGE OF THE WILDERNESS   MINNESOTA

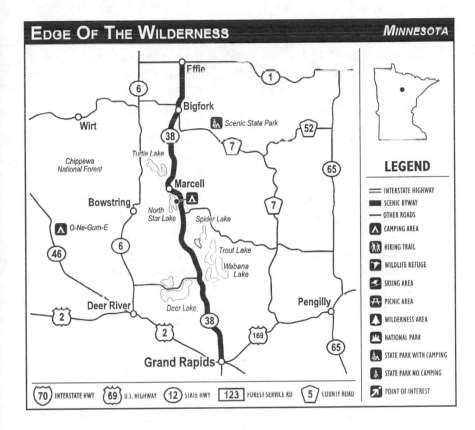

Route Location

The Edge Of The Wilderness byway is located in north-central Minnesota and begins in Grand Rapids. The scenic byway travels north through the Chippewa National Forest and ends in the community of Effie.

Roads Traveled

The 47 mile route follows Minnesota State Highway 38 which is a two-lane paved road suitable for all vehicles. The entire route has been designated a National Scenic Byway by the Federal Highway Administration. The 22 mile portion that runs through the national forest has been designated a National Forest Scenic Byway.

Travel Season

The byway is normally open year-round with possible delays in the winter for snow removal.

Description

The Edge Of The Wilderness scenic byway winds through forests of oak, birch, and aspen, skirting the shores of numerous lakes. The variety of trees along the byway create a beautiful show of fall color. Wildlife observers will want to be on the lookout for beaver, white-tailed deer, osprey, and eagles. Coyotes and the gray wolf also inhabit this region of Minnesota.

The many lakes adjacent to the byway provide opportunities for boating and fishing. Those interested in fishing will find northern pike, muskie, walleye, bass, and sunfish. Lake trout can also be found in some of the lakes.

Local Information

Chippewa National Forest
Route 3 - Box 244
Cass Lake, MN 56633
Phone: 218-335-2226

Chippewa National Forest
Cass Lake Ranger District
Rt 3 - Box 219
Cass Lake, MN 56633
Phone: 218-335-2283

Grand Rapids Area C of C
One NW Third St.
Grand Rapids, MN 55744
Phone: 218-326-6619

Scenic State Park
HC 2, Box 17
Bigfork, MN 56628
Phone: 218-743-3362

For those wishing to lengthen their stay here will find a developed national forest campground at North Star Lake. The campground has 42 sites for tents and recreational vehicles, drinking water, restrooms, picnic tables, and fire rings. Additionally, there are primitive national forest campsites on Spider, Trout, and Wabana Lakes.

Approximately 7 miles east of Bigfork on County Road 7 is the Scenic State Park. This park offers 117 campsites, some with electrical hookups. Facilities include restrooms, showers, drinking water, and a dump station. Picnicking, swimming, fishing, and boating are among the activities available here. Boat rentals are available for those that didn't bring their own boat. The park also offers miles of hiking, cross-country skiing, and snowmobiling trails.

Nearby Routes

Avenue Of Pines, page 191

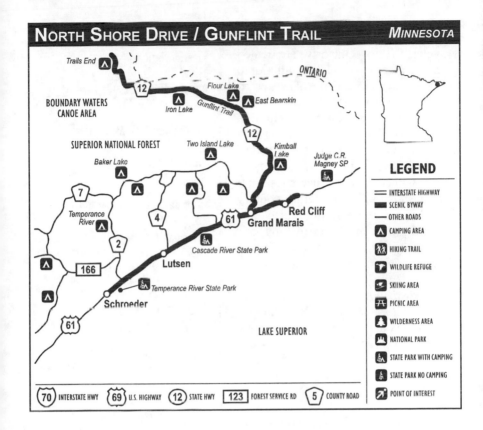

NORTH SHORE DRIVE / GUNFLINT TRAIL   *MINNESOTA*

Route Location

The North Shore Drive / Gunflint Trail is located in northeastern Minnesota approximately 80 miles northeast of Duluth. The Northshore Drive portion begins in Schroeder and travels northeast to the national forest boundary, east of Red Cliff. The Gunflint Trail section starts in Grand Marais and travels north to the road's end near the Canadian border.

Roads Traveled

The 100-mile route follows U.S. Highway 61 and Gunflint Trail, also known as County Road 12. Both roads are two-lane paved roads suitable for all vehicles. The 58-mile drive along U.S. Highway 61 has been designated a National Forest Scenic Byway.

Travel Season

Both routes are open year-round although caution should be exercised during the winter months.

Description

Travelers to this scenic drive are treated to spectacular views of Lake Superior to the south and a vast expanse of hardwood forests to the north. U.S. Hwy. 61 follows the shoreline as it passes through the Superior National Forest. The forest offers numerous opportunities for camping, picnicking, hiking, and fishing. During the winter, this area becomes a haven for snowmobile and cross-country ski enthusiasts. Opportunities also exist for spotting deer and moose making their way through the woods or gazing at eagles soaring gracefully in the sky.

Many side roads tempt the traveler to turn off the main route and explore the wilderness. If you do find yourself tempted, you'll be rewarded with beautiful scenery. These side roads also provide access to miles of hiking trails and crystal-clear lakes for paddling a canoe.

The Gunflint Trail will take you through the Boundary Waters Canoe Area Wilderness and deeper into the national forest. The Gunflint Trail offers anglers the opportunity for trying their luck at catching brook and rainbow trout, walleye, bass, and northern pike. Those interested in hiking will find access to the Superior Hiking Trail, Border Route Trail, and Kekekabic Trail. In winter, there are miles of well groomed trails for cross-country skiing, snowmobiling and snowshoeing. For additional detailed information on the recreational possibilities refer to *The Gunflint Trail Association* listed below.

Local Information

Superior National Forest
515 W. First St.
Duluth, MN 55801
Phone: 218-720-5324

The Gunflint Trail Association
P.O. Box 205
Grand Marais, MN 55604
Phone: 800-338-6932

Silver Bay Area Chamber of Commerce
P.O. Box 26
Silver Bay, MN 55614
Phone: 218-226-4870

Grand Marais Chamber of Commerce
P.O. Box 1048
Grand Marais, MN 55604
Phone: 218-387-2524

Temperance River State Park
MN Dept. of Natural Resources
500 Lafayette Rd.
St. Paul, MN 55155
Phone: 612-296-6157

Cascade River State Park
HC 3, Box 450
Lutsen, MN 55612
Phone: 218-387-1543

Judge C.R. Magney State Park
P.O. Box 500
Grand Marais, MN 55604
Phone: 218-387-2929

Lodging Directory

Cascade Lodge - Lutsen, page 445 — Resort
The Gunflint Trail Association - Grand Marais, page 446 — Bed & Breakfast / Inns, Cabin / Cottage / Guest Ranch & Campground / RV Park

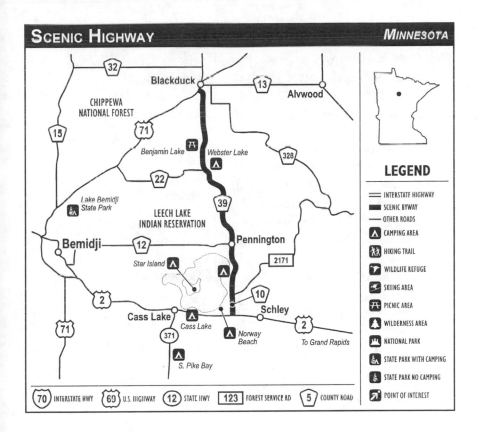

Route Location

The Scenic Highway is located in north-central Minnesota, about 20 miles east of Bemidji. The byway's northern terminus is near Blackduck on U.S. Highway 71. The byway travels south through the Chippewa National Forest and ends at its junction with U.S. Highway 2.

Roads Traveled

The byway follows Beltrami County Road 39 and Cass County Road 10. Both roads are two-lane paved roads safe for travel by all types of vehicles. The entire 28-mile drive is designated a National Forest Scenic Byway.

Travel Season

Delays are possible during the winter for snow removal, otherwise the byway is normally open all year.

Description

The Scenic Highway crosses the Chippewa National Forest through mixed stands of hardwood trees, evergreens, and wetlands. The southern portion of the byway travels adjacent to the shores of Cass Lake. Beautiful fall colors decorate the byway with colors of orange, red, and gold. White-tailed deer can sometimes be seen from the byway foraging among the open wetlands. These areas are also good locations for spotting a great blue heron or two.

Local Information

Chippewa National Forest
Route 3 - Box 244
Cass Lake, MN 56633
Phone: 218-335-2226

Bemidji Area Chamber of Commerce
300 Bemidji Ave.
Bemidji, MN 56601
Phone: 218-751-3541

Lake Bemidji State Park
3401 State Park Road NE
Bemidji, MN 56601
Phone: 218-755-4073

Cass Lake is a large lake on the west side of the byway with numerous opportunities for boating, fishing, and camping. When Lewis Cass explored this area, he thought the waters of the lake were the headwaters of the Mississippi River. Several archaeological sites are located near the dam and along the river with artifacts of historic significance having been discovered here.

Near the Benjamin Lake Recreation Area is the Camp Rabideau Historic Site. This Civilian Conservation Corps camp was built in 1935 to house the men that constructed fire towers, bridges, roads, and trails in the area. Four of the camp's 15 buildings have been restored and are open to the public for touring during the summer.

There are several national forest campgrounds surrounding Cass Lake providing a total of 227 campsites from which to choose. Facilities vary but most provide drinking water, picnic tables, and fire rings. Near the byway's northern end is the Webster Lake Campground with 24 campsites. To the west of the byway, north of Bemidji is the Lake Bemidji State Park. There are 98 campsites available with many having RV hookups. The park also offers miles of hiking, snowmobiling, and cross-country skiing trails.

Nearby Routes

Avenue Of Pines, page 191

NATCHEZ TRACE PARKWAY   *MISSISSIPPI*

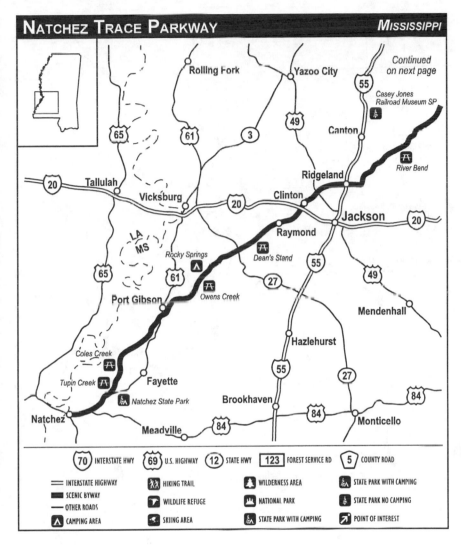

This historic route generally follows the old Indian trace, or trail, between Nashville, Tennessee and Natchez, Mississippi. By 1810, the trace was an important wilderness road and the most heavily traveled pass/trail in the Old Southwest.

Alabama section see page 14 / Tennessee portion see page 334

Route Location

The Natchez Trace Parkway is a 445-mile drive between Natchez, Mississippi and Nashville, Tennessee. This is the longest portion of the parkway as it travels across all of Mississippi from Natchez in the south to the Ala-

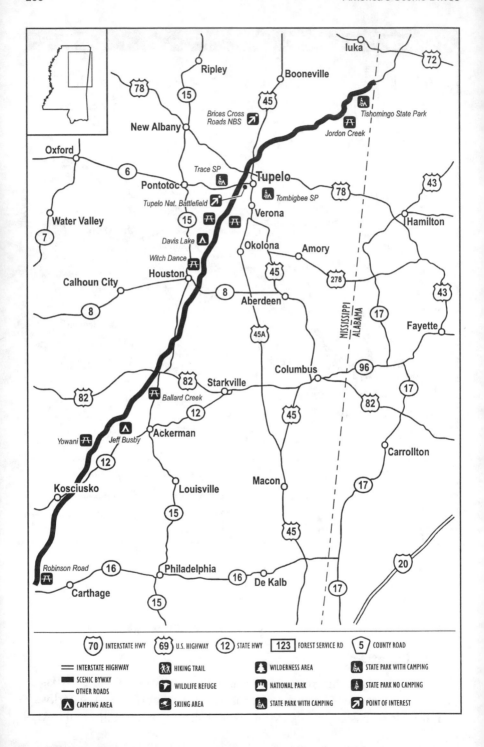

Iuka
72
Ripley
Booneville
78
15
45
Brices Cross Roads NBS
Tishomingo State Park
Jordon Creek
New Albany
Oxford
6
Trace SP
Tupelo
43
Pontotoc
78
Tombigbee SP
Tupelo Nat. Battlefield
Hamilton
Water Valley
15
Verona
7
Davis Lake
Okolona
Amory
Witch Dance
Houston
45
278
Calhoun City
8
43
8
Aberdeen
45A
Fayette
MISSISSIPPI
ALABAMA
17
Columbus
96
82
Starkville
17
82
Ballard Creek
12
45
82
Yowani
Jeff Busby
Ackerman
Carrollton
12
Kosciusko
Louisville
Macon
17
15
45
Robinson Road
16
Philadelphia
20
16
De Kalb
Carthage
15
17

70 INTERSTATE HWY	69 U.S. HIGHWAY	12 STATE HWY	123 FOREST SERVICE RD	5 COUNTY ROAD
INTERSTATE HIGHWAY	HIKING TRAIL	WILDERNESS AREA	STATE PARK WITH CAMPING	
SCENIC BYWAY	WILDLIFE REFUGE	NATIONAL PARK	STATE PARK NO CAMPING	
OTHER ROADS	SKIING AREA	STATE PARK WITH CAMPING	POINT OF INTEREST	
CAMPING AREA				

bama state line, northeast of Tupelo.

Roads Traveled

The Natchez Trace Parkway is a two-lane paved route suitable for all vehicles. This portion across Mississippi is nearly 310 miles in length. The byway is designated a National Parkway by the National Park Service and an All-American Road by the Federal Highway Administration. A 17-mile portion through the Tombigbee National Forest is designated a National Forest Scenic Byway.

Travel Season

The route is open year-round.

Description

Once trekked by Indians and trampled into a rough road by traders, trappers, and missionaries, the Parkway is now a scenic 445-mile road traveling from Natchez, Mississippi to Nashville, Tennessee. In the late 1700s and early 1800s, "Kaintucks," as the river merchants were called, would float downriver on flatboats loaded with their merchandise to be sold in New Orleans. Since there wasn't any practical way to return by river, the boats were dismantled and the lumber sold. The Natchez Trace would be the only pathway home. At that time, the trace was a dangerous path to take. Travelers waded through swamps and swam streams and fended off attacks by wild animals and poisonous snakes, not to mention keeping an eye open for mur-

Local Information

National Park Service
Natchez Trace Parkway
RR 1, NT- 143
Tupelo, MS 38801
Phone: 601-842-1572

National Forest In Mississippi
Tombigbee Ranger District
Rt. 1- Box 98A
Ackerman, MS 39735
Phone: 601-285-3264

Natchez - Adams County C of C
P.O. Box 1403
Natchez, MS 39121
Phone: 601-445-4611

Port Gibson - Claiborne County C of C
P.O. Box 491
Port Gibson, MS 39150
Phone: 601-437-4351

Clinton Chamber of Commerce
100 E. Leake
Clinton, MS 39060
Phone: 601-924-5912

Metro Jackson Chamber of Commerce
P.O. Box 22548
Jackson, MS 39225
Phone: 601-948-7575

Madison County Chamber of Commerce
P.O. Box 202
Canton, MS 39046
Phone: 601-859-1606

Leake County Chamber of Commerce
103 N. Pearl St.
Carthage, MS 39051
Phone: 601-267-9231

derous bandits and Indian attacks. The terrain of the trace was rough, too. A broken leg of a lone traveler would often mean certain death. The dangers of the route earned the Trace the nickname "Devil's Backbone." Modern-day travelers don't have these dangers to face as they travel this historic route. Now you can safely travel the route in the comfort of your own vehicle.

You can begin your drive on the parkway in the historic town of Natchez. Natchez boasts an incredible 500 antebellum structures, including homes, churches, and public buildings. Prior to the Civil War, more than half of the millionaires in the United States lived in Natchez. Several of the beautiful mansions are open year-round for guided tours.

In the picturesque town of Port Gibson you will find numerous historic homes and churches. Port Gibson was a major objective for Ulysses S. Grant in his 1863 campaign for Vicksburg during the Civil War. After overcoming Port Gibson, Grant departed from his "scorched earth" policy, declaring the town "too beautiful to burn." Today, Port Gibson proudly displays the beautiful homes and churches that prevented Grant from burning the town.

The city of Jackson was torched on three separate occasions during the Civil War, reducing the community to a series of ruins nicknamed "Chimneyville." There were only a

Local Information

Kosciusko-Attala Chamber of Commerce
P.O. Box 696
Kosciusko, MS 39090
Phone: 601-289-2981

Chickasaw Dev. Foundation
P.O. Box 505
Houston, MS 38851
Phone: 601-456-2321

Okolona Chamber of Commerce
219 Main St.
Okolona, MS 38860
Phone: 601-447-5913

Verona Chamber of Commerce
194 Main St.
Verona, MS 38879
Phone: 601-566-2211

For general information on all State Parks contact:

Mississippi State Parks
P.O. Box 23093
Jackson, MS 39225
Phone: 601-364-2123

Natchez State Park
Phone: 601-442-2658

Trace State Park
Phone: 601-489-2958

Tombigbee State Park
Phone: 601-842-7669

Tishomingo State Park
Phone: 601-438-6914

Casey Jones Railroad Museum State Park
Phone: 601-673-9864

handful of historic buildings that survived the war. Today, Jackson is a large city offering all of the cultural and recreational activities associated with a large city.

On the parkway's northern end is the city of Tupelo. It is here that the parkway headquarters and visitor center are located. A museum located within the visitor center houses artifacts and displays chronicling the history and development of the old Natchez Trace and the modern parkway. Audiovisual programs tell the story of the historic trail. A nature trail is also found here.

Recreational activities are plentiful along the parkway. The Rocky Springs recreation area, north of Port Gibson, offers 22 campsites, a picnic area, and interpretive trails. Jeff Busby Park, west of Ackerman, offers an 18-site campground, picnic area, trails, and an exhibit shelter and overlook atop Little Mountain. At 603 feet in elevation, Little Mountain is one of the highest points along the parkway in Mississippi. The only service station and campstore directly along the parkway are also located here. In addition to the National Park Service campgrounds, several picnic areas have been developed along the route.

A small portion of the Natchez Trace Parkway travels through the Tombigbee National Forest. This 17-mile portion is a National Forest Scenic Byway. The national forest offers the Davis Lake Recreation Area which provides a 24-site campground suitable for tents or trailers. Some of the campsites have electrical hookups. The lake is stocked with largemouth bass, catfish, crappie, and bream. The Witchdance picnic area provides access to hiking and horseback riding trails, in addition to picnic facilities.

There are several state parks located along or a short distance from the parkway. The parks offer numerous campsites for tents and recreational vehicles, many having electrical hookups. Other facilities vary but most offer drinking water, restrooms, picnic areas, and nature trails.

LODGING DIRECTORY

Cabot Lodge Jackson North - Ridgeland, page 444 —— Hotel / Motel
Fairview Inn - Jackson, page 444 —— Bed & Breakfast / Inns

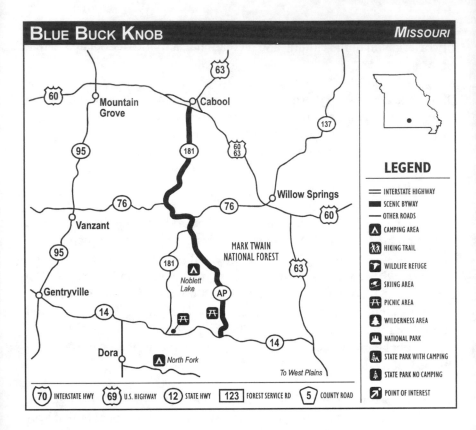

Route Location

The Blue Buck Knob scenic drive is located in south-central Missouri, about 75 miles east of Springfield. The byway begins in Cabool off U.S. Highway 60 and travels south through the Mark Twain National Forest to the byway's end at the intersection with Missouri State Highway 14.

Roads Traveled

The byway follows Missouri State Highways 76, 181, and "AP" which are all two-lane paved roads suitable for all types of vehicles. The byway is approximately 28 miles long with all but 4 miles being officially designated a National Forest Scenic Byway.

Travel Season

The roads followed are usually open all year long, however, caution should be exercised when driving the byway during the winter.

Description

The Blue Buck Knob scenic byway travels through Missouri's Ozark hill country within the Mark Twain National Forest. The scenic drive twists and turns through farmland, open pastures, and densely wooded hillsides. Many tree-lined spur roads tempt the byway traveler to take a side trip and further explore the national forest.

Noblett Recreation Area provides diverse recreational opportunities for the byway traveler. Noblett is a 27-acre lake that was constructed by the Civilian Conservation Corps during the 1930s. The remains of the CCC camp are accessible just a few miles away by gravel road. A boat ramp provides access to this scenic lake set among the hardwood trees. A 9-mile walking trail encircles the lake. The northern trailhead of the Ridge Runner National Recreation Trail is also located here. This hiking trail heads south through the forest to the North Fork Recreation Area. A campground located in the Noblett Recreation Area offers 25 tree shaded sites with picnic tables and fire rings. No hookups are provided. Fishermen may wish to spend some time trying to pull bass, bluegill, crappie, or catfish from the lake.

Other recreational activities are available throughout the national forest. Wildlife observers will want to be on the lookout for white-tailed deer or wild turkey that were reintroduced to Missouri in the 1930s. The North Fork of the White River offers canoeing enthusiasts a pleasurable float along towering rock outcrops and densely wooded forests. Horseback riding, hunting, and hiking are also popular recreational opportunities on the Mark Twain National Forest.

Local Information

Mark Twain National Forest
Ava Ranger District
P.O. Box 188
Ava, MO 65608
Phone: 417-683-4428

Greater West Plains Area C of C
401 Jefferson
West Plains, MO 65775
Phone: 417-256-4433

Willow Springs Area C of C
P.O. Box 5
Willow Springs, MO 65793
Phone: 417-469-3944

Mountain Grove Area C of C
P.O. Box 434
Mountain Grove, MO 65711
Phone: 417-926-4135

Cabool Area Chamber of Commerce
P.O. Box 285
Cabool, MO 65689
Phone: 417-962-3002

GLADE TOP TRAIL   MISSOURI

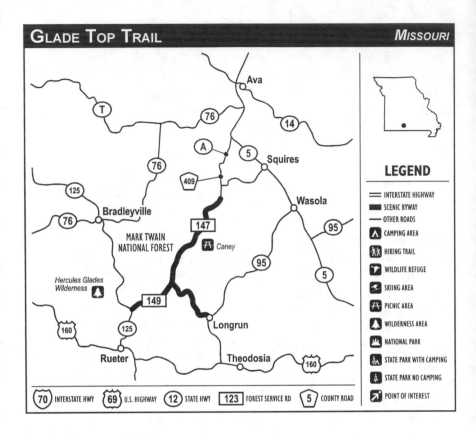

Route Location

The Glade Top Trail is located in southwestern Missouri, about 55 miles southeast of Springfield near the Arkansas border. To reach the northern end of the byway from Ava, follow State Hwy. 5 south to State Hwy. "A". Take State Hwy. "A" to the intersection with County Road 409 and follow this road to the national forest entrance where the byway officially begins. The byway travels south to Longrun with a side trip leading to State Hwy. 125.

Roads Traveled

The 23-mile byway follows Forest Service Roads 147 and 149 which are two-lane well maintained gravel roads suitable for most vehicles. The entire route is designated a National Forest Scenic Byway.

Travel Season

The roads followed are generally open year-round. Caution should be exercised when driving during the winter.

Description

The Glade Top Trail cuts across the Mark Twain National Forest traveling through narrow ridge tops above the surrounding rolling countryside. Numerous scenic vistas of the Springfield Plateau to the west and the St. Francis and Boston Mountains to the south reward the traveler of this byway. The changing seasons paint the area with brilliant colors of red and orange in autumn. Dogwood, serviceberry, redbud, and wild fruit trees make their presence known in the spring.

Local Information

Mark Twain National Forest
Ava Ranger District
P.O. Box 188
Ava, MO 65608
Phone: 417-683-4428

Ava Area Chamber of Commerce
P.O. Box 83
Ava, MO 65608
Phone: 417-683-4594

Branson / Lakes Area C of C
P.O. Box 1897
Branson, MO 65615
Phone: 417-334-4136

Wildlife observers will delight in the numerous species inhabiting this region of Missouri. White-tailed deer, wild turkey, bobwhite, quail, squirrels, rabbits, and many varieties of songbirds are among the wildlife seen along the byway. The glades also provide a home for wildlife not often encountered in the Ozarks, such as the roadrunner.

Developed recreational facilities are limited along this byway. There are no public campgrounds along the byway, however, the Caney Picnic Area provides a nice spot for taking a break and enjoying lunch. A short hiking trail here will lead to a small but interesting cave. The nearest national forest camping facilities are 30 miles northwest on State Highway 125.

The Mark Twain National Forest provides other recreational pursuits in addition to picnicking. Numerous side roads make for a pleasurable drive, taking you further into the national forest. They also offer a challenge to those interested in bicycling. The Hercules Glades Wilderness to the west of the byway has several trails for hiking or horseback riding. The many rivers and streams running through the forest provide the angler with the opportunity for catching bass, bluegill, catfish, or crappie.

Branson lies approximately 30 miles west of the byway and offers music shows, a scenic train ride, and opportunities for outdoor recreation.

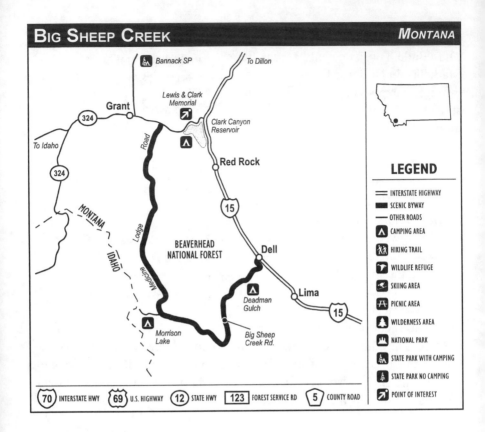

Route Location

The Big Sheep Creek scenic drive is located in southwestern Montana, about 25 miles south of Dillon. The byway forms an open loop route from Dell on Interstate 15, encircles Beaverhead National Forest, and ends at the intersection with Montana State Highway 324.

Roads Traveled

The 50-mile route follows Big Sheep Creek and Medicine Lodge Roads. The byway travels over two-lane gravel roads with a short stretch of one-lane dirt road. The route can safely be driven by a two-wheel drive vehicle although motorhomes and vehicles pulling trailers should not attempt the entire route. The byway is designated a BLM Type I Back Country Byway.

Travel Season

The roads are generally open from May through early October and then closed by winter snows.

Description

From Dell, the Big Sheep Creek Back Country Byway makes its way through steep canyon walls with the waters of Big Sheep Creek flowing alongside. This spring-fed creek attracts bighorn sheep and deer which are commonly seen in the evening. Numerous side roads tempt the byway traveler to further explore the canyon on foot, by bicycle, or in the comfort of your vehicle.

Once through the canyon, the byway heads north through the open spaces of the Medicine Lodge Valley, surrounded by the Tendoy Mountains to the east and the Bitterroot Range to the west. Through this portion of the byway, the waters of Medicine Lodge Creek flow nearby. Side roads from here will take you into the Beaverhead National Forest for hiking and back packing opportunities.

Developed recreational facilities are nearly non-existent on this back country route. The Bureau of Land Management maintains the primitive Deadman Gulch Campground. A pit toilet is provided but no drinking water is available. Camping is permitted anywhere along the byway as long as your campsite is on BLM land.

More developed camping facilities may be found in the Clark Canyon Reservoir area and Bannack State Park. The state park is the site of Montana's first major gold discovery and a well-preserved ghost town. The town once boasted of a population of more than 3,000 and became the state's first territorial capital in 1864. There are 30 campsites available for tents and recreational vehicles, however, no hookups are provided.

Local Information

BLM - Butte District Office
106 N. Parkmont
Butte, MT 59702
Phone: 406-494-5059

BLM -Dillon Resource Area
1005 Selway Drive
Dillon, MT 59725
Phone: 406-683-2337

Beaverhead National Forest
420 Barrett St.
Dillon, MT 59725
Phone: 406-683-3900

Beaverhead Chamber of Commerce
125 S. Montana
Dillon, MT 59725
Phone: 406-683-5511

Bannack State Park
Montana State Parks Division
1420 E 6th Ave.
Helena, MT 59620
Phone: 406-834-3413

Nearby Routes

Pioneer Mountains, page 218 / Lewis & Clark, page 157

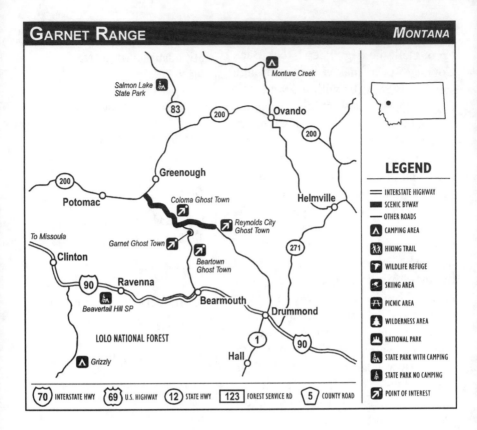

Route Location

The Garnet Range Back Country Byway is approximately 30 miles east of Missoula in western Montana. The byway begins south of Greenough on Montana State Highway 200. The byway travels east and officially ends just north of the Reynolds City ghost town.

Roads Traveled

The 12-mile route follows the Garnet Range Road which is marked and groomed as a National Winter Recreation Trail. The entire route is designated a BLM Type IV Back Country Byway.

Travel Season

This byway is a National Winter Recreation Trail marked and groomed by the Bureau of Land Managment from January 1 through April 30 for snowmobile and cross-country skiing. The byway is accessible by car in good weather from May through October.

Description

From State Highway 200, the Garnet Range scenic byway climbs 2,000 feet into the evergreen forest of the Garnet Mountains and offers spectacular views of the Mission, Rattlesnake, Swan, and Sapphire mountain ranges. The byway provides access to one of the best-preserved ghost towns remaining in Montana, the gold mining town of Garnet.

The town of Garnet grew around a stamp mill erected in 1895 by Dr. Armistead Mitchell. Soon after the mill was constructed, Sam Ritchey hit a rich vein of ore in his mine just west of town. The rush was on. By early 1898, nearly 1,000 people resided in Garnet. After 1900 the gold, however, became scarce and difficult to mine. By 1905 many of the mines were abandoned and Garnet's population shrunk to 150. Fire in 1912 destroyed much of the town and the advent of World War I in 1914 drew most of the remaining residents away to defense-related jobs. By the 1920s, Garnet had become a ghost town.

The Garnet Range byway is part of a 55-mile system of snowmobile and cross-country ski trails in the Garnet Range. A visitor center is located in Garnet and offers more detailed information on the town and the recreational opportunities found in the area. During the winter, there are two cabins in Garnet that are available for rent.

Camping facilities may be found at the Salmon Lake State Park (25 sites), Beavertail Hill State Park (25 sites), and several national forest campgrounds throughout Lolo National Forest.

Local Information

BLM - Garnet Resource Area
3255 Fort Missoula Rd.
Missoula, MT 59801
Phone: 406-329-3914

Missoula Area Chamber of Commerce
P.O. Box 7577
Missoula, MT 59807
Phone: 406-543-6623

Powell County Chamber of Commerce
P.O. Box 776
Deer Lodge, MT 59722
Phone: 406-846-2094

Seeley Lake Area Chamber of Commerce
P.O. Box 516
Seeley Lake, MT 59868
Phone: 406-677-2880

Lincoln Valley Chamber of Commerce
P.O. Box 985
Lincoln, MT 59639
Phone: 406-362-4949

Philipsburg Chamber of Commerce
P.O. Box 661
Philipsburg, MT 59858
Phone: 406-859-3388

Montana State Parks
1420 East 6th Avenue
Helena, MT 59620
Phone: 406-444-2535

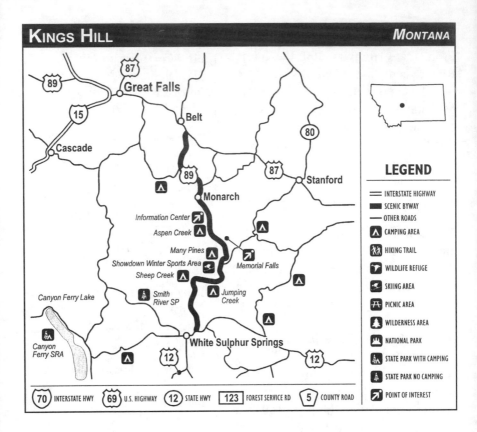

Route Location

The Kings Hill scenic byway is located in central Montana, about 25 miles southeast of Great Falls. The byway's northern terminus is near Belt on U.S. Highway 87. The scenic drive then travels south across the Lewis & Clark National Forest to its end at the intersection with U.S. Highway 12, northeast of White Sulphur Springs.

Roads Traveled

Kings Hill is approximately 70 miles long and follows U.S. Highway 89 which is a two-lane paved road safe for travel by all types of vehicles. The byway is officially designated a National Forest Scenic Byway.

Travel Season

The byway is generally open all year long. Snow and ice during winter months require drivers to use extra caution.

Description

The Kings Hill National Forest Scenic Byway travels through dense forests, limestone canyons, and grassy meadows as it crosses the Little Belt Mountains. The byway crosses Kings Hill Pass at an elevation of 7,393 feet. An observation tower near the pass provides panoramic views of the surrounding mountains. The meandering Belt Creek follows alongside most of the byway from Kings Hill Pass northward.

A variety of wildlife is found within the national forest and this part of Montana. Mule deer and elk may be seen grazing along streams or in meadows. Flying on the winds of above you may catch a glimpse of golden eagles or red-tailed hawks. Another form of wildlife inhabiting this area that you may not necessarily wish to see is the black bear.

The byway traveler is provided with numerous opportunities for outdoor recreation. Winter brings cross-country skiers and snowmobilers to the area for its many miles of groomed trails. Downhill skiing is also a popular wintertime activity.

The warmer months bring fishermen to the banks of the area's numerous lakes and streams. Fishermen will find the lakes and streams filled with rainbow, cutthroat, and brook trout, among other species.

There are several camping areas located directly along the byway and within the national forest that can accommodate tents and recreational vehicles. Facilities will vary but most provide campsites with picnic tables and fire rings, restrooms, and drinking water. A couple of miles north of the Many Pines Campground is a short hiking trail that will take you to the scenic Memorial Falls.

Local Information

Lewis And Clark National Forest
1101 15th St. North
Great Falls, MT 59403
Phone: 406-791-7700

Meagher County Chamber of Commerce
P.O. Box 356
White Sulphur Springs, MT 59645
Phone: 406-547-3932

Great Falls Area Chamber of Commerce
P.O. Box 2127
Great Falls, MT 59403
Phone: 406-761-4434

Smith River State Park
Montana State Parks Division
1420 E. 6th Ave.
Helena, MT 59620
Phone: 406-444-4475

Canyon Ferry State Recreation Area
P.O. Box 200701
Helena, MT 59620
Phone: 406-444-4952

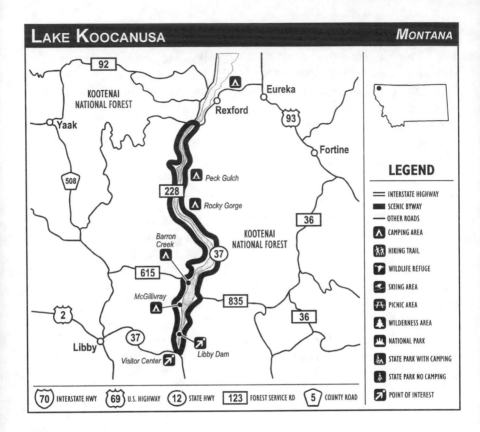

Route Location

The Lake Koocanusa scenic byway is located in northwestern Montana, northwest of Libby. The byway forms a loop drive around Lake Koocanusa between Libby and Eureka. The byway can be reached from Libby on U.S. Highway 2 by traveling east on Montana State Highway 37. From U.S. Highway 93 in Eureka, take State Highway 37 west.

Roads Traveled

The 88-mile route follows Montana State Highway 37 and Forest Service Road 228 which are two-lane paved roads suitable for all vehicles. The byway is officially designated a National Forest Scenic Byway.

Travel Season

The entire route is generally open year-round although temporary closures are possible in the winter due to heavy snowfall.

Description

The Lake Koocanusa scenic byway travels across the Kootenai National Forest through ponderosa pine, lodgepole pine, and Douglas fir along the shores of Lake Koocanusa. The lake is a 90-mile long reservoir reaching into Canada that was created by the construction of Libby Dam. Numerous scenic turnouts provide excellent views of the lake and the surrounding mountains. A visitor center at the dam provides information and guided tours of the 370-foot high structure.

Excellent fishing in the lake has given the area the reputation as one of the best salmon fisheries. The lake and Kootenai River below the dam provide excellent opportunities for catching rainbow, westslope, cutthroat, bull trout, kokanee salmon, and brook trout.

Local Information

Kootenai National Forest
506 U.S. Highway 2 West
Libby, MT 59923
Phone: 406-293-6211

Libby Area Chamber of Commerce
905 W. 9th St.
Libby, MT 59923
Phone: 406-293-4167

Tobacco Valley Board of Commerce
P.O. Box 186
Eureka, MT 59917
Phone: 406-296-2024

Lake Koocanusa
U.S. Army Corps of Engineers
P.O. Box 3755
Seattle, WA 98124
Phone: 206-764-3750

Several recreation areas are located along the byway. Rocky Gorge provides 120 campsites suitable for tents and recreational vehicles. A boat ramp provides access to the lake. Peck Gulch provides restrooms, a boat ramp, and plenty of sites for picnicking or camping. The Barron Creek Recreation Site has a boat ramp and dispersed camping areas. McGillivray Recreation Site is a campground and day use area with group picnic shelters. Overnight camping, ball fields, a swimming beach, and a boat ramp are available. A short boat ride from this recreation area will take you to Yarnell Islands which have camping and picnicking facilities.

Several side roads from the byway will take you further into the Kootenai National Forest. The forest offers a total of 35 camping areas with over 600 campsites available. The national forest also permits dispersed camping nearly anywhere on public lands. Five national recreation trails are within the national forest providing hiking and backpacking opportunities for those interested. The Little North Fork Trail is near the byway and will take you to a scenic waterfall.

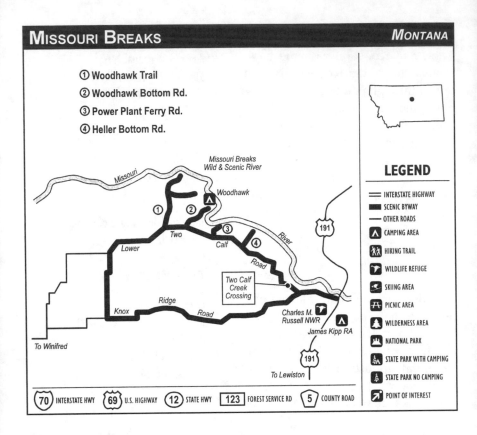

Route Location

The Missouri Breaks byway is about 40 miles north of Lewiston in north-central Montana. The eastern access is located off U.S. Highway 191 in the Charles M. Russell National Wildlife Refuge. The byway travels north-west forming a loop drive back to U.S. Highway 191. Several spur roads lead to overlooks of the Missouri River.

Roads Traveled

The 73-mile loop follows the Lower Two Calf and Knox Ridge Roads which are mostly two-lane gravel and dirt roads that can be negotiated by passenger cars in dry weather. Large RVs and vehicles pulling trailers should not attempt to access the route from U.S. Highway 191. Nor should they attempt the Two Calf Creek crossing or any of the spur roads off of Lower Two Calf Road. The byway is officially designated a BLM Type II Back Country Byway.

Travel Season

The route is generally open from May through October and then closed in the winter and spring due to snow and mud.

Description

The Missouri Breaks Back Country Byway crosses a ruggedly beautiful landscape alongside portions of the Upper Missouri National Wild & Scenic River. A 149-mile segment of the river was designated in 1976 as a wild and scenic river to preserve the river and its natural surroundings. Much of the river is the same today as Lewis & Clark saw it in May of 1805 on their journey to the Pacific Northwest.

Local Information

BLM - Lewistown District Office
P.O. Box 1160
Lewiston, MT 59457
Phone: 406-538-7461

Malta Area Chamber of Commerce
P.O. Drawer 1420
Malta, MT 59538
Phone: 406-654-1776

Lewistown Area Chamber of Commerce
408 N.E. Main
Lewistown, MT 59457
Phone: 406-538-5436

Charles M Russell Nat'l. Wildlife Refuge
Box 110
Lewistown, MT 59457

Several side trips off the main route will lead to scenic overlooks on the Missouri River. Woodhawk Trail takes you to Sunshine and Deweese Ridges where the river flows almost directly beneath you. Woodhawk Bottom Road will take you down to the banks of the river. A BLM campground here provides 5 sites with picnic tables for those interested in staying overnight or longer.

A diversity of wildlife inhabits the area of the byway. Some 60 species of mammals, 233 species of birds, and 20 species of amphibians and reptiles may be found here. Wildlife observers will want to be on the lookout for antelope, white-tailed deer and mule deer, elk, and bighorn sheep. Prairie dogs, beaver, pheasant, sage grouse, and a large variety of song birds may also be seen along the byway.

Camping is available at the Woodhawk Campground and at James Kipp Recreation Area in the Charles M. Russell National Wildlife Refuge. The James Kipp Recreation Area provides 28 sites with picnic tables and fire rings. A boat ramp provides access to the river. Pit toilets and drinking water are also provided.

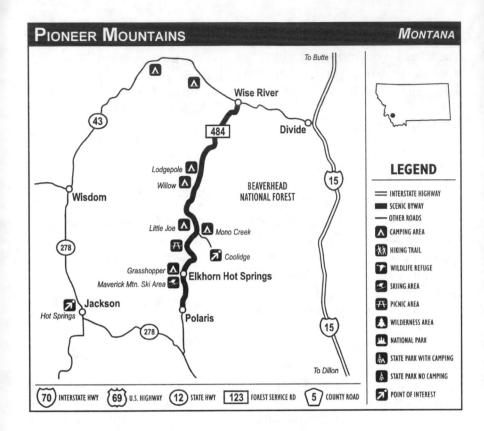

Route Location

The scenic route is located in southwestern Montana, about 35 miles southwest of Butte near the Idaho border. The Pioneer Mountains scenic byway travels across the Beaverhead National Forest between Wise River and Polaris. The northern terminus of the byway can be reached from Interstate 15 by taking Exit #105 and traveling west on State Highway 43.

Roads Traveled

The Pioneer Mountains byway is approximately 40 miles long and follows Forest Service Road 484. This forest road is primarily a two-lane paved road suitable for all vehicles. There is a segment of road that is a narrow, gravel-surfaced road requiring slow speeds. This segment of road near Elkhorn Hot Springs is not recommend for travel by motorhomes or vehicles pulling trailers. Twenty-seven miles of this byway are designated a National Forest Scenic Byway.

Travel Season

The byway is normally open from mid-May through mid-November and then closed by winter snows.

Description

The scenic byway crosses the Beaverhead National Forest as it travels through lodgepole pine forests and across numerous parks and meadows. Outstanding views of the Pioneer Mountain Range are provided as the byway ascends the divide separating the Wise River and Grasshopper Creek drainages. Both Wise River and Grasshopper Creek flow alongside the byway.

Local Information

Beaverhead National Forest
420 Barrett St.
Dillon, MT 59725
Phone: 406-683-3900

Butte - Silver Bow C of C
2950 Harrison Ave.
Butte, MT 59701
Phone: 406-494-5595

Beaverhead Chamber of Commerce
125 S. Montana
Dillon, MT 59725
Phone: 406-683-5511

The national forest offers nearly unlimited opportunities for outdoor recreation. The forest's many rivers and creeks provide excellent fishing for grayling, rainbow, brook, and cutthroat trout. There are many hiking trails accessible along the route ranging from short, easy walks to longer, more strenuous hikes. The Pioneer Loop Trail is a strenuous 35-mile National Scenic Trail that will take you along the western peaks of the Pioneer Mountains.

Those wishing to prolong their stay in the area will find many national forest campgrounds from which to choose. Lodgepole and Willow Campgrounds provide a total of 12 campsites set among pine trees along the Wise River. Little Joe offers 4 sites on the river, while Mono Creek Campground has 5 sites set back about 1 mile from the byway. Grasshopper is the largest of the campgrounds as it has 24 campsites available. All of the campgrounds except Little Joe can accommodate recreational vehicles up to 16 feet in length.

A short side trip off the byway will take you to the ghost town of Coolidge. This historic town was built in the 1920s to provide a homebase for miners who worked in the Elkhorn silver mine. Remnants of the Elkhorn Mill remain for inspection by visitors.

Nearby Routes

Big Sheep Creek, page 208

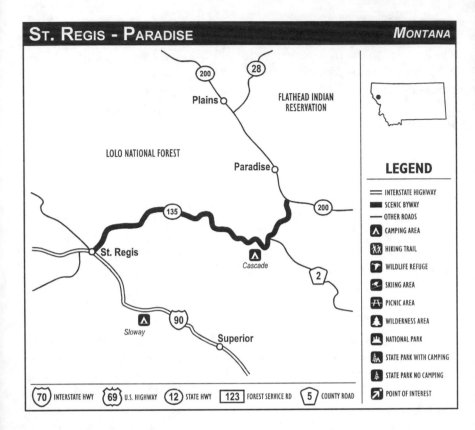

Route Location

The St. Regis - Paradise scenic byway is located in western Montana, about 70 miles northwest of Missoula near the Idaho border. The byway travels across the Lolo National Forest between St. Regis on Interstate 90 and Paradise on State Highway 200. The byway officially ends at its junction with State Highway 200, south of Paradise.

Roads Traveled

This scenic drive is a 22-mile byway following Montana State Highway 135 which is a two-lane paved road that is safe for travel by all types of vehicles. The byway is designated a National Forest Scenic Byway.

Travel Season

Although the byway is generally open year-round, winter driving conditions may require drivers to use extra caution.

Description

Originally a meandering trail used by homesteaders in the late 1800s, the St. Regis - Paradise scenic byway is now a pleasurable drive along the scenic Clark Fork River. The byway travels through the flat, forested Dolan Flats into the canyon walls of the Clark Fork River which divides the Coeur d'Alene and Cabinet Mountain ranges. Elk, deer, and bighorn sheep inhabit the canyon region and the heavily forested mountains surrounding the route. Bald eagles are occasionally seen, especially during the fall and winter months.

Local Information

Lolo National Forest
Plains Ranger District
P.O. Box 429
Plains, MT 59859
Phone: 406-826-3821

Plains - Paradise C of C
P.O. Box 714
Plains, MT 59859
Phone: 406-826-3662

Superior Area Chamber of Commerce
Box 483
Superior, MT 59872
Phone: 406-822-4672

The Clark Fork River provides excellent opportunities for those interested in fishing or rafting. The river rapids are of varying levels of difficulty, offering a challenging float trip for all skill levels. If you're not interested in rafting, there are numerous spots where you can enjoy a lunch while watching others float on the river.

Those interested in camping will find only one national forest campground along the byway. The Cascade Campground has 10 sites that can accommodate recreational vehicles up to 22 feet in length. The campground is open from mid-May to the end of October. Other facilities available include drinking water, restrooms, a boat ramp, and hiking trail. The Sloway Campground is about 7 miles southeast of St. Regis off Interstate 90. The campground offers 16 sites, picnic tables, drinking water, restrooms, and fishing opportunities on the Clark Fork River. This campground is usually open from Memorial Day to Labor Day.

About 25 miles east of the northern end of this byway is the 19,000-acre National Bison Range. This natural grassland area was established in 1908 to protect one of the most important remaining herds of American bison. About 400 of these shaggy animals roam the land. Self-guided auto tours are available year-round. A visitor center here provides more information on the bison and the area. Other wildlife seen in this area includes white-tailed deer, mule deer, bighorn sheep, and pronghorns.

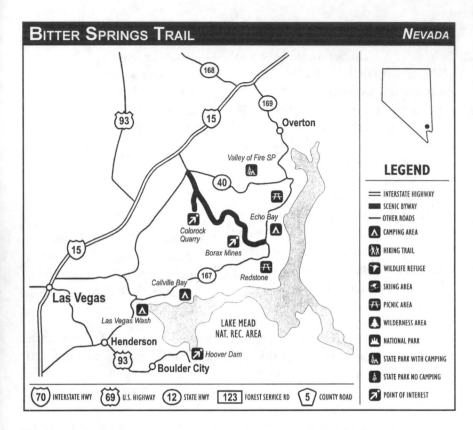

Route Location

The Bitter Springs Trail Back Country Byway is about 45 miles north-east of Las Vegas in southeastern Nevada. The western terminus is located at the junction of Nevada State Highway 40 and the Bitter Springs Road, off Interstate 15. The byway then travels southeast to the junction of Northshore Drive / State Highway 167 in the Lake Mead National Recreation Area.

Roads Traveled

The 28-mile byway follows the Bitter Springs Road which is a single-lane dirt road that requires a two-wheel drive, high-clearance vehicle. The route is officially designated a BLM Type II Back Country Byway.

Travel Season

The entire byway is usually open all year long.

Description

The Bitter Springs Trail travels through the foothills of the Muddy Mountains, past abandoned mining operations, and brightly colored sandstone hills. One of the more interesting sites encountered along the route is the Bitter Ridge, a sweeping arc that cuts for 8 miles across a rolling valley. Side roads invite the byway traveler to explore the many canyons, but unless you're in a four-wheel drive vehicle, it is not recommended that you attempt to take these side roads.

Remnants of the American Borax mining operation can be seen along the byway. Several mine buildings still stand, along with 30-foot deep cisterns that were once used to hold water, mine tunnels, and adits (horizontal passages). Evidence of early human inhabitants is also found along the byway for on many of the canyon walls are pictographs and petroglyphs.

Developed recreational facilities are non-existent along this byway, however, camping areas are not far away. The Valley of Fire State Park offers 50 campsites with shaded picnic tables. The park also has drinking water, restrooms, and shower facilities. Near the byway's eastern terminus is the Echo Bay Campground in Lake Mead National Recreation Area. The campground offers over 150 sites with picnic tables and grills. The area also offers a dump station, restrooms, drinking water, a marina, and a lodge.

Local Information

BLM - Las Vegas District Office
4765 Vegas Dr.
Las Vegas, NV 89107
Phone: 702-647-5000

Moapa Valley Chamber of Commerce
P.O. Box 361
Overton, NV 89040
Phone: 702-397-2160

Henderson Chamber of Commerce
590 S. Boulder Hwy.
Henderson, NV 89015
Phone: 702-565-8951

Boulder City Chamber of Commerce
1305 Arizona St.
Boulder City, NV 89005
Phone: 702-293-2034

Las Vegas Chamber of Commerce
711 E. Desert Inn Rd.
Las Vegas, NV 89109
Phone: 702-735-1616

Valley of Fire State Park
Box 515
Overton, NV 89040
Phone: 702-397-2088

Lake Mead National Recreation Area
601 Nevada Hwy.
Boulder City, NV 89005
Phone: 702-293-8907

Nearby Routes

Gold Butte, page 231

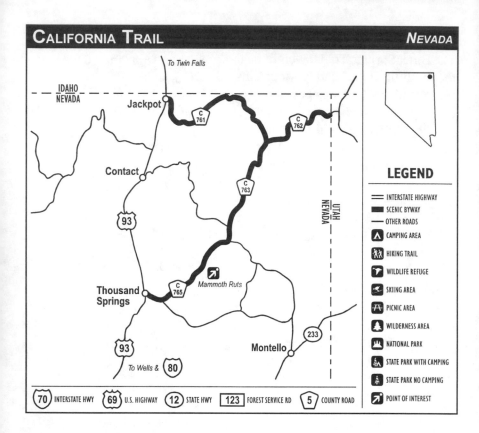

Route Location

The California Trail scenic byway is located in the northeastern corner of Nevada, approximately 75 miles northeast of Elko. The byway can be accessed from U.S. Highway 93 in either Jackpot or Thousand Springs. The route forms an open loop drive beginning and ending on U.S. Highway 93 with a spur road taking you to the Utah state line.

Roads Traveled

The 76-mile byway follows Elko County Roads C765, C763, C761, and C762. All of the roads are gravel-surfaced roads suitable for passenger cars except under adverse weather conditions. The entire route has been designated a BLM Type I Back Country Byway.

Travel Season

The byway is normally open from May through October. Mud and snowfall make the roads impassable the rest of the year.

Description

The California Trail Back Country By-way follows the footsteps and wagon trains of the settlers who used this route as the path to a better life in California. Trailmarkers along the byway identify the California Trail. The wagon wheel ruts made by the pioneers can still be seen at many places along the byway. The Mammoth Ruts site is located on private property, please respect the land-owners rights and obtain permission before exploring this site.

As you travel this scenic byway, you will also be retracing part of the path of the old Magic City Freight Line. This route was once used by horse-drawn wagons to haul goods between Toana, Nevada and Magic City, Idaho (now known as Twin Falls).

Local Information

BLM - Elko District Office
3900 E. Idaho St.
Elko, NV 89803
Phone: 702-753-0200

Wells Chamber of Commerce
279 Clover Ave.
Wells, NV 89835
Phone: 702-752-3540

Jackpot Visitor Information
P.O. Box 508
Jackpot, NV 89825
Phone: 702-755-2321

Twin Falls Area Chamber of Commerce
858 Blue Lakes Blvd. N.
Twin Falls, ID 83301
Phone: 208-733-3974

Though this byway travels through isolated countryside, opportunities for outdoor recreation are plentiful. Photographers and wildlife observers will delight in the many opportunities for spotting mule deer or photographing natures work of art. Several streams and creeks, especially Rock Spring Creek and Thousand Springs Creek provide opportunities for the angler.

Although there are no developed campgrounds along the byway, the Bureau of Land Management does permit dispersed camping anywhere on BLM land. It is best to obtain maps from the BLM that will delineate public lands from private property before setting up camp. Developed camping areas can be found in the Toiyabe National Forest which lies to the west of the byway.

Nearby Routes

Lamoille Canyon Road, page 233 / Silver Island Mountains, page 375 / Transcontinental Railroad, page 379 / City Of Rocks, page 155

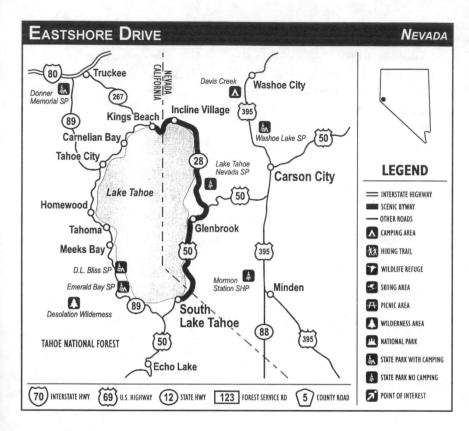

EASTSHORE DRIVE   NEVADA

Route Location

The East Shore Drive is located in west-central Nevada, about 15 miles west of Carson City, and travels along the shores of North America's largest alpine lake, Lake Tahoe. The byway's northern terminus is King's Beach in California and its southern terminus is in South Lake Tahoe, also on the California side.

Roads Traveled

East Shore Drive is a 30-mile scenic byway that follows State Highway 28 and U.S. Highway 50. All but two miles of the route are designated a National Scenic Byway by the Federal Highway Administration. The East Shore Drive scenic byway is a two-lane paved route that is safe for travel by all types of vehicles.

Travel Season

State Highway 28 and U.S. Highway 50 are normally open year-round.

Description

The East Shore Drive follows alongside the shores of Lake Tahoe through pine wood forests of the Toiyabe National Forest and Lake Tahoe State Park. Lake Tahoe is the largest alpine lake in North America. It stretches for 22 miles north to south and is 12 miles wide. It is said that a white dinner plate can be seen in these crystal-clear waters to a depth of 75 feet. A tram near the lake's south shore takes visitors up 2,000 feet above the lake for spectacular panoramic views of the lake and Lake Tahoe Basin.

Near the byway's northern end is Incline Village. Located here is the site of the Ponderosa Ranch which was the filming site for the television show "Bonanza" and is now a theme park featuring a petting farm, saloon and a museum. Visitors can stroll through the original Cartwright ranch house and a recreated Western town. The museum displays automobiles, carriages and an antique gun collection.

Recreational opportunities are plentiful along this scenic byway. In winter, the area provides excellent opportunities for cross-country skiing, downhill skiing, snowmobiling, and sledding. Lake Tahoe finds sailboats and water-skiers on its waters during the warmer months. Miles of alpine beaches can be found within the Lake Tahoe Nevada State Park and around the lake that provide the perfect spot for a family outing. Numerous side roads and trails provide hiking and mountain biking opportuni-

Local Information

Tahoe National Forest
22830 Foresthill Rd.
Foresthill, CA 95631
Phone: 916-367-2224

Incline Village - Crystal Bay C of C
969 Tahoe Blvd.
Incline Village, NV 89451
Phone: 702-831-4440

Carson City Chamber of Commerce
1900 S. Carson St.
Carson City, NV 89701
Phone: 702-882-1565

South Lake Tahoe Chamber of Commerce
3066 Lake Tahoe Blvd.
South Lake Tahoe, CA 96150
Phone: 916-541-5255

Lake Tahoe Nevada State Park
2005 Hwy. 28
Incline Village, NV 89452
Phone: 702-831-0494

Mormon Station State Historic Park
Foothill Road
Genoa, NV 89411
Phone: 702-687-4379

Washoe Lake State Recreation Area
4855 E. Lake Blvd.
Carson City, NV 89704
Phone: 702-687-4319

Emerald Bay State Park
State Route 89
Tahoe City, CA 96142
Phone: 916-525-7277

ties. The 63,475-acre Desolation Wilderness on the California side offers hiking, backpacking, and horseback riding. The Pacific Crest National Scenic Trail also passes through here.

Those interested in camping will find numerous private and public campgrounds along the byway and around the lake. Although there are no camping facilities within the Lake Tahoe Nevada State Park, numerous public campgrounds can be found a short drive from the byway in the national forests surrounding the lake or at other state parks.

The Washoe Lake State Park is located north of Carson City off U.S. Highway 395. The campground here has 50 sites for tents and recreational vehicles with some sites having hookups. The campground also offers drinking water, picnic areas, restrooms, a dump station, and a boat ramp.

In South Lake Tahoe is a county park offering 170 campsites. Hookups are available at many of the sites. The park also offers restrooms, picnic areas, shower facilities, and a boat ramp.

On the California side is the 593-acre Emerald Bay State Park. There are 100 campsites suitable for tents and recreational vehicles. Just north of this state park is the D.L. Bliss State Park which has 167 campsites. This 1,237-acre park also offers miles of hiking trails.

Local Information

D.L. Bliss State Park
P.O. Box 266
Tahoma, CA 96142
Phone: 916-525-7232

Donner Memorial State Park
P.O. Box 9210
Truckee, CA 95737
Phone: 916-582-7892

Nearby Routes

Fort Churchill To Wellington, page 229 / Carson Pass Highway, page 71 / Yuba Donner, page 114

Lodging Directory

Carson Station Hotel & Casino - Carson City, page 435 — Hotel / Motel
Coachland RV Park - Truckee, page 436 — Campground / RV Park
Lampliter Motel - South Lake Tahoe, page 436 — Hotel / Motel
Tahoe Colony Inn - South Lake Tahoe, page 436 — Hotel / Motel
Viking Motor Lodge - South Lake Tahoe, page 436 — Hotel / Motel

FORT CHURCHILL TO WELLINGTON — *NEVADA*

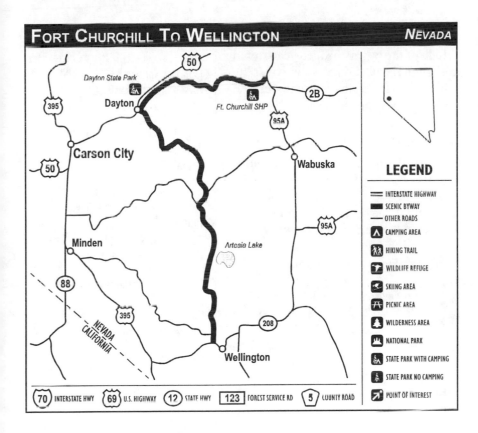

LEGEND

- ▬▬ INTERSTATE HIGHWAY
- ■ SCENIC BYWAY
- — OTHER ROADS
- 🄰 CAMPING AREA
- 🄰 HIKING TRAIL
- 🄰 WILDLIFE REFUGE
- 🄰 SKIING AREA
- 🄰 PICNIC AREA
- 🄰 WILDERNESS AREA
- 🄰 NATIONAL PARK
- 🄰 STATE PARK WITH CAMPING
- 🄰 STATE PARK NO CAMPING
- 🄰 POINT OF INTEREST

(70) INTERSTATE HWY   (69) U.S. HIGHWAY   (12) STATE HWY   [123] FOREST SERVICE RD   (5) COUNTY ROAD

Route Location

The Fort Churchill To Wellington scenic byway is located in west-central Nevada, 10 miles east of Carson City. The southern access is located off Nevada State Highway 208 near the town of Wellington. The byway travels north to Dayton and then east to the junction of Alternate U.S. Highway 95, near the Fort Churchill State Historical Park.

Roads Traveled

The 67-mile byway follows Nevada State Highway 2B and the Como, Sunrise Pass, and Upper Colony Roads. The roads vary from relatively smooth gravel to rough unsurfaced roads. The gravel sections are mostly two-lane while the rough segment is a single-lane road with steep grades. A four-wheel drive vehicle is necessary to safely drive the entire byway although a two-wheel drive, high-clearance vehicle can travel most of the route. This BLM Back Country Byway has 38 miles designated as Type I and 29 miles of Type II road.

Travel Season

Much of the byway is open year-round although the portion traveling over the Pine Nut Mountains is usually closed from heavy winter snows.

Description

The scenic drive retraces a portion of the historic Pony Express Trail with the waters of the Carson River flowing alongside. The byway then heads south, crossing the rugged Pine Nut Mountains and through peaceful valleys before it ends near Wellington.

Near the eastern end is Fort Churchill State Historic Park. This military establishment was erected in 1860 to defend settlers and riders of the Pony Express Trail against feared Indian attacks. The stone buildings were used for less than a decade and abandoned in 1869. The fort once had more than 60 buildings. The remains of these stone structures invite exploration. A visitor center here has more information on the history of the fort.

Local Information

BLM - Carson City District Office
1535 Hot Springs Rd., Suite 300
Carson City, NV 89706
Phone: 702-885-6000

Virginia City Chamber of Commerce
P.O. Box 464
Virginia City, NV 89440
Phone: 702-847-0311

Carson City Chamber of Commerce
1900 S. Carson St.
Carson City, NV 89701
Phone: 702-882-1565

Dayton Area Chamber of Commerce
P.O. Box 408
Dayton, NV 89403
Phone: 702-246-7909

Dayton State Park
Hwy. 50 East - Box 412
Dayton, NV 89403
Phone: 702-687-5678

Ft. Churchill State Historic Park
Old Fort Churchill Rd.
Silver Springs, NV 89429
Phone: 702-577-2345

Leaving the fort, you continue west along the banks of the Carson River, retracing the Pony Express Trail for 21 miles. From Dayton, the byway heads south across the rugged Pine Nut Mountains. This region is home to wild horses, mountain lions, mule deer, bobcats, and coyotes. Once across the mountains, the route smooths out a bit as it travels between the Pine Nut Mountains on the west and the Buckskin Range on the east. Camping facilities can be found in the Fort Churchill SHP and Dayton SP. The Dayton State Park's 10-site campground and picnic area were built on the site of the Rock Point Quartz Mill which dates to 1861.

Nearby Routes

Eastshore Drive, page 226 / Pyramid Lake, page 237 / Carson Pass Highway, page 71

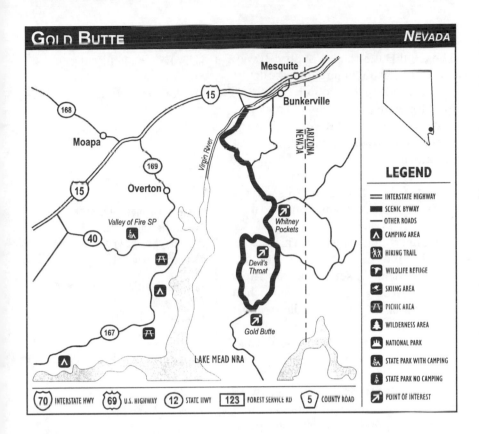

Route Location

The Gold Butte byway is in southeastern Nevada about 80 miles northeast of Las Vegas. The byway begins several miles south of Mesquite off Nevada State Highway 170 and travels south to the ghost town of Gold Butte.

Roads Traveled

The byway is a 62-mile route that follows the Gold Butte Road, splitting at Devil's Throat. The first 24 miles is along a narrow paved road suitable for passenger cars. The 19 mile portion heading east of Devil's Throat travels on a relatively smooth gravel road also suitable for passenger cars. The 19 mile portion heading west from Devil's Throat follows a lightly maintained dirt road that requires a high-clearance, two-wheel or four-wheel drive vehicle. Gold Butte is a Type II Back Country Byway.

Travel Season

The byway's roads are usually open all year long.

Description

The Gold Butte Back Country Byway is a back road traveling across the desert landscape along the foothills of the Virgin Mountains set among red rock formations. The Virgin River can be seen peacefully flowing alongside the first several miles of this byway. To the east you'll see Virgin Peak towering 8,000 feet above the desert floor. Side roads can take you to the top of this mountain peak.

This area is rich in history. Three separate Native American cultures are known to have settled here. Their petroglyph carvings can be seen etched into the rocks. Early non-Indian explorers were followed by the Mormon colonizers who settled in the Mesquite and Bunkerville area in 1877.

Desert wildlife thrives along the byway. Wildlife observers will want to remain alert for they may see bighorn sheep and mule deer. Mountain lions and the desert tortoise also make their home in this area. The patient observer may occasionally catch a glimpse of wild horses or herds of burro.

The byway passes colorful sandstone rock formations in the area of Whitney Pockets. This area was partially named for a local family and the pockets that have been etched into the cliffs by erosion. The remnants of a Civilan Conservation Corps projects can also be seen in this area.

The byway continues to a split in the road at Devil's Throat, a 100-foot wide by 100-foot deep sinkhole that continues to expand. Whether you turn left or right at this point, you'll end up at the historic mining town of Gold Butte. This town was established in 1908 to service the many mining operations in the area. The town once boasted of a store, hotel, stable, and post office.

Nearby Routes

Bitter Springs Trail, page 222

Local Information

BLM - Las Vegas District Office
4765 Vegas Dr.
Las Vegas, NV 89107
Phone: 702-647-5000

Moapa Valley Chamber of Commerce
P.O. Box 361
Overton, NV 89040
Phone: 702-397-2160

Mesquite Chamber of Commerce
250 W. Mesquite Blvd.
Mesquite, NV 89024
Phone: 702-346-2902

Lake Mead National Recreation Area
601 Nevada Hwy.
Boulder City, NV 89005
Phone: 702-293-8907

Valley of Fire State Park
Box 515
Overton, NV 89040
Phone: 702-397-2088

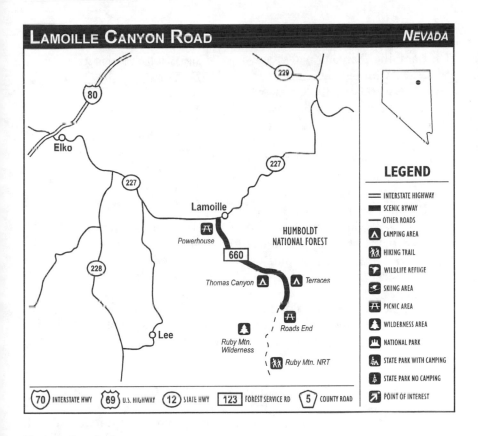

LAMOILLE CANYON ROAD — NEVADA

LEGEND

- ═══ INTERSTATE HIGHWAY
- ▬▬ SCENIC BYWAY
- ── OTHER ROADS
- 🅰 CAMPING AREA
- 🚶 HIKING TRAIL
- 🦌 WILDLIFE REFUGE
- 🎿 SKIING AREA
- 🍽 PICNIC AREA
- 🌲 WILDERNESS AREA
- 🏔 NATIONAL PARK
- 🏕 STATE PARK WITH CAMPING
- 🏕 STATE PARK NO CAMPING
- ⚑ POINT OF INTEREST

70 INTERSTATE HWY 69 U.S. HIGHWAY 12 STATE HWY 123 FOREST SERVICE RD 5 COUNTY ROAD

Route Location

The Lamoille Canyon Road byway is located in northeastern Nevada, approximately 20 miles southeast of Elko on Interstate 80. The byway can be reached from Elko by taking Nevada State Highway 227 south to the byway's entrance, just west of Lamoille. The byway travels south across the Humboldt National Forest to the Roads End Picnic Area.

Roads Traveled

The 12-mile byway follows Forest Service Road 660 which is a two-lane paved road suitable for all types of vehicles. Travelers will need to retrace the route back to State Highway 227. The byway is designated a National Forest Scenic Byway.

Travel Season

The byway's roads are usually open from May through October, after which heavy winter snows make the route impassable.

Description

The Lamoille Canyon Road scenic byway travels through the rugged canyon carved by the Lamoille Creek which flows alongside much of the byway. The canyon is a beautifully rugged canyon with three perennial streams, sheer rock cliffs, and scenic ribbon-like waterfalls. Two other canyons can be seen from the byway, Right Fork Lamoille Canyon and Thomas Canyon. These canyons and the rivers which carved them provide excellent fishing opportunities. A small stand of Bristlecone pine exists within the Thomas Canyon.

Local Information

Humboldt National Forest
976 Mountain City Hwy.
Elko, NV 89801
Phone: 702-738-5171

Humboldt National Forest
Ruby Mountin Ranger District
P.O. Box 246
Wells, NV 89825
Phone: 702-752-3357

Elko Chamber of Commerce
1601 Idaho St.
Elko, NV 89801
Phone: 702-738-7135

Some of the wildlife seen along the byway includes mule deer, yellow-bellied marmots, red-tailed hawks, cottontail rabbits, and coyotes. Other wildlife inhabiting the region includes snow partridge, mountain goats, and bighorn sheep.

Byway travelers will find two national forest campgrounds in Lamoille Canyon. The Thomas Canyon Campground offers 42 campsites with picnic tables and fire rings. The Terraces Campground is more primitive with only 9 tent camping sites. Two picnic areas provide the perfect spot for enjoying an afternoon sack lunch. The Powerhouse Picnic Area is located near the byway's beginning with the Roads End Picnic Area being, where else, at the end of the byway.

The Ruby Mountain National Recreation Trail can be accessed from the Roads End Picnic Area. This trail extends south for 40 miles through some spectacular scenery. There are 8 lakes, with excellent opportunities for fishing, that can be reached from the Ruby Mountain Trail. Other hiking trails can be found along the route providing opportunities for those interest in hiking, backpacking, mountain biking, or horseback riding.

Nearby Routes

California Trail, page 224

LODGING DIRECTORY

Shilo Inn - Elko, page 442 — Hotel / Motel

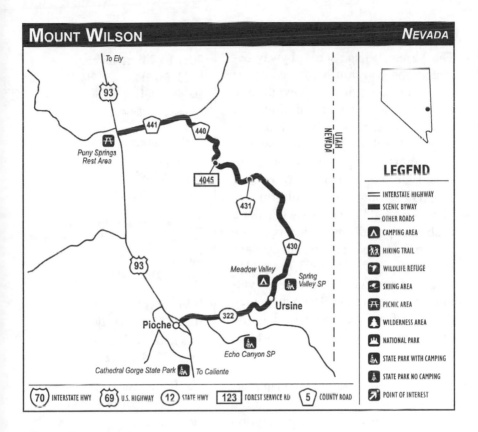

MOUNT WILSON   NEVADA

LEGEND

- ═══ INTERSTATE HIGHWAY
- ▬ SCENIC BYWAY
- — OTHER ROADS
- △ CAMPING AREA
- 🚶 HIKING TRAIL
- 🦆 WILDLIFE REFUGE
- 🎿 SKIING AREA
- ⛱ PICNIC AREA
- 🌲 WILDERNESS AREA
- 🏛 NATIONAL PARK
- STATE PARK WITH CAMPING
- STATE PARK NO CAMPING
- POINT OF INTEREST

(70) INTERSTATE HWY (69) U.S. HIGHWAY (12) STATE HWY [123] FOREST SERVICE RD (5) COUNTY ROAD

Route Location

The Mount Wilson Back Country Byway is approximatley 90 miles south of Ely in eastern Nevada. The northern access is located off U.S. Hwy. 93 at the Pony Springs rest area (milepost 147.9). The byway then travels southeast forming an open loop drive back to U.S. Hwy.93, near the town of Pioche.

Roads Traveled

The byway is 62 miles long and follows County Roads 441, 440, 431, and 430, BLM Road 4045, and Nevada State Highway 322. The routes travel over a combination of paved and gravel-surfaced roads that can be safely driven in a two-wheel drive, high-clearance vehicle. The Mount Wilson byway is a Type II Back Country Byway.

Travel Season

The roads are generally open from May through October and then closed due to snowfall. The byway may also become impassable after heavy rains.

Description

The Mount Wilson scenic byway begins in the arid, brush-covered desert landscape common to Nevada and takes you to the forested slopes of Mount Wilson. The byway passes through the thick pinyon-juniper forest, climbing into pockets of ponderosa pine, fir, mountain mahogany, and aspen. The spring offers a colorful display as the wildlfowers growing along the byway proudly make their presence known. Not to be outdone, fall displays its own show of colors, with the golden color of aspen set among leaves of yellow, red, and orange. The byway then descends from the mountains into the broad valleys of Camp and Meadow Valleys.

The back country byway offers numerous opportunies for outdoor recreation. Numerous side roads invite exploration by the hiker and mountain biker. There's never a bad time for looking for wildlife which includes such species as mule deer, coyotes, hawks, and various lizards. Wild horses can also be seen at times.

Local Information

BLM - Ely District Office
HC 33, Box 150
Ely, NV 89301
Phone: 702-289-4865

Pioche Chamber of Commerce
P.O. Box 127
Pioche, NV 89043
Phone: 702-962-5850

Caliente Chamber of Commerce
P.O. Box 553
Caliente, NV 89008
Phone: 702-726-3129

Spring Valley State Park
Star Rt. 89063 - Box 201
Pioche, NV 89043
Phone: 702-962-5102

Echo Canyon State Park
Star Rt. 295 - Box 295
Pioche, NV 89043
Phone: 702-962-5103

Cathedral Gorge State Park
US Hwy. 93 - Box 176
Panaca, NV 89042
Phone: 702-728-4467

Those interested in fishing will find a 65-acre lake stocked with brown trout, rainbow trout, and Alabama striped bass in the Spring Valley State Park. The park also offers the opportunity to camp overnight at any one of its 37 sites. Some of the campsites have electrical hookups. Several pioneer ranches, old stone homes, and a cemetery dating to the pioneer days exist within the park.

Situated in a narrow, steep-walled canyon is the BLM operated Meadow Valley Campground. Here the visitor will find 6 tent-only campsites with picnic tables and fire rings. Pit toilets are provided but there is no drinking water. You can stay here up to 14 days if you want to.

PYRAMID LAKE   NEVADA

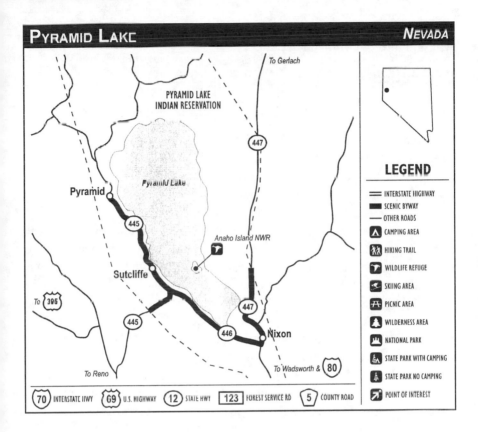

Route Location

The Pyramid Lake scenic drive is located in west-central Nevada, approximately 30 miles north of Reno. The byway lies entirely within the boundary of the Pyramid Lake Indian Reservation. The main route travels from Pyramid southeast to Nixon and then north to officially end at the boundary of the reservation. A side road heads south from the main route to the reservation boundary heading towards Mullen Pass.

Roads Traveled

Pyramid Lake follows Nevada State Highways 445, 446 and 447 which are two-lane paved routes suitable for all types of vehicles. This scenic route is designated a National Scenic Byway by the Federal Highway Administration and is also a state scenic byway. The byway is about 40 miles long.

Travel Season

The roads followed are generally open year-round. Severe winter storms

may occasionally close Nevada Highway 445 through Mullen Pass.

Description

The Pyramid Lake scenic drive travels
along the beautiful shores of Pyramid
Lake, named for the rock formation that
resembles a pyramid. The byway travels in the shadows of the rugged Virginia Mountains which lie to the south
of the byway. A side trip from the main

Local Information

Pyramid Lake Paiute Tribe
P.O. Box 256
Nixon, NV 89424
Phone: 702-574-1000

Greater Reno - Sparks C of C
P.O. Box 3499
Reno, NV 89505
Phone: 702-686-3030

route of the byway takes you into this mountain range where Sugarloaf Peak
stands a proud 5,291 feet above sea level. Other mountain peaks in this
mountain range reach heights above 8,000 feet. Another mountain range
lies to the north of Pyramid Lake where Pah-Rah peak stretches towards the
sky at 7,800 feet.

Pyramid Lake is the largest natural lake in Nevada, measuring approximately 30 miles long and 7 to 9 miles wide. The Cui-ui, an endangered
species of fish, make their home in these waters as do Cutthroat trout. White
pelicans and various other shorebirds also inhabit this region; their safe
haven being the 750-acre Anaho Island National Wildlife Refuge.

Recreation along the scenic byway is mostly in the form of boating and
fishing. A marina is located in Sutcliffe and provides all the necessary equipment for such activities. Swimming is also a popular activity on the lake.
Beaches can be found at Pelican Point and Warrior Point. The mountains
that surround the lake offer excellent opportunities for hiking, horseback
riding, and backpacking. Please note that Tribal permits are required for
fishing and boating and may be obtained in Sutcliffe

At present, there are no developed facilities for overnight camping. The
nearest privately-owned camping facilities are found in Reno, some 30 miles
to the south. Public campgrounds may be found within the Toiyabe National
Forest which is further south of Reno.

Nearby Routes

Fort Churchill To Wellington, page 229

RED ROCK CANYON   *NEVADA*

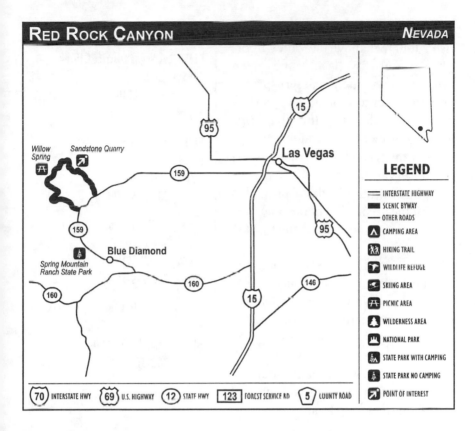

Willow Spring · Sandstone Quarry · Las Vegas

LEGEND

- ═══ INTERSTATE HIGHWAY
- ▬▬ SCENIC BYWAY
- ── OTHER ROADS
- ◭ CAMPING AREA
- 🏃 HIKING TRAIL
- 🦌 WILDLIFE REFUGE
- ⛷ SKIING AREA
- ⛱ PICNIC AREA
- 🌲 WILDERNESS AREA
- 🏔 NATIONAL PARK
- STATE PARK WITH CAMPING
- STATE PARK NO CAMPING
- ↗ POINT OF INTEREST

Blue Diamond
Spring Mountain Ranch State Park

(70) INTERSTATE HWY   (69) U.S. HIGHWAY   (12) STATE HWY   [123] FOREST SERVICE RD   (5) COUNTY ROAD

Route Location

The Red Rock Canyon byway is located in southern Nevada, about 20 miles west of Las Vegas. The byway forms an open loop drive beginning and ending on Nevada State Highway 159.

Roads Traveled

The byway follows Red Rock Canyon Road which is a one-way, paved road that is safe for travel by all types of vehicles. The byway is approximately thirteen miles long and has been designated a Type I Back Country Byway by the Bureau of Land Management.

Travel Season

The byway is normally open all year.

Description

The Red Rock Canyon Back Country Byway traverses the arid desert landscape passing rock formations that rise 2,000 feet above the valley floor. The sheer cliff walls are cut by deep canyons where hidden desert springs provide water to support the diversity of wildlife inhabiting this area. Bighorn sheep can be seen along the byway by the watchful eye of the wildlife observer. Cougars, kit fox, coyotes, bobcat, and birds of prey also inhabit the area. Wild horses and burros can also be seen along the byway.

This scenic drive travels through the 67,500-acre Red Rock Canyon National Conservation Area. This area provides opportunities for hiking, backpacking, horseback riding, rock climbing, and mountain biking. You'll most likely encounter many mountain bikers on the byway, be cautious and share the road with them.

Local Information

BLM - Las Vegas District Office
4765 Vegas Dr.
Las Vegas, NV 89107
Phone: 702-647-5000

BLM - Caliente Resource Area
P.O. Box 237
Caliente, NV 89008
Phone: 702-726-8100

Las Vegas Chamber of Commerce
711 E. Desert Inn Rd.
Las Vegas, NV 89109
Phone: 702-735-1616

Spring Mountain Ranch State Park
Box 124
Blue Diamond, NV 89004
Phone: 702-875-4141

A visitor center is located at the entrance of the byway. Here you will find information and exhibits on the area and its recreational opportunities. For example, a brochure is available that lists and briefly describes 15 hiking trails. Other materials provide information on the plant and animal life of this rugged desert area.

One site of interest you'll encounter along the byway is Sandstone Quarry. A short walk will take you to an historic quarry dating from the turn of the century. Trailheads here will take you further into the conservation area.

Nearby Routes

East Mojave National Scenic Area, page 75

KANCAMAGUS HIGHWAY   NEW HAMPSHIRE

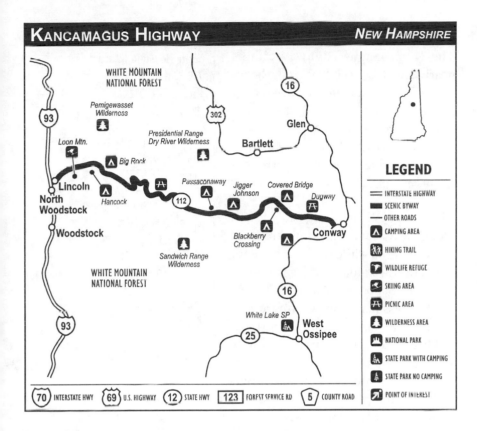

Route Location

The Kancamagus Highway is located in central New Hampshire, approximately 60 miles north of Concord. The western terminus is located off Interstate 93 in the town of Lincoln. The byway travels east across the White Mountain National Forest to the junction of New Hampshire State Highway 16, south of Conway.

Roads Traveled

The 28-mile route follows New Hampshire State Highway 112 which is a two-lane paved road suitable for all types of vehicles. The entire route has been designated a National Forest Scenic Byway and a National Scenic Byway by the Federal Highway Administration.

Travel Season

The route is open year-round although winter driving conditions from November through May can be hazardous.

Description

The Kancamagus Highway climbs nearly 3,000 feet as it crosses the beautiful White Mountains. The waters of Swift River flow alongside the byway once you cross Kancamagus Pass. Several scenic vistas along the route provide panoramic views of the surrounding mountains.

There are several hiking trails found along the byway. Some trails are short walking trails while others are longer and more strenuous. A pleasant walk along the Sabbaday Brook Trail, west of the Passaconaway Campground, will lead you to the beautiful Sabbaday Falls. Other trails near here will take you to the top of 4,140-foot Mt. Tripyramid. Wilderness areas surround the byway. These pristine areas offer excellent hiking, back country camping, and horseback riding. The Appalachian National Scenic Trail can be accessed in the Pemigewasset and Presidential Range-Dry River Wilderness Areas.

The White Mountain National Forest has developed numerous camping and picnicking areas along this scenic byway. There are 6 public campgrounds from which to choose for an overnight stay. The Jigger Johnson Campground is the largest with 75 sites. Hancock Campground follows in size with 56 campsites. Forty-nine sites are available at Covered Bridge; Passaconaway has 33 sites; Big Rock offers 28 campsites; Blackberry Crossing has 20 sites. Facilities found in each campground includes drinking water, picnic tables, and restrooms. None of the campgrounds offer electrical hookups for recreational vehicles.

Local Information

White Mountain National Forest
719 N. Main St.
Laconia, NH 03247
Phone: 603-528-8721

Conway Village Chamber of Commerce
P.O. Box 1019
Conway, NH 03818
Phone: 603-447-2639

Lincoln - Woodstock C of C
P.O. Box 358
Lincoln, NH 03251
Phone: 603-745-6621

White Lake State Park
Route 16
Tamworth, NH 03886
Phone: 603-323-7350

Lodging Directory

Kancamagus Motor Lodge - Lincoln, page 442 — Hotel / Motel
Three Rivers House - N. Woodstock, page 442 — Bed & Breakfast / Inns

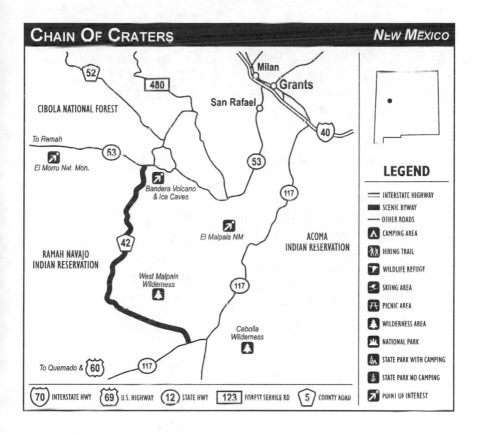

CHAIN OF CRATERS — NEW MEXICO

LEGEND

- ══ INTERSTATE HIGHWAY
- ▬ SCENIC BYWAY
- ─ OTHER ROADS
- ⚠ CAMPING AREA
- 🏃 HIKING TRAIL
- 🦅 WILDLIFE REFUGE
- 🎿 SKIING AREA
- 🏕 PICNIC AREA
- 🌲 WILDERNESS AREA
- 🏛 NATIONAL PARK
- 🏕 STATE PARK WITH CAMPING
- 🏕 STATE PARK NO CAMPING
- 🔼 POINT OF INTEREST

(70) INTERSTATE HWY (69) U.S. HIGHWAY (12) STATE HWY [123] FOREST SERVICE RD (5) COUNTY ROAD

Route Location

The Chain Of Craters is located in west-central New Mexico, approximately 25 miles southwest of Grants. The northern access is located off New Mexico State Highway 53 with the junction of County Road 42. The byway travels south to the junction of New Mexico State Highway 117.

Roads Traveled

The 36-mile byway follows County Road 42 which is a dirt road requiring a two-wheel drive, high-clearance vehicle. A four-wheel drive vehicle is recommended during wet weather. The byway has been designated a BLM Type II Back Country Byway.

Travel Season

Usually, the byway is open year-round although the road is likely to be impassable during and after periods of inclement weather.

Description

The Chain Of Craters Back Country Byway travels through portions of the El Malpais National Monument and National Conservation Area. The byway crosses the brush-covered landscape with views of sandstone bluffs rising above the desert floor.

This rugged and desolate area was once inhabited by Indians, and crossed by Spanish and American explorers who carved their names in the sandstone. Inscription Rock can be seen to the west of this byway in the El Morro National Monument. The earliest inscription dates to 1605 by Juan de Onate, a Spanish governer and colonizer of New Mexico. Native American symbols and pictures are also carved in the rock.

The 40,000-acre West Malpais Wilderness offers opportunities for exploring. Hiking on the lava rocks in this area is very rugged and not recommended for the inexperienced hiker. Numerous side roads provide easier hiking for those interested in exploring the area on foot. These side roads are also used by mountain bikers. Four-wheel vehicles and mountain bikes are prohibited from the wilderness area. The Continental Divide National Scenic Trail follows a portion of the byway along the northern area.

There are no developed public campgrounds along the byway, however, dispersped camping is permitted on BLM land. Be sure to bring your own water as none is available.

Local Information

BLM - Albuquerque District Office
435 Montano Rd. NE
Albuquerque, NM 87107
Phone: 505-761-8700

BLM
El Malpais National Conservation Area
P.O. Box 846
Grants, NM 87020
Phone: 505-285-5406

Grants / Cibola County C of C
100 N. Iron Ave.
Grants, NM 87020
Phone: 800-748-2142

El Malpais National Monument
P.O. Box 939
Grants, NM 87020
Phone: 505-285-5406

El Morro National Monument
RR 2, Box 43
Ramah, NM 87321
Phone: 505-783-4226

Bandera Volcano & Ice Caves
12000 Ice Caves Road
Grants, NM 87020
Phone: 505-783-4303

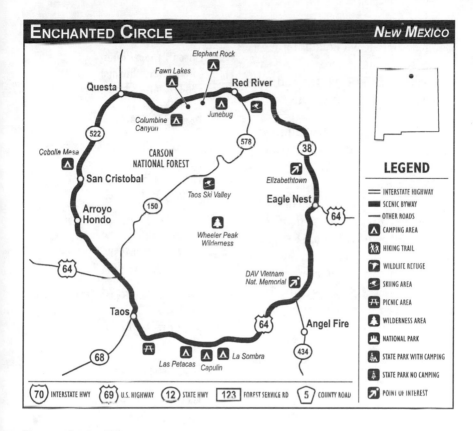

Route Location

The Enchanted Circle scenic byway is in north-central New Mexico, near the Colorado state line, approximately 70 miles northeast of Santa Fe. The byway forms a loop drive beginning and ending in Taos.

Roads Traveled

The 84-mile route follows New Mexico State Highways 38, and 522, and U.S. Highway 64 which are two-lane paved roads suitable for all vehicles. The entire route has been designated a National Forest Scenic Byway.

Travel Season

The byway's roads are normally open year-round.

Description

The Enchanted Circle crosses the Carson National Forest forming a circle around the 13,161-foot Wheeler Peak, New Mexico's highest point. The byway climbs the southern portion of the Sangre de Cristo Mountains through forests of spruce and fir, crosses wide mountain valleys and meadows, and follows alongside meandering streams and rivers.

The ghost town of Elizabethtown lies on the byway's eastern portion, just north of the U.S. Highway 64 intersection. This town was established in 1870 after gold was discovered in the area and was New Mexico's first incorporated town. The town is reported to have been a wild and wooly place, with thousands of residents, seven saloons, and three dance halls. The remains of the town are a short drive west of the byway on County Road B-20 across Moreno Creek.

Further south of Elizabethtown is another monument to American history. The Vietnam Veterans National Memorial, now operated by the Disabled American Veterans, was originally built by Dr. Victor Westphall in memory of his son who died in the Vietnam War. The memorial is open daily and has special Memorial Day Services each year.

Local Information

Carson National Forest
Forest Service Building
208 Cruz Alta Rd.
Taos, NM 87571
Phone: 505-758-6200

Taos County Chamber of Commerce
1139 Paseo del Pueblo Sur
Taos, NM 87571
Phone: 800-732-8267

Red River Chamber of Commerce
P.O. Box 870
Red River, NM 87558
Phone: 800-348-6444

Angel Fire Resort Chamber of Commerce
P.O. Box 547
Angel Fire, NM 87710
Phone: 505-377-6661

Eagle Nest Chamber of Commerce
P.O. Box 322
Eagle Nest, NM 87718
Phone: 505-377-2420

DAV Vietnam National Memorial
Hwy. 64
Angle Fire, NM 87710
Phone: 505-377-6900

Plenty of opportunities exist for extending your stay along the byway. The national forest has developed several campgrounds providing numerous shaded sites with picnic tables. The national forest also permits dispersed camping nearly anywhere within the forest.

Nearby Routes

Lodging Directory

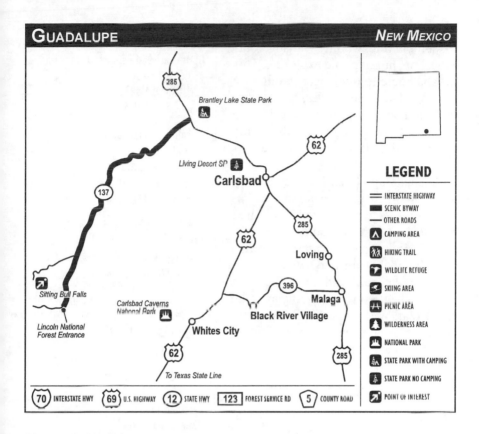

Route Location

The Guadalupe Back Country Byway is located in southeastern New Mexico. The byway begins about 12 miles north of Carlsbad and travels south to the boundary of the Lincoln National Forest.

Roads Traveled

The scenic drive follows New Mexico Highway 137 which is a two-lane paved road suitable for all types of vehicles. The 30 mile route is designated a Type I Back Country Byway by the Bureau of Land Management.

Travel Season

New Mexico Highway 137 is generally open year-round.

Description

Visitors to this back country byway will ascend nearly 3,000 feet from the landscape of the Chihuahuan Desert at the beginning of the byway to the

Guadalupe Mountains. Opportunities exist for hiking, wildlife viewing, four-wheeling, hunting, and exploring. This area is home to mule deer, pronghorn antelope, hawks and eagles, coyotes, lizards, and rattle snakes. A short side trip from the byway takes you to the scenic Sitting Bull Falls and a picnic area.

The Guadalupe Back Country Byway is rich in history. Stone spearheads or dartpoints have been found in this area that are between 8,000 and 9,000 years old. Various types of pottery have also been found that are associated with the ancient Anasazi Indians. The first ranchers began arriving shortly after the Civil War. West Texas ranchers would also pass through here with their cattle, headed for the railheads in Kansas. Today this area is used for livestock grazing and oil and gas exploration.

Nearby is the Carlsbad Caverns National Park which has more than 70 underground caverns, some of which are among the largest in the world. In addition to touring the caverns, the national park offers hiking and picnicking opportunities. Camping facilities can be found in the Brantley Lake State Park, located north of the byway. The state park also offers picnicking, fishing, swimming, and boating opportunities.

Local Information

BLM - Carlsbad Resource Area
630 East Greene
Carlsbad, NM 88220
Phone: 505-234-5272

Lincoln National Forest
Federal Bldg.
1101 New York Ave.
Alamogoroo, NM 88310
Phone: 505-437-6030

Carlsbad Chamber of Commerce
P.O. Box 910
Carlsbad, NM 88220
Phone: 505-887-6516

Cave Country Chamber of Commerce
P.O. Box 128
White's City, NM 88268
Phone: 505-785-2291

Brantley Dam State Park
P.O. Box 2288
Carlsbad, NM 88221
Phone: 505-457-2384

Living Desert State Park
1504 Miehls Dr.
Carlsbad, NM 88220
Phone: 505-887-5516

Carlsbad Caverns National Park
3225 National Parks Highway
Carlsbad, NM 88220
Phone: 505-785-2232

Travelers along the byway may wish to continue driving through Lincoln National Forest to the Dog Canyon Ranger Station in Guadalupe National Park. The national park contains what is considered to be one of the finest examples of an ancient marine fossil reef in the world. The park is also home to Guadalupe Peak, the highest point in Texas at 8,749 feet. A small campground is located near the ranger station as is access to hiking trails that lead to back country camping areas and Guadalupe Peak.

INNER LOOP - GILA CLIFF DWELLINGS   NEW MEXICO

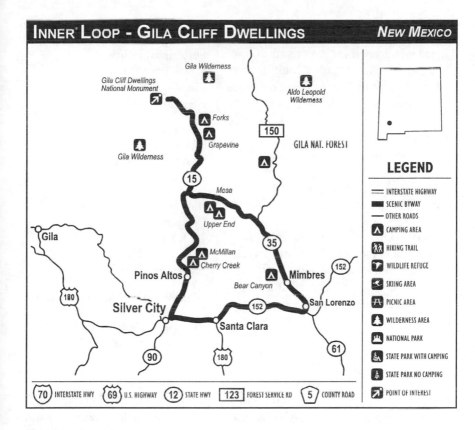

Route Location

The Inner Loop - Gila Cliff Dwellings scenic byway is in southwestern New Mexico, about 100 miles northwest of Las Cruces. The byway begins in Silver City and heads east to San Lorenzo. It then travels northwesterly to the Gila Cliff Dwellings National Monument. From here, the byway heads south, retracing part of the byway, to end back in Silver City.

Roads Traveled

The 110-mile route follows New Mexico State Highways 15, 35, and 152, and U.S. Highway 180. All of the roads are two-lane paved roads. Vehicles over 17 feet should not attempt the portion of State Highway 15 between Pinos Altos and the junction with State Highway 35 as this segment is narrow with sharp curves. The byway is a National Forest Scenic Byway.

Travel Season

The entire byway is generally open year-round.

Description

This scenic drive travels across the Gila National Forest through a high desert and mountainous landscape, crossing the Continental Divide twice. Located all along the byway are scenic turnouts that provide panoramic views of the surrounding mountains or a nice spot to enjoy a picnic lunch. State Hwy. 15 to the Gila Cliff Dwellings NM is enshrouded by the pristine Gila Wilderness.

The Gila Cliff Dwellings National Monument is the site of six cliff dwellings inhabited by the Mogollans in the late 13th century. Over 40 masonry rooms were built within the six caves. A moderately easy trail takes you through these historic cliff dwellings. Hiking trails found here will lead you into the Gila Wilderness.

Local Information

Gila National Forest
2610 N. Silver St.
Silver City, NM 88061
Phone: 505-388-8201

Silver City - Grant County C of C
1103 N. Hudson St.
Silver City, NM 88061
Phone: 800-548-9378

Truth or Consequences / Sierra County Chamber of Commerce
201 S. Foch St.
T or C, NM 87901
Phone: 800-831-9487

Gila Cliff Dwellings National Monument
Rt. 11 - Box 100
Silver City, NM 88061
Phone: 505-536-9344

Wildlife observes will want to remain alert for bald eagles flying overhead. Golden eagles and red-tailed hawks can also be seen. In the mountains and valleys of the Gila National Forest you'll also find elk, mule deer, and wild turkeys. Black bear also inhabit the area.

For those wanting to prolong their stay within this area, the national forest has developed several public campgrounds along the byway. Most of the campgrounds are set among the trees along bubbling streams or rivers. The Mesa and Upper End Campgrounds are situated on the shores of 75-acre Lake Roberts. Those interested in a more primitive setting are invited to explore the Gila Wilderness area and may camp anywhere they desire.

Nearby Routes

Lake Valley, page 251

Lodging Directory

Holiday Motor Hotel - Silver City, page 441 — Hotel / Motel
Silver City KOA Kampground - Silver City, page 441 — Campground / RV Park

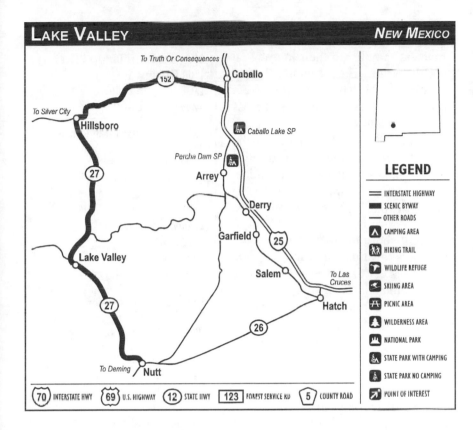

Route Location

The Lake Valley byway is located in southwestern New Mexico, 50 miles northwest of Las Cruces. The byway begins south of Caballo at Exit #63 on Interstate 25. The byway travels west to Hillsboro and then heads south to end at the intersection with New Mexico State Highway 26 in Nutt.

Roads Traveled

New Mexico State Highways 27 and 152 are the roads followed on this 44-mile scenic drive. The highways are narrow, two-lane paved roads safe for travel by all types of vehicles. The byway is officially designated a Type I Back Country Byway.

Travel Season

Both state highways are usually open all year. Several low water crossings are encountered along the byway. It is best not to attempt crossing these areas when water is present.

Description

Travelers may begin their journey on the Lake Valley Back Country Byway by taking the Hillsboro exit from I-25. From here the byway heads west across the desert landscape with views of distant Animas Peak and Black Peak to the north. Before reaching Hillsboro you'll see the remains of an open copper mine. You may want to spend some time in Hillsboro exploring the historic buildings.

From Hillsboro the byway turns south and heads towards the nearly deserted town of Lake Valley. The byway passes through mountain scrubland with stands of juniper and pinyon trees. This is an excellent area for spotting mule deer. Between Hillsboro and Lake Valley, you'll be following the route of the Kingston-Lake Valley Stage Line which ran through here during the 1880s. Soldiers were stationed in Hillsboro and Lake Valley to protect settlers from Apache attacks. Lake Valley was once a thriving mining town of over 4,000 inhabitants, not including wildlife. The devaluation of silver in 1893 led to the eventual decline of this town. A few historic structures remain, among them the schoolhouse which is still used by the locals for weddings and dances.

Once through Lake Valley the byway continues through the desert landscape with views of Monument Peak and Nutt Mountain. Wildlife inhabiting this area includes antelope, deer, roadrunners, red-tailed hawks, and coyotes. The byway ends in Nutt, originally a stop on the Atchison, Topeka, and Santa Fe Railway.

There are no public campgrounds along the byway, however, two state parks are near the byway's northern terminus. Caballo Lake State Park has 130 sites for tents and recreational vehicles, many with electrical hookups. The Percha Dam State Park has 60 sites, some also with hookups.

Nearby Routes

Inner Loop - Gila Cliff Dwellings, page 249

Local Information

BLM - Las Cruces District Office
1800 Marquess St.
Las Cruces, NM 88005
Phone: 505-525-4300

Hatch Valley Chamber of Commerce
224 Elm St.
Hatch, NM 87937
Phone: 505-267-5050

Truth or Consequences / Sierra County Chamber of Commerce
201 S. Foch St.
T or C, NM 87901
Phone: 800-831-9487

Caballo Lake State Park
Caballo, NM 87931
Phone: 505-743-3942

Percha Dam State Park
Caballo, NM 87901
Phone: 505-267-9394

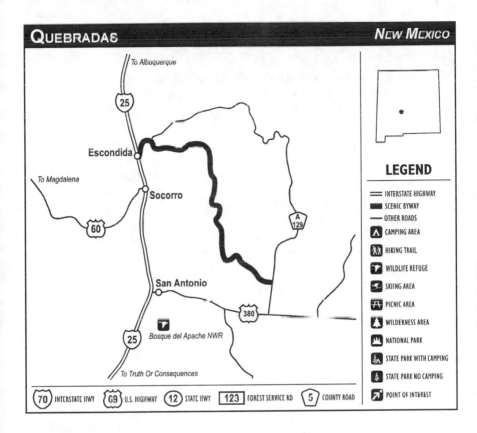

Route Location

The Quebradas Back Country Byway is approximately 75 miles south of Albuquerque in central New Mexico. The northern access is located off Interstate 25 in Escondida. The byway travels southeast to the junction of County Road A129, a few miles north of U.S. Highway 380.

Roads Traveled

The 24-mile route follows the Quebradas Road which is a dirt road requiring a two-wheel drive, high-clearance vehicle. A four-wheel drive vehicle is recommended during wet weather. The Quebradas is a BLM Type II Back Country Byway.

Travel Season

The route is normally open year-round but heavy rains can make the dry wash crossings impassable.

Description

The Quebradas Back Country Byway traverses a ruggedly scenic desert landscape east of the Rio Grande Valley. The byway crosses the Rio Grande River just east of Escondida. The river valley and surrounding area provides habitat for a variety of wildlife including mule deer, gray fox, coyote, bobcat, opossum, and jack rabbit. Bird watchers will need to be on the lookout for the red-tailed hawk, horned lark, snow goose, and sandhill crane. The endangered whooping crane may also be seen occasionally along the river.

The byway continues east of Escondida for several miles before turning south where it crosses several arroyos that drain into the Rio Grande

Local Information

BLM - Las Cruces District Office
1800 Marquess St.
Las Cruces, NM 88005
Phone: 505-525-4300

BLM - Socorro Resource Area
198 Neel Ave. NW
Socorro, NM 87801
Phone: 505-835-0412

Socorro County Chamber of Commerce
103 Francisco de Avondo
Socorro, NM 87801
Phone: 505-835-0424

Bosque del Apache NWR
P.O. Box 1246
Socorro, NM 87801
Phone: 505-835-1878

River. These crossings can contain deep pockets of sand and should not be crossed during or immediately following heavy rain. Views of the Loma de las Canas come into view as you continue driving southward. Near vertical, multi-colored cliffs and narrow box canyons dominate the view through here. This area provides excellent opportunities for exploring the back country on foot and is popular with hikers and back-packers.

To the south of the byway lies the 57,000-acre Bosque del Apache National Wildlife Refuge. Nearly 300 species of birds either inhabit this area or migrate through on a seasonal basis. The whooping crane has also made its presence known in this area.

Although there are no developed public campgrounds along the byway, the Bureau of Land Management permits camping nearly anywhere on BLM-managed land. To the west of the byway is the Cibola National Forest which offers public camping facilities.

Route Location

The Sandia Crest Road is about 23 miles northeast of downtown Albuquerque in central New Mexico. The byway begins at the junction of New Mexico State Highways 14 and 536. The scenic drives heads west across the Cibola National Forest and ends near the summit of Sandia Peak.

Roads Traveled

The 11-mile byway follows New Mexico State Highway 536 which is a two-lane paved road suitable for all vehicles although there are some sharp curves. Travelers will need to retrace the route back to either State Highway 165 or 14. The scenic drive is a National Forest Scenic Byway.

Travel Season

The Sandia Crest Road is usually open year-round. Winter driving conditions can be hazardous in the higher elevations. Chains or snow tires are sometimes required.

Description

The Sandia Crest Road climbs nearly 4,000 feet as it travels through the high desert and dense forests of the Sandia Mountains. The byway switchbacks up the mountain to 10,678-foot Sandia Crest where observation platforms provide spectacular panoramic views. Come nightfall, visitors are treated to a beautiful display of Albuquerque's twinkling city lights.

The Sandia Mountains are home to a variety of wildlife. Wildlife observers will want to keep a watchful eye for mule deer, golden eagles, or bighorn sheep. Mountain lions, bobcats, and black bear also inhabit the area but are rarely seen.

Local Information

Cibola National Forest
2113 Osuna Rd. NE, Suite A
Albuquerque, NM 87113
Phone: 505-761-4650

Cibola National Forest
Sandia Ranger District
11776 Highway 14 South
Tijeras, NM 87059
Phone: 505-281-3304

Greater Albuquerque C of C
401 Second St., N.W.
Albuquerque, NM 87125
Phone: 505-764-3700

South Valley Chamber of Commerce
1625 Rio Bravo Blvd. SW, #26-106
Albuquerque, NM 87105
Phone: 505-873-0551

Trailheads located along the byway provide access to the Sandia Mountain Wilderness. This 37,232-acre mountain wilderness provides excellent opportunities for hiking, backpacking, and horseback riding. The Crest Trail is a 28-mile hiking trail following the mountain ridgeline from Tijeras Canyon to Placitas.

Visitors to the Sandia Crest Road will find a lot of picnic areas that provide a good spot for relaxing a bit and enjoying a lunch or an early dinner. No public campgrounds have been developed along the byway, nor is car camping permitted. The nearest public campground is found in the Coronado State Park, approximately 20 miles west of the byway. There are 25 campsites here for tents and recreational vehicles. Shower facilities and electrical hookups are available.

Lodging Directory

Sandia Mountain Hostel - Cedar Crest, page 454 — Hostel

Route Location

Located in north-central New Mexico in Santa Fe. The southern access is in downtown Santa Fe at the corner of Palace and Washington Avenues. The scenic byway travels northeast to the road's end near the Santa Fe Ski Area.

Roads Traveled

The Santa Fe scenic byway is a 15-mile drive following New Mexico State Highway 475 which is a narrow two-lane paved road with sharp curves and steep grades. Caution should be used by all drivers. The byway also follows Washington Avenue in Santa Fe north to the intersection with State Highway 475. Travelers will need to retrace the route back to Santa Fe. The byway is designated a National Forest Scenic Byway.

Travel Season

The entire route is open year-round although winter driving conditions can be hazardous and temporary delays are possible for snow removal.

Description

The scenic byway begins near the historic Palace of the Governors. This adobe structure was built in 1610 by the Spanish government and is the oldest continuously occupied public building in the United States. From this point, drive north on Washington Ave. for several blocks and then turn east on Artist Road which is also State Hwy. 475.

Once you're on SH 475, the byway begins climbing the Sangre de Cristo Mountains. You first pass through picturesque Tesuque Canyon and then enter dense stands of ponderosa pine which eventually give way to the mixed conifer and apsen forests at the 10,400-foot level of the ski area.

A trailhead for the Winsor Trail is at the byway's end and provides access to the Pecos Wilderness. Numerous other trails can be found at the campgrounds and picnic areas along the byway, all offering the opportunity for a short walk among the trees or a more intense backpacking journey.

Local Information

Santa Fe National Forest
1220 St. Francis Dr.
Santa Fe, NM 87504
Phone: 505-988-6940

Santa Fe National Forest
Espanola Ranger District
P.O. Drawer R
Espanola, NM 87532
Phone: 505-753-7331

Santa Fe County Chamber of Commerce
P.O. Box 1928
Santa Fe, NM 87504
Phone: 505-983-7317

Hyde State Park
State Rt. 475
Santa Fe, NM 87504
Phone: 505-983-7175

Santa Fe Ski Area
1210 Luisa St.
Santa Fe, NM 87505
Phone: 505-983-9155

Camping areas are not in short supply along this scenic byway. The national forest maintains 3 campgrounds and the New Mexico State Parks and Recreation Department offers the Hyde State Park for byway travelers. The state park offers nearly 400 acres of land completely surrounded by national forest land. There are 45 campsites available with picnic tables and fire rings. Some sites have electrical hookups. The Black Canyon Campground is the next largest campground with 41 sites. Hookups are also available at many of the campsites. Big Tesuque and Aspen Basin Campgrounds are a little more primitive but offer a total of 17 campsites with picnic tables. Neither campground has drinking water or hookups.

Lodging Directory

Residence Inn by Marriott - Santa Fe, page 454 — Hotel / Motel

SUNSPOT   NEW MEXICO

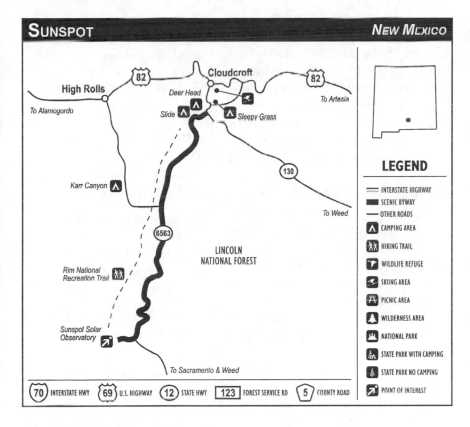

Route Location

The Sunspot scenic drive is located in south-central New Mexico, approximately 85 miles east of Las Cruces. The northern terminus is located off U.S. Highway 82 a couple of miles south of Cloudcroft. The byway travels south across the Lincoln National Forest to its end at the Sunspot Solar Observatory.

Roads Traveled

The byway follows New Mexico State Highway 6563 which is a two-lane paved road suitable for all vehicles. The 14-mile scenic drive has been officially designated a National Forest Scenic Byway.

Travel Season

State Highway 6563 is normally open all year.

Description

Traversing the Lincoln National Forest, the Sunspot scenic byway travels along the front rim of the Sacramento Mountains through a mixed forest of Douglas-fir, white fir, Southwestern white pine, ponderosa pine, and aspen. Mule deer, black bears, elk, and the occasional eagle and spotted owl can be seen from the byway. Turnouts along the route provide spectacular views of the Tularosa Basin and the shifting sand dunes of the nearby White Sands National Monument. On a clear day you can see the space port for the landing of the space shuttle.

Local Information

Lincoln National Forest
1101 New York Ave.
Alamogoroo, NM 88310
Phone: 505-437-6030

Alamogordo Chamber of Commerce
P.O. Box 518
Alamogordo, NM 88310
Phone: 505-437-6120

Cloudcroft Chamber of Commerce
P.O. Box 1290
Cloudcroft, NM 88317
Phone: 505-682-2733

In the fall, the aspen and maple-covered canyons and hillsides to the west of the byway display brilliant colors of yellow, orange, and red.

At the byway's southern end is the Sunspot Solar Observatory. There are two research facilities open to the public, the Vacuum Tower Telescope and the John W. Evans Solar Facility. The Vacuum Tower Telescope is the largest of the telescopes located hear. Over 200 feet of this telescope is buried beneath the surface of Sacramento Peak. The John W. Evans Solar Facility is used for studying the sun's surface.

There are several scenic turnouts along the byway that not only provide panoramic vistas of the surrounding landscape, but also opportunities for taking a break and enjoying a picnic under the shade of a tree. Those that enjoy hiking will find 13 miles of the Rim National Recreation Trail running alongside the byway. The many side roads off the byway also invite exploration by the hiker or mountain biker.

If you're interested in staying overnight or longer, the national forest has developed several campgrounds that should provide just the right spot. The campgrounds provide sites for tents and recreational vehicles, however, no hookups are provided. All of the campsites have picnic tables and fire rings. Most of the campgrounds have drinking water and restrooms.

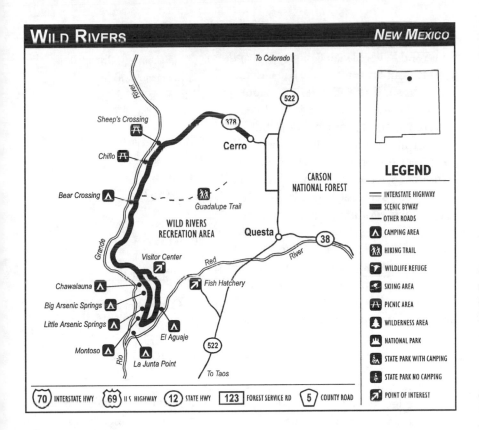

Route Location

The Wild Rivers scenic drive is located in north-central New Mexico, about 25 miles north of Taos and 17 miles south of the Colorado state line. The scenic byway begins in the town of Cerro which is west of New Mexico State Highway 522. The byway then travels south along the Rio Grande River through the Wild Rivers Recreation Area.

Roads Traveled

The 13-mile byway follows the Wild Rivers Road also known as New Mexico State Highway 378 which is a two-lane paved road safe for travel by all types of vehicles. The Wild Rivers drive is a BLM Type I Back Country Byway.

Travel Season

The scenic byway is generally open year-round, however, the road is not maintained during the winter and heavy snows may restrict access.

Description

The Wild Rivers Back Country Byway is a pleasant drive along the Rio Grande River around the Guadalupe Mountains. The byway crosses a landscape covered with sagebrush and stands of pinyon and juniper. The byway will take you to a point overlooking the confluence of the Rio Grande River and Red River 800 feet beneath you. The Guadalupe Mountains rise above the desert floor to the east of you. A hiking trail can be accessed from the byway that will take you deep into these rugged mountains. Several scenic overlooks are also provided along the byway that give you the chance to gaze at the river flowing way down below.

There are trails along the byway that will take you down the gorge to the river's edge. Here you may wish to cast a line in hopes of finding a brown trout attached to the other end. There are campgrounds located along the river's edge if you discover that you need to spend some more time trying to pull the fish from the water.

Those not interested in fishing can spend the day looking for wildlife. There are plenty of species inhabiting this area. Mule deer can often be seen along the roadside foraging among the grass. Red-tailed hawks and turkey vultures may be spotted flying over the canyon rims, almost effortlessly floating upon the wind currents. The cold winter snows force the beautiful elk from the higher elevations to the lower elevations in search of food.

Visitors to the byway will find plenty of opportunities for pitching a tent or parking your recreational vehicle. Some of the campgrounds are situated on the rim of the gorge, while others are located along the river's edge. Campfire programs are offered from Memorial Day through Labor Day.

Local Information

BLM - Albuquerque District Office
435 Montano Rd. NE
Albuquerque, NM 87107
Phone: 505-761-8700

BLM - Taos Resource Area
224 Cruz Alta Rd.
Taos, NM 87571
Phone: 505-758-8851

Carson National Forest
P.O. Box 558
Taos, NM 87571
Phone: 505-758-6200

Taos County Chamber of Commerce
1139 Paseo del Pueblo Sur
Taos, NM 87571
Phone: 800-732-8267

Nearby Routes

Enchanted Circle, page 245 / Los Caminos Antiguos, page 128

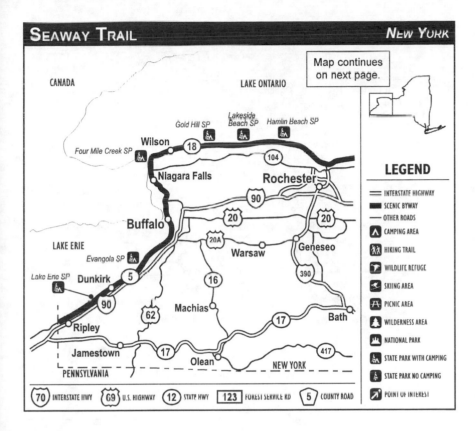

Route Location

The Seaway Trail follows the shoreline of Lake Erie and Lake Ontario as it travels from the southwest corner of New York to the state's northeastern region. The byway begins at the Pennsylvania-New York state line near the town of Ripley and travels northeasterly to Rooseveltown.

Roads Traveled

The Seaway Trail is a 454-mile scenic drive that follows a series of two-lane paved roads that are suitable for travel by all types of vehicles. For a detailed listing of the routes followed, please see the sidebar titled "Following The Seaway Trail." The entire route is designated a New York State Scenic Byway and a National Scenic Byway.

Travel Season

The roads followed along this route are generally open year-round, however, winter driving conditions may call for extra caution.

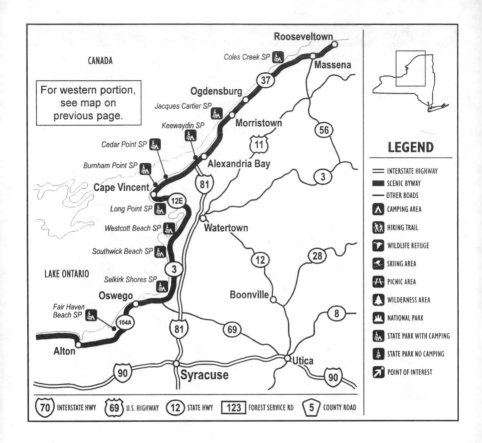

Description

The 454-mile route of the Seaway Trail travels along the shores of New York's Great Lakes, the Niagara River, and St. Lawrence River, connecting quaint villages, historic sites, picturesque bays, and rolling farmland. The route is a part of the National Park Service's National Recreational Trail system and is the longest such trail in the United States. Several scenic overlooks offer spectacular views of the Great Lakes.

During the months of September and October, the Seaway Trail is ablaze with fall colors of red, orange, and gold. Fall foliage tours can be taken by car, boat, floatplane, and train. Farmer's markets and roadside stands offer autumn's harvest of fruits and vegetables, or you may desire to pick your own.

The winter months bring cross-country skiers and snowmobilers to the trail. Miles of well groomed trails are found all along the route. Niagara Falls celebrates the season with its Festival of Lights illuminating the majestic waterfalls. In February, visitors can enjoy a frosty hot air balloon ride at the Thousand Island Winter Balloon Festival in Clayton. Farther north along the trail, the Ogensburg "River Shiver" reenacts its War of 1812 battle history.

Fishing opportunities are plentiful along the scenic drive. Both warm and coldwater fish make their home along the Seaway Trail. Fishermen will find bass, walleye, muskellunge, Atlantic and Pacific salmon, brown and rainbow trout, northern pike, and a variety of exotic species. Guides are available for hire that will take you onto the waters of Lake Erie or Lake Ontario.

For those interested in camping, there are many state parks and privately owned campgrounds along the route that accommodate all types of camping interests—tents, recreational vehicles, cottages, and cabins. New York's state parks also offer hiking trails and picnic areas in addition to fishing, boating, and swimming opportunities. Some state parks offer interpretive sites of historical significance. History buffs will find 42 historical markers along the route providing information of events that occurred along the trail in the War of 1812. Historic lighthouses can also be found along the drive.

Lodging Directory

The Vineyard Motel - Dunkirk, page 455 — Hotel / Motel

Local Information

Seaway Trail, Inc.
Madison Barracks
109 Barracks Drive
Sackets Harbor, NY 13685
Phone: 800-SEAWAY-T

Northern Chautauqua C of C
212 Lake Shore Dr.
Dunkirk, NY 14048
Phone: 716-366-6200

Greater Buffalo Chamber of Commerce
300 Main Place Tower
Buffalo, NY 14202
Phone: 716-852-7100

Niagara Falls Area Chamber of Commerce
345 Third St., #500
Niagara Falls, NY 14303
Phone: 716-285-9141

Eastern Niagara Chamber of Commerce
151 W. Genesee St.
Lockport, NY 14094
Phone: 716-433-3828

Greater Rochester Metro C of C
55 St. Paul St.
Rochester, NY 14624
Phone: 716-454-2220

Greater Oswego Chamber of Commerce
P.O. Box 3046
Oswego, NY 13126
Phone: 315-343-7681

Cape Vincent Chamber of Commerce
P.O. Box 482
Cape Vincent, NY 13618
Phone: 315-654-2481

Following the Seaway Trail

Beginning at the Pennsylvania - New York state line near the town of Ripley, the Seaway Trail follows State Route 5 in a northeasterly direction toward the village of Silver Creek to a point where Route 5 merges with U.S. Highway 20.

The trail continues along Routes 5 and 20 to the community of Irving, where the trail leaves the routes and then follows the Old Lake Shore Road, running roughly along the Lake Erie shoreline, to the community of Wanakah.

At Wanakah, the trail picks up State Route 5 again and continues northeasterly and then northerly to the city of Lackawanna and proceeds across the Skyway to the Delaware Avenue exit.

The trail then follows Delaware Avenue to Niagara Square in the city of Buffalo and then around Niagara Square to Niagara Street and along Niagara Street to the River Road, State Route 265.

The trail continues along the River Road, Route 265 through the cities of Tonawanda and North Tonawanda to Buffalo Avenue. Following Buffalo Avenue, the trail then turns onto the westbound lanes of the Robert Moses State Parkway until it reaches the Quay Street exit in the city of Niagara Falls.

Local Information

Alexandria Bay Chamber of Commerce
P.O. Box 365
Alexandria Bay, NY 13607
Phone: 315-482-9531

Greater Ogdensburg C of C
1020 Park St.
Ogdensburg, NY 13669
Phone: 315-393-3620

Greater Massena Chamber of Commerce
P.O. Box 387
Massena, NY 13662
Phone: 315-769-3525

Many of New York's 150 state parks are located along and near the Seaway Trail. For a free copy of "New York State Parks Guide" contact the address listed below. The guide describes each area, contains a locator map, and includes information on facilities and activities.

Office of Parks, Recreation & Historic Preservation
Empire State Plaza
Agency Building 1
Albany, NY 12238
Phone: 518-474-0456

The trail then leaves the Robert Moses State Parkway and follows Quay Street until it reaches Rainbow Boulevard. The trail then continues northerly along Rainbow Boulevard, being State Route 384, until it intersects with Niagara Street.

The trail then turns westerly onto Niagara Street and continues until it reaches the Rainbow Bridge. From the Rainbow Bridge in the city of Niagara Falls, the trail follows State Route 104E to the community of Lewiston, where the trail intersects with Route 18F.

Following the Seaway Trail *cont.*

The trail continues along Route 18F until it merges into State Route 18. Following Route 18, the trail passes the villages of Roosevelt Beach, Olcott, Ashwood and Kuckville. Once inside Lakeside Beach State Park, the trail leaves route 18 and follows Lake Ontario State Parkway. In the town of Irondequoit, Lake Ontario State Parkway joins with Stutson Street. The trail then follows Stutson Street, turns right onto Saint Paul Boulevard, then left onto Lake Shore Boulevard.

The trail continues east on Lake Shore Boulevard to Culver Road. The trail then turns right onto Culver Road, then left onto Empire Boulevard, State Route 104, then left onto Bay Road and then right onto Lake Road. The trail follows Lake Road through the community of Pultneyville and continues to the village of Sodus Point.

At Sodus Point, the trail bears south on State Route 14 to Alton, where it intersects Ridge Road. Following Ridge Road, the trail passes through the villages of Resort and Wolcott. Once outside of Wolcott, the trail picks up Old Ridge Road until it reaches the village of Red Creek. There it joins State Route 104A.

The trail continues north on Route 104A through the village of Fair Haven, Sterling and Southwest Oswego to the city of Oswego, then north on State Route 104 through the community of Scriba to State Route 104B. Proceeding north through the community of Texas, the trail follows Route 104B to the intersection with State Route 3. There it joins Route 3 north through Port Ontario, and roughly parallel to the Lake Ontario shoreline.

At Baggs Corners, the trail picks up State Route 180 and travels north through the village of Dexter to the intersection of State Route 12E at Limerick. The trail then follows Route 12E west through the village of Chaumont to the village of Cape Vincent, and north along the St. Lawrence River to Clayton where it connects with State Route 12 north.

The trail follows Route 12 past the village of Alexandria Bay, Chippewa Bay and Oak Point. Near Morristown, the trail joins State Route 37 north to the city of Ogdensburg. The trail follows State Route 124 onto the state arterial, then north on State street (State Routes 68/87), and then east on Washington street. The trail turns onto North Rossell street, then left on Ford street. The trail turns left onto Proctor Avenue, then turns right onto State Route 812 and south to State Route 37.

After passing through the village of Waddington, the trail continues on 37 through the town of Louisville, connecting by a left turn onto State Route 131. The trail turns right at the intersection of Tunnel Road, still on Route 131. At the junction with County Route 42, the trail continues straight over the Grass River Bridge to the junction with State Route 37 north. The trail turns left onto Route 37 north to the trail's northern terminus at the Rooseveltown International Bridge to Canada.

BLUE RIDGE PARKWAY   NORTH CAROLINA

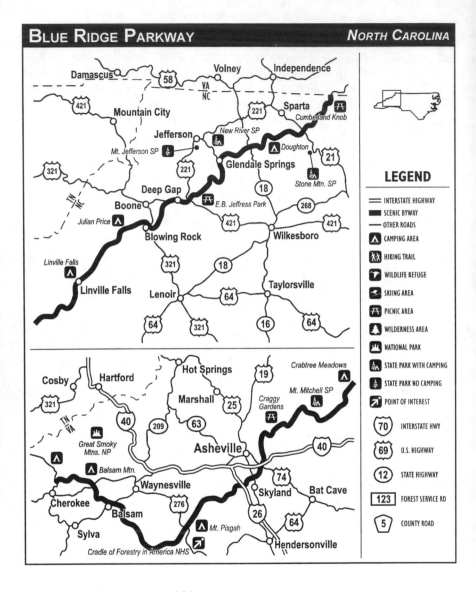

Virginia section see page 383

Route Location

The Blue Ridge Parkway is a 469-mile drive between Shenandoah National Park in Virginia and the Great Smoky Mountains National Park in North Carolina. This portion of the parkway is in western North Carolina, traveling north and south between the Virginia state line and Great

Smoky Mountains National Park.

Roads Traveled

The Blue Ridge Parkway is a two-lane paved route that is suitable for travel by most types of vehicles. Portions of the route travel through small tunnels cut into the rock and may prohibit trailer traffic. The entire byway is designated a National Parkway by the National Park Service. The North Carolina portion of the byway is 252 miles in length and has also been designated an All-American Road by the Federal Highway Administration.

Travel Season

The route is generally open year-round, however, from November through mid-April portions of the byway may be closed due to snow and ice.

Description

The Blue Ridge Parkway follows the Appalachian Mountain chain, twisting and turning through the beautiful mountains. From the Shenandoah National Park, the scenic drive travels along the Blue Ridge Mountains for 355 miles. Then, for the remaining 114 miles, it skirts the southern end of the Black Mountains, weaves through the Craggies, the Pisgahs, and the Balsams before finally ending in the Great Smokies. The Blue Ridge Parkway was authorized in 1933 and became a unit of the National Park Service in 1936.

Local Information

National Park Service
Blue Ridge Parkway
200 BB&T Building, One Park Square
Asheville, NC 28801
Phone: 704-271-4779

Pisgah National Forest
National Forests in North Carolina
P.O. Box 2750
Asheville, NC 28802
Phone: 704-257-4203

Cherokee Chamber of Commerce
P.O. Box 460
Cherokee, NC 28719
Phone: 704-497-9195

Haywood County Chamber of Commerce
107 Woodland Dr.
Waynesville, NC 28786
Phone: 704-456-3021

Asheville Area Chamber of Commerce
151 Haywood St.
Asheville, NC 28802
Phone: 704-258-6101

Blowing Rock Chamber of Commerce
P.O. Box 406
Blowing Rock, NC 28605
Phone: 704-295-7851

Boone Area Chamber of Commerce
208 Howard St.
Boone, NC 28607
Phone: 704-264-2225

Alleghany County Chamber of Commerce
P.O. Box 1237
Sparta, NC 28675
Phone: 910-372-5473

The North Carolina portion of the Blue Ridge Parkway is a beautiful drive from the Virginia state line to the Great Smoky Mountains National Park. Cumberland Knob is the first stopping point when traveling the route from north to south. This is a good spot to walk through fields and woodlands on a loop trail to Cumberland Knob or enjoy a picnic lunch. A longer trail here will take you into Gully Creek Gorge. Allow 2 hours to complete the walk. A visitor center is also located here and has information on the parkway.

Doughton Park, located near the northern end of the route, is a 7,000-acre recreation area with miles of hiking trails. Those interested in staying overnight will find camping facilities for tents and trailers in addition to a lodge, complete with food service and gasoline. Picnicking facilities can also be found here.

Another large recreation area is the 4,344-acre Julian Price Memorial Park. Camping, picnicking, fishing, and hiking are among the recreational opportunities here. Located just north of this park is the Moses H. Cone Memorial Park which has many miles of horse and carriage trails. The historic Cone Manor House and Parkway Craft Center are also located near here.

The National Park Service has also developed several smaller recreation areas along the byway. At the Linville Falls Recreation Area, visitors will find a walking trail that leads to overlooks of the scenic falls. The falls plummet through a dramatic, rugged gorge, an area that was donated to the parkway by John D. Rockefeller. Visitors will also find camping and picnicking facilities here. A visitor center is also here.

Local Information

Mt. Mitchell State Park
Route 5, Box 700
Burnsville, NC 28714
Phone: 704-675-4611

New River State Park
P.O. Box 48
Jefferson, NC 28640
Phone: 910-982-2587

Mt. Jefferson State Park
1481 Mt. Jefferson SP Road
West Jefferson, NC 28694
Phone: 910-246-9653

Stone Mtn. State Park
2643 Stone Mtn. Rd.
Roaring Gap, NC 28668
Phone: 910-957-8185

Cradle of Forestry in America NHS
100 S. Broad St.
Brevard, NC 28712
Phone: 704-884-5713

Great Smoky Mountains National Park
107 Park Headquarters Rd.
Gatlinburg, TN 37738
Phone: 615-436-1220

Crabtree Meadows is a 250-acre recreation area that is painted a beautiful pink in the spring. A picnic area provides a pleasant setting for enjoying a lunch. Scenic waterfalls can be reached by taking a walk on a short hiking trail. Visitors will also find a campground here.

The Blue Ridge Parkway ends at the Great Smoky Mountains National Park. The park preserves over 500,000 acres of the heavily forested Appalachian Mountains. For hikers, the Appalachian Trail runs through the park as do numerous other trails. Visitors will also find short, self-guided nature trails. There are 10 developed camping areas in the park. The campgrounds have tent sites, limited trailer space, drinking water, fire rings, picnic tables, and restrooms. No hookups or shower facilities are provided.

Fall is a special time of the year to be traveling the Blue Ridge Parkway. Dogwood, sourwood, and blackgum turn a deep red in late September. Tulip-trees and hickories turn bright yellow, sassafras a vivid orange. The various oak trees add russet and maroon while the red maples proudly display their fall colors. All of this vivid color is set against a backdrop of the evergreen Virginia pine, white pine, hemlock, spruce, and fir.

Wildlife is abundant along the route. Woodchucks, chipmunks, raccoon, and opossum are the more commonly seen among the wildlife, however, white-tailed deer and black bears are also present in the woods.

Nearby Routes

Forest Heritage, page 272 / Cherohala Skyway, page 332 / Mount Rogers, page 390

LODGING DIRECTORY

Chestnut Street Inn - Asheville, page 431 — Bed & Breakfast / Inns
Lindridge House - Blowing Rock, page 432 — Bed & Breakfast / Inns
Maple Lodge - Blowing Rock, page 432 — Bed & Breakfast / Inns
Oak Park Inn - Waynesville, page 432 — Hotel / Motel
Stone Pillar Bed & Breakfast - Blowing Rock, page 432 — Bed & Breakfast / Inns
Sunset Motel - Brevard, page 433 — Hotel / Motel

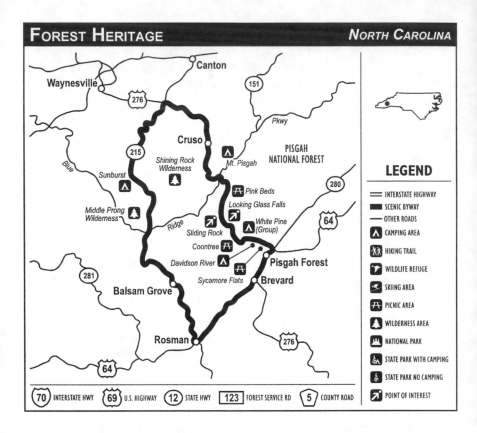

Route Location

The Forest Heritage scenic byway is located in western North Carolina, about 30 miles southwest of Asheville. The byway forms a loop drive through the Pisgah National Forest. Byway travelers can begin their scenic journey at the forest visitor center near the junction of U.S. Highway 64 and North Carolina Highway 280.

Roads Traveled

The 79-mile route follows North Carolina State Highway 215 and U.S. Highways 276 and 64 which are two-lane paved roads suitable for all types of vehicles. The byway is a National Forest Scenic Byway.

Travel Season

The roads followed are normally open year-round although occasional snow and ice may require the use of chains.

Description

The Forest Heritage scenic byway crosses the spruce and fir-covered mountains of the Pisgah National Forest. Many beautiful rivers and streams flow alongside the byway. Scenic waterfalls can be seen along the byway such as the Looking Glass Falls which tumble 60 feet to the creek below.

Adjacent to the Pink Beds Picnic Area is the Cradle of Forestry in America, a National Historic Site commemorating the birthplace of scientific forestry and forestry education in America. The area offers a visitor center with exhibits and historical film, gift shop, snack bar, and two interpretive trails. The 1-mile paved Biltmore Forest School Campus Trail leads visitors to reconstructed and restored buildings used by forestry students at the turn of the century. The other trail, Forest Festival Trail, features early 1900s exhibits including a 1915 Climax logging locomotive and a steam-powered sawmill. The historical site is open May through October from 10:00 a.m. to 6:00 p.m.

Campgrounds along the byway provide the perfect spot for staying overnight or longer. The Davidson River Campground offers 161 sites for tents and recreational vehicles. It is recommend that reservations for a campsite be made at least two weeks in advance. Sunburst is a smaller campground situated on the banks of the West Fork of the Pigeon River. There are 10 sites available here. The White Pine camping area is a group campground that can accomodate groups of 25 or less.

Sliding Rock is a 60-foot smooth rock natural waterslide. You can watch others slide into the pool of cold water or take part in the activity.

Nearby Routes

Blue Ridge Parkway, page 268 / Oscar Wigington, page 324

LODGING DIRECTORY

Oak Park Inn - Waynesville, page 439 — Hotel / Motel
Sunset Motel - Brevard, page 439 — Hotel / Motel

Local Information

Pisgah National Forest
Pisgah Ranger District
1001 Pisgah Hwy.
Pisgah Forest, NC 28768
Phone: 704-877-3350

Brevard - Transylvania C of C
35 W. Main St.
Brevard, NC 28712
Phone: 704-883-3700

Haywood County Chamber of Commerce
P.O. Drawer 600
Waynesville, NC 28786
Phone: 704-456-3021

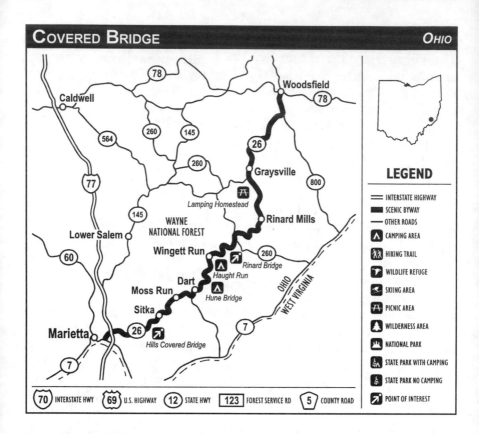

LEGEND

▬▬▬ INTERSTATE HIGHWAY
▬ SCENIC BYWAY
— OTHER ROADS
🅰 CAMPING AREA
🚶 HIKING TRAIL
🦌 WILDLIFE REFUGE
🎿 SKIING AREA
🍽 PICNIC AREA
🌲 WILDERNESS AREA
🏛 NATIONAL PARK
🏕 STATE PARK WITH CAMPING
🌲 STATE PARK NO CAMPING
↗ POINT OF INTEREST

70 INTERSTATE HWY   69 U.S. HIGHWAY   12 STATE HWY   123 FOREST SERVICE RD   5 COUNTY ROAD

Route Location

Covered Bridge scenic byway is located in southeastern Ohio, east of Marietta near the West Virginia border. The byway begins at the junction of Ohio State Highways 7 and 26, east of downtown Marietta. The byway travels northeasterly across the Wayne National Forest to its end in the town of Woodsfield.

Roads Traveled

The Covered Bridge scenic drive follows Ohio State Highway 26 which is a narrow, two-lane paved road suitable for most vehicles. All but 3 miles of the 47-mile byway has been designated a National Forest Scenic Byway.

Travel Season

The entire route is normally open year-round.

Description

The Covered Bridge scenic drive winds through the pretty hills and valleys of southeastern Ohio as it travels across the Wayne National Forest. The waters of the Little Muskingum River flow alongside much of the byway and provide good fishing and canoeing. Wildlife that may be seen along the byway includes white-tailed deer, turkeys, beavers, red foxes, raccoons, and minks. This scenic byway is especially beautiful when driven in the fall when the route is covered with brilliant colors of red, orange, and yellow. You'll want to visit the Forest Service office in Marietta before taking this byway to pick up a brochure that highlights 10 points of interest along the way.

Local Information

Wayne-Hoosier National Forest
Marietta Field Office
Rt. I - Box 132
Marietta, OH 45750
Phone: 614-373-9055

Marietta Area Chamber of Commerce
316 Third St.
Marietta, OH 45750
Phone: 614-373-5176

Monroe County Chamber of Commerce
P.O. Box 643
Woodsfield, OH 43793
Phone: 614-472-5499

Ohio once boasted of 2,000 covered bridges, more than any other state. As you travel this byway, you'll come across three of these historical bridges. These bridges were covered with a roof not to protect travelers from the elements of weather, but to keep the main structural timbers dry. If left exposed to rain, the timber would quickly rot.

Visitors to the Covered Bridge scenic byway will find two national forest campgrounds. The Hune Bridge area has only two campsites with picnic tables. The Haught Run Recreation Area has three campsites. No drinking water is available at either campground.

The many rivers and streams within the national forest provide excellent opportunities for fishing. Anglers will find a large variety of fish including largemouth bass, smallmouth bass, bluegill, catfish, and crappie. The rivers also provide pleasant canoe trips. Outfitters can provide you with all that you need to enjoy a leisurely float down the river.

If you feel like stretching your legs a bit, you can catch the North Country National Scenic Trail from the byway. This portion of the trail winds through the national forest between Woodsfield and the Hune Covered Bridge.

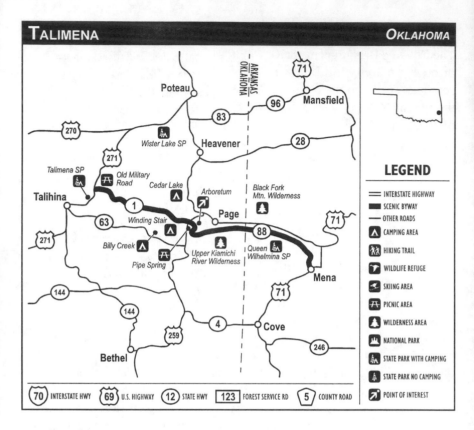

Route Location

The Talimena scenic byway is located in southeastern Oklahoma and southwestern Arkansas. The western access is located off U.S. Highway 271 north of Talihina which is about 70 miles southwest of Fort Smith, Arkansas. The byway travels east across the Ouachita National Forest to end in Mena, Arkansas which is about 82 miles south of Fort Smith.

Roads Traveled

The 54-mile route follows Oklahoma State Highway 1 and Arkansas State Highway 88. The routes are two-lane paved roads with some steep grades and sharp curves, but are suitable for all vehicles. The entire route has been designated a National Forest Scenic Byway.

Travel Season

The route is generally open year-round although occasional winter snows can close the byway temporarily for snow removal.

Description

The Talimena scenic byway rides atop the forested Ouachita Mountains, one of America's oldest land masses. These mountains are unique because they stretch east to west rather than north and south. The byway also cuts through the 26,445-acre Winding Stair Mountain National Recreation Area. Several scenic turnouts are located along the route providing beautiful panoramic views of the surrounding wilderness. Side roads shooting off the byway invite the traveler to further explore these heavily forested mountains. Wildflowers in spring proudly display their colors while autumn, not to be outdone, also puts on its own beautiful display.

The Talimena scenic drive offers unlimited opportunities for outdoor recreation. Wilderness areas adjacent to the byway offer seclusion for hikers, backpackers, and horseback riders. Also popular with the hiker or backpacker is the Ouachita National Recreation Trail which can be accessed from the byway.

Local Information

Ouachita National Forest
P.O. Box 1270
Hot Springs, AR 71902
Phone: 501-321-5202

Talihina Chamber of Commerce
P.O. Box 548
Talihina, OK 74571
Phone: 918-567-3434

Heavener Chamber of Commerce
600 W. First St.
Heavener, OK 74937
Phone: 918-653-4303

Mena / Polk County C of C
524 Sherwood Ave.
Mena, AR 71953
Phone: 501-394-2912

Talimena State Park
Talihina, OK 74571
Phone: 918-567-2052

Queen Wilhelmina State Park
3877 Hwy. 88 West
Mena, AR 71953
Phone: 501-394-2863

Several national forest campgrounds are located along or a short drive off the byway. Cedar Lake Campground is one of the larger camping areas. It is situated on the shores of the 90-acre lake and offers 98 sites for tents or recreational vehicles. Some of the sites have water and electrical hookups. The campground also provides drinking water, restrooms, a boat ramp, shower facilities, hiking trails, fishing, and swimming. This area also provides hundreds of miles of horseback riding trails. The Billy Creek Campground is a short drive off the byway and has 11 units. The Winding Stair Campground is located along the byway and provides 26 campsites with picnic tables. Drinking water and restrooms are also provided.

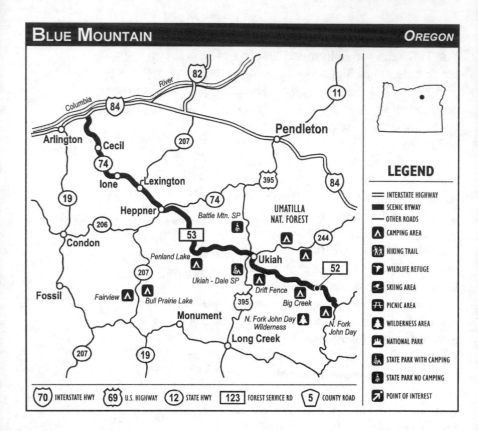

Route Location

The Blue Mountain byway is located in northeastern Oregon. The byway's northern terminus can be reached by taking Exit #147 on Interstate 84, approximately 62 miles west of Pendleton. The byway then travels south, ending at the intersection with Forest Service Road 73 in the Umatilla National Forest which is part of the Elkhorn Drive scenic byway.

Roads Traveled

The byway is about 130 miles long and follows Oregon State Highway 74 and Forest Service Roads 52 and 53. All of the roads are two-lane paved roads suitable for all types of vehicles. The route is designated a National Forest Scenic Byway.

Travel Season

Most of the byway is open all year long. The portion running through the national forest is usually open from May through mid-November and then closed the rest of the year due to snow.

Description

The Blue Mountain byway begins on the southern bank of the mighty Columbia River and climbs south through rolling grasslands alongside the tumbling waters of Willow Creek. The landscape changes dramatically as you climb up the Blue Mountains through forests of pine and fir, separated by valleys and meadows covered with wildflowers. Wildlife observers will want to be looking for white-tailed deer and bighorn sheep. Other wildlife found here includes mountain lions, black bears, an occasional bald eagle, and numerous species of songbirds.

Historic Oregon Trail crosses the byway near the community of Cecil. In the mid-1800s wagon trains wore deep ruts in the land as more pioneers moved westward. Evidence of the Oregon Trail wagon wheel ruts can be seen near Wells Spring 13 miles east of Cecil.

Visitors to the byway will find plenty of opportunities for outdoor recreation. The Ukiah-Dale State Park is situated on the banks of Camas Creek and offers 25 campsites for tents. The park also provides picnic tables and drinking water. Umatilla National Forest offers numerous campgrounds directly along or a short distance from the byway. Three small campgrounds are near the byway's eastern terminus. Drift Fence has three sites for tent camping, Big Creek has two. There are five sites suitable for either tents or recreational vehicles at the North Fork John Day Campground. None of the campgrounds have drinking water.

Nearby Routes

Elkhorn Drive, page 288

Local Information

Umatilla National Forest
2517 SW Hailey Ave.
Pendleton, OR 97801
Phone: 541-278-3716

Arlington Chamber of Commerce
P.O. Box 2000
Arlington, OR 97812
Phone: 541-454-2143

Heppner Chamber of Commerce
P.O. Box 1232
Heppner, OR 97836
Phone: 541-676-5536

Condon Chamber of Commerce
P.O. Box 315
Condon, OR 97823
Phone: 541-384-2421

Pendleton Chamber of Commerce
25 SE Dorin
Pendleton, OR 97801
Phone: 541-276-7411

Oregon Parks & Rec. Dept.
1115 Commercial St. NE
Salem, OR 97310
Phone: 503-378-6305

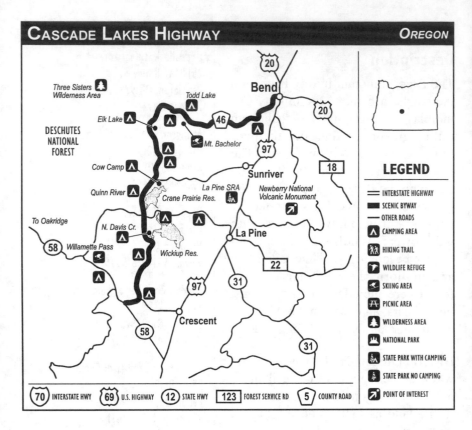

Route Location

The Cascade Lakes Highway is located in central Oregon. The byway begins in Bend at the intersection of Galveston Avenue and 14th Street. The byway heads west from there and then south across the Deschutes National Forest to its end at the intersection with State Highway 58.

Roads Traveled

The byway is approximately 79 miles in length and follows County Road 46 which is a two-lane paved road suitable for all types of vehicles. The route is designated a National Forest Scenic Byway.

Travel Season

The portion of the route from Bend to the Mt. Bachelor Ski and Summer Resort is usually open year-round. The remaining portion is closed by heavy winter snows.

Description

The scenic byway travels through the Deschutes National Forest offering magnificent views of snow-covered peaks of the Cascade Mountain Range. The byway travels through dense forests of pine and fir, skirting the shores of numerous mountain lakes. Wildlife observers will want to be on the lookout for mule deer, bald eagles, and a variety of hawks. This area is also inhabited by black bear.

The 200,000-acre Three Sisters Wilderness lies northwest of the byway. This pristine wilderness area offers over 100 alpine lakes for excellent fishing opportunities. The wilderness is also home to Collier Glacier, Oregon's largest glacier which is located on the North Sister mountain peak. Trailheads are found along the byway that lead into this unspoiled wilderness area. Since the wilderness is closed to all forms of motorized transportation, it is an excellent area for those seeking solitude, whether on foot or horseback.

Local Information

Deschutes National Forest
1645 Hwy. 20 East
Bend, OR 97701
Phone: 541-388-2715

Bend Chamber of Commerce
63085 N. Hwy. 97
Bend, OR 97701
Phone: 541-382-3221

Sunriver Area Chamber of Commerce
P.O. Box 3246
Sunriver, OR 97707
Phone: 541-593-8149

La Pine Chamber of Commerce
P.O. Box 616
La Pine, OR 97739
Phone: 541-536-9771

La Pine State Recreation Area
Oregon Parks & Recreation Dept.
20310 Empire Ave., Suite B1
Bend, OR 97701
Phone: 541-388-6211

Those interested in pitching a tent or parking an RV should not have any problem finding a spot as their are hundreds of campsites available. Most of the national forest campgrounds have drinking water and restrooms available. Some have shower facilities, however, none have electrical hookups. Boat ramps at many of the campgrounds provide access to the lakes. The La Pine State Recreation Area offers 145 campsites, 95 with full hookups and 50 with electrical. The recreation area also has drinking water, shower facilities, a dump station, and hiking trails.

Nearby Routes

Christmas Valley, page 282 / Lower Crooked River, page 300 / McKenzie - Santiam Pass Loop, page 304 / Robert Aufderheide Memorial Drive, page 308

LODGING DIRECTORY

Shilo Inn Suites Hotel - Bend, page 434 — Hotel / Motel

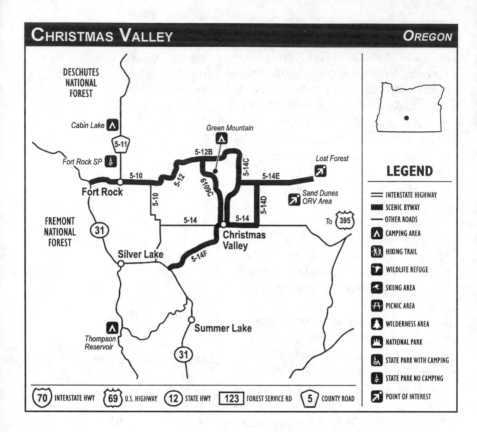

Route Location

Located in south-central Oregon, about 60 miles southeast of Bend. The north-western terminus is located off Oregon State Hwy. 31 west of Fort Rock. The route follows a series of roads traveling east and south of the northwestern terminus and eventually ends back on State Hwy. 31, east of Silver Lake.

Roads Traveled

The 102-mile byway follows Lake County Roads 5-10, 5-12, 5-12B, 5-14, 5-14C, 5-14D, 5-14E, and 5-14F, and BLM Road 6109C. The route travels over a combination of paved and gravel roads suitable for most passenger cars except for BLM Road 6109C which requires a high-clearance or four-wheel drive vehicle. The byway is officially designated a BLM Type I and Type II Back Country Byway.

Travel Season

Much of the route is open year-round although some sections will close in the winter from heavy snowfall. Portions of the byway can also become impassable after periods of heavy rain or because of extremely muddy conditions from March through May.

Description

The Christmas Valley Back Country Byway travels across the high desert landscape covered with sagebrush and shifting sand dunes. A unique feature to this desert landscape, however, is the isolated forest of pine trees. The Lost Forest area preserves a 9,000-acre stand of ponderosa pine growing among the high desert landscape common to this part of Oregon. This stand of ponderosa pine is about 35 miles east of the nearest ponderosa pine forest.

Adjacent to this oddity of nature is the 15,000-acre Christmas Valley Sand Dunes Off-Road Vehicle Area. Some of the sand dunes here rise 60 feet above the desert floor. Ten thousand acres are open to the public for recreational purposes. Vehicle use outside the dunes is restricted to roads or trails posted as open to vehicular travel.

Developed campgrounds are nonexistent along the byway. There is a BLM campground in the Green Mountain region, however, no facilities are provided. There are no designated campsites, but picnic tables are provided. The BLM does, however, permit dispersed camping nearly anywhere on public land. To the north of the byway in the Deschutes National Forest is the Cabin Lake national forest campground. There are 14 campsites and drinking water available here. The Thompson Reservoir lies to the south in the Fremont National Forest. Two campgrounds are available here with a total of 32 campsites. Drinking water and boat ramps are also provided.

Nearby Routes

Cascade Lakes Highway, page 280

Local Information

BLM - Lakeview District Office
1000 Ninth St. S
Lakeview, OR 97630
Phone: 541-947-2177

Fremont National Forest
524 North G St.
Lakeview, OR 97630
Phone: 541-947-2151

Lake County Chamber of Commerce
126 North E St.
Lakeview, OR 97630
Phone: 541-947-6040

Fort Rock State Park
Oregon Parks & Rec. Dept.
1115 Commercial St. NE
Salem, OR 97310
Phone: 503-378-6305

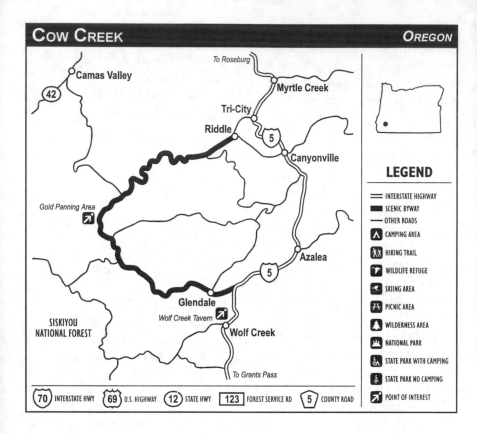

Route Location

The Cow Creek scenic byway is located in southwestern Oregon, about 25 miles north of Grants Pass. The byway forms an open loop drive west of Interstate 5 between the communities of Glendale and Riddle. The byway can be reached from Interstate 5 in the south by taking Exit #80 or from the north at Exit #103.

Roads Traveled

The byway follows the Cow Creek Road which is a two-lane paved road suitable for all types of vehicles. The entire 45-mile route has been designated a BLM Type I Back Country Byway.

Travel Season

Cow Creek Road is normally open all year long.

Description

The cool waters of Cow Creek flow alongside the Cow Creek Back Country Byway as it makes its way through a mixed conifer forest. Railroad tracks of the historic Oregon & California Railroad also accompany you for most the byway. Rugged rock bluffs, railroad bridges, tunnels, and retaining walls are among some of the views offered to the byway traveler. The railroad tracks, tunnels, and bridges are now used by Southern Pacific Railroad. Wildlife observers will want to be looking for osprey nests along the creek as well as mule deer. In spring the wildflowers proudly make their presence known along the byway.

The area encompassing Cow Creek has long been a popular mining area, and still is to this day. Nickel Mountain with its nickel mine can be seen from the byway. The BLM maintains a recreational gold panning area midway along the route with day-use facilities including picnic tables and restrooms.

Although there are no developed campgrounds along the byway, the Bureau of Land Management does permit camping nearly anywhere on public lands. Private lands may surround lands operated by the BLM so it is best to obtain detailed maps showing private and public lands before choosing your campsite. Public campgrounds can be found along the nearby scenic byways and in the nearby Siskiyou National Forest.

Local Information

BLM - Medford District Office
3040 Biddle Rd.
Medford, OR 97504
Phone: 541-770-2200

Siskiyou National Forest
P.O. Box 440
Grants Pass, OR 97526
Phone: 541-471-6500

Canyonville Chamber of Commerce
250 NW Main
Canyonville, OR 97417
Phone: 541-839-4258

Grants Pass / Josephine County C of C
1501 NE 6th St.
Grants Pass, OR 97526
Phone: 800-547-5927

Roseburg Area Chamber of Commerce
410 SE Spruce St.
Roseburg, OR 97470
Phone: 541-672-2648

Nearby Routes

Galice - Hellgate, page 290 / Grave Creek To Marial, page 292 / Rogue Umpqua - North Umpqua River, page 312

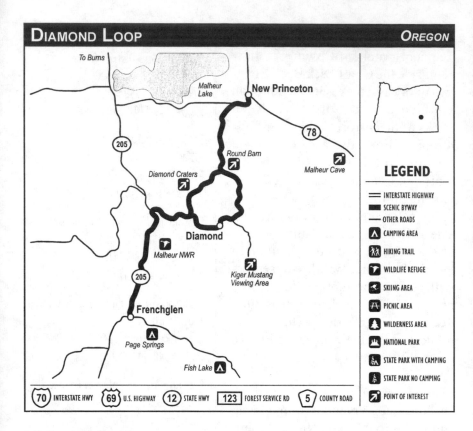

DIAMOND LOOP   OREGON

LEGEND

═══ INTERSTATE HIGHWAY
▬▬ SCENIC BYWAY
─── OTHER ROADS
🄰 CAMPING AREA
🏃 HIKING TRAIL
🌲 WILDLIFE REFUGE
⛷ SKIING AREA
🎪 PICNIC AREA
🌲 WILDERNESS AREA
🏛 NATIONAL PARK
🏕 STATE PARK WITH CAMPING
🚶 STATE PARK NO CAMPING
↗ POINT OF INTEREST

70 INTERSTATE HWY   69 U.S. HIGHWAY   12 STATE HWY   123 FOREST SERVICE RD   5 COUNTY ROAD

Route Location

The Diamond Loop Back Country Byway is located in southeastern Oregon, about 40 miles southeast of Burns. The byway's northern terminus is located off Oregon State Hwy. 78 in the town of New Princeton. The route travels south to Frenchglen with a loop drive through the community of Diamond.

Roads Traveled

The 64-mile route follows a series of county and state secondary roads which are a combination of paved and gravel-surfaced roads. The route can be safely traveled by passenger cars although vehicles towing a trailer or larger RVs should check with the BLM about current road conditions. The Diamond Loop is a Type I Back Country Byway.

Travel Season

The entire route is usually open year-round although the graveled sections can be difficult during and after inclement weather.

Description

The Diamond Loop route travels through a patchwork of high desert terrains, from mountain vistas and sagebrush-covered hills to red rimrock canyons and grassy marshes and valleys. Numerous species of wildlife can be seen including wild horses, mule deer, pronghorn antelope, hawks, and eagles. For viewing wild horses, the best place is the established Kiger Mustang Viewing Area located approximately 14 miles east of Diamond. The road to this area requires the use of a high-clearance vehicle and is passable only in dry weather.

Local Information

BLM - Burns District Office
HC74-12533 Hwy. 20 West
Hines, OR 97738
Phone: 541-573-5241

Harney County Chamber of Commerce
18 West D St.
Burns, OR 97720
Phone: 541-573-2636

Malheur National Wildlife Refuge
P.O. Box 245
Princeton, OR 97721
Phone: 541-493-2612

The Round Barn on the northern end of the loop was designed and built by Peter French, the manager of the historic Frenchglen Livestock Company. The barn was built in the late 1870s or early 1880s and was used to break horses during the long and bitter cold Oregon winters.

Another point of interest found along the byway is the Diamond Craters, an outstanding natural area. This 17,000-acre area displays some of the most diverse volcanic features in America. A self-guided tour identifies the craters, cinder cones, and lave tubes found in the area. The Malheur National Wildlife Refuge, managed by the U.S. Fish and Wildlife Service, was dedicated in 1908 by President Theodore Roosevelt. The area is popular with birdwatchers as there are over 200 species of birds in this area.

There are no developed camping areas found along the byway, however, dispersed camping is permitted on public lands. Check with the local office for more information and maps showing private lands among the public lands before setting up camp. Campgrounds can be found along the Steens Mountain byway which is to the south of this byway.

Nearby Routes

Lakeview To Steens, page 296 / Steens Mountain, page 320

LODGING DIRECTORY

McCoy Creek Ranch - Diamond, page 435 —— Bed & Breakfast / Inns

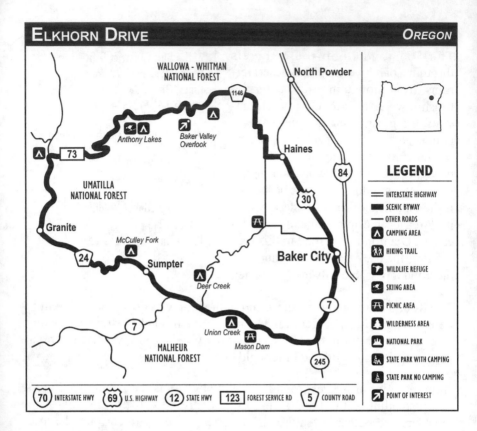

Route Location

The Elkhorn Drive is located in northeast Oregon starting in Baker City. This scenic byway forms a loop drive through the Wallowa-Whitman National Forest and ends back in Baker City.

Roads Traveled

The 106-mile route follows Oregon State Highway 7, County Road 24, Forest Service Road 73, County Road 1146, and U.S. Highway 30. All of the roads are two-lane paved roads suitable for all vehicles. The byway has been designated a National Forest Scenic Byway.

Travel Season

Most of the byway is open year-round. The portion between Granite and Anthony Lake is not plowed during the winter and remains closed from mid-November through mid-June.

Description

The Elkhorn Drive cuts through dense forests of ponderosa pine, Douglas-fir, and Engelmann spruce as it winds through the Elkhorn Mountains of the Wallowa-Whitman National Forest. The byway passes beautiful mountain lakes and rivers, all providing excellent fishing opportunities. Gold was discovered in this area in 1862 by five ex-Confederate soldiers. Visitors may wish to pan for gold near the Deer Creek Campground or McCulley Fork Campground at the areas set aside for this purpose.

Be sure to take some time and ride the rails of the historic Sumpter Valley Railroad. A five-mile section of the original tracks have been restored between Sumpter and the McEwen Station. The ten-mile round trip ride is powered by a steam locomotive. The narrow-gauge train operates on weekends and holidays throughout the summer.

Those interested in hiking or just taking a walk among the trees will find numerous trails along the byway. Hikers can access the Elkhorn Crest National Recreation Trail which is a 22½-mile trail following the ridge-top of the Elkhorn Mountains. Other shorter trails can be found that lead to placid mountain lakes and secluded spots.

If you wish to extend your stay in the area, the national forest provides several campgrounds to choose from. The largest campground along the byway is Union Creek situated on the banks of Phillips Lake. Here visitors will find 58 campsites that can accommodate tents or recreational vehicles. Drinking water, restrooms, electrical hookups, a boat ramp, and swimming area are among the facilities found here. The Deer Creek Campground is a small six-site campground for tent campers. The Anthony Lakes area offers four campgrounds with a total of 56 sites.

Local Information

Wallowa-Whitman National Forest
Baker Ranger District
3165 10th St.
Baker City, OR 97814
Phone: 541-523-4476

Umatilla National Forest
2517 SW Hailey Ave.
Pendleton, OR 97801
Phone: 541-278-3716

Malheur National Forest
141 NE Dayton St.
John Day, OR 97845
Phone: 541-575-1731

Baker County Chamber of Commerce
490 Campbell St.
Baker City, OR 97814
Phone: 541-523-5855

Nearby Routes

Blue Mountain, page 278 / Hells Canyon, page 294 / Snake River - Mormon Basin, page 314

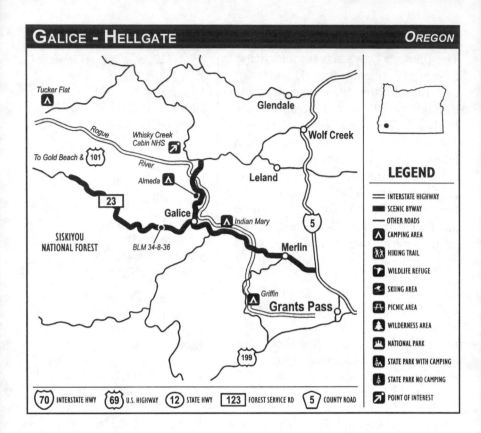

Route Location

The Galice - Hellgate scenic byway is located in the southwestern corner of Oregon, about four miles northwest of Grants Pass. The eastern access is located off Exit #61 on Interstate 5. The byway heads west to the Siskiyou National Forest with a small portion traveling north to Grave Creek.

Roads Traveled

The 39-mile route follows the Merlin-Galice, Hellgate, and BLM 34-8-36 roads and Forest Service Road 23. The scenic drive is composed of paved, single-lane and two-lane roads suitable for passenger car travel. Caution should be exercised on the single-lane portions. The byway has been designated a BLM Type I Back Country Byway.

Travel Season

The byway is generally open year-round except the portions that travel through the Siskiyou National Forest which closes due to heavy snowfall.

Description

The Galice - Hellgate byway begins off Interstate 5 and travels through forested hills and open pastures filled with grazing cattle until it reaches the Rogue River. Here the landscape changes dramatically as the National Wild and Scenic River cuts through the rugged canyon bordered by forested slopes. In Galice, you can continue the drive for eight miles north with the Rogue River keeping you company. If you decide to head west, you'll begin climbing away from the river canyon into the heavily forested Siskiyou Mountains.

The Rogue River provides some excellent river rafting opportunities. Outfitters in the area can provide everything you need to enjoy a rafting trip on this scenic river. If you're more interested in pulling fish from the water, you'll find chinook salmon, cutthroat trout, and rainbow trout among others. The BLM operates a visitor center north of Galice; the folks here are happy to provide information on the river and its recreational opportunities.

There are two developed campgrounds along the byway, both situated on the banks of the river. The Indian Mary Campground provides 95 sites with picnic tables, drinking water, full hookups, shower facilities, and access to the river. The Almeda Park is smaller with 25 campsites, drinking water, and a boat ramp.

Local Information

BLM - Medford District Office
3040 Biddle Rd.
Medford, OR 97504
Phone: 541-770-2200

Siskiyou National Forest
P.O. Box 440
Grants Pass, OR 97526
Phone: 541-471-6500

Grants Pass / Josephine County C of C
1501 NE 6th St.
Grants Pass, OR 97526
Phone: 800-547-5927

Gold Beach Chamber of Commerce
1225 S. Ellensburg Ave., #3
Gold Beach, OR 97444
Phone: 800-525-2334

Nearby Routes

Cow Creek, page 284 / Grave Creek To Marial, page 292 / Rogue - Coquille, page 310 / Rogue Umpqua - North Umpqua River, page 312 / Smith River, page 102 / State Of Jefferson, page 104

LODGING DIRECTORY

Shilo Inn - Grants Pass, page 439 — Hotel / Motel

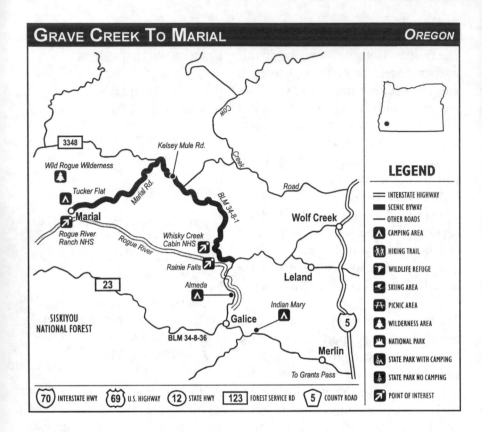

GRAVE CREEK TO MARIAL   OREGON

Route Location

The Grave Creek To Marial byway is located in southwest Oregon, about 28 miles northwest of Grants Pass. The byway can be reached from the Cow Creek scenic byway or the Galice - Hellgate byway. The byway begins at Grave Creek and travels northwest to the roads end in Marial.

Roads Traveled

The byway is approximately 33 miles long and follows the Mt. Reuben (BLM 34-8-1), Kelsey Mule, and Marial Roads. The route travels over a combination of one-lane paved and gravel surfaced roads that are suitable for passenger cars. Motorhomes and vehicles pulling trailers should not attempt the drive. The byway has been officially designated a BLM Type I Back Country Byway.

Travel Season

The byway is closed in the winter due to heavy snowfall.

Description

This byway is an excellent extension of the Galice - Hellgate byway. The route climbs out of the Rogue River Canyon and winds through the beautiful mountains before descending back to the river and the Rogue River Ranch. Spectacular views of the wild river are found along the byway. Wildlife observers will want to look for elk, deer, and wild turkeys as well as an occasional black bear.

Near the beginning of this byway is a hiking trail that will take you to the scenic Rainie Falls. Also near here is the trailhead to the Rogue River National Recreation Trail. Hikers and backpackers can take the trail along the banks of the river from Grave Creek to Marial, a distance of 24 miles. The trail continues south from Marial along the river for an additional 16 miles to Illahe, crossing the Siskiyou National Forest.

The historic Rogue River Ranch lies at the end of the byway. The Rogue River Ranch has a history dating back to the late 1800s when all that existed was a one-room "sugar pine shake" cabin. In the years that followed, the pioneer Billings family added more buildings including a barn and a trading post. The ranch was sold to the Bureau of Land Management in 1970 and now operates a museum depicting the ranch's history.

Camping is available at the Tucker Flat Campground which offers 10 sites. Be prepared to bring your own water or draw from Mule Creek. Be sure to purify the water from the creek before consuming.

Local Information

BLM - Medford District Office
3040 Biddle Rd.
Medford, OR 97504
Phone: 541-770-2200

Siskiyou National Forest
P.O. Box 440
Grants Pass, OR 97526
Phone: 541-471-6500

Grants Pass / Josephine County C of C
1501 NE 6th St.
Grants Pass, OR 97526
Phone: 800-547-5927

Gold Beach Chamber of Commerce
1225 S. Ellensburg Ave., #3
Gold Beach, OR 97444
Phone: 800-525-2334

Nearby Routes

Cow Creek, page 284 / Galice - Hellgate, page 290 / Rogue - Coquille, page 310

Lodging Directory

Shilo Inn - Grants Pass, page 439 — Hotel / Motel

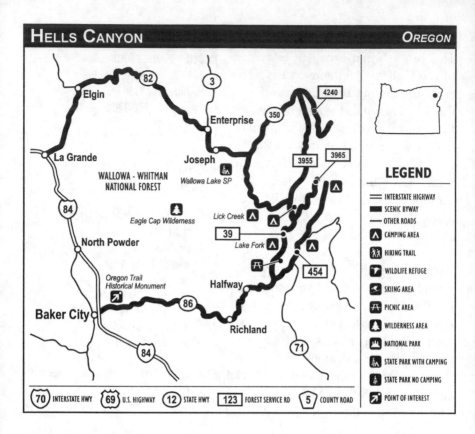

Route Location

Located in northeastern Oregon, the byway forms an open loop drive east of Interstate 84 with access points in Baker City and La Grande.

Roads Traveled

The 314-mile route follows a series of state highways and national forest roads. The main loop follows State Highways 82 and 86 and Forest Service Road 39 which are two-lane paved roads suitable for all vehicles. The spur roads are State Hwy. 350 and Forest Service Roads 454, 3955, 3965, and 4240. These roads vary from two-lane paved roads to gravel-surfaced roads. The side roads are suitable for automobile travel but vehicles pulling trailers or larger RVs may have difficulty in turning around. This scenic drive is designated a National Forest Scenic Byway.

Travel Season

Most of the route is open year-round although winter driving conditions can be hazardous and portions will temporarily close in the winter.

Description

The Hells Canyon scenic byway takes the traveler through the forested mountains and valleys of the Wallowa-Whitman National Forest to the scenic splendor which is the Hells Canyon National Recreation Area. This 652,488-acre recreation area protects the free-flowing Snake River in Hells Canyon and its surrounding landscape.

The byway offers access to numerous opportunities for outdoor recreation. Nearly a thousand miles of trails can be found in the National Recreation Area alone. Some trails are easy to travel providing quiet walks while other trails are difficult to find and a challenge to the experienced hiker.

In addition to the Snake River, the byway provides access to other rivers, lakes, and streams, all offering excellent boating and fishing. Wallowa Lake is situated in a forest of pine and fir and offers boating, swimming, skiing, and fishing opportunities. The state park here offers 210 campsites, 121 with full hookups and 89 for tent campers. Hiking trails here provide access to the 200,416-acre Eagle Cap Wilderness.

Nearby Routes

Elkhorn Drive, page 288 / Snake River - Mormon Basin, page 314

LODGING DIRECTORY

Shilo Inn Troy Wilderness Retreat - Enterprise, page 439 — Cabin / Cottage / Guest Ranch & Campground / RV Park

Local Information

Wallow - Whitman National Forest
1550 Dewey Ave.
Baker City, OR 97814
Phone: 541-523-6391

Baker County Chamber of Commerce
490 Campbell St.
Baker City, OR 97814
Phone: 541-523-5855

La Grande - Union County C of C
1912 Fourth St., #200
La Grande, OR 97850
Phone: 800-848-9969

Wallowa County Chamber of Commerce
P.O. Box 427
Enterprise, OR 97828
Phone: 541-426-4622

Joseph Chamber of Commerce
P.O. Box 13
Joseph, OR 97848
Phone: 541-432-1015

Elgin Chamber of Commerce
P.O. Box 1001
Elgin, OR 97827
Phone: 541-437-1971

Hells Canyon National Recreation Area
88401 Hwy. 82
Enterprise, OR 97828
Phone: 541-426-4978

Wallowa Lake State Park
72214 Marina Ln.
Joseph, OR 97846
Phone: 541-432-4185

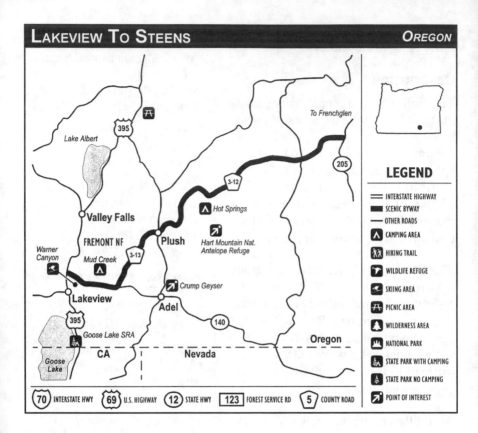

Route Location

This byway is located in southeastern Oregon, beginning 5 miles north of Lakeview. The byway begins at the junction with U.S. Hwy. 395 and travels northeast to the intersection with Oregon State Hwy. 205, south of Frenchglen.

Roads Traveled

The 90-mile scenic drive follows State Highway 140 and County Roads 3-13 and 3-12. The state highway and County Road 3-13 are two-lane paved roads safe for travel by all types of vehicles. County Road 3-12 is a gravel road that requires the use of a high-clearance vehicle. Vehicles pulling trailers are not recommended on the gravel portion. The byway is a BLM Type I and II Back Country Byway.

Travel Season

The byway is usually open all year, however, severe storms in the winter can result in brief periods of closure or rough driving conditions.

Description

The Lakeview To Steens Back Country Byway crosses a portion of the Fremont National Forest traveling through the Warner Mountains and crosses a vast expanse of high desert country. After crossing the mountains, the byway descends into Warner Valley and crosses the Warner Wetlands. Spring and fall brings hundreds of migrating birds to this area including cranes, herons, egrets, ducks, and swans. The route then climbs the escarpment of Hart Mountain through the Hart Mountain National Antelope Refuge. In addition to herds of pronghorn antelope, the refuge provides habitat for sage grouse, burrowing owls, and coyotes in the lower elevations and mule deer, bighorn sheep, and prairie falcons in the higher elevations.

Developed recreational facilities are nearly nonexistent along the byway. A primitive campground is located in the antelope refuge a few miles south of the refuge headquarters. Dispersed camping is permitted nearly anywhere on lands managed by the Bureau of Land Management. Check with the district office in Lakeview regarding any private land that may exist along the byway before choosing your campsite.

The Fremont National Forest offers Mud Creek Campground which has eight campsites and drinking water. The campground is a few miles north of State Highway 140. About fifteen miles south of Lakeview off U.S. Highway 395 is the Goose Lake State Recreation Area. Visitors will find 48 campsites here with electrical hookups. The park also has shower facilities, picnic areas, and a trailer dump station.

Nearby Routes

Diamond Loop, page 286 / Steens Mountain, page 320 / Barrel Springs, page 65

Local Information

BLM - Lakeview District Office
1000 Ninth St. S
Lakeview, OR 97630
Phone: 541-947-2177

Fremont National Forest
524 North G St.
Lakeview, OR 97630
Phone: 541-947-2151

Lake County Chamber of Commerce
126 North E St.
Lakeview, OR 97630
Phone: 541-947-6040

Harney County Chamber of Commerce
18 West D St.
Burns, OR 97720
Phone: 541-573-2636

Goose Lake State Recreation Area
Oregon Parks & Rec. Dept.
1115 Commercial St. NE
Salem, OR 97310
Phone: 503-378-6305

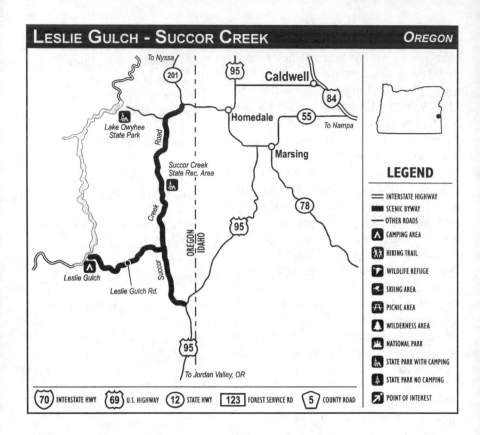

Route Location

The scenic byway is about 100 miles southeast of Baker City in eastern Oregon, near the Idaho state line. The northern terminus is at the junction with State Hwy. 201. The route travels south and includes a side road traveling west. The southern end of the byway intersects with U.S. Hwy. 95.

Roads Traveled

The 52-mile byway follows Succor Creek Road and Leslie Gulch Road. Both roads consist of a graded dirt and gravel surface. A high-clearance, two-wheel drive vehicle is recommended to travel the entire route. Larger RVs and vehicles pulling trailers are strongly discouraged from traveling the Leslie Gulch Road because of its sustained 11% road grade. The road is also steep and narrow within Succor Creek Canyon, the area through the state recreation area. The route is designated a BLM Type I and Type II Back Country Byway.

Travel Season

The byway is generally open from mid-April through October. The roads are closed during winter months because of snow and mud. Severe summer rainstorms and flashflooding may cause the byway to become impassable.

Description

The Leslie Gulch - Succor Creek Back Country Byway travels through the beautifully rugged landscape found here in eastern Oregon. The scenic byway first crosses sagebrush-covered hills and then down into the rugged canyon carved by the waters of Succor Creek. The byway then climbs back out of Succor Creek Canyon to rolling stretches of open landscape. The side trip on Leslie Gulch Road is a neat drive through a narrow and winding canyon of steep cliffs and towering rock spires. This road ends on the banks of 53-mile long Lake Owyhee.

Those interested in staying awhile will find camping areas courtesy of the Bureau of Land Management and the state of Oregon. Located along the byway is the Succor Creek State Recreation Area where you will find 19 primitive campsites with picnic tables. The Lake Owyhee State Park offers 40 campsites with 10 having electrical hookups for recreational vehicles. The park also provides a dump station, shower facilities, and access to Lake Owyhee. The BLM campground at the bottom of Leslie Gulch has 12 sites and a boat ramp.

Local Information

BLM - Vale District Office
100 Oregon St.
Vale, OR 97918
Phone: 541-473-3144

Nyssa Chamber of Commerce
145 South 3rd St.
Nyssa, OR 97913
Phone: 541-372-3091

Homedale Chamber of Commerce
P.O. Box 845
Homedale, ID 83628
Phone: 208-337-4611

Caldwell Chamber of Commerce
P.O. Box 819
Caldwell, ID 83606
Phone: 208-459-7493

Lake Owyhee State Park
1298 Owyhee Dam
Adrian, OR 97901
Phone: 541-339-2331

Succor Creek State Recreation Area
Oregon Parks & Rec. Dept.
1115 Commercial St. NE
Salem, OR 97310
Phone: 503-378-6305

Nearby Routes

Owyhee Uplands, page 161 / Ponderosa Pine, page 163

Lodging Directory

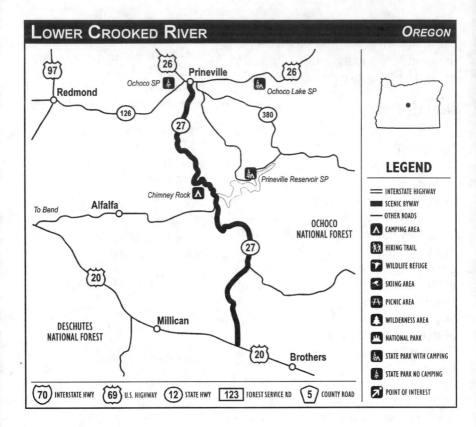

Route Location

The Lower Crooked River is located in central Oregon, approximately 35 miles east of Bend. The northern terminus of the byway is in the community of Prineville on U.S. Highway 26. The byway heads south from Prineville and ends at the intersection with U.S. Highway 20, about seven miles northwest of Brothers.

Roads Traveled

The 43-mile byway follows Oregon State Hwy. 27. The highway is a two-lane paved road for approximately 21 miles from Prineville. The remaining portion is an all-weather gravel road. The byway can be safely driven by all types of vehicles. This scenic drive is a BLM Type I Back Country Byway.

Travel Season

State Highway 27 is usually open year-round although the gravel portion can become muddy after heavy rains and snow.

Description

This back country byway begins in Prineville and heads south through the steep-walled canyon carved by the Crooked River. The river flows alongside the byway until you reach Prineville Reservoir, formed by the construction of the Arthur R. Bowman dam on the river. The segment of river along the byway has been designated a National Wild and Scenic River. The river, besides being scenic, provides excellent fishing for native rainbow trout. Wildlife seen along this stretch of the byway includes deer, coyotes, and numerous birds of prey. Black bear inhabit the area as do bald eagles during winter.

Once you cross Bear Creek the landscape begins to change. As you continue driving south, the canyon walls give way to the vast expanse of sagebrush. This is Oregon's high desert. Here you can spot mule deer, antelope, sage grouse, and coyotes.

There are several primitive BLM campgrounds along the byway in addition to the Chimney Rock Campground which offers 16 campsites with picnic tables. Although not located directly along the byway, there are two state parks that offer camping facilities. The Ochoco State Park has 22 primitive sites situated on the shore of Ochoco Lake. The Prineville Reservoir State Park is more developed with 22 sites offering full hookups and 48 sites for tent campers. Shower facilities and a swimming beach are among the facilities available here.

Local Information

BLM - Prineville District Office
185 E. 4th St.
Prineville, OR 97754
Phone: 541-447-4115

Ochoco National Forest
P.O. Box 490
Prineville, OR 97754
Phone: 541-447-6247

Deschutes National Forest
1645 Hwy. 20 East
Bend, OR 97701
Phone: 541-388-2715

Prineville - Crook County C of C
390 N. Fairview
Prineville, OR 97754
Phone: 541-447-6304

Bend Chamber of Commerce
63085 N. Hwy. 97
Bend, OR 97701
Phone: 541-382-3221

Ochoco Lake State Park
91677 Parkland Dr.
Prineville, OR 97754
Phone: 541-447-4363

Prineville Reservoir State Park
91677 Parkland Dr.
Prineville, OR 97754
Phone: 541-447-4363

Nearby Routes

Cascade Lakes Highway, page 280 / McKenzie - Santiam Pass Loop, page 304

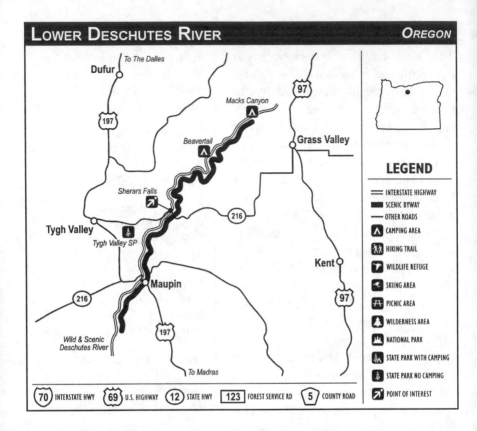

Route Location

The Lower Deschutes River scenic byway is approximately 40 miles south of Interstate 84 and The Dalles in north-central Oregon. The byway can be accessed from U.S. Highway 197 in Maupin or off Oregon State Highway 216 between Tygh Valley and Grass Valley. The byway travels along the banks of the Deschutes River both north and south of Maupin.

Roads Traveled

The 36-mile byway follows the Deschutes River Road, an old railroad grade. Nine miles are paved with the rest being a rough gravel road. The road is suitable for most types of vehicles, however, vehicles pulling trailers are discouraged from traveling the eight mile portion south of Maupin. Also, there are some narrow, sharp curves with limited sight distance on the gravel portion. This scenic drive is a Type I Back Country Byway.

Travel Season

The entire length of the byway is normally open year-round.

Description

This back country byway cuts through the scenic canyon created by the flowing waters of the Deschutes River as it twists its way to the Columbia River. Native Americans used to fish for salmon here at the beautiful Sherar's Falls. Peter Skene Ogden came exploring the Deschutes River Canyon in 1826 and was followed by John C. Fremont and Kit Carson in 1843. Today the river is part of the National Wild and Scenic River System and is used by rafters for its challenging whitewater rapids. There are several good spots along the byway for watching these rafters or you may decide you'd like to float the river yourself.

If you're not interested in floating the river, then perhaps you would like to

Local Information

BLM - Prineville District Office
185 E. 4th St.
Prineville, OR 97754
Phone: 541-447-4115

The Dalles Area Chamber of Commerce
404 W. 2nd St.
The Dalles, OR 97058
Phone: 541-296-2231

Madras - Jefferson County C of C
197 SE 5th St.
Madras, OR 97741
Phone: 541-475-2350

Tygh Valley State Park
Oregon Parks & Rec. Dept.
1115 Commercial St. NE
Salem, OR 97310
Phone: 503-378-6305

spend some time trying to pull rainbow trout, steelhead, or chinook salmon from the river. Or you may be interested in finding a quiet, secluded spot to read and enjoy a picnic lunch. There's a variety of wildlife to be looking for, too. The watchful eye may catch glimpses of mule deer, osprey, or the great blue heron.

There are two developed and numerous primitive campgrounds along the byway for those interested in extending their stay. The two developed campgrounds are Beavertail and Macks Canyon. The Beavertail Campground has 20 campsites with picnic tables and fire rings. Macks Canyon Campground offers 16 sites, also with picnic tables and fire rings. Drinking water and pit toilets are provided in both campgrounds. Both also provide boat access to the river. A small fee is charged for the use of each campground. The remains of a prehistoric pithouse village can be seen at the Macks Canyon recreation area.

This back country byway is heavily used by outdoor recreationists during the spring and summer months. Exercise caution while driving the byway.

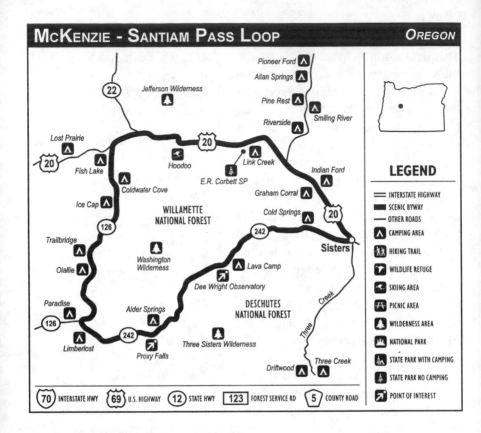

Route Location

The McKenzie - Santiam Pass Loop is located in west-central Oregon, about 22 miles northwest of Bend. The byway begins in Sisters on U.S. Highway 20 and travels westward through the Deschutes and Willamette National Forests forming a loop drive back to Sisters.

Roads Traveled

The byway is 82 miles in length and follows Oregon State Highways 126 and 242, and U.S. Highway 20. All of the routes are two-lane paved roads suitable for all vehicles. Motor homes over 22 feet long and vehicles pulling trailers are not recommended on Oregon State Highway 242. This is a National Forest Scenic Byway.

Travel Season

U.S. Highway 20 and State Highway 126 normally remain open year-round. State Highway 242 is usually closed from November through early July.

Description

This scenic drive crosses the Deschutes and Willamette National Forests through forests of ponderosa pine and stands of aspen, across Oregon's high desert landscape, and skirts the shores of numerous mountain lakes. Scenic vistas along the byway provide spectacular views of the Three Sisters mountain peaks as well as the surrounding wilderness. Mount Washington, standing proudly at 7,794 feet, may also be seen at times along the byway.

Flowing alongside the winding State Highway 126 are the bubbling waters of McKenzie River. The McKenzie River National Recreation Trail also follows along the banks of this river. Several scenic waterfalls reward the hiker and offer a nice place to take a break and relax a bit. There are numerous access points along this part of the byway. There's a ½-mile trail off State Highway 242 that leads to the beautiful Proxy Falls. Both the upper and lower falls drop about 200 feet over moss-covered cliffs. The Pacific Crest National Scenic Trail can also be accessed from the byway. Several other trails provide opportunities for a short stroll or a long day hike.

The Dee Wright Observatory is located at the summit of McKenzie Pass. This observatory was named for Dee Wright, a Forest Service packer from 1910 to 1934. He was also the foreman of the Civilian Conservation Corps crew that built the observatory. Views from the observatory include Mt. Hood, Mt. Washington, Mt. Jefferson, and Three Fingered Jack as well as the Three Sisters. The Lava River Trail is an interpretive trail beginning at the observatory and winds through interesting volcanic features.

Local Information

Willamette National Forest
211 E. Seventh Ave.
Eugene, OR 97440
Phone: 541-465-6521

Deschutes National Forest
1645 Hwy. 20 East
Bend, OR 97701
Phone: 541-388-2715

Sisters Area Chamber of Commerce
P.O. Box 430
Sisters, OR 97759
Phone: 541-549-0251

Sweet Home Chamber of Commerce
1575 Main St.
Sweet Home, OR 97386
Phone: 541-367-6186

E.R. Corbett Memorial State Park
Oregon Parks & Rec. Dept.
1115 Commercial St. NE
Salem, OR 97310
Phone: 503-378-6305

Nearby Routes

Cascade Lakes Highway, page 280 / Lower Crooked River, page 300 / Robert Aufderheide Memorial Drive, page 308

NESTUCCA RIVER   OREGON

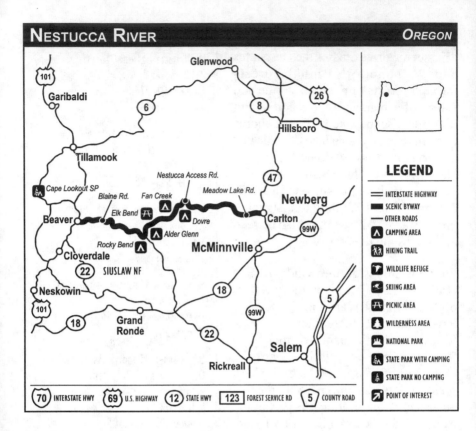

Route Location

The Nestucca River byway is located in northwestern Oregon, approximately 32 miles north of Salem. The byway begins in Carlton on State Highway 47 and travels west to Beaver on U.S. Highway 101.

Roads Traveled

The 45-mile byway follows Meadow Lake County Road, BLM's Nestucca Access Road, and Blaine Road. The roads followed are two-lane paved roads suitable for all types of vehicles. There is a small portion of the byway that is not paved. Eleven miles of this route are officially designated a BLM Type I Back Country Byway.

Travel Season

The byway is usually open year-round, however, snow and ice can make the road hazardous or impassable during the winter.

Description

The Nestucca River back country by-way travels through Oregon's old growth forest where Douglas firs reach heights of 200 feet and over 400 years old. The byway also cuts through the moss-covered canyon walls carved by the Nestucca River. The byway is kept company by the tumbling waters of this scenic river for most of its length. Wild-flowers growing alongside the byway provide a diversity of colors through-out much of the year. Wildlife observ-ers need to be on the lookout for elk and deer which are common to the area. The byway traveler may also catch a glimpse of a bald eagle flying overhead.

There are four BLM operated recre-ation areas and one Siuslaw National Forest campground along the byway. The Dovre Campground offers 10 campsites with picnic tables and fire rings. Fan Creek Campground has 12 sites and Alder Glen has 11, each with picnic tables. Elk Bend is primarily a day use area but does offer 4 campsites. West of the Alder Glen recreation area, the byway enters the Siuslaw National Forest. Here, visitors will find the 12-site Rocky Bend Campground. This is the only campground where drink-ing water is not available. The campgrounds are situated on the banks of Nestucca River and provide excellent places for fishing or swimming.

Local Information

BLM - Salem District Office
1717 Fabry Rd. SE.
Salem, OR 97306
Phone: 503-375-5646

Siuslaw National Forest
P.O. Box 1148
Corvallis, OR 97339
Phone: 541-757-4480

Tillamook Chamber of Commerce
3705 Hwy. 101 N.
Tillamook, OR 97141
Phone: 503-842-7525

McMinnville Chamber of Commerce
417 N. Adams St.
McMinnville, OR 97128
Phone: 503-472-6196

West Valley Chamber of Commerce
P.O. Box 98
Sheridan, OR 97378
Phone: 503-843-4964

Cape Lookout State Park
Oregon Parks & Rec. Dept.
1115 Commercial St. NE
Salem, OR 97310
Phone: 503-378-6305

LODGING DIRECTORY

Sandlake Country Inn - Cloverdale, page 444 — Bed & Breakfast / Inns
Shilo Inn - Newberg, page 445 — Hotel / Motel
Shilo Inn - Tillamook, page 445 — Hotel / Motel

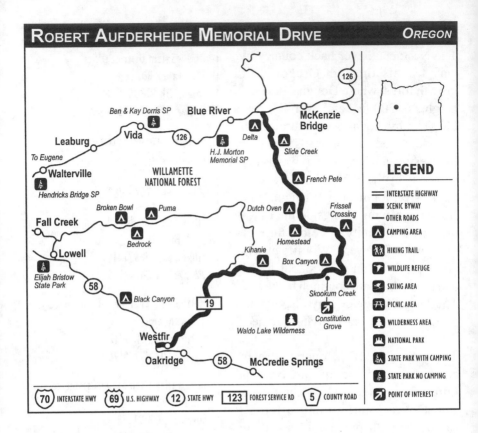

ROBERT AUFDERHEIDE MEMORIAL DRIVE — OREGON

LEGEND

- ▬▬ INTERSTATE HIGHWAY
- ▬ SCENIC BYWAY
- — OTHER ROADS
- ▲ CAMPING AREA
- 🏃 HIKING TRAIL
- 🦅 WILDLIFE REFUGE
- ⛷ SKIING AREA
- 🎪 PICNIC AREA
- 🌲 WILDERNESS AREA
- 🏔 NATIONAL PARK
- 🏕 STATE PARK WITH CAMPING
- 🏕 STATE PARK NO CAMPING
- 🎯 POINT OF INTEREST

(70) INTERSTATE HWY (69) U.S. HIGHWAY (12) STATE HWY [123] FOREST SERVICE RD (5) COUNTY ROAD

Route Location

The Robert Aufderheide Memorial Drive is located in west-central Oregon, about 40 miles east of Eugene. The byway begins east of Blue River at the intersection of Forest Service Road 19 and State Highway 126. The byway then heads south through the Willamette National Forest and ends at the junction with State Highway 58.

Roads Traveled

The 65-mile route follows Forest Service Road 19 which is a two-lane paved road suitable for all vehicles. Travelers can pick up an audio cassette tape of the tour, free of charge, from the ranger stations in either Blue River or Oakridge and return it at the other end of the drive. This byway has been designated a National Forest Scenic Byway.

Travel Season

The byway is generally open from early April through October and is then closed by heavy winter snows.

Description

The Robert Aufderheide Memorial Drive is named in honor of a man who devoted 24 years of his life to Forestry. Mr. Aufderheide was the Supervisor of Willamette National Forest from 1954 until his death in 1959.

This scenic byway travels through the mixed conifer and hardwood forests alongside the South Fork of the McKenzie River and the North Fork of the Middle Fork of the Willamette River, a long name but a scenic river. This river is part of the National Wild and Scenic River System and provides good opportunities for catching rainbow and cutthroat trout.

Those interested in hiking, backpacking, or horseback riding will find a lot of trails along the byway. There's the Waldo Wilderness Trail that takes you into the Waldo Wilderness. Another trail is called the Grasshopper Trail which will take you through the Chucksney Roadless Area, not a designated wilderness but offers seclusion just the same. There is a self-guided trail in the area of Constitution Grove that will lead you among a grove of trees over 200 years old.

Travelers to the byway could easily spend a week or longer here. The national forest has developed numerous campgrounds providing hundreds of campsites to choose from. Most of the campgrounds are situated on the banks of pretty meandering rivers and streams. Plan on finding a spot and staying awhile.

Local Information

Willamette National Forest
211 E. Seventh Ave.
Eugene, OR 97440
Phone: 541-465-6521

Oakridge - Westfir C of C
P.O. Box 217
Oakridge, OR 97463
Phone: 541-782-4146

Eugene Area Chamber of Commerce
1401 Willamette St.
Eugene, OR 97440
Phone: 541-484-1314

Elijah Bristow State Park
Ben and Kay Dorris State Park
H.J. Morton Memorial State Park
Hendricks Bridge State Park

Oregon Parks and Recreation Dept.
1115 Commercial St. NE
Salem, OR 97310
Phone: 503-378-6305

Nearby Routes

Cascade Lakes Highway, page 280 / Mckenzie - Santiam Pass Loop, page 304

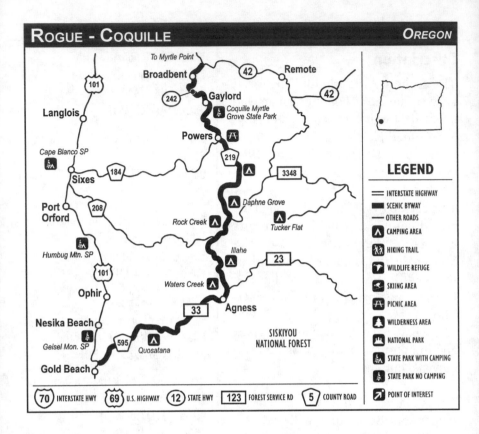

Route Location

The Rogue - Coquille scenic drive is situated in southwestern Oregon, approximately 25 miles southeast of Coos Bay. The byway's northern terminus is located at the junction with Oregon State Highway 42. The byway travels south, crossing the Siskiyou National Forest, and ends at the intersection with U.S. Highway 101 north of Gold Beach.

Roads Traveled

The 83-mile byway follows State Highway 242, County Roads 219 and 595, and Forest Service Road 33. All of the roads followed are two-lane paved roads suitable for all types of vehicles. This scenic route is officially designated a National Forest Scenic Byway.

Travel Season

The byway is generally open all year long.

Description

The Rogue - Coquille National Forest Scenic Byway travels alongside the Wild and Scenic Rogue River between Gold Beach and Agness, then leaves the river to climb over the gentle divide and descend into the Coquille River Basin. Here the byway begins to follow the course dictated by the Coquille River through a narrow canyon rimmed with high cliffs. The river canyon eventually gives way to the wide open valley near Powers to the byway's northern end. The Rogue River was one of eight rivers initially included in the National Wild and Scenic Rivers Act of 1968 and is popular with fishermen, river rafters, and photographers.

There are numerous pullouts along the byway that provide beautiful panoramic vistas of the forest's rivers and surrounding mountains. These places are always good spots for enjoying a picnic, taking photos, or looking for wildlife. The national forest supports a variety of wildlife including deer, bobcats, mountain lions, bald eagles, and river otters. You'll also find hiking trails at some turnouts that invite you to explore the forest. There are some short hiking trails that reward you with a cascading waterfall.

There are several national forest campgrounds found along the byway that provide the perfect spot for an overnight stay or longer. To the west of the byway are state parks with hundreds of developed campsites.

Near the byway's southern terminus is Battle Rock, located at the mouth of Lobster Creek. This was the site of a bloody battle between settlers and Native Americans living in the Rogue River corridor in the 1800s. Nearly all of the Indians involved in the battle lost their lives.

Local Information

Siskiyou National Forest
200 NE Greenfield Rd.
Grants Pass, OR 97526
Phone: 541-471-6500

Gold Beach Chamber of Commerce
1225 S. Ellensburg Ave., #3
Gold Beach, OR 97444
Phone: 800-525-2334

Myrtle Point Chamber of Commerce
P.O. Box 265
Myrtle Point, OR 97458
Phone: 541-572-2626

Cape Blanco State Park
Coquille Myrtle Grove State Park
Humburg Mountain State Park

Oregon Parks and Recreation Dept.
1115 Commercial St. NE
Salem, OR 97310
Phone: 503-378-6305

Nearby Routes

Galice Hellgate, page 290 / Grave Creek To Marial, page 292

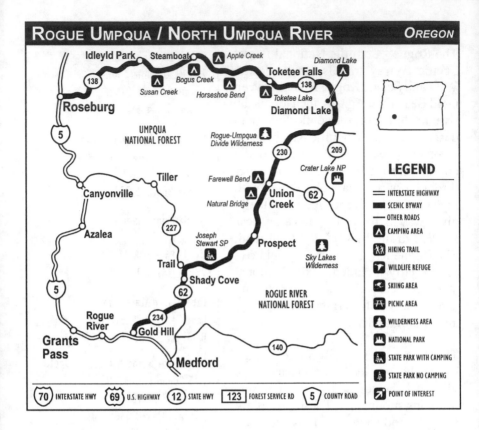

Route Location

Located in southwestern Oregon, 70 miles south of Eugene. The byway begins in Roseburg and travels east to Diamond Lake and then south to Gold Hill.

Roads Traveled

This 172-mile byway follows State Highways 62, 138, 230 and 234 which are two-lane paved roads suitable for all types of vehicles. This byway is both a BLM Type I Back Country Byway and a National Forest Scenic Byway. The portion designated by the BLM begins near Idleyld Park and ends at the national forest boundary, a distance of about 11 miles.

Travel Season

The byway is usually open year-round. Use caution in the winter months.

Description

This scenic drive takes the traveler through a diverse landscape from rural countryside dotted with farms and open pastures to thick forests of Douglas fir and lodgepole pine. Wildflowers bloom along the byway making their colorful presence known. Travelers are also treated to views of the beautiful Cascade Mountains, meandering mountain streams, and scenic cascading waterfalls. The byway provides unlimited opportunities for outdoor recreation. There are hiking trails ranging from short easy walks to pretty waterfalls to longer, more arduous trails that are enjoyed by experienced hikers and backpackers. Wilderness areas surrounding the byway provide opportunities for hiking or horseback riding to secluded places.

Numerous campgrounds are provided along the entire length of the route by the Bureau of Land Management, the National Forest Service, the Corps of Engineers, and the state of Oregon. You're bound to find a campsite that interests you, whether you seek a primitive, secluded site or one that is highly developed.

The byway winds along two National Wild and Scenic Rivers, the North Umpqua and Upper Rogue. These rivers, and the many others found within the forest, provide excellent fishing and rafting opportunities.

Local Information

Rogue River National Forest
333 West 8th St.
Medford, OR 97501
Phone: 541-776-3600

Umpqua National Forest
P.O. Box 1008
Roseburg, OR 97470
Phone: 541-672-6601

Roseburg Area Chamber of Commerce
410 SE Spruce St.
Roseburg, OR 97470
Phone: 541-672-2648

Grants Pass / Josephine County C of C
1501 NE 6th St.
Grants Pass, OR 97526
Phone: 800-547-5927

Rogue River Area C of C
P.O. Box 457
Rogue River, OR 97537
Phone: 541-582-0242

Chamber of Medford / Jackson County
101 W. 8th St.
Medford, OR 97501
Phone: 541-779-4847

Crater Lake National Park
P.O. Box 128
Crater Lake, OR 97604
Phone: 541-594-2511

Nearby Routes

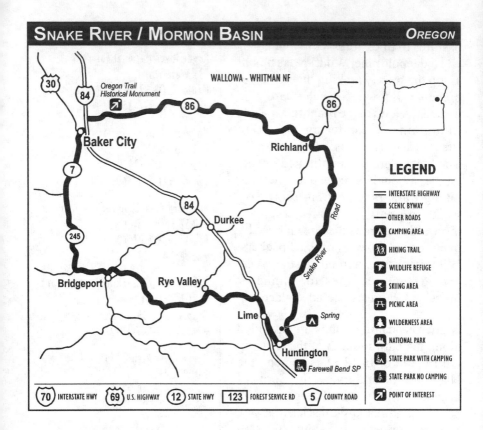

Route Location

The Snake River / Mormon Basin byway is located in northeastern Oregon. The byway begins in Baker City and travels southeasterly to form a loop drive back to Baker City. Part of this scenic drive shares the road with the Hells Canyon and Elkhorn Drive scenic byways.

Roads Traveled

The 150-mile route follows portions of Oregon State Highways 7, 86, and 245, and a series of county roads marked with "Snake River / Mormon Basin" signage. The roads are a combination of paved, gravel, and narrow dirt roads, requiring the use of a high-clearance vehicle. The byway is a Type I and II Back Country Byway. Due to the narrow segments, the byway is not recommend for travel by large RVs or vehicles pulling trailers.

Travel Season

The byway is usually open year-round although winter driving conditions may be hazardous. The route can also become impassable at times during the winter or after periods of severe thunderstorms.

Description

This rugged back country byway begins in Baker City and heads east along State Highway 86, crossing the rural countryside before descending into the walled canyon of the Powder River.

Passing through Richland, the byway heads south along the shores of the Powder Arm of Brownlee Reservoir, onto

Local Information

BLM - Vale District Office
100 Oregon St.
Vale, OR 97918
Phone: 541-473-3144

Baker County Chamber of Commerce
490 Campbell St.
Baker City, OR 97814
Phone: 541-523-5855

Farewell Bend State Park
Hwy 30 East
Huntington, OR 97907
Phone: 541-869-2365

the dirt Snake River Road. From here the byway travels through the Snake River Breaks with the waters of Snake River flowing alongside. The byway comes across the BLM Spring Recreation Site where you can pitch a tent and take in the scenery or continue driving. This campground does not have any designated campsites, but picnic tables and drinking water are available.

Continue driving north on old Highway 30 and then Interstate 84 for a few short miles. Take the Rye Valley exit and head west. Through this portion of the byway you're kept company by the waters of Dixie Creek as you travel through rangeland into pinyon juniper country. In Rye Valley the byway narrows and begins climbing the heavily forested slopes of ponderosa pine, juniper, and Douglas fir to the crest of Mormon Basin.

At a four-way intersection, the byway heads northwest up Glengarry Gulch alongside Clarks Creek through aspen, pine, and juniper forests. The waters of Cottonwood Creek will join Clarks Creek as you continue. Shortly, you'll begin heading west along the Burnt River through Bridgeport Valley until you link up with State Highway 245.

You'll want to head north on State Highway 245 where you will enter the Wallowa-Whitman National Forest, taking numerous hairpin turns until you come to the State Highway 7 junction. Continue north on SH 7 through forests of pine, aspen, and fir until you return to Baker City.

Nearby Routes

Elkhorn Drive, page 288 / Hells Canyon, page 294

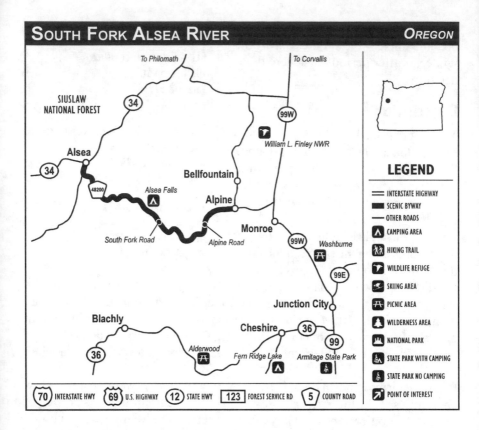

Route Location

The South Fork Alsea River byway is located in northwestern Oregon, about 30 miles northwest of Eugene. The eastern access is located west of Oregon State Highway 99W in the town of Alpine. The byway travels west to the junction with Oregon State Highway 34 in the town of Alsea.

Roads Traveled

The 19 mile route follows the Alpine Road, BLM's South Fork Access Road, and County Road 48200. The byway travels over a combination of paved and gravel-surfaced roads suitable for all vehicles. Visitors to the byway should be cautious of logging trucks in the area. Eleven miles of this route are officially designated a BLM Type I Back Country Byway.

Travel Season

The byway's roads are maintained throughout the year.

Description

The South Fork Alsea River scenic byway follows the path dictated by the twisting and turning river flowing through Oregon's Coastal Range. The byway passes through the Douglas fir forest where some trees may reach heights of 200 feet. Some of these old-growth trees have attained the honorable age of 400 years or more. From mid-summer through autumn, red vine maples proudly display their color. The competing wildflowers growing along the byway bloom much of the year and need not beg for your attention.

The beautiful waterfalls of the South Fork of the Alsea River is perhaps the main attraction to this scenic byway. Here the water tumbles over a 20-foot series of rock steps to the pool formed below. Visitors will find a 16-site BLM campground here, all with picnic tables and fire rings. Drinking water and comfort stations are also provided. Take some time and spend a few days relaxing here. A trail here will lead you to the base of the waterfalls, a nice spot for reading a book or enjoying a picnic. Anglers can spend their days attempting to pull coho salmon, chinook salmon, steelhead, or cutthroat trout from the river. Wildlife observers can enjoy the byway in search of deer or elk. Black bears and bobcats also inhabit the area but are not seen very often.

To the south of the byway is the Corps of Engineers project, Fern Ridge Lake. There are day use parks surrounding the lake that offer swimming beaches and picnic areas. There's also a campground here situated on the south shore. The campground provides hookups, drinking water, restrooms, swimming beach, and a boat ramp. The lake is also a popular spot for sailboating, waterskiing, and fishing.

Local Information

BLM - Salem District Office
1717 Fabry Rd. SE
Salem, OR 97306
Phone: 503-375-5646

Siuslaw National Forest
P.O. Box 1148
Corvallis, OR 97339
Phone: 541-757-4480

Junction City-Harrisburg Area C of C
565 Greenwood St.
Junction City, OR 97448
Phone: 541-998-6154

Corvallis Area Chamber of Commerce
420 NW 2nd St.
Corvallis, OR 97330
Phone: 541-757-1505

Eugene Area Chamber of Commerce
P.O. Box 1107
Eugene, OR 97440
Phone: 541-484-1314

Armitage State Park
90064 Coburg Rd.
Eugene, OR 97408
Phone: 541-686-7884

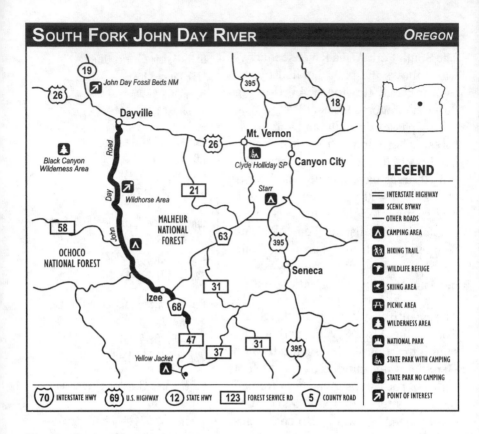

Route Location

The South Fork John Day River byway is located in central Oregon, about 140 miles south of Pendleton. The byway begins in Dayville at the intersection of Park Avenue and South Fork John Day Road. The byway travels south to the Malheur National Forest boundary, a few miles south of Izee.

Roads Traveled

The 50-mile byway follows the South Fork John Day Road and County Road 68. Most of the byway travels on a gravel-surfaced road varying in width from a single-lane road to two lanes. The portion south of Izee on County Road 68 is paved. The byway is designated a Type I and Type II Back Country Byway.

Travel Season

The byway is usually open all year, however, sections may become impassable during winter or spring because of snowy and muddy conditions.

e

Description

The South Fork John Day River byway leads travelers through the scenic river canyon, along the hillsides covered with sagebrush, juniper, and scattered stands of ponderosa pine. The canyon narrows as the byway climbs into the higher elevations where the sagebrush and juniper landscape gives way to forests of ponderosa pine and the occasional Douglas fir and white fir. Willows, shrubs, and hardwood trees line the banks of the river.

The byway passes the Murderer's Creek Wildhorse Management Area about 10 miles south of Dayville. This 150,000-acre area is home to approximately 100 wild horses. This is also an excellent area for viewing mule deer, elk, and bighorn sheep. Other wildlife found in the area includes black bear, coyotes, eagles, and hawks.

The South Fork of the John Day River flows alongside the byway from start to finish. This part of the river is a National Wild and Scenic River, preserving its free-flowing waters. All along the byway anglers are provided excellent opportunties for trout fishing. Private parcels of land do exist along the byway, so obtain permission from land owners before crossing private property. The BLM has maps of the area that shows public and private lands.

Local Information

BLM - Prineville District Office
185 E. 4th St.
Prineville, OR 97754
Phone: 541-447-4115

Malheur National Forest
141 NE Dayton St.
John Day, OR 97845
Phone: 541-575-1731

Ochoco National Forest
P.O. Box 490
Prineville, OR 97754
Phone: 541-447-6247

Grant County Chamber of Commerce
281 W. Main St.
John Day, OR 97845
Phone: 800-769-5664

Harney County Chamber of Commerce
18 West D St.
Burns, OR 97720
Phone: 541-573-2636

John Day Fossil Beds Nat'l. Monument
420 W Main St.
John Day, OR 97845
Phone: 541-987-2333

Clyde Holiday State Park
Oregon Parks & Rec. Dept.
1115 Commercial St. NE
Salem, OR 97310
Phone: 503-378-6305

About 23 miles south of Dayville is a primitive campground with sites for tents and recreational vehicles. There are no facilities available. Camping is permitted anywhere along the byway on BLM land.

Route Location

The Steens Mountain byway is located in southeastern Oregon, approximately 60 miles south of Burns. The byway forms a loop drive beginning in Frenchglen on State Highway 205.

Roads Traveled

The 66-mile route follows the Steens Mountain Loop Road and Oregon State Highway 205. The state highway is a two-lane paved road while the remaing portion of the byway is gravel. Portions of the byway are narrow, rough, and steep requiring the use of a high-clearance vehicle. Passenger cars, recreational vehicles, and vehicles pulling trailers are not recommended on this byway. This scenic drive is a Type II Back Country Byway.

Travel Season

The entire length of the byway is generally open from mid-July through October. Five gates are located at various elevations to control access during wet or snowy conditions. The lower gates are usually opened by May 1 while the upper gates open around mid-July.

Description

The Steens Mountain Back Country Byway travels across Oregon's high desert country and up through the ruggedly beautiful Steens Mountain. Several scenic overlooks along the byway provide spectacular views of Kiger Gorge, wild horses, and the vast expanse of the sagebrush-covered Alvord Desert. In almost every season of the year wildflowers bloom, elegantly displaying their brilliant colors of purple, yellow, and pink.

Local Information

BLM - Burns District Office
HC74-12533 Hwy. 20 West
Hines, OR 97738
Phone: 541-573-5241

Lake County Chamber of Commerce
126 North E St.
Lakeview, OR 97630
Phone: 541-947-6040

Harney County Chamber of Commerce
18 West D St.
Burns, OR 97720
Phone: 541-573-2636

There is a variety of wildlife to be on the lookout for. In the lower elevations, you're likely to see pronghorn antelope and higher up, the majestic bighorn sheep. Mule deer and Rocky Mountain elk are most likely seen near cover and water in the evening and early morning. Overhead, the byway traveler will want to be searching for golden eagles, hawks, and falcons.

For staying overnight or longer, you'll find three campgrounds maintained by the Bureau of Land Management. Page Springs Campground is the first campground encountered east of Frenchglen. There are 30 sites here with picnic tables and fire rings. Fish Lake Campground provides 24 campsites with picnic tables and grills. The lake found here is stocked with cutthroat and rainbow trout. Jackman Park Campground provides six sites. Drinking water and comfort stations are provided in each camping area.

Frenchglen was named for Peter French and his father-in-law, Dr. Hugh Glen. Frenchglen was originially known as P Station and was part of French's P Ranch. The remains of Mr. French's former headquarters for his cattle ranch can be seen about one mile east of Frenchglen. The historic Frenchglen Hotel, built in 1924, is listed on the National Registry of Historic Places and is owned by the state of Oregon. The hotel still accepts guests from March through November.

Nearby Routes

Diamond Loop, page 286 / Lakeview To Steens, page 296

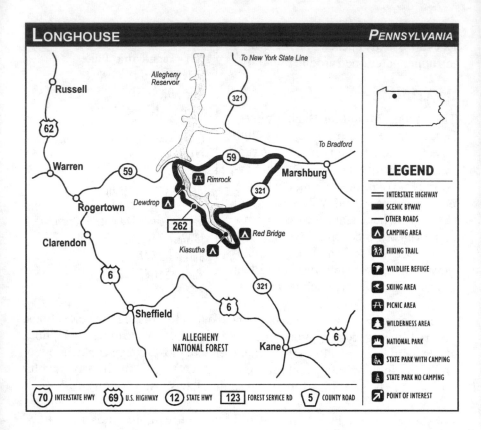

Route Location

The Longhouse scenic drive is located in northwestern Pennsylvania, approximately 15 miles east of Warren. The byway begins at the Forest Service Ranger Station near the junction of State Highways 59 and 321. The byway forms a loop drive back to the ranger station.

Roads Traveled

This 29-mile scenic byway follows Pennsylvania State Highways 59 and 321, and Forest Service Road 262. All of the roads are two-lane paved roads suitable for all types of vehicles. The Longhouse is a National Forest Scenic Byway.

Travel Season

State Highways 59 and 321 are normally open all year long. Forest Service Road 262 is closed from about mid-December through March due to winter snow.

Description

The Longhouse scenic byway travels through the hardwood forests of Allegheny National Forest as it makes its way around the Kinzua Arm of the Allegheny Reservoir. Scenic turnouts along the route provide beautiful vistas of the forest's valleys, rugged rock outcrops, and the lakes blue waters. Fall paints the byway in brilliant colors of red, orange, and gold.

Allegheny Reservoir is a 12,080-acre lake formed by the construction of a dam on the Allegheny River. The dam was constructed by the Corps of Engineers, creating this lake that stretches into New York. The lake provides excellent opportunities for fishing, swimming, boating, and waterskiing.

Local Information

Allegheny National Forest
Bradford Ranger District
Star Rt. 1 - Box 88
Bradford, PA 16701
Phone: 814-362-4613

Warren County Chamber of Commerce
P.O. Box 942
Warren, PA 16365
Phone: 814-723-3050

Kane Chamber of Commerce
14 Greeves St.
Kane, PA 16735
Phone: 814-837-6565

Bradford Area Chamber of Commerce
10 Main St.,Seneca Bldg.
Bradford, PA 16701
Phone: 814-368-7115

Wildlife observers will delight in the many species inhabiting this area. The best time for viewing white-tailed deer is early in the morning or evening. If you look above, you're likely to spot an eagle, osprey, or hawk riding on the wind currents. There's other forms of wildlife here including black bears, turkeys, an abundance of rabbits, and the great blue heron, usually seen fishing along the banks and streams of the reservoir.

Those interested in extending their stay here will find three developed national forest campgrounds to choose from. The Red Bridge Campground offers 55 campsites with picnic tables and grills. Drinking water, restrooms, a dump station, shower facilities, and a playground are provided here. Kiasutha Campground is more developed and has 90 sites for tents and recreational vehicles. The campground also offers drinking water, restrooms, a boat ramp, showers, trailer dump station, and playground equipment. The third camping area is the Dewdrop Campground with 74 sites, drinking water, restrooms, dump station, playground, and boat access to the lake. None of the campgrounds provide hookups.

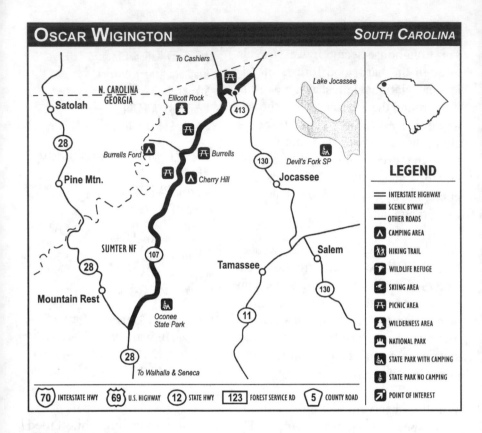

Route Location

The Oscar Wigington scenic byway is in northwestern South Carolina about 53 miles west of Greenville. The byway begins at the intersection with South Carolina Highway 28 and travels north across the Sumter National Forest, ending at the North Carolina state line. Another segment of the byway heads east and ends at the intersection with State Highway 130.

Roads Traveled

The byway is 20 miles long and follows State Highways 107 and 413. The highways are two-lane paved roads suitable for all types of vehicles. Fourteen miles are officially designated a National Forest Scenic Byway.

Travel Season

Normally the byway is open year-round, however, icy conditions may exist in January and February and can temporarily close the roads.

Description

The scenic byway winds through the hardwood forest along the crest of the Blue Ridge Mountains. Turnouts along the byway provide scenic vistas of the surrounding mountains. Fall is a popular time with many for driving the byway as the area is ablaze with colors of orange, red, and gold.

Hikers, backpackers, and horseback riders will be interested in the 9,015-acre Ellicott Rock Wilderness Area. There are miles of trails here running through these beautiful mountains. Maps of the wilderness area and its trails is available from the Andrew Pickens Ranger District in Walhalla. Other trails throughout the forest provide opportunities for short walks to longer day hikes.

The Chattooga River crosses the national forest and is in fact the boundary line between Georgia and South Carolina. Portions of this scenic river have been designated a National Wild and Scenic River. The river offers whitewater rapids for those interested in floating. Outfitters can provide you with all you need to enjoy a float trip down this wild and scenic river. Anglers will find the river provides enjoyable trout fishing.

Local Information

Francis Marion & Sumter N. F.
1835 Assembly St., Room 333
Columbia, SC 29201
Phone: 803-765-5222

Greater Walhalla Area C of C
214 E. Main St.
Walhalla, SC 29691
Phone: 803-638 2727

Cashiers Area Chamber of Commerce
P.O. Box 238
Cashiers, NC 28717
Phone: 704-743-5191

Greater Seneca Chamber of Commerce
P.O. Box 855
Seneca, SC 29679
Phone: 864-882-2097

Discover Upcountry Carolina Assn.
P.O. Box 3116
Greenville, SC 39602
Phone: 800-849-4766

Oconee State Park
624A State Park Rd.
Walhalla, SC 29691
Phone: 864-638-5353

Devils Fork State Park
161 Holcombe Circle
Salem, SC 29676
Phone: 864-944-2639

Those interested in camping will find one national forest campground directly along the byway. This campground provides 22 tree-shaded sites with picnic tables. Drinking water, restrooms, and shower facilities are provided. The Oconee State Park is near the southern end of the byway and provides 140 sites with water and electrical hookups.

Nearby Routes

Russell - Brasstown, page 151 / Blue Ridge Parkway, page 268

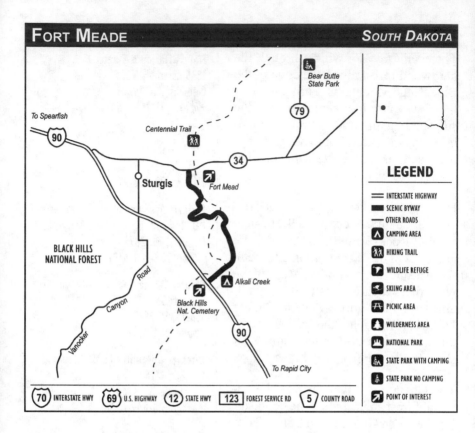

Route Location

The Fort Meade byway is located in west-central South Dakota, just east of Sturgis. The byway begins at the intersection with South Dakota State Highway 34 and travels south to Interstate 90.

Roads Traveled

This scenic drive is a short five-mile route that follows Fort Meade Road which is a two-lane gravel-surfaced road suitable for all types of vehicles. The byway is officially designated a Type I Back Country Byway.

Travel Season

The entire route is usually open year-round.

Description

The Fort Meade Back Country Byway travels through rolling hills covered with ponderosa pine to the historic calvary post of Fort Meade. Historically, this region of the Black Hills was home to Sioux, Cheyenne, and Arapahoe Indian tribes. The settlement of this area by pioneers generated disputes among the Native Americans and the newcomers. By 1878, these conflicts prompted the government to establish this military post situated between Fort Laramie and the Montana forts. Many of the old buildings remain intact and are listed on the National Register of Historic Places. A museum contains exhibits and many historic artifacts.

In addition to the history of the area, the byway does offer outdoor recreation opportunities. The Centennial Trail can be accessed from the byway for those interested in hiking. This 111-mile trail extends from the Wind Cave National Park to Black Butte State Park, about 12 miles north of the byway. Alkali Creek flows alongside the trail near the southern end of the byway.

Those interested in camping will find a six-site BLM campground near the southern terminus. A separate campground for riders and their horses is located adjacent to the Alkali Creek Campground. Additional public campgrounds can be found in the Black Hills National Forest to the south. To the north of the byway is the Black Butte State Park. There are fifteen sites for tents and recreational vehicles, however, no hookups are provided.

Local Information

BLM - South Dakota Resource Area
310 Roundup St.
Belle Fourche, SD 57717
Phone: 605-892-2526

Black Hills National Forest
Rt 2 - Box 200
Custer, SD 57730
Phone: 605-673-2251

Sturgis Area Chamber of Commerce
606 Anna St.
Sturgis, SD 57785
Phone: 605-347-2556

Rapid City Area Chamber of Commerce
444 Mt. Rushmore Rd. N.
Rapid City, SD 57709
Phone: 605-343-1744

Deadwood / Lead Area C of C
735 Main St.
Deadwood, SD 57732
Phone: 605-578-1876

Black Hills, Badlands & Lakes Assn.
900 Jackson Blvd.
Rapid City, SD 57702
Phone: 605-341-1462

Bear Butte State Park
P.O. Box 688
Sturgis, SD 57785
Phone: 605-347-5240

Nearby Routes

Peter Norbeck, page 328 / Spearfish Canyon Highway, page 330

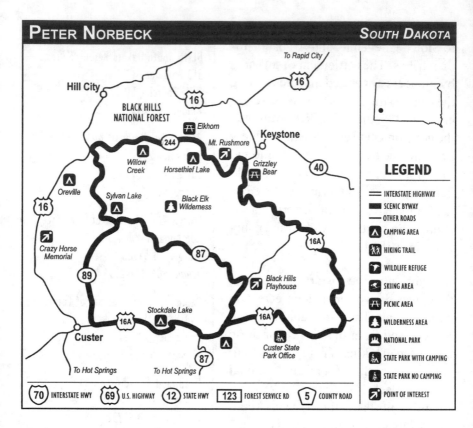

Route Location

Located in southwestern South Dakota, about 20 miles southwest of Rapid City. Beginning east of Custer at the intersection of U.S. Hwy. 16A and State Hwy. 89 the byway forms a loop drive across the Black Hills National Forest.

Roads Traveled

The 70-mile route follows South Dakota State Highways 87, 89, and 244, and U.S. Highway 16A. All of the routes are two-lane paved roads suitable for most vehicles. Vehicles pulling trailers and motorhomers may want to inquire locally before attempting to travel Highways 16A and 87. These routes have many curves and narrow tunnels along with short radius pig-tailed bridges. The byway is designated a National Forest Scenic Byway and a National Scenic Byway by the Federal Highway Administration.

Travel Season

Most of the route is open year-round with the exception of State Highway

87 and sections of U.S. Highway 16A which are closed due to heavy winter snow from December through March.

Description

The Peter Norbeck scenic byway travels through forests of pine, spruce, and groves of aspen as it twists and turns through the beautiful Black Hills. Overlooks along the byway provide spectacular vistas of the surrounding mountains and rugged rock outcrops.

Wildlife observers will be thrilled at the variety of wildlife found here. The American bison, lots of them, can be seen in the area of Custer State Park. Bighorn sheep, pronghorn antelope, wild burros, and pairie dogs can also be seen in the park. Other wildlife frequently seen along the byway includes white-tailed deer, mule deer, and wild turkeys. Rocky Mountain elk, coyotes, red fox, and bobcats also inhabit the area but are seen less frequently. Bird watchers will want to be on the lookout for golden eagles, hawks, woodpeckers, wrens, warblers, and swallows. Bald eagles can be seen from late fall to early spring.

Local Information

Black Hills National Forest
Route 2 - Box 200
Custer, SD 57730
Phone: 605-673-2251

Custer County Chamber of Commerce
447 Crook St.
Custer, SD 57730
Phone: 800-992-9818

Rapid City Area Chamber of Commerce
444 Mt. Rushmore Rd. N
Rapid City, SD 57709
Phone: 605-343-1744

Hot Springs Area Chamber of Commerce
801 S. 6th St.
Hot Springs, SD 57747
Phone: 605-745-4140

Custer State Park
HC83 - Box 70
Custer, SD 57730
Phone: 605-255-4515

Mount Rushmore National Memorial
P.O. Box 268
Keystone, SD 57751
Phone: 605-574-2523

Hikers, backpackers, and horseback riders will find miles of trails within the 9,824-acre Black Elk Wilderness. Some of the hiking trails lead to the summit of 7,242-foot Harney Peak for spectacular panoramic views of the Black Hills. There are numerous other trails accessed along the byway.

Those interested in extending their stay will find many public campgrounds to choose from. The 73,000-acre Custer State Park offers over 300 campsites in several campgrounds along the byway. The state park also offers resorts for those seeking a little more comfort.

Nearby Routes

Fort Meade, page 326 / Spearfish Canyon Highway, page 330

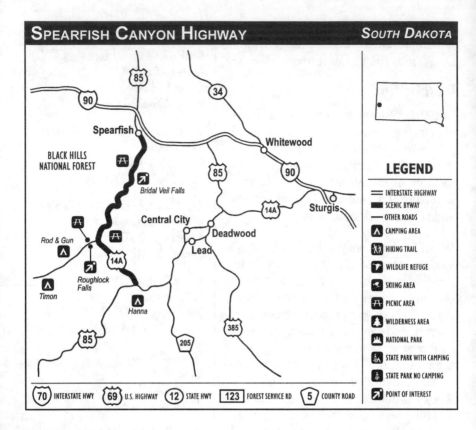

SPEARFISH CANYON HIGHWAY   SOUTH DAKOTA

LEGEND

= INTERSTATE HIGHWAY
■ SCENIC BYWAY
— OTHER ROADS
🄰 CAMPING AREA
🏃 HIKING TRAIL
🐦 WILDLIFE REFUGE
⛷ SKIING AREA
🄰 PICNIC AREA
🌲 WILDERNESS AREA
🏔 NATIONAL PARK
🅰 STATE PARK WITH CAMPING
🅰 STATE PARK NO CAMPING
↗ POINT OF INTEREST

70 INTERSTATE HWY   69 U.S. HIGHWAY   12 STATE HWY   123 FOREST SERVICE RD   5 COUNTY ROAD

Route Location

Spearfish Canyon Highway is located in west-central South Dakota,
approximately 47 miles northwest of Rapid City. The northern access
is located off Interstate 90 in the town of Spearfish. The byway travels
south across the Black Hills National Forest and ends at the intersection with U.S. Highway 85.

Roads Traveled

The 20-mile scenic byway follows U.S. Highway 14A which is a two-lane
paved road safe for travel by all types of vehicles. The Spearfish Canyon
Highway is a National Forest Scenic Byway.

Travel Season

The byway is usually open year-round.

Description

Crossing the Black Hills National Forest, the Spearfish Canyon Highway takes you through the narrow canyon created by the tumbling waters of adjacent Spearfish Creek. The byway twists and turns, following the path dictated by the creek. Spruce, pine, aspen, birch, and oak trees cover much of the hillsides, with limestone cliffs piercing the sky above the forested slopes. In fall the canyon explodes with color as the aspens, birch, and oak prepare for the coming of winter.

Wildlife observers will want to be searching the canyon for white-tailed deer or mule deer. Occasionally raccoons can be seen climbing or wandering among the trees. Overhead, eagles or hawks may be seen riding on the wind currents. Numerous songbirds fill the canyon with their music.

Outdoor recreational opportunities are bountiful along the byway. Spearfish Creek and its tributaries offers one the opportunity for enjoying a lazy afternoon fishing for brown, brook, or rainbow trout. Bridal Veil Falls can be seen from the road as the water plummets 40 feet into the creek over the cliffs up above. The many side canyons offer hikers the opportunity to explore the scenic treasures hidden within.

There are two national forest campgrounds located off the byway down Forest Service Road 222. Rod & Gun offers seven campsites scattered along the banks of Little Spearfish Creek. Timon Campground also offers seven sites situated along the creek. Near the byway's southern end is the Hanna Campground. Visitors will find thirteen sites from which to choose.

Local Information

Black Hills National Forest
Spearfish Ranger District
2014 N. Main St.
Spearfish, SD 57783
Phone: 605-642-4622

Spearfish Area Chamber of Commerce
115 E. Hudson
Spearfish, SD 57783
Phone: 605-642-2626

Deadwood / Lead Area C of C
735 Main St.
Deadwood, SD 57732
Phone: 605-578-1876

Nearby Routes

Fort Meade, page 326 / Peter Norbeck, page 328

Lodging Directory

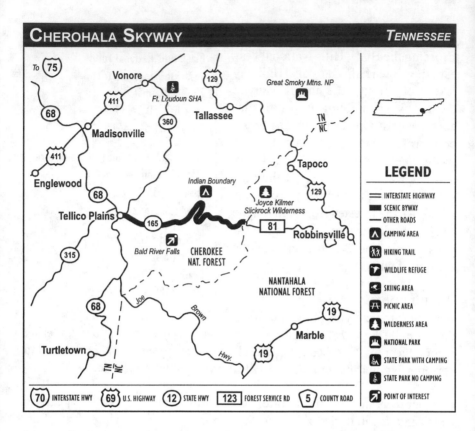

Route Location

The Cherohala Skyway is located in southeastern Tennessee, approximately 60 miles southwest of Knoxville. The byway begins in the town of Tellico Plains and travels east through the Cherokee National Forest to end at the North Carolina state line. The byway can be reached from the North Carolina side by traveling west on Forest Service Road 81 out of Robbinsville.

Roads Traveled

This 23-mile byway follows Tennessee Highway 165 which is a two-lane paved road suitable for all types of vehicles. The scenic drive is both a National Forest Scenic Byway and a National Scenic Byway designated by the Federal Highway Administration.

Travel Season

The Cherohala Skyway is usually open year-round.

Description

The Cherohala Skyway passes through the woodlands, mountains, and valleys found in this part of Tennessee. From Tellico Plains, the byway follows alongside a portion of the Tellico River, a popular spot for trout fishing, canoeing, and kayaking. A short drive off the byway on Forest Development Road 221 (Tellico River Road) will lead to the scenic Bald River Falls. This is also a good spot for fishing, hiking, or enjoying a picnic.

A variety of wildlife is found in this part of Tennessee including bear, wild boar, deer, and a wide variety of birds. The northern flying squirrel, found at high elevations along the Skyway, is listed as a threatened species.

Several overlooks along the route provide scenic vistas of the surrounding mountains. Short loop trails can also be found at the overlooks. The trails vary in length from 3 to 8 miles and are rated from easy to strenuous. Trails may also be accessed that lead into the wilderness area. These trails are generally primitive, rugged, and oftentimes steep.

Local Information

Cherokee National Forest
2800 N. Ocoee St.
Cleveland, TN 37320
Phone: 615-476-9700

Nantahala National Forest
National Forests in North Carolina
P.O. Box 2750
Asheville, NC 28802
Phone: 704-257-4203

Monroe County Chamber of Commerce
P.O. Box 37
Madisonville, TN 37354
Phone: 423-442-4588

Graham County Chamber of Commerce
P.O. Box 1206
Robbinsville, NC 28771
Phone: 704-479-3790

Great Smoky Mtns. National Park
107 Park Headquarters Rd.
Gatlinburg, TN 37738
Phone: 423-436-1200

Ft. Loudoun State Historical Area
338 Fort Loudoun Rd.
Vonore, TN 37885
Phone: 423-884-6217

Those interested in camping will find that the Indian Boundary Recreation Area offers 120 campsites that can accommodate tents or trailers up to 22 feet long. A picnic area, 90-acre lake, swimming area, and a bicycle trail are also found here. Bicycles are available for rent at the Ketoowah Interpretive Center. The Indian Boundary Recreation Area is located off Forest Development Road 345.

Nearby Routes

Ocoee, page 337 / Blue Ridge Parkway, page 228

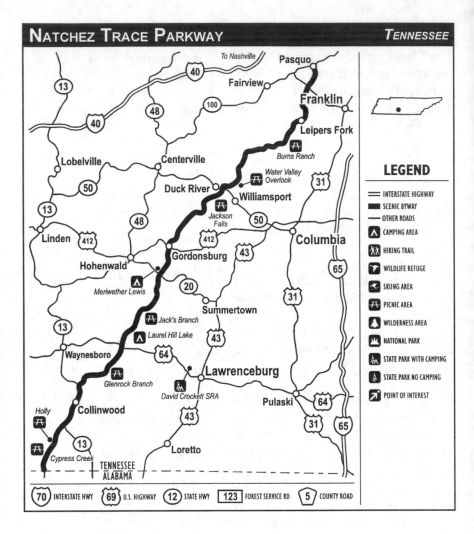

This historic route generally follows the old Indian trace, or trail, between Nashville, Tennessee and Natchez, Mississippi. By 1810, the trace was an important wilderness road and the most heavily traveled pass/trail in the Old Southwest.

Alabama section see page 14 / Mississippi portion see page 199

Route Location

The Natchez Trace Parkway is a 445 mile drive between Natchez, Mississippi and Nashville, Tennessee. This portion of the Natchez Trace Parkway travels across central Tennessee from Nashville to the Alabama state line.

Roads Traveled

The Natchez Trace Parkway is a two-lane paved route that is suitable for all types of vehicles. This portion in Tennessee is about 103 miles in length. The byway has been designated a National Parkway by the National Park Service and an All-American Road by the Federal Highway Administration.

Travel Season

The route is generally open year-round.

Description

Once trekked by Indians and trampled into a rough road by traders, trappers, and missionaries, the Natchez Trace Parkway is now a scenic 445 mile road travelling from Natchez, Mississippi to Nashville, Tennessee. In the late 1700s and early 1800s, "Kaintucks," as the river merchants were called, would float downriver on flatboats loaded with their merchandise to be sold in New Orleans. Since there wasn't any practical way to return by river, the boats were dismantled and the lumber sold. The Natchez Trace would be the only pathway home. At that time, the trace

Local Information

National Park Service
Natchez Trace Parkway
RR I, NT-143
Tupelo, MS 38801
Phone: 601-680-4025

Wayne County Chamber of Commerce
P.O. Box 675
Waynesboro, TN 38485
Phone: 615-722-9022

Lewis County Chamber of Commerce
P.O. Box 182
Hohenwald, TN 38462
Phone: 615-796-4084

Williamson County Chamber of Commerce
P.O. Box 156
Franklin, TN 37065
Phone: 615-794-1225

Lawrence County Chamber of Commerce
P.O. Box 86
Lawrenceburg, TN 38464
Phone: 615-762-4911

David Crockett State Recreation Area
P.O. Box 398
Lawrenceburg, TN 38464
Phone: 615-762-9408

was a dangerous path to take. Travelers waded through swamps, swam streams and fended off attacks by wild animals and poisonous snakes, not to mention keeping an eye open for murderous bandits and Indian attacks. The terrain of the trace was rough, too. A broken leg of a lone traveler would often mean certain death. The dangers of the route earned the Trace the nickname "Devil's Backbone." Modern-day travelers don't have these dangers to face as they travel this historic route. Now you can safely travel the route in the comfort of your own vehicle.

On the parkway's northern end lies the historic city of Nashville which was incorporated in 1806. Early in the 19th century, Nashville became a bustling river port known for shipping cotton. During the Civil War, Nashville was a strategic military post for the Confederacy, but was captured by Union troops in 1862. The Confederates unsuccessfully attempted to retake the city in the Battle of Nashville in December of 1864. Today Nashville is known as "Music City USA," the place to be for country-and-western musicians and fans.

There are many parks developed by the National Park Service along the route. Most of the parks provide picnic facilities and nature trails, some of the trails follow the original Natchez Trace. Camping is available at the Meriwether Lewis Park. This park is the site of Grinder's Inn, where Meriwether Lewis, the noted member of the Lewis and Clark expedition, died of gunshot wounds in 1809. A monument designed as a broken shaft marks his grave. There are 32 campsites for tents or recreational vehicles. A pioneer cemetery, exhibit room, and picnic tables are also found here.

Another option for camping is not too far from the parkway, the David Crockett State Park near Lawrenceburg. The state park offers over 100 campsites for tents and recreational vehicles. A small lake here provides fishing, boating, and swimming opportunities. There are also nature trails and bicycling trails.

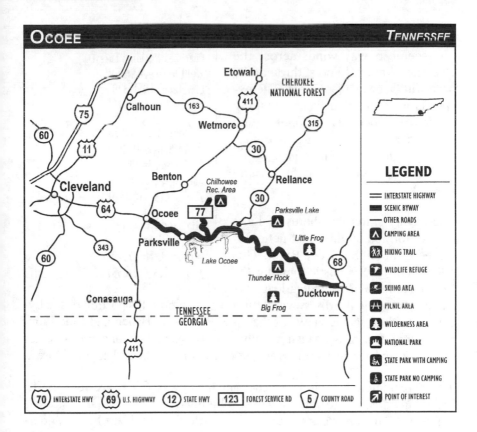

Route Location

The Ocoee scenic drive is located in the southeastern corner of Tennessee, just about 10 miles southeast of Cleveland. The byway's western terminus is in Ocoee on U.S. Highway 411. The byway travels eastward from Ocoee across the Cherokee National Forest and ends in the community of Ducktown on State Highway 68. Another part of the byway heads north off the main route and ends at the Chilhowee Recreation Area.

Roads Traveled

Ocoee is a 29-mile byway following U.S. Highway 64 and Forest Service Road 77. These roads are two-lane paved roads that are safe for all types of vehicles. Twenty-six miles of this scenic drive are officially designated a National Forest Scenic Byway.

Travel Season

The entire length of the byway is normally open year-round.

Description

The scenic byway winds across the Cherokee National Forest through the beautiful Ocoee River Gorge. The byway is accompanied by the rushing waters of Ocoee River, popular with white-water rafters. Several scenic overlooks provide panoramic vistas of the surrounding forested mountains and Lake Ocoee.

The byway skirts the shores of Lake Ocoee, formed by the construction of Ocoee Dam on the Ocoee River. This 1,950-acre lake is nestled among the forested mountains with Sugarloaf Peak standing proudly nearby. Several turnouts are along this portion of the byway providing scenic views of the lake. Parksville Beach and Mac Point Swimming Area provide visitors a chance to relax and go for a dip. A visitor center located nearby has maps and brochures of the lake and national forest.

There are numerous trails accessed along the byway. There are horse trails, bicycling trails, nature trails, and longer hiking trails. Two wilderness areas are near the byway's eastern end. Both Little Frog and Big Frog Wilderness Areas provide opportunities for hiking to secluded spots.

The side trip up Forest Service Road 77 is a steady climb up Chilhowee Mountain. From here, the panoramic vistas extend beyond Lake Ocoee, across the Tennessee Valley to the distant Cumberland Mountains. The large recreation area here offers a 68-site campground, a 7-acre lake with swimming beach, and picnicking areas. Those wishing to camp will find two other campgrounds in addition to the Chilhowee Recreation Area. Parksville Lake offers 32 sites that can accommodate tents or RVs. Thunder Rock is a smaller campground with only six sites with picnic tables and grills. Drinking water and comfort stations are available in both camping areas.

Local Information

Cherokee National Forest
2800 N. Ocoee St. NW
Cleveland, TN 37320
Phone: 615-476-9700

Cherokee National Forest
Ocoee Ranger District
Rt. I - Box 348D
Benton, TN 37307
Phone: 615-338-5201

Cleveland / Bradley C of C
2145 Keith St.
Cleveland, TN 37320
Phone: 615-472-6587

Nearby Routes

Cherohala Skyway, page 332 / Russell - Brasstown, page 151

LODGING DIRECTORY

Lake Ocoee Inn & Marina - Benton (Information), page 447 — Resort (On Lake Ocoee)

BEAVER CANYON   UTAH

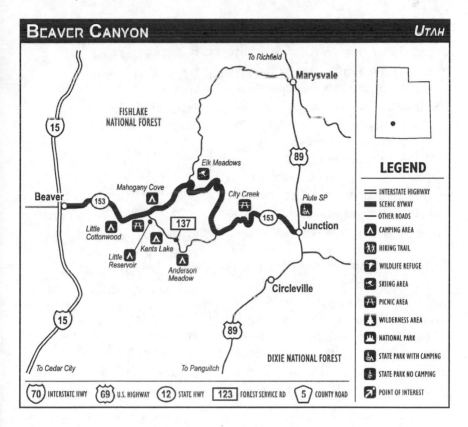

Route Location

The Beaver Canyon byway is located in southwestern Utah, about 50 miles northeast of Cedar City. The byway begins off Interstate 15 in Beaver and travels east across the Fishlake National Forest to end in Junction.

Roads Traveled

The 40-mile byway follows Utah State Highway 153. The byway is a two-lane paved road suitable for all types of vehicles from Beaver to the Elk Meadows Ski Area. State Highway 153 from the ski area to Junction is an unpaved, dry-weather-only road. Seventeen miles of the drive are designated a state scenic byway and National Forest Scenic Byway.

Travel Season

State Highway 153 from Beaver to the ski area is usually open year-round. The rest of the route is closed in winter and may also become impassable after heavy rainfall.

Description

Travelers of this scenic byway are treated to the scenic Beaver Canyon. From Beaver, the byway begins climbing through the forested canyon filled with pine, aspen, and maple. The byway climbs the western slopes of the Tushar Mountains. Several scenic turnouts provide panoramic vistas of the surrounding mountains. The waters of Beaver River will flow alongside you for much of your scenic journey.

Early in the morning or late evening is the best time for spotting mule deer or elk. Wild turkeys can also be seen occasionally. If you look towards the sky you may catch glimpses of eagles, hawks, or falcons. Other wildlife inhabiting the national forest includes moose, mountain goat, bobcat, and mountain lion.

Local Information

Fishlake National Forest
Beaver Ranger District
575 S. Main
Beaver, UT 84713
Phone: 801-438-2436

Dixie National Forest
82 N. 100 E.
Cedar City, UT 84720
Phone: 801-865-3700

Beaver Valley Chamber of Commerce
P.O. Box 760
Beaver, UT 84713
Phone: 801-438-2975

Piute State Park
P.O. Box 43
Antimony, UT 84712
Phone: 801-624-3268

There are two national forest campgrounds along the byway and three a short side trip up Forest Service Road 137. The first campground you come across is situated on the banks of the river. This is the Little Cottonwood Campground. There are fourteen sites here, with two barrier-free sites. Further up the byway is Mahogany Cove Campground. There are seven campsites here set among mountain mahogany and pinyon pine.

About one mile up FDR 137 is Little Reservoir and its campground with eight sites. Little Reservoir is stocked with rainbow and brown trout. Four miles further along is the Kents Lake Campground with seventeen sites surrounding the lake. Continue on another four miles and you'll come across the Anderson Meadow Campground. This campground is 9,350 feet above sea level and has ten campsites and good fishing in the nearby reservoir.

Nearby Routes

Brian Head - Panguitch Lake, page 345 / Fishlake, page 353

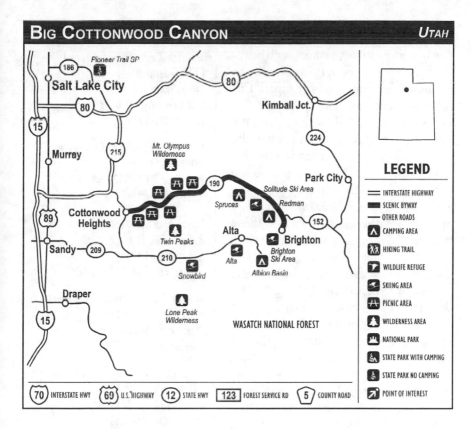

Route Location

The Big Cottonwood Canyon is located in north-central Utah, about 13 miles south of downtown Salt Lake City. The scenic byway begins in Cottonwood Heights at the intersection of Wasatch Boulevard and Utah State Highway 190. The byway travels east and ends in Brighton.

Roads Traveled

This scenic byway is approximately 15 miles in length and follows State Highway 190 which is a two-lane paved road suitable for all vehicles. This is a National Forest Scenic Byway and a state scenic byway.

Travel Season

State Highway 190 is generally open year-round although delays or closure is possible during the winter due to avalanche danger. Snow tires or chains may be required from November through April.

Description

The byway provides visitors with beautiful mountain scenery as it climbs through thick stands of fir, aspen, Engelmann spruce, and lodgepole pine. Big Cottonwood Creek flows alongside the byway and will remain with you to the end. The byway is surrounded by two wilderness areas, Mt. Olympus to the north and Twin Peaks to the south. Several scenic turnouts found along the way provide breathtaking views into these two pristine mountain wilderness areas.

Wildlife observers will delight in the variety of species found along the byway. If you look closely, you may catch glimpses of elk or mule deer foraging among the woods. Moose also inhabit the region but are not seen as often. Other wildlife calling the area home are bobcats, mountain lions, coyotes, beavers, and the snowshoe hare. Birdwatchers will want to be looking for golden eagles, hawks, and a large variety of songbirds.

During the warmer months, byway travelers enjoy picnicking, camping, hiking, and bicycling. At the Birches Picnic Area you can see a water flume clinging to the canyon wall. Winter sport enthusiasts come to this area in search of snowmobiling, downhill skiing, and cross-country skiing. Those interested in hiking will find trails that lead deep into the surrounding wilderness areas. The Doughnut Falls Trail will take you to an unusual waterfall where the waters of Mill D South Fork tumble through a hole in the rock. The Spruces Campground provides 97 campsites for tents and RVs. Redman Campground is set at an elevation of 8,300 feet and offers 38 sites.

Local Information

Wasatch-Cache National Forest
8236 Federal Bldg.
125 S. State St.
Salt Lake City, UT 84138
Phone: 801-524-5030

Park City Chamber of Commerce
P.O. Box 1630
Park City, UT 84060
Phone: 801-649-6100

Sandy Area Chamber of Commerce
8807 S. 700 E.
Sandy, UT 84070
Phone: 801-566-0344

Murray Area Chamber of Commerce
111 E. 5600 S., #104
Murray, UT 84107
Phone: 801-263-2632

Salt Lake Area Chamber of Commerce
175 E. 400 S., # 600
Salt Lake City, UT 84111
Phone: 801-364-3631

Pioneer Trail State Park
2601 Sunnyside Ave.
Salt Lake City, UT 84108
Phone: 801-584-8391

Nearby Routes

Little Cottonwood Canyon, page 359 / Mirror Lake, page 365 / Pony Express, page 373

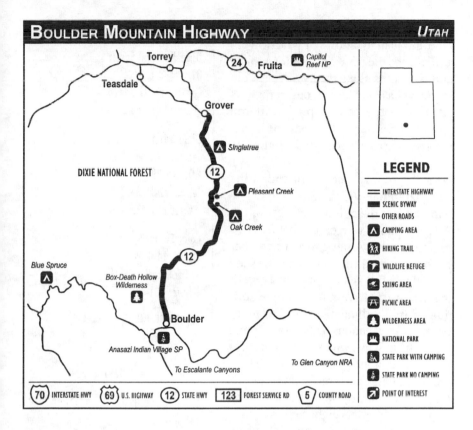

Route Location

The Boulder Mountain Highway is approximately 150 miles east of Cedar City in south-central Utah. The byway begins in Boulder and travels north across the Dixie National Forest to end in the community of Grover.

Roads Traveled

The 30-mile route follows Utah State Highway 12 which is a two-lane paved road suitable for all types of vehicles. The Boulder Mountain Highway is both a National Forest Scenic Byway and a state scenic byway.

Travel Season

State Highway 12 usually remains open all year long. Closure during the winter months is possible after heavy snowfall.

Description

The scenic drive takes travelers from the sagebrush and grassy pastures of

Boulder through stands of ponderosa
pine and lush meadows of wildflowers
as it climbs the edge of Boulder Mountain. Turnouts along the byway provide
scenic vistas of the lower desert regions
set against the backdrop of scattered
mountain peaks. Isolated stands of aspen provide a splash of gold in autumn.

Near the byway's southern end is the
Anasazi Indian Village State Park. The
park depicts the cultural aspects of the
Anasazi Indian who once inhabited this
region. Native American artifacts dating back to the 11th century can be seen
as well as a full-scale replica of a dwell-
ing believed to have existed here. A self-
guided trail will take you to the site of
on-going excavations. Other trails found
along the byway lead to scenic lakes for
fishing or enjoying a picnic lunch. There
are three national forest campgrounds
located along the byway. The Oak Creek
Campground offers eight camping units
situated on the creek. You'll also find
fishing and hiking opportunities here.
Further north of this campground is the
Pleasant Creek Campground with eighteen sites. The Singletree Campground
is the largest of the three with twenty-
six sites and two group camping areas.

Local Information

Dixie National Forest
82 N. 100 E.
Cedar City, UT 84720
Phone: 801-865-3700

Dixie National Forest
Teasdale Ranger District
P.O. Box 99
Teasdale, UT 84773
Phone: 801-425-3702

Color Country
906 N. 1400 W.
St George, UT 84771
Phone: 801-628-4171

Capitol Reef National Park
HC70 - Box 15
Torrey, UT 84775
Phone: 801-425-3791

Glen Canyon National Recreation Area
P.O. Box 1507
Page, AZ 86040
Phone: 602-645-8200

Anasazi Indian Village State Park
400 N. Hwy. 12
Boulder, UT 84716
Phone: 801-335-7308

Nearby Routes

Bull Creek Pass, page 347 / Fishlake, page 353

LODGING DIRECTORY

Boulder View Inn - Torrey, page 433 — Hotel / Motel
Cactus Hill Ranch Motel - Teasdale, page 433 — Cabin / Cottage / Guest Ranch & Hotel / Motel
Cockscomb Inn & Cottage B & B - Teasdale, page 433 — Bed & Breakfast / Inns & Cabin /
Cottage / Guest Ranch
Thousand Lakes RV Park - Torrey, page 434 — Cabin / Cottage / Guest Ranch & Campground / RV Park

BRIAN HEAD - PANGUITCH LAKE   *UTAH*

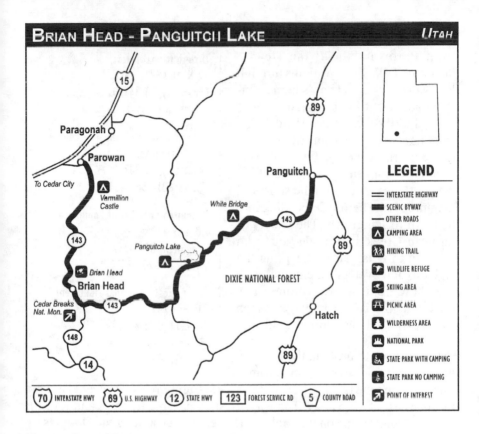

LEGEND

━━━ INTERSTATE HIGHWAY
▬▬ SCENIC BYWAY
━ OTHER ROADS
🅰 CAMPING AREA
🏃 HIKING TRAIL
🦌 WILDLIFE REFUGE
⛷ SKIING AREA
🌳 PICNIC AREA
🌲 WILDERNESS AREA
🏔 NATIONAL PARK
🏕 STATE PARK WITH CAMPING
🎣 STATE PARK NO CAMPING
🚏 POINT OF INTEREST

(70) INTERSTATE HWY   (69) U.S. HIGHWAY   (12) STATE HWY   [123] FOREST SERVICE RD   (5) COUNTY ROAD

Route Location

The Brian Head - Panguitch Lake scenic byway is located in southwestern Utah. The byway begins in Parowan which is about 20 miles north of Cedar City off Interstate 15. The scenic drive then travels south to the Cedar Break National Monument. From there it heads northeast and ends in the town of Panguitch.

Roads Traveled

The 55-mile route follows Utah State Highway 143 which is a two-lane paved road suitable for all types of vehicles. The byway has been designated a National Forest Scenic Byway and a Utah Scenic Byway.

Travel Season

Utah State Highway 143 is generally open year-round. Winter driving conditions may call for extra caution.

Description

From Parowan, the Brian Head - Panguitch Lake byway climbs through Parowan Canyon to Utah's highest incorporated city of Brian Head. Nearby is the 11,305-foot Brian Head Peak. From here the byway cuts through the northeastern corner of Cedar Breaks National Monument, turns northeasterly and continues on to pass the shores of Panguitch Lake before descending into the town of Panguitch. The waters of Parowan Creek will guide you from Parowan to Brian Head, tempting the angler to pull over and attempt to catch a rainbow trout or two. Autumn is a good time to drive the byway as aspen leaves display their colors of gold.

Local Information

Dixie National Forest
82 N. 100 E.
Cedar City, UT 84720
Phone: 801-865-3700

Cedar City Area Chamber of Commerce
286 N. Main St.
Cedar City, UT 84720
Phone: 801-586-4484

Panguitch Chamber of Commerce
P.O. Box 400
Panguitch, UT 84759
Phone: 801-676-8128

Cedar Breaks National Monument
P.O. Box 749
Cedar City, UT 84720
Phone: 801-586-9451

Those wishing to prolong their stay in the area will find several public campgrounds along the byway. Vermillion Castle Campground is located a short distance east of the byway. There are 16 sites suitable for tents and RVs up to 24 feet long sitting on the banks of Bowery Creek among the Douglas fir and pinyon pines. Drinking water and flush toilets are available.

Panguitch Lake sits in a sagebrush basin with aspen and pine trees covering the surrounding hillsides. The lake is stocked with rainbow and brown trout. There are two campgrounds here, Panguitch Lake North and Panguitch Lake South. The northern campground offers 49 sites suitable for tents and RVs. Drinking water, flush toilets, and a dump station are among the facilities found here. The southern campground has 18 sites for tent campers only. Drinking water is not available, but there are comfort stations.

Further up the byway from Panguitch Lake is the White Bridge Campground. Campers will find 28 sites among the cottonwoods lining Panguitch Creek suitable for tents and recreational vehicles up to 24 feet in length. Drinking water and flush toilets are provided.

Nearby Routes

Beaver Canyon, page 339 / Cedar Breaks, page 349 / Markaguant, page 363

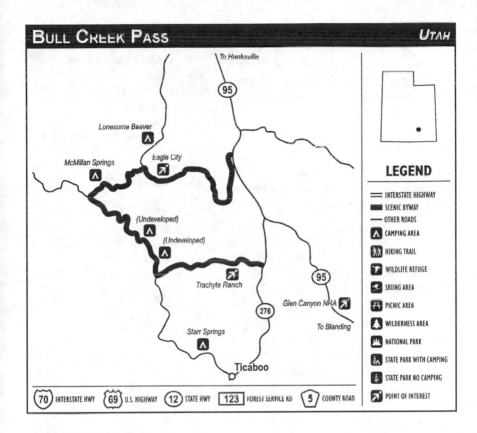

Route Location

Bull Creek Pass is located in southeastern Utah between Capitol Reef National Park and Canyonlands National Park. The byway forms an open loop drive west of State Highways 95 and 276. The northern access is located off Utah State Highway 95 twenty-one miles south of Hanksville. The byway's southern access is from State Highway 276, approximately five miles south of the junction with State Highway 95

Roads Traveled

The 68-mile route travels through remote country along the Bull Creek Pass Road which is a one-lane dirt road. There are numerous rough sections, steep grades, and blind curves. A four-wheel drive vehicle is strongly recommended for traveling this BLM Type III Back Country Byway.

Travel Season

This back country route is generally open from July through October and then the higher elevations may be closed by winter snows. The lower elevations are normally passable year-round although heavy thunderstorms during the summer can wash out sections of the road.

Description

The Bull Creek Pass Back Country Byway takes travelers from the desert floor at an elevation around 5,000 feet to Bull Creek Pass in the Henry Mountains, a height of 10,485 feet above sea level. The view from the pass is truly spectacular. To the west you'll see the Waterpocket Fold, the Circle Cliffs, and Boulder Mountain. In the east are tributaries of the Dirty Devil River, Canyonlands National Park, and the distant Abajo Mountains. The Henry Mountains were the last to be explored and named in continental United States.

As you travel this byway, you'll come across the remains of Eagle City on Cresent Creek. Eagle City was founded in the 1890s after gold was discovered in nearby Bromide Basin. The town once boasted of a hotel, two saloons, a dance hall, three stores, and a post office. By 1900 the gold boom went bust and the town became a ghost town.

There are three developed campgrounds along or near the byway that are maintained by the Bureau of Land Management. Lonesome Beaver Campground offers five sites with picnic tables and fire rings. McMillan Springs has ten sites and Starr Springs offer twelve. All of the campgrounds provide drinking water and vault toilets. There are also two primitive campgrounds along the byway. Camping is also permitted anywhere along BLM lands. Check with the BLM office in Hanksville for more information.

Nearby Routes

Boulder Mountain Highway, page 343

Local Information

BLM - Richfield District Office
150 E. 900 N.
Richfield, UT 84701
Phone: 801-896-8221

BLM - Henry Mountain Resource Area
P.O. Box 99
Hanksville, UT 84734
Phone: 801-542-3461

Color Country
906 N. 1400 W.
St George, UT 84771
Phone: 801-628-4171

Canyon Lands South
P.O. Box 490
Monticello, UT 84535
Phone: 801-587-3235

Blanding Chamber of Commerce
P.O. Box 792
Blanding, UT 84511
Phone: 801-678-2539

Glen Canyon National Recreation Area
P.O. Box 1507
Page, AZ 86040
Phone: 602-645-8200

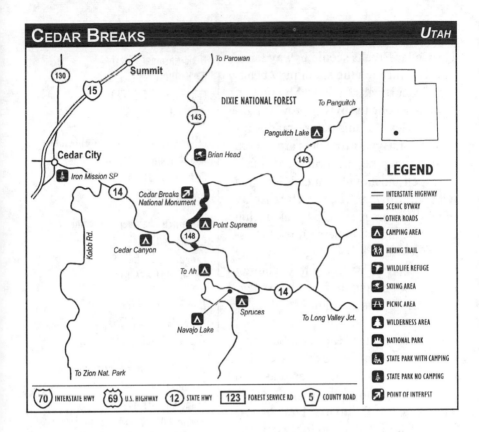

Route Location

The Cedar Breaks scenic byway is located in southwestern Utah, approximately 14 miles east of Cedar City. The byway begins at the junction of Utah State Highways 14 and 148 and travels north along the Cedar Breaks National Monument to end at the intersection with State Highway 143.

Roads Traveled

This short six-mile byway follows Utah State Highway 148 which is a two-lane paved road safe for travel by all types of vehicles. The byway is designated a National Forest Scenic Byway and a Utah Scenic Byway.

Travel Season

The byway is passable throughout most of the year but is closed during the winter months.

Description

The Cedar Breaks scenic byway takes travelers through the stunningly beautiful Cedar Breaks National Monument. Turnouts along the byway provide panoramic views of this nature-made amphitheater. Byway travelers are treated to forests of pine, fir, spruce, and quaking aspen and mountain meadows filled with wildflowers. The colorful display of wildflowers reaches its peak during July and August. In September, the aspen trees turn a bright gold. Byway travelers are most likely to encounter mule deer grazing in the meadows every morning and evening.

The visitor center near Point Supreme Campground offers exhibits on the plants and animals of the area as well as the formation of the amphitheater. The Wasatch Ramparts Trail begins here and follows the rim for two miles, taking you to panoramic overlooks. Along the trail at Spectra Point is a stand of bristlecone pine, some trees being over 1,500 years old.

Local Information

Dixie National Forest
82 N. 100 E.
Cedar City, UT 84720
Phone: 801-865-3700

Cedar City Area Chamber of Commerce
286 N. Main St.
Cedar City, UT 84720
Phone: 801-586-4484

Panguitch Chamber of Commerce
P.O. Box 400
Panguitch, UT 84759
Phone: 801-676-8128

Zion National Park
Springdale, UT 84767
Phone: 801-772-3256

Cedar Breaks National Monument
P.O. Box 749
Cedar City, UT 84720
Phone: 801-586-9451

Iron Mission State Park
585 N. Main St.
Cedar City, UT 84720
Phone: 801-586-9451

About midway along the scenic drive is the Alpine Pond Trail. This is a short, easy, self-guided trail that will lead you to Alpine Pond where wildflowers grow along the shore. A stand of bristlecone pine can be found near the Chessman Ridge Overlook.

A campground and picnic area is located near Point Supreme. The campground offers 30 sites for tents and recreational vehicles. Drinking water and comfort stations are among the facilities available.

Nearby Routes

Brian Head - Panguitch Lake, page 345 / Markaguant, page 363

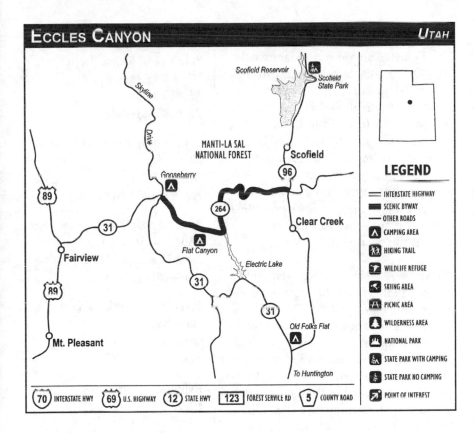

Route Location

The Eccles Canyon scenic drive is located in central Utah, approximately 50 miles southeast of Provo. The byway's eastern access point is between Scofield and Clear Creek at the intersection with State Highways 96 and 264. The western terminus is at the junction with State Highway 31, a few miles northeast of Fairview.

Roads Traveled

The 16-mile route follows Utah State Highway 264 which is a two-lane paved road suitable for all vehicles. The byway is a National Forest Scenic Byway and a state scenic drive.

Travel Season

State Highway 264 is generally open year-round although winter driving conditions may require the use of extra caution. Snow tires or chains may be required at times from October through April.

Description

The Eccles Canyon travels across the 10,000 foot Wasatch Plateau offering beautiful panoramic vistas of the Manti-La Sal National Forest and descends 2,500 feet to the Eccles Canyon. The meandering waters of Upper Huntington Creek will greet you midway along this route and will accompany you for several miles. Wildflowers growing in the meadows provide a colorful display set against the backdrop of the evergreens.

Those interested in staying overnight or longer will find two public campgrounds along the byway. The Gooseberry Campground is near the byway's western terminus and provides eight sites, two of which can accommodate recreational vehicles up to 25 feet. Flat Canyon Campground has thirteen sites set among Engelmann spruce and subalpine fir. All of the campsites can accommodate recreational vehicles up to 30 feet. Near this campground is Boulger Reservoir which is stocked with rainbow trout. Both campgrounds are open from mid-June through mid-September.

Local Information

Manti - La Sal National Forest
599 W. Price River Dr.
Price, UT 84501
Phone: 801-637-2817

Carbon County Chamber of Commerce
P.O. Box 764
Price, UT 84501
Phone: 801-637-2788

Mount Pleasant Chamber of Commerce
115 W. Main St., City Hall
Mount Pleasant, UT 84647
Phone: 801-462-2456

Emery County Chamber of Commerce
410 E. Main
Castle Dale, UT 84513
Phone: 801-381-2547

Scofield State Park
P.O. Box 166
Price, UT 84501
Phone: 801-448-9449

To the north of the byway's eastern end is the Scofield State Park. There are 134 campsites here, most suitable for tent campers only. Drinking water, restrooms, and shower facilities are found here. The park also offers miles of groomed snowmobile and cross-country skiing trails for winter sport enthusiasts.

Nearby Routes

Huntington Canyon, page 357 / Nine Mile Canyon, page 369

Lodging Directory

Larsen House Bed & Breakfast - Mt. Pleasant, page 437 — Bed & Breakfast / Inns

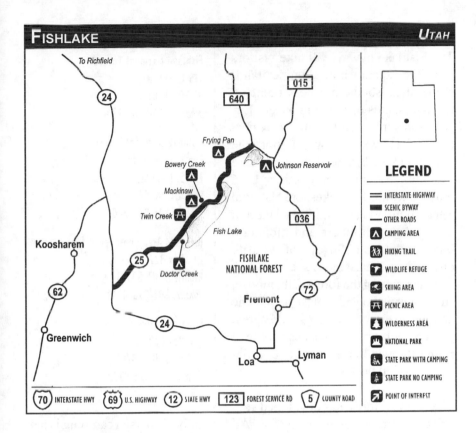

Route Location

The Fishlake scenic byway is located in south-central Utah, approximately 30 miles southeast of Richfield. The byway begins at the junction of Utah State Highways 24 and 25 and travels northeast across Fishlake National Forest. The byway ends at the intersection with Forest Service Road 036, also known as the Fremont River Road.

Roads Traveled

The byway is about 16 miles long and follows Utah State Highway 25 which is a two-lane paved road suitable for all types of vehicles. Thirteen miles of this route are designated a National Forest Scenic Byway and a Utah Scenic Byway.

Travel Season

The state highway is usually open year-round. Driving the byway in winter may require drivers to use extra caution.

Description

The Fishlake byway will take visitors from the sagebrush and juniper landscape at its southern access point up through stands of quaking aspen, Engelmann spruce, and white fir. A portion of the byway follows the shoreline of Fish Lake, a beautiful mountain lake extending 5½ miles in length and 1½ miles in width. The Lakeshore National Recreation Trail surrounds the lake and is popular with hikers and mountain bikers. The watchful eye of wildlife observers will most likely see mule deer foraging among the forest. Elk, moose, and mountain lions also make their home here but are not commonly seen. Osprey, golden eagles, and hawks can be seen riding the wind currents above, especially around the lake.

Local Information

Fishlake National Forest
115 E. 900 N.
Richfield, UT 84701
Phone: 801-896-9233

Fishlake National Forest
Loa Ranger District
138 S. Main St.
Loa, UT 84747
Phone: 801-836-2800

Richfield Area Chamber of Commerce
P.O. Box 327
Richfield, UT 84701
Phone: 801-896-4241

Panoramaland
P.O. Box 820
Richfield, UT 84701
Phone: 801-896-9222

The national forest has developed several campgrounds along the byway. Additionally, dispersed camping is permitted anywhere on national forest land. The Doctor Creek camping area offers 31 sites, 15 that can accommodate recreational vehicles up to 22 feet long. The Mackinaw Campground has 68 sites suitable for tent campers and recreational vehicles up to 22 feet. Bowery Creek Campground is the second largest along the byway with 43 sites. All of the campsites here can accommodate recreational vehicles up to 22 feet and have complete hookups. The Frying Pan camping area offers 12 sites suitable for tents and recreational vehicles.

Many of the campgrounds are situated on picturesque Fish Lake, a natural lake surrounded by rolling mountains. Anglers will find rainbow and brown trout in the lake among other species. Johnson Reservoir is a smaller lake but also provides good fishing opportunities.

Nearby Routes

Beaver Canyon, page 339 / Boulder Mountain Highway, page 343

FLAMING GORGE - UINTAS   UTAH

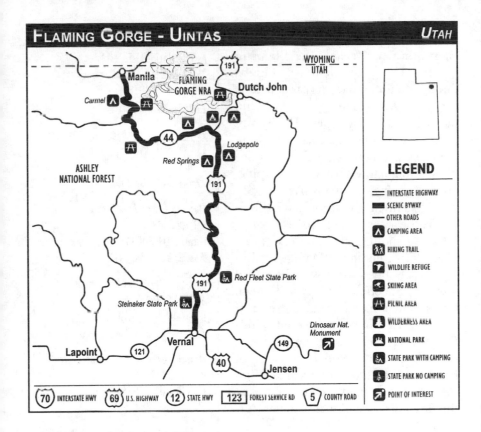

Route Location

The Flaming Gorge - Uintas scenic byway is located in northeastern Utah, beginning in Vernal which is about 30 miles west of the Colorado state line. The byway travels north from Vernal across the Ashley National Forest, enters the Flaming Gorge National Recreation Area, and ends in the small community of Manila.

Roads Traveled

The 67-mile byway follows U.S. Highway 191 and State Highway 44. Both routes are two-lane paved roads suitable for all vehicles. The byway is designated a National Forest Scenic Byway and state scenic drive.

Travel Season

U.S. Highway 191 and State Highway 44 usually remain open year-round. Caution should be exercised when driving the route during winter, especially in the higher elevations.

Description

Beginning in Vernal, the Flaming Gorge - Uintas scenic byway climbs through sculptured layers of sandstone and steep slopes of juniper, pinyon, and patches of quaking aspen. The byway continues its winding course, climbing the eastern flank of the Uinta Mountains, through forests of lodgepole pine, ponderosa pine, and aspen, passing open meadows filled with colorful wildflowers. These areas provide good opportunities for spotting elk, moose, or mule deer. Before ending in Manila, the byway treats the visitor with beautiful views of Sheep Creek Bay and Sheep Creek Canyon as it descends a steep cliff along the twisting, turning road. Wildlife observers will want to keep one eye on the road and the other in search of bighorn sheep through this area. Visitors can obtain maps and brochures at the national forest offices in either Vernal or Manila.

The Flaming Gorge National Recreation Area is loaded with outdoor recreation opportunities. Flaming Gorge Reservoir is a 91-mile lake formed when the Bureau of Reclamation constructed a dam on the Green River. The huge lake extends into Wyoming and offers excellent boating and fishing opportunities. Fishermen will find lake trout, rainbow trout, smallmouth bass, and Kokanee salmon. Boat ramps provide access to the lake and can be found in many of the campgrounds surrounding the lake. Several campgrounds in the area provide beautiful spots for pitching a tent or parking your RV for a few days.

Local Information

Ashley National Forest
355 N. Vernal Ave.
Vernal, UT 84078
Phone: 801-789-1181

Vernal Area Chamber of Commerce
134 W. Main
Vernal, UT 84078
Phone: 801-789-1352

Flaming Gorge Area C of C
P.O. Box 122
Manila, UT 84046
Phone: 801-784-3417

Dinosaur National Monument
4545 U.S. Hwy. 40
Dinosaur, CO 81610
Phone: 970-374-3000

Flaming Gorge National Rec. Area
P.O. Box 278
Manilla, UT 84046
Phone: 801-784-3445

Steinaker State Park
4335 N. Hwy. 191
Vernal, UT 84078
Phone: 801-789-4432

Red Fleet State Park
4335 N. Hwy. 191
Vernal, UT 84078
Phone: 801-789-4432

Nearby Routes

Nine Mile Canyon, page 369

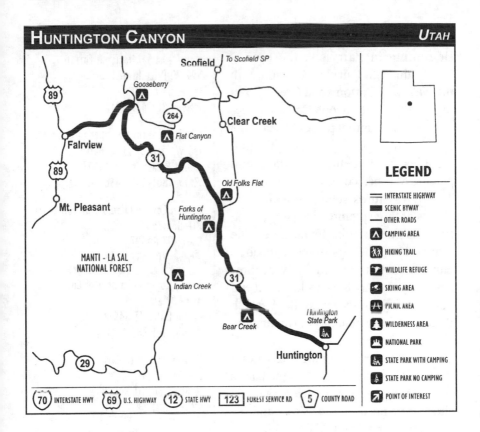

Route Location

The Huntington Canyon byway is located in central Utah, about 21 miles southwest of Price. The byway's eastern terminus is located in Huntington at the intersection with State Highways 10 and 31. The western end of the byway is in Fairview on U.S. Highway 89.

Roads Traveled

The Huntington Canyon scenic drive is approximately 48 miles long following State Highway 31, a two-lane paved road safe for traveling by all types of vehicles. This scenic route is a National Forest Scenic Byway and a Utah Scenic Byway.

Travel Season

The entire route is generally open year-round although winter driving conditions may be hazardous. Snow tires or chains may be required at times from October through April.

Description

Beginning in Fairview, the byway climbs through Fairview Canyon with the waters of Cottonwood Creek flowing nearby. Cottonwood Creek will accompany you until it passes beneath the byway through the Narrows Tunnel. Douglas fir, Engelmann spruce, and patches of aspen cover the steep slopes. The byway turns south and skirts the shores of three picturesque lakes; good trout fishing may be found here. The byway continues its descent through Huntington Canyon and is now accompanied by Huntington Creek. You'll end your scenic journey across the Wasatch Plateau in the community of Huntington.

There are several camping areas along the byway, many situated on the banks of bubbling creeks. Gooseberry is a short drive north of the byway and offers eight campsites. Old Folks Flat also offers eight sites set among spruce and fir trees. The campsites can accommodate tents or recreational vehicles up to 30 feet. Forks of Huntington Campground lies on the banks of Huntington Creek and has six tent-only campsites. A hiking trail accessed here will take you along Left Fork Creek. Bear Creek is a county-maintained campground with twenty sites for tents and recreational vehicles. Two miles east of Huntington is a state park with twenty-two sites, some with hookups.

Local Information

Manti - La Sal National Forest
599 W. Price River Dr.
Price, UT 84501
Phone: 801-637-2817

Mount Pleasant Chamber of Commerce
115 W. Main St., City Hall
Mount Pleasant, UT 84647
Phone: 801-462-2456

Carbon County Chamber of Commerce
P.O. Box 764
Price, UT 84501
Phone: 801-637-2788

Emery County Chamber of Commerce
410 E. Main
Castle Dale, UT 84513
Phone: 801-381-2547

Huntington State Park
P.O. Box 1343
Huntington, UT 84528
Phone: 801-687-2491

Scofield State Park
P.O. Box 166
Price, UT 84501
Phone: 801-448-9449

Nearby Routes

Eccles Canyon, page 351 / Nebo Loop, page 367 / Nine Mile Canyon, page 369

Lodging Directory

Larsen House Bed & Breakfast - Mt. Pleasant, page 440 — Bed & Breakfast / Inns

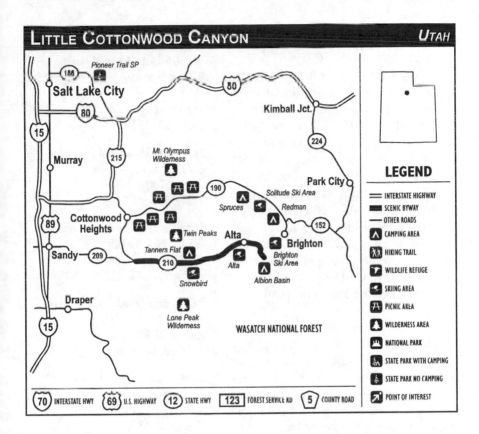

Route Location

Little Cottonwood Canyon is located in north-central Utah, about 18 miles south of downtown Salt Lake City. The byway begins at the junction of Utah State Highways 209 and 210 and travels east to end three miles east of Alta near the Albion Basin Campground.

Roads Traveled

The 12-mile byway follows Utah State Highway 210 which is a narrow two-lane paved road to Alta with the remaining portion being graveled. The byway is safe for travel by all types of vehicles. This is a state scenic drive and a National Forest Scenic Byway.

Travel Season

The paved portion of the byway is usually open year-round. The graveled portion from Alta to Albion Basin is closed from November through May because of heavy snowfall.

Description

The Little Cottonwood Canyon is a scenic journey through the narrow, sheer-walled canyon of Little Cottonwood Creek. Near the mouth of the canyon is the site where Mormon pioneers quarried huge granite blocks used to construct the Salt Lake Temple. Today, the canyon is used by those in pursuit of outdoor recreation. The area attracts downhill and cross-country skiers during winter and hikers, campers, and photographers during the warmer months. A beautiful display of colorful wildflowers rewards the byway travelers who reach the end of the road.

Wildlife observers will want to be on the lookout for mule deer, elk, and moose. Golden eagles and hawks can sometimes be seen riding the wind currents above the canyon walls. If you decide to camp among the stars, hooting of the great horned owl may break the nighttime silence. During the day, numerous songbirds will be heard speaking to one another in a language only known to them. Other wildlife inhabiting the area but rarely seen includes coyotes, mountain lions, and bobcats.

For a breathtaking view of the surrounding mountains and its wilderness areas, be sure to take the Snowbird Tram to the top of 11,000-foot Hidden Peak. There are two wilderness areas along the byway. Twin Peaks Wilderness to the north protects 11,796 acres of the rugged landscape and separates Big Cottonwood Canyon from Little Cottonwood Canyon. To the south of the byway is 30,088-acre Lone Peak Wilderness. Both wilderness areas provide back country exploration for the experienced hiker. Tanners Flat Campground provides 36 sites suitable for tents and RVs. Albion Basin Campground is set 9,500 feet above sea level and has 21 campsites.

Nearby Routes

Big Cottonwood Canyon, page 341 / Pony Express, page 373

Local Information

Wasatch-Cache National Forest
8236 Federal Bldg.
125 S. State
Salt Lake City, UT 84138
Phone: 801-524-5030

Sandy Area Chamber of Commerce
8807 S. 700 E.
Sandy, UT 84070
Phone: 801-566-0344

Salt Lake Area Chamber of Commerce
175 E. 400 S., #600
Salt Lake City, UT 84111
Phone: 801-364-3631

Murray Area Chamber of Commerce
111 E. 5600 S., # 104
Murray, UT 84107
Phone: 801-263-2632

Pioneer Trail State Park
2601 Sunnyside Ave
Salt Lake City, UT 84108
Phone: 801-584-8391

LOGAN CANYON HIGHWAY   UTAH

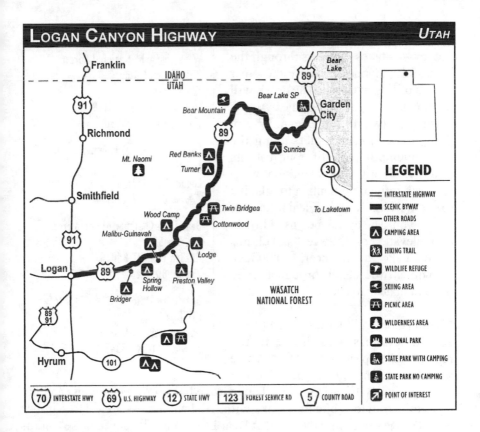

Route Location

The Logan Canyon Highway is located in northern Utah near the Idaho state line. The byway begins in Logan, 47 miles north of Ogden, and travels northeast across the Wasatch-Cache National Forest to the small community of Garden City.

Roads Traveled

Logan Canyon Highway is a 40-mile byway following U.S. Highway 89. The highway is a two-lane paved road suitable for all types of vehicles. The byway has been designated a National Forest Scenic Byway and a Utah Scenic Byway.

Travel Season

Winter driving conditions, especially in the higher elevations, may dictate the use of extra caution, otherwise the byway is generally open all year.

Description

The byway takes travelers through the beautiful canyon carved by the clear waters of Logan Creek. The creek will accompany you for most of the byway's journey eastward from Logan. You're likely to see many anglers along the creek attempting to pull trout from its water. The nearly vertical limestone walls and rock formations contain fossils that speak much of the geological history of the canyon. The byway begins in Logan at an elevation of 4,525 feet and climbs to Bear Lake Summit, nearly 7,800 feet, then quickly descends through a series of switchbacks to end in Garden City.

Mount Naomi Wilderness is a 44,964-acre wilderness area, home to the region's tallest peak at 9,980 feet. A side trip west of the byway near Turner Campground will lead to scenic Tony Grove Lake. From here you can hike a 4½-mile trail to White Pine Lake within the wilderness area. The Limber Pine Trail is a one-mile loop trail at Bear Lake Summit near Sunrise Campground that is a pleasant walk providing scenic vistas of Bear Lake ten miles away. Another one-mile trail near the Cottonwood Picnic Area will take you to Logan Canyon's Wind Caves. The caves offer an outstanding example of a series of arches and rooms formed by wind and ice erosion.

Malibu-Guinavah is the largest campground offering 40 sites for tents and RVs up to 25 feet. Sunrise is the next largest and has 27 campsites. Bridger, Lodge, and Turner Campgrounds each has ten sites with picnic tables and fire rings. Twelve campsites for tents and RVs await the byway traveler in the Red Banks and Spring Hollow Campgrounds. Preston Valley offers eight sites while Wood Camp has six. All of the campgrounds can accommodate RVs up to 20 feet except Malibu-Guinavah. The campgrounds have a seven day length of stay limit.

Local Information

Wasatch-Cache National Forest
8236 Federal Bldg.
125 S. State
Salt Lake City, UT 84138
Phone: 801-524-5030

Cache Chamber of Commerce
160 N. Main
Logan, UT 84321
Phone: 801-752-2161

Bear Lake Chamber of Commerce
P.O. Box 55
Garden City, UT 84028
Phone: 801-946-2901

Bear Lake State Park
P.O. Box 184
Garden City, UT 84028
Phone: 801-946-3343

Nearby Routes

Ogden River, page 371 / Transcontinental Railroad, page 379 / Bear Lake - Caribou, page 153

MARKAGUANT   UTAH

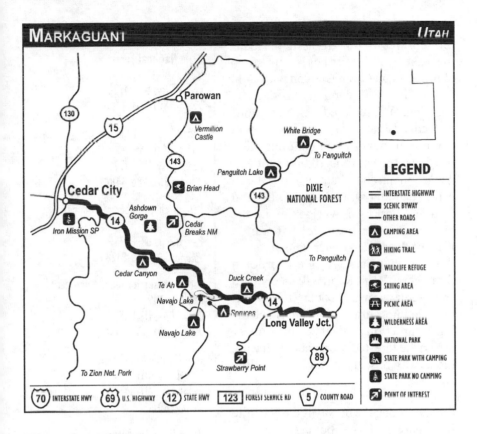

Route Location

The Markaguant scenic byway is located in southwestern Utah. The byway begins off Interstate 15 in Cedar City and travels east across the Dixie National Forest to U.S. Highway 89 in Long Valley Junction.

Roads Traveled

Maraguant is approximately 40 miles long and follows Utah State Highway 14. The highway is a two-lane paved road safe for travel by all types of vehicles. This scenic drive has been officially designated a National Forest Scenic Byway and a state scenic drive.

Travel Season

State Highway 14 is maintained year-round, however, winter driving conditions may call for extra caution.

Description

The byway begins in historic Cedar City where pioneers first arrived in

1851 and soon established the first iron refinery west of the Mississippi. Heading east, the byway begins its steep climb through Cedar Canyon with Coal Creek quietly flowing alongside. The stunning, multi-colored rock formations of Cedar Breaks National Monument come into view as you continue eastward. To the south is 10,000-foot Cedar Mountain and a bumpy, four-wheel-drive road that will take you into Zion National Park. An overlook along the byway offers a beautiful panoramic view of the distant towers and buttes of this national park. A side trip down Strawberry Point Road will take you to spectacular views of southern Utah extending into Zion National Park. Nearing completion of your scenic journey across the forested Markaguant Plateau, the byway descends into Long Valley Junction.

Situated along the byway is the 3½-mile long Navajo Lake, popular with the trout fisher. There are also three national forest campgrounds here. The Spruces Campground has 28 campsites with picnic tables. The Navajo Lake Campground also offers 28 campsites for tents and RVs up to 24 feet long. There are 42 sites available in the Te-Ah Campground. All of the campgrounds have drinking water, flush toilets, and boat access to the lake. Visitors can stay at any one site for up to two weeks.

Other national forest camping areas can be found in the Cedar Canyon and Duck Creek Campgrounds. Cedar Canyon, the smaller of the two, offers 19 sites with picnic tables. The campsites here can accommodate tents and RVs up to 24 feet long. Duck Creek has 79 sites for tents and RVs up to 35 feet long.

Local Information

Dixie National Forest
82 N. 100 E.
Cedar City, UT 84720
Phone: 801-865-3700

Cedar City Area Chamber of Commerce
286 N. Main St.
Cedar City, UT 84720
Phone: 801-586-4484

Panguitch Chamber of Commerce
P.O. Box 400
Panguitch, UT 84759
Phone: 801-676-8128

Cedar Breaks National Monument
P.O. Box 749
Cedar City, UT 84720
Phone: 801-586-9451

Iron Mission State Park
585 N. Main St
Cedar City, UT 84720
Phone: 801-586-9451

Brian Head Ski Resort
223 Hunter Ridge Dr.
Brian Head, UT 84719
Phone: 801-677-2035

Nearby Routes

Brian Head - Panguitch Lake, page 345 / Cedar Breaks, page 349 / Smithsonian Butte, page 377

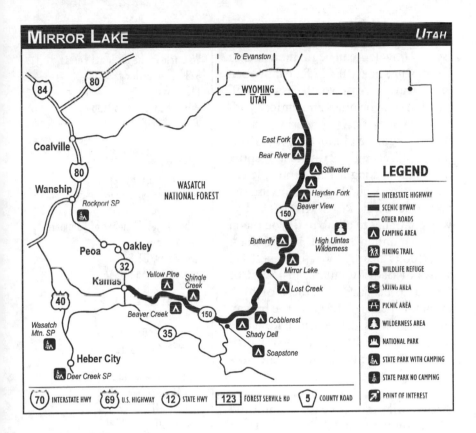

Route Location

The Mirror Lake scenic drive is located in north-central Utah, 45 miles east of Salt Lake City. The byway begins in the community of Kamas and travels northeast, crossing Bald Mountain Pass before descending to its end at the Wyoming state line.

Roads Traveled

Mirror Lake is a 65-mile route following Utah State Highway 150. This highway is a two-lane paved road suitable for all types of vehicles. The byway has been officially designated a National Forest Scenic Byway and a Utah Scenic Byway.

Travel Season

The entire length of the byway is generally open from Memorial Day through mid-October. The rest of the year, the portion from Soapstone to Beaver River is closed by snow. This portion is used as a snowmobile trail.

Description

Byway travelers can begin their scenic journey in Kamas, 6,437 feet above sea level. Traveling east, you'll pass through stands of pinyon pines and juniper with Beaver Creek flowing nearby. As the byway begins to climb, the pinyon-juniper landscape gives way to lodgepole pine and quaking aspen. You'll leave Beaver Creek and begin following the course set by the Provo River. The byway continues to climb until you reach Bald Mountain Pass at 10,715 feet. Overlooks nearby provide beautiful views of Bald Mountain, just west of you, and the vast wilderness of high mountain peaks to the east. The byway then begins its descent to end at the Wyoming state line, all the while providing spectacular views of the surrounding landscape.

A two-mile trail accessed near Bald Mountain Pass will take you to the top of Bald Mountain. The panoramic view from this mountain peak is breathtaking. Another short walking trail, this one paved, will take you to the Provo River Falls Overlook. Trails near the Lost Creek Campground will lead you among many alpine lakes. The ten-mile Notch Mountain Trail will leave the byway from this area, take you along beautiful mountain lakes, and return you to the byway at Bald Mountain Pass.

If you're interested in staying overnight or longer there are over twenty campgrounds to choose from offering a total of nearly 700 sites. The campgrounds are generally open from Memorial Day through September. All of the campgrounds can accommodate tents or RVs. Most provide drinking water and comfort stations; none have hookups.

Local Information

Wasatch-Cache National Forest
8236 Federal Bldg.
125 S. State
Salt Lake City, UT 84138
Phone: 801-524-5030

Evanston Chamber of Commerce
36 10th St.
Evanston, WY 82931
Phone: 307-789-2757

Heber Valley Chamber of Commerce
475 N. Main St.
Heber City, UT 84032
Phone: 801-654-3666

Rockport State Park
9040 N. Hwy. 32
Peoa, UT 84061
Phone: 801-336-2241

Wasatch Mountain State Park
P.O. Box 10
Midway, UT 84049
Phone: 801-654-1791

Deer Creek State Park
P.O. Box 257
Midway, UT 84049
Phone: 801-654-0171

Nearby Routes

Big Cottonwood Canyon, page 341 / Ogden River, page 371

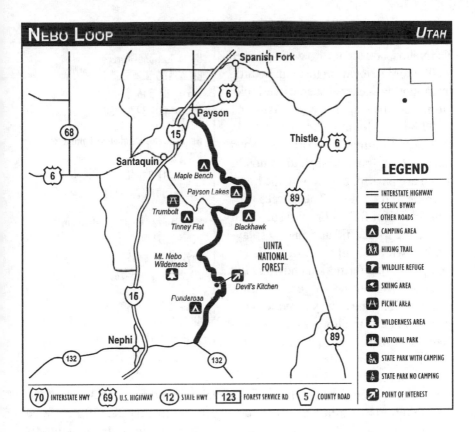

Route Location

The Nebo Loop scenic byway is approximately 15 miles south of Provo in central Utah. The byway begins in Payson off Interstate 15 and travels south across the Uinta National Forest. The scenic drive's southern terminus is at the intersection with Utah State Highway 132.

Roads Traveled

This is a 38-mile scenic byway following Nebo Loop Road which is also known as Forest Service Road 015. The forest road is a two-lane paved road safe for travel by all types of vehicles. The byway has been designated a National Forest Scenic Byway and a Utah Scenic Byway.

Travel Season

Nebo Loop is generally open from May through November. Heavy winter snows make the route impassable the rest of the year.

Description

The Nebo Loop scenic drive climbs over 9,000 feet in elevation through beautiful mountain scenery. Scenic overlooks along the byway provide vistas of 11,877-foot Mount Nebo and 10,931-foot Bald Mountain. Colorful canyons lined with maples, oaks, and stands of aspen are passed, beseeching the hiker to come and explore. These trees provide beautiful fall colors and stand out among the spruce, fir, and pine. Displaying its own brilliant color of red is the sandstone rock formation known as the Devil's Kitchen. An overlook constructed along the byway provides visitors the chance to photograph this ruggedly beautiful work of nature.

Local Information

Uinta National Forest
88 W. 100 N.
Provo, UT 84601
Phone: 801-377-5780

Nephi Area Chamber of Commerce
P.O. Box 71
Nephi, UT 84648
Phone: 801-623-5203

Payson Area Chamber of Commerce
P.O. Box 21
Payson, UT 84651
Phone: 801-465-2634

Spanish Fork Area C of C
40 S. Main
Spanish Fork, UT 84660
Phone: 801-798-8352

The Mount Nebo Wilderness lies to the west of this scenic route. Hikers, backpackers, and horseback riders will find hundreds of miles of trails running through this 28,170-acre area. Trailheads can be found at various points along the byway leading into the wilderness, some taking you to the top of the mountain peak. Shorter trails can also be found for those interested in just taking a stroll among the trees. If you do take a hike, be sure to look for mule deer, elk, or moose grazing around the lakes.

There are several campgrounds located along the byway for those wishing to prolong their stay here. Payson Lakes is the largest with 100 units available. The campground provides barrier-free facilities for the handicapped. All of the sites provide picnic tables, grills, and access to drinking water. The Blackhawk Campground is the next largest with 38 sites. Ponderosa Campground has 22 sites; Maple Bench offers 10 sites set among Rocky Mountain maples.

Nearby Routes

Huntington Canyon, page 357 / Pony Express, page 373

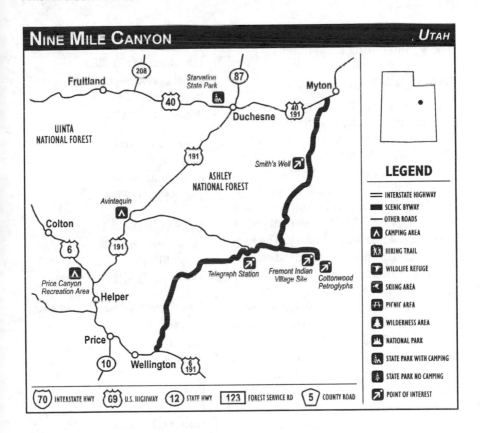

NINE MILE CANYON   UTAH

LEGEND

- ═══ INTERSTATE HIGHWAY
- ▬▬▬ SCENIC BYWAY
- ─── OTHER ROADS
- △ CAMPING AREA
- 🚶 HIKING TRAIL
- 🛡 WILDLIFE REFUGE
- SKIING AREA
- PICNIC AREA
- WILDERNESS AREA
- NATIONAL PARK
- STATE PARK WITH CAMPING
- STATE PARK NO CAMPING
- POINT OF INTEREST

(70) INTERSTATE HWY   (69) U.S. HIGHWAY   (12) STATE HWY   [123] FOREST SERVICE RD   (5) COUNTY ROAD

Route Location

The Nine Mile Canyon scenic byway is located in east-central Utah, about 81 miles southeast of Provo. The byway begins east of Wellington at the junction with U.S. Highway 6 and Nine Mile Canyon Road. The byway travels north to end at the intersection with U.S. Highway 40 near Myton.

Roads Traveled

The 78-mile route follows the Nine Mile Canyon Road which is a two-lane graded gravel and dirt road suitable for most vehicles. The first 12 miles from Wellington are two lanes of paved road. Large RVs or vehicles pulling trailers are not recommended on this route because of occasional steep grades and sharp turns. A four-wheel drive vehicle is recommended for exploring the side roads. The byway is designated a Type I Back Country Byway.

Travel Season

The byway can generally be driven year-round, however, several dry wash crossings can become impassable after heavy rains during the summer.

Description

The byway takes travelers through a high desert landscape with surrounding hills dotted with aspen and Douglas fir. From the south, the byway enters Soldier Creek Canyon with the cottonwood lined Soldier Creek meandering nearby. The byway then leaves Soldier Creek to enter Nine Mile Canyon offering glimpses of this area's history. The Fremont Indians once inhabited the region, leaving behind petroglyphs and pictographs on the canyon's walls. After the Civil War, the military built a major supply road through here to Myton. A stone structure at Telegraph Station served as a home and telegraph office between Price and Duchesne. Telegraph wire was strung on metal poles that still stand along the byway.

Further into the canyon, byway travelers can see the remains of a Fremont Indian village on the terrace above the road. Small boulders indicate where structures once stood.

Local Information

BLM - Moab District Office
82 E. Dogwood
Moab, UT 84532
Phone: 801-259-6111

Uinta National Forest
88 W. 100 N.
Provo, UT 84601
Phone: 801-377-5780

Ashley National Forest
355 N. Vernal Ave.
Vernal, UT 84078
Phone: 801-789-1181

Carbon County Chamber of Commerce
P.O. Box 764
Price, UT 84501
Phone: 801-637-2788

Duchesne County Area C of C
P.O. Box 1417
Roosevelt, UT 84066
Phone: 801-722-4598

Starvation State Park
Duchesne, UT 84021
Phone: 801-738-2326

Once you've completed your exploration of Nine Mile Canyon, continue driving north on the byway. Leaving the canyon, you'll come across the site of a stage stop once operated by Owen Smith. Mr. Smith and his family constructed nine buildings including a restaurant, blacksmith shop, and a small hotel to serve the needs of passengers on the Myton to Price stage line. From here the byway once again crosses the sagebrush covered hills to its end near Myton.

Nearby Routes

Eccles Canyon, page 351 / Flaming Gorge - Uinta's, page 355 / Huntington Canyon, page 357

OGDEN RIVER   *UTAH*

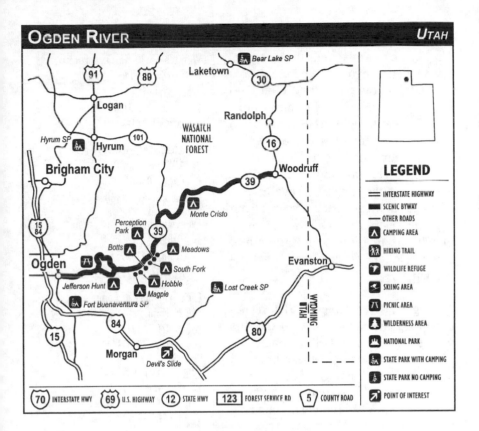

Route Location

The Ogden River scenic byway travels across the Wasatch-Cache National Forest in northern Utah. The byway's western end can be reached from Interstate 15 by taking Exit #347 and traveling east through Ogden. The byway's eastern terminus is in Woodruff at the intersection with Utah State Highway 16.

Roads Traveled

The 60-mile route follows Utah State Highway 39 which is a two-lane paved road suitable for all vehicles. Thirty-three miles of this route are designated a National Forest Scenic Byway and a Utah Scenic Byway.

Travel Season

State Highway 39 is open from late April through mid-December and then closed by winter's snow. The portion crossing the national forest becomes a snowmobile route during the winter.

Description

The scenic byway travels through narrow Ogden Canyon, around the shores of Pineview Reservoir, and climbs to Monte Cristo Summit. From the summit, the byway begins its descent to end in the community of Woodruff. Spectacular views of Monte Cristo Peak come into view as the byway traveler approaches the summit. Travelers are taken through a diverse landscape; from the sagebrush covered hills in the lower elevations to forests of Engelmann spruce, Douglas fir, and stands of quaking aspen.

The Ogden River scenic drive takes visitors alongside cottonwood-lined rivers where mule deer and elk can be seen. The best times to spot these graceful animals are early morning or evening. Beavers can also sometimes be seen working dutifully, building or repairing their dams. Bald eagles can occasionally be seen around Pineview Reservoir. Other wildlife inhabiting the area but not commonly seen includes moose, bobcats, mountain lions, and coyotes.

If you're interested in camping overnight or longer, you'll have over 200 campsites to choose from among the several national forest campgrounds. All have picnic tables, drinking water, and comfort stations available. Most of the campgrounds are open from mid-May through October.

Nearby Routes

Logan Canyon Highway, page 361
Mirror Lake, page 365 / Transcontinental Railroad, page 379

Local Information

Wasatch-Cache National Forest
8236 Federal Bldg.
125 S. State
Salt Lake City, UT 84138
Phone: 801-524-5030

The Chamber - Ogden / Weber
2404 Washington Blvd., #1100
Ogden, UT 84401
Phone: 801-621-8300

Evanston Chamber of Commerce
36 10th St.
Evanston, WY 82931
Phone: 307-789-2757

Cache Chamber of Commerce
160 N. Main
Logan, UT 84321
Phone: 801-752-2161

Brigham City Area C of C
P.O. Box 458
Brigham City, UT 84302
Phone: 801-723-3931

Bear Lake State Park
P.O. Box 184
Garden City, UT 84028
Phone: 801-946-3343

Ft. Buenaventura State Park
624 W. 21st St
Ogden, UT 84401
Phone: 801-392-5581

Lost Creek State Park
Hyrum State Pake

Utah Division of Parks and Recreation
1636 W North Temple, Suite 116
Salt Lake City, UT 84116
Phone: 801-538-7221

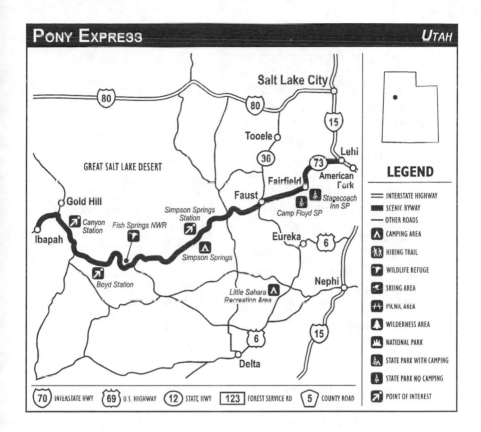

PONY EXPRESS   UTAH

LEGEND

━━ INTERSTATE HIGHWAY
▬▬ SCENIC BYWAY
── OTHER ROADS
🅐 CAMPING AREA
🕴 HIKING TRAIL
🚩 WILDLIFE REFUGE
🎿 SKIING AREA
🔀 PICNIC AREA
🌲 WILDERNESS AREA
🏔 NATIONAL PARK
🏕 STATE PARK WITH CAMPING
🏕 STATE PARK NO CAMPING
🡵 POINT OF INTEREST

(70) INTERSTATE HWY   (69) U.S. HIGHWAY   (12) STATE HWY   [123] FOREST SERVICE RD   (5) COUNTY ROAD

Route Location

Located in west-central Utah, about 30 miles south of Salt Lake City. The byway begins in Lehi and can be reached from I-15 by taking either Exit #281 or #285. The byway heads west from Lehi and ends in Ibapah.

Roads Traveled

The 160-mile route follows State Hwy. 73 and the Pony Express Road, which is marked with stone pillars. State Hwy. 73 is a two-lane paved road suitable for all vehicles. The remainder of the route travels over a dirt and gravel-surfaced road. A two-wheel drive, high-clearance vehicle is recommended on this segment. RVers and vehicles pulling trailers should inquire with the BLM about current road conditions. The BLM has designated 133 miles of this route, from Fairfield to Ibapah, a Type II Back Country Byway.

Travel Season

The byway is generally open year-round although heavy thunderstorms can cause flash floods and wash out sections of the road.

Description

Byway visitors will be retracing the path followed by the historic Pony Express Trail. This mail route lasted only eighteen months from April 1860 to October 1861. The trail was made obsolete when the first transcontinental telegraph system was completed. The byway takes travelers across the arid desert landscape of the Great Salt Lake Desert. No gas is available between Faust and Ibapah.

Visitors may wish to begin their journey back in time at the Stage Coach Inn State Park. The adobe inn, built in 1858, was an overnight stop for riders of the Pony Express Trail. Nearby is the Camp Floyd State Park which was established in 1858 as a military post.

The Simpson Springs Station was one of the most dependable watering points in this desert region. A stone building has been restored and closely resembles the original that was built around 1860. The BLM campground is located just east of the station and has fourteen campsites. Boyd Station offers only a rock wall remaining from the building that once housed the station keeper, a spare rider, and a blacksmith. The Canyon Station was originally located northwest of the present site and consisted of a log house, a stable, and a dugout where meals were served.

Nearby Routes

Big Cottonwood Canyon, page 341
Little Cottonwood Canyon, page 359
Nebo Loop, page 367

Local Information

BLM - Richfield District Office
150 E. 900 N.
Richfield, UT 84701
Phone: 801-896-8221

Lehi Chamber of Commerce
P.O. Box 154
Lehi, UT 84043
Phone: 801-768-9264

Tooele County Chamber of Commerce
P.O. Box 414
Tooele, UT 84074
Phone: 801-882-0690

American Fork Chamber of Commerce
31 N. Church St.
American Fork, UT 84003
Phone: 801-756-5110

Delta Area Chamber of Commerce
80 N. 200 W.
Delta, UT 84624
Phone: 801-864-4316

Nephi Area Chamber of Commerce
P.O. Box 71
Nephi, UT 84648
Phone: 801-623-5203

Salt Lake Area Chamber of Commerce
175 E. 400 S., #600
Salt Lake City, UT 84111
Phone: 801-364-3631

Stagecoach Inn State Park
18035 W. 1540 N.
Cedar Valley, UT 84013
Phone: 801-768-8932

Camp Floyd State Park
18035 W. 1540 N.
Cedar Valley, UT 84013
Phone: 801-768-8932

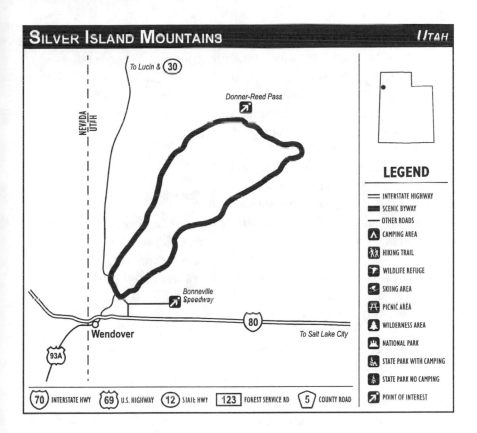

Route Location

The Silver Island Mountains byway is located in northwestern Utah, 122 miles west of Salt Lake City. The byway begins north of Wendover and can be reached from Exit #4 on Interstate 80. The byway forms a loop drive around the Silver Island Mountains.

Roads Traveled

The 54-mile route follows the Silver Island Mountains Road, a graded gravel and dirt road requiring a two-wheel drive, high-clearance vehicle. RVers and vehicles pulling trailers should inquire with the BLM about any vehicle limitations and the current road conditions. This is a Type II Back Country Byway and a Utah Scenic Backway.

Travel Season

The byway can usually be driven all year, however, portions of the route can be muddy after periods of rain.

Description

The Silver Island Mountains Back Country Byway takes travelers around the rugged and isolated Silver Island Mountains. The byway is surrounded by the vast expanse of the Bonneville Salt Flats; deposits of salt and minerals left behind by the evaporated and ancient Lake Bonneville. Views can often become distorted with distances running together or becoming disguised in the heat.

Numerous side roads will take you into the rugged mountains for exploring. A four-wheel drive vehicle is a must if you wish to drive into the mountains. The mountains do, however, provide excellent opportunities for hikers. These bumpy roads also provide challenges to experienced mountain bikers.

The Silver Island Mountains have seen mountain men, explorers, and wagon trains cross it peaks and valleys. Pilot Peak, eleven miles to the northwest, was named by John C. Fremont in 1845. This mountain peak became a beacon for later travelers passing through the area. The Donner-Reed Party attempted this route on their way to California but abandoned their wagons in the soft mud east of here. You can see part of their fateful route near Donner-Reed Pass.

By the 1930s, the Bonneville Salt Flats had become known as the place to be for setting world land speed records. Some of the mountain peaks in the Silver Island Mountains are named for famous racers associated with the salt flats.

Local Information

BLM - Salt Lake District Office
2370 S. 2300 W.
Salt Lake City, UT 84119
Phone: 801-977-4300

Tooele County Chamber of Commerce
P.O. Box 414
Tooele, UT 84074
Phone: 801-882-0690

Danger Cave State Park
Utah Division of Parks & Recreation
1636 W North Temple - Suite 116
Salt Lake City, UT 84116
Phone: 801-538-7221

Nearby Routes

Transcontinental Railroad, page 379 / California Trail, page 224

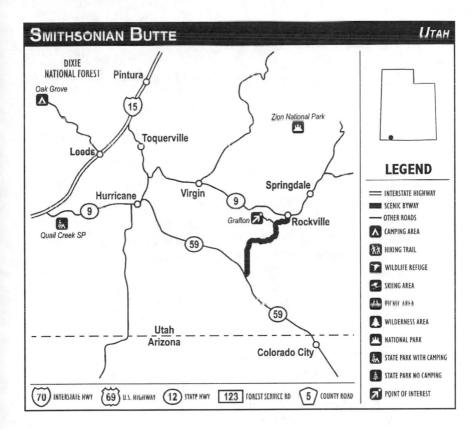

Route Location

The Smithsonian Butte byway is located in southwestern Utah, approximately 40 miles northeast of St. George. The byway's southern entry point can be reached from Utah State Highway 59, fourteen miles south of Hurricane. The byway's northern terminus is in Rockville.

Roads Traveled

The nine-mile byway follows Smithsonian Butte County Road which is a graded unsurfaced road but is suitable for most vehicles. Due to sharp curves and a half-mile section of steep grade, large RVs and travel trailers are discouraged from traveling the byway. This byway is a Type I Back Country Byway and a Utah Scenic Backway.

Travel Season

The byway can normally be traveled year-round when dry. The segment of road located on the north-facing slope of Smithsonian Butte can remain snow-covered during winter. Travelers should not attempt to drive the byway after rain or snowstorms.

Description

The Smithsonian Butte Back Country Byway is best driven from south to north for the spectacular views into Zion National Park. The turn onto the byway from State Highway 59 is tight for southbound travelers, please use caution. Once you're on the byway heading north, you are treated to views of Smithsonian Butte ahead of you. To the east is Canaan Mountain and the Vermilion Cliffs. Nearly three miles into your scenic journey you'll reach Grafton Wash Canyon. From here you can see the distant Pine Valley Mountains to the northwest as you have reached the byway's highest point at 4,920 feet.

The byway begins heading east, winding across Wire Mesa. Soon you begin the steep descent from Wire Mesa into Horse Valley Wash. Before you is a spectacular view of the Virgin River Valley. Be cautious, though, because this portion of the road descends 800 feet in a little more than ½ mile.

Once you've safely descended from Wire Mesa, you'll come to a junction. You can turn left (west) and visit the ghost town of Grafton or head east and end your scenic experience in Rockville. The present site of Grafton was settled in 1862 after the original town was washed away in the big flood of 1859. The town was abandoned in the early 1900s.

Nearby Routes

Markaguant, page 363

Lodging Directory

Snow Family Guest Ranch B & B - Virgin, page 457 — Bed & Breakfast / Inns & Cabin / Cottage / Guest Ranch

Local Information

BLM - Cedar City District Office
176 East D.L. Sargent Dr.
Cedar City, UT 84720
Phone: 801-865-3053

Hurricane Valley Chamber of Commerce
P.O. Box 101
Hurricane, UT 84737
Phone: 801-635-3402

Rockville Board of Trade
144 E. 250 S.
Rockville, UT 84763
Phone: 801-772-3472

Zion National Park
Springdale, UT 84767
Phone: 801-772-3256

Quail Creek State Park
P.O Box 1943
St George, UT 84770
Phone: 801-879-2378

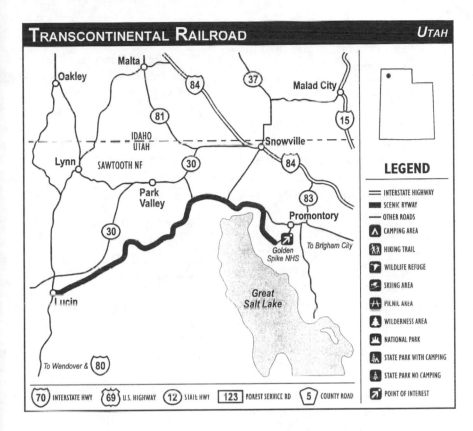

Route Location

The Transcontinental Railroad byway is located in northwestern Utah, approximately 30 miles west of Brigham City. The eastern access is located west of the Golden Spike National Historic Site off State Highway 83. The byway travels west across the desert and ends in Lucin.

Roads Traveled

This is a 90-mile byway following the Transcontinental Railroad Road which is a narrow, gravel and dirt-surfaced road. The route requires a two-wheel drive, high-clearance vehicle. Vehicles longer than 30 feet are discouraged from traveling the byway. Inquire locally on road conditions before attempting the drive. The BLM has designated this byway as a Type II Back Country Byway. It is also a Utah Scenic Backway.

Travel Season

The entire route is usually passable throughout the year, however, hazardous driving conditions exist after periods of rain. Portions of the road may become impassable.

Description

This back country byway takes travelers across the abandoned Central Pacific Railroad grade through the old town sites of Kelton, Terrace, and Watercress. The landscape today looks much the same as it did in 1869 when Central Pacific's tracks met Union Pacific's rails. The Golden Spike National Historic Site preserves the site where these two railroads joined their rails with a gold spike on May 10, 1869. A visitor center here offers movies and exhibits of this historic event. Take your time to stop and read the more than 30 interpretive sites along the byway. Byway travelers will come across original trestles and culverts as well as remains of two railroad communities and several workers' camps.

Local Information

BLM - Salt Lake District Office
2370 S. 2300 W.
Salt Lake City, UT 84119
Phone: 801-977-4300

Sawtooth National Forest
2647 Kimberly Rd. East
Twin Falls, ID 83301
Phone: 208-737-3200

Brigham City Area C of C
P.O. Box 458
Brigham City, UT 84302
Phone: 801-723-3931

Tooele County Chamber of Commerce
P.O. Box 414
Tooele, UT 84074
Phone: 801-882-0690

Golden Spike National Historic Site
P.O. Box 897
Brigham City, UT 84302
Phone: 801-471-2209

The byway crosses the northern reaches of the Great Salt Lake Desert. The eastern portion provides broad vistas of the northern end of Great Salt Lake. As you travel the western segment of the byway, you are rewarded with views of the Pilot, Newfoundland, Grouse Creek, and Raft River mountain ranges. Please be cautious as you travel this byway as portions of it may be used by bicyclists. Also, there are no services along the byway. Gasoline is available in Snowville, Brigham City, and Wendover.

Nearby Routes

Logan Canyon Highway, page 361 / Ogden River, page 371 / Silver Island Mountains, page 375 / City Of Rocks, page 155 / California Trail, page 224

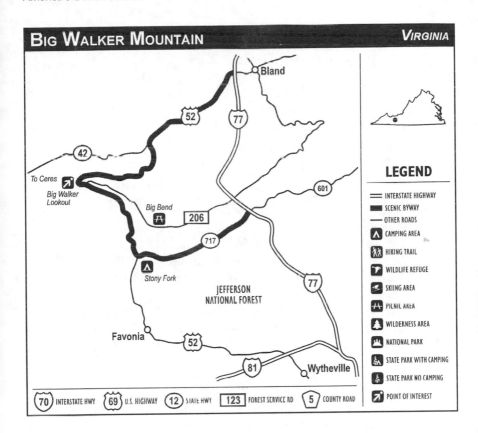

Route Location

The Big Walker Mountain scenic byway is located in southwestern Virginia, approximately 90 miles west of Roanoke. The byway forms an open loop drive west of Interstate 77, crossing the Jefferson National Forest. Travelers can access the byway from the south at Exit #47 or from the north, west of Bland, at Exit #52.

Roads Traveled

Big Walker Mountain is a 16-mile byway following U.S. Highway 52 and Virginia State Highway 717. Both highways are two-lane paved roads safe for travel by all types of vehicles. The entire length of the byway is officially designated a National Forest Scenic Byway.

Travel Season

The roads followed are usually open year-round.

Description

The scenic byway takes the traveler through forests of oak, hickory, and white pine as it ascends Big Walker Mountain. In the spring colorful wildflowers bloom, beseeching your admiration. Flowering trees compete with the wildflowers, adding their own dash of color to the landscape. In fall the byway is painted in beautiful colors of red and gold. Among the trees within the mountains, one finds a diversity of wildlife. White-tailed deer can sometimes be seen along the byway, usually in the early morning or evening. Wild turkeys tend to be more secretive, but they oc-

Local Information

Jefferson National Forest
210 Franklin Road, SW
Roanoke, VA 24001
Phone: 540-982-6270

Jefferson National Forest
Wythe Ranger District
1625 W. Lee Hwy.
Wytheville, VA 24382
Phone: 540-228-5551

Wytheville - Wythe - Bland C of C
P.O. Box 563
Wytheville, VA 24382
Phone: 540-228-3211

casionally allow themselves to be seen. The numerous songbirds inhabiting the area joyfully sing their songs of welcome to visitors. Meandering creeks along the byway add to the symphony with their bubbling and gurgling sounds.

Once atop Big Walker Mountain, visitors will find a privately-owned 100-foot tower open to tourists for a small fee. The view from here is spectacular, encompassing the surrounding densely-forested mountains and wide open valleys. An historical marker here tells the story of Mary Tynes warning the people of Wytheville of an impending Union Calvary raid led by Colonel John Toland in 1863.

A side trip on Forest Service Road 206 near the tower will take you to the Big Bend Picnic Area, constructed by the Civilian Conservation Corps in the 1930s. Set amidst orchard grass under a canopy of oaks, the picnic site offers vistas of the ridge and valley terrain to the south. This is a good spot to take a break and breathe in the surrounding landscape.

A national forest campground is located on the banks of East Fork of the Stony Fork Creek off State Highway 717. The Stony Fork Campground offers 53 sites for tents and recreational vehicles. Drinking water, comfort stations, and a dump station are among the facilities available. A 1½-mile nature trail leads you among the trees and flowers.

Nearby Routes

Mount Rogers, page 390 / Blue Ridge Parkway, page 383

BLUE RIDGE PARKWAY   VIRGINIA

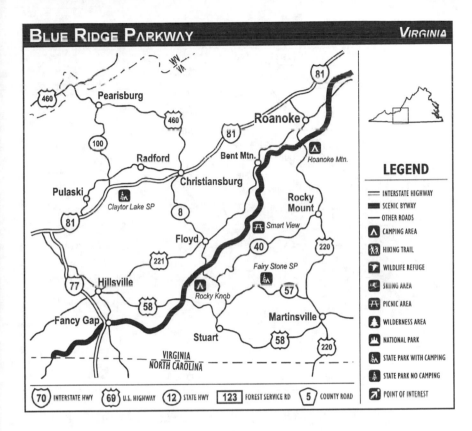

LEGEND

- ═══ INTERSTATE HIGHWAY
- ▬▬ SCENIC BYWAY
- ── OTHER ROADS
- CAMPING AREA
- HIKING TRAIL
- WILDLIFE REFUGE
- SKIING AREA
- PICNIC AREA
- WILDERNESS AREA
- NATIONAL PARK
- STATE PARK WITH CAMPING
- STATE PARK NO CAMPING
- POINT OF INTEREST

(70) INTERSTATE HWY   (69) U.S. HIGHWAY   (12) STATE HWY   [123] FOREST SERVICE RD   (5) COUNTY ROAD

North Carolina portion see page 268

Route Location

The Blue Ridge Parkway is a 469-mile drive between the Shenandoah and Great Smoky Mountains National Parks. This portion of the scenic byway lies in western Virginia and travels between Shenandoah National Park and the North Carolina state line.

Roads Traveled

The Blue Ridge Parkway is a two-lane paved route that is suitable for travel by all types of vehicles. The byway is designated a National Parkway by the National Park Service. This portion of the byway is approximately 217 miles in length.

Travel Season

The route is generally open year-round, however, from November through

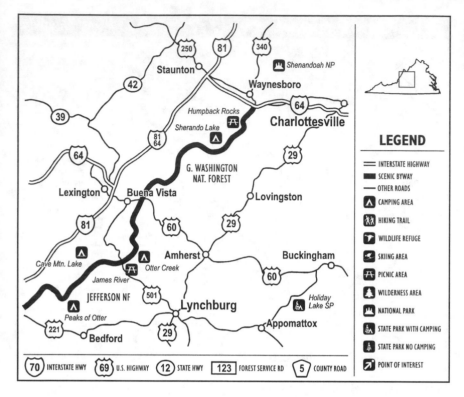

mid-April portions of the route may be closed due to snow and ice.

Description

The Parkway follows the Appalachian Mountain chain, twisting and turning through the beautiful mountains. From the Shenandoah National Park, the scenic drive travels along the Blue Ridge Mountains for 355 miles. Then, for the remaining 114 miles, it skirts the southern end of the Black Mountains, weaves through the Craggies, the Pisgahs, and the Balsams before finally ending in the Great Smokies. The Parkway was authorized in 1933 and became a unit of the National Park Service in 1936.

Local Information

National Park Service
Blue Ridge Parkway
200 BB&T Building, One Park Square
Ashville, NC 28801
Phone: 704-271-4779

George Washington National Forest
101 N. Main St.
Harrisonburg, VA 22801
Phone: 540-433-2491

Floyd County Chamber of Commerce
P.O. Box 510
Floyd, VA 24091
Phone: 540-745-4407

Carroll County Chamber of Commerce

This 217-mile portion of the Parkway is a beautiful drive through the Blue Ridge Mountains in Virginia. Much of the Appalachian Trail parallels the drive for the first 100 miles from the national park to just north of Roanoke. Portions of this 2,147 mile National Scenic Trail may be accessed from the byway.

Waynesboro, Virginia is the starting point of the parkway when traveling north to south. To the north lies the vast Shenandoah National Park and the Skyline Drive, which winds 105 miles through the park. To the south is the Blue Ridge Parkway and the George Washington National Forest. The national forest covers more than a million acres of mountains and valleys in Virginia and West Virginia. Sherando Lake is a national forest recreation area that offers camping, fishing, boating, hiking, picnicking, and swimming opportunities. Further south lies the Jefferson National Forest. Numerous camping and picnicking areas are situated around the Cave Mountain Lake area.

The National Park Service also provides areas for camping and picnicking. Otter Creek, Peaks of Otter, and Rocky Knob are just a few examples. In addition to tent and trailer campsites, Peaks of Otter and Rocky Knob also offer lodging. Food service and gasoline are also available in Peaks of Otter. Several picnic areas with scenic vistas of the surrounding mountains are found in Humpback Rocks and James River recreation areas. Many of the parks also have visitor centers where you can obtain detailed brochures and maps of the Blue Ridge Parkway.

Local Information

P.O. Box 1184
Hillsville, VA 24343
Phone: 540-728-5397

Roanoke Regional Chamber of Commerce
310 First St. S.W.
Roanoke, VA 24011
Phone: 540-983-0700

Bedford Area Chamber of Commerce
305 E. Main St.
Bedford, VA 24523
Phone: 540-586-9401

Buena Vista Chamber of Commerce
2202 Magnolia Ave.
Buena Vista, VA 24416
Phone: 540-261-2880

Waynesboro Chamber of Commerce
301 W. Main St.
Waynesboro, VA 22980
Phone: 540-949-8203

Shenandoah National Park
Route 4, Box 348
Luray, VA 22835
Phone: 540-999-2243

Fairy Stone State Park
Route 2, Box 723
Stuart, VA 24171
Phone: 540-930-2424

Nearby Routes

Big Walker Mountain, page 381 / Highlands Scenic Tour, page 388 / Mount Rogers, page 390

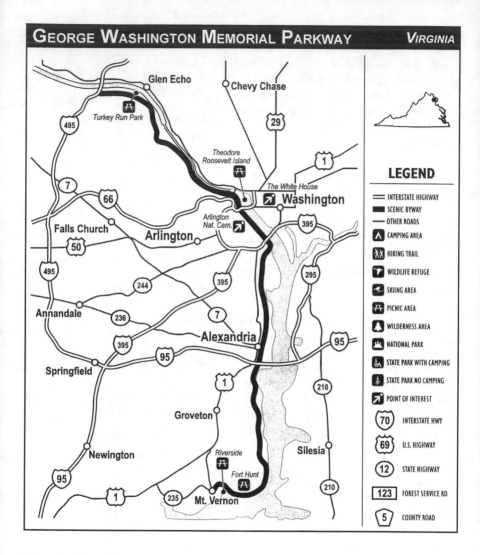

GEORGE WASHINGTON MEMORIAL PARKWAY   *VIRGINIA*

LEGEND

━━━ INTERSTATE HIGHWAY
■ SCENIC BYWAY
─ OTHER ROADS
Ⓐ CAMPING AREA
Ⓐ HIKING TRAIL
Ⓐ WILDLIFE REFUGE
Ⓐ SKIING AREA
🅰 PICNIC AREA
Ⓐ WILDERNESS AREA
Ⓐ NATIONAL PARK
Ⓐ STATE PARK WITH CAMPING
Ⓐ STATE PARK NO CAMPING
🅰 POINT OF INTEREST
⑦⓪ INTERSTATE HWY
⑥⑨ U.S. HIGHWAY
⑫ STATE HIGHWAY
⟦123⟧ FOREST SERVICE RD
⑤ COUNTY ROAD

Maryland section see page 183

Route Location

The George Washington Memorial Parkway is located in northeastern Virginia and south-central Maryland. Portions of the scenic drive pass through Washington, D.C. This portion of the parkway travels between Mount Vernon in the south to its junction with Interstate 495.

Roads Traveled

The route is primarily four lanes of divided highway, safe for travel by all vehicles. The byway is named George Washington Memorial Parkway except in Alexandria where the route follows Washington Street. This portion in Virginia is approximately 24 miles in length and has been designated a National Parkway.

Travel Season

The parkway is open year-round.

Description

The Parkway preserves the natural scenery along the Potomac River, connecting historic sites from Mount Vernon, past the Nation's Capital, to the Great Falls of the Potomac. The many historic sites are complemented by the scenic countryside. The banks of the Potomac River are covered with willows, elders, and birches. Fall brings vibrant colors to the parkway as the red maples, oaks, sumacs, and hickories proudly display their autumn attire.

Mount Vernon, the parkway's southern terminus, is the home of George Washington. The Washington mansion, beautifully situated on a hill, was built in 1743 by Washington's half brother, Lawrence. George Washington inherited the home in 1752. Both he and his wife are buried in an ivy-covered mausoleum not far from the house.

The parkway passes through historic Alexandria which was founded in 1749. Some historical sites of interest include the Christ Church, where George Washington worshipped, Gadsby's Tavern, frequented by Washington and other patriots, and the boyhood home of Confederate general Robert E. Lee.

In addition to the numerous other points of historical interest, the parkway is also used for recreational purposes. Dyke Marsh is home to over 250 species of birds and is a nice spot for fishing or hiking. Fort Hunt Park offers 156 acres for picnicking, hiking, or bicycling. A boat ramp can be found in Daingerfield Island as well as picnicking facilities.

Local Information

George Washington Memorial Parkway
Turkey Run Park
McLean, VA 22101
Phone: 703-285-2598

Arlington Chamber of Commerce
2009 N. 14th St., #111
Arlington, VA 22201
Phone: 703-525-2400

Alexandria Chamber of Commerce
801 N. Fairfax St., #402
Alexandria, VA 22313
Phone: 703-549-1000

Mt. Vernon - Lee Chamber of Commerce
7686 Richmond Hwy., #103
Alexandria, VA 22306
Phone: 703-660-6602

For information on the various parks and historical sites in the District of Columbia area contact:

National Capital Parks
National Capital Region
1100 Ohio Drive, S.W.
Washington, DC 20242
Phone: 202-619-7222

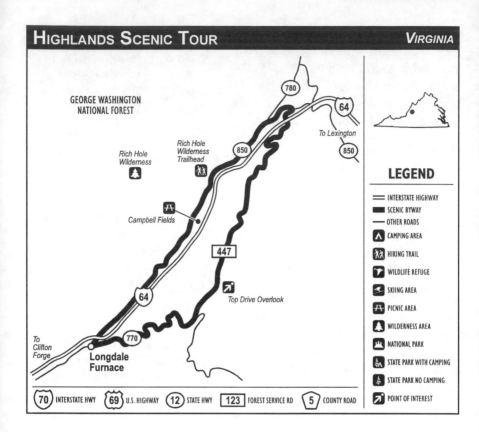

Route Location

The Highlands Scenic Tour is located in west-central Virginia, about 50 miles northwest of Roanoke. The southern access is located in the town of Longdale Furnace south of Interstate 64. From here the byway heads north-easterly to form a loop drive back to Longdale Furnace.

Roads Traveled

The 20-mile route follows Virginia State Highways 770 and 850, and Forest Service Road 447. The routes travel over a combination of paved and gravel-surfaced roads. The roads are suitable for all vehicles with the exception of State Highway 770 which is narrow with steep hairpin turns. This portion is not recommended for vehicles pulling trailers. The byway has been designated a National Forest Scenic Byway.

Travel Season

State Route 850 is open year-round while State Route 770 and Forest Service Road 447 are not maintained during the winter months and are typically impassable from December to early March.

Description

The Highlands Scenic Tour travels through the hardwood forests of the George Washington National Forest, riding the crest of North Mountain on Forest Service Road 447 and alongside the Rich Hole Wilderness on State Highway 850. In spring, flowering trees provide beautiful colors of red and pink set against the green leaves of the forested hillsides. The trees are given their chance to show off their colors when

Local Information

George Washington National Forest
Harrison Plaza
101 N. Main St.
Harrisonburg, VA 22801
Phone: 540-433-2491

Lexington - Rockbridge County C of C
10 E. Washington St.
Davidson Tucker House #1
Lexington, VA 24450
Phone: 540-463-5375

Alleghany Highlands C of C
203 Commercial Ave.
Clifton Forge, VA 24422
Phone: 540-862-4969

autumn arrives. If you can look beyond the colorful display, chances are pretty good that you may see white-tailed deer foraging among the trees. Perhaps unnoticed by the deer are the numerous songbirds serenading the mountains in thanksgiving for the beautiful habitat. Other wildlife living peacefully among the others are black bears, wild turkeys, ruffed grouse, and squirrels. Red-tailed hawks can also be seen soaring overhead.

To the west of the byway is the 6,450-acre Rich Hole Wilderness. Visitors to the byway may want to take some time to walk the six-mile, moderately strenuous trail running through this wilderness area. The trail will take you along the North Fork of the Simpson Creek through stands of poplar, oak, and hickory. If interested, you can spend some time trying to pull brook and rainbow trout from the creek.

Large motorhomes and vehicles pulling trailers will want to plan their trip so they travel south on Forest Service Road 447. There is a large turnaround point at the Top Drive Overlook so these vehicles can avoid the steep switchbacks of State Highway 770. Otherwise, this portion of the byway provides beautiful views of the Alleghany Highlands in the southwest and the Blue Ridge Mountains to the east.

Nearby Routes

Blue Ridge Parkway, page 383 / Highland Scenic Highway, page 402

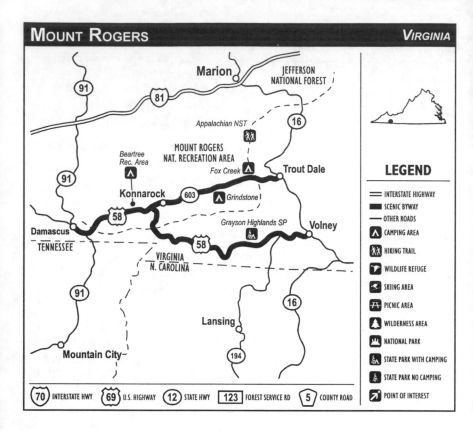

Route Location

The Mount Rogers scenic byway is approximately 30 miles east of Bristol in southwestern Virginia. The byway begins in Damascus on U.S. Highway 58 and heads east to end at the intersection with Virginia State Highway 16. The byway splits near Konnarock, one route heading southeast and the other continuing east. The northern segment ends in Trout Dale and the southern portion in Volney.

Roads Traveled

The 56-mile route follows U.S. Highway 58 and Virginia State Highway 603 which are two-lane paved roads. Because of sharp curves and a winding route, U.S. Highway 58 is not recommended for vehicles longer than 35 feet. The byway is a National Forest Scenic Byway.

Travel Season

The roads followed are usually open year-round.

Description

The Mount Rogers scenic byway winds through hardwood forests and rural countryside as it crosses the Jefferson National Forest and Mount Rogers National Recreation Area. Mount Rogers stands proudly at 5,729 above sea level and can be seen at various points along the drive. It also has the honor of being Virginia's highest point.

Mount Rogers National Recreation Area encompasses 114,000 acres and is part of the Jefferson National Forest. Visitors will find numerous opportunities for outdoor recreation. The Mount Rogers National Recreation Trail is found here as is the Appalachian National Scenic Trail. Enjoy just walking a short distance on either of these trails or plan a more extensive backpacking adventure. Either way, you'll be treated to hardwood forests, numerous songbirds, and trickling streams. You might even spot a deer or two. Altogether there are over 400 miles of trails available to the hiker, mountain biker, backpacker, and horseback rider.

Local Information

Jefferson National Forest
Mt. Rogers Ranger District
Rt. I - Box 303
Marion, VA 24354
Phone: 540-783-5196

Washington County C of C
179 E. Main St.
Abingdon, VA 24210
Phone: 540-628-8141

Chamber of Commerce of Smyth County
124 W. Main St.
Marion, VA 24354
Phone: 540-783-3161

Alleghany County C of C
348 S. Main St.
Sparta, NC 28675
Phone: 910-372-5473

Mt. Rogers National Recreation Area
Rt. I - Box 303
Marion, VA 24354
Phone: 540-783-5196

Grayson Highlands State Park
Rt. 2 - Box 141
Mouth of Wilson, VA 24363
Phone: 540-579-7092

Those interested in a more passive activity will find numerous places to pull over and enjoy a good book or picnic. The Grayson Highlands State Park is also a good place to find lots of picnic areas. The 4,754-acre park also offers camping opportunities. There are nearly 100 campsites available to tent campers and RVers. The park also has comfort stations, shower facilities, and hookups at some campsites. The national forest also offers camping areas but none have hookups.

Nearby Routes

Big Walker Mountain, page 381 / Blue Ridge Parkway, page 383 (VA), page 268 (NC)

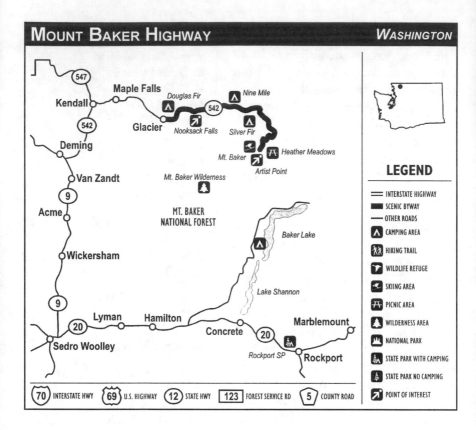

Route Location

The Mount Baker Highway is about 35 miles east of Bellingham in northwestern Washington. The byway's western terminus is located on Washington State Highway 542 in the town of Glacier. The byway travels east from Glacier to the road's end at Artist Point.

Roads Traveled

The 24-mile route follows Washington State Highway 542 which is a two-lane paved road suitable for all vehicles. The byway will need to be retraced back to Glacier. The Mount Baker Highway is officially designated a National Forest Scenic Byway.

Travel Season

Most of the route is open year-round except the last three miles to the Heather Meadows Recreation Area which is subject to closure from November to mid-July, depending on weather conditions.

Description

Travelers of the Mount Baker Highway are treated to beautiful mountain scenery as they climb through the narrow valley of the Nooksack River to the rugged timberline of the North Cascades. Artist Point is the destination. From there you are rewarded with spectacular views of Mount Baker, standing tall at 10,775 feet above the ocean level, and the wilderness area which encompasses the mountain peak. The tumbling waters of the North Fork of the Nooksack River will gracefully flow alongside you for much of your journey. Be sure to take in one of the prettiest gifts the river has to offer, the thundering Nooksack Falls.

The Mount Baker Wilderness envelops the mountain peak for which it is named and nearly 118,000 acres of the surrounding landscape filled with mountain streams and lakes. This area is a haven for hikers, backpackers, horseback riders, and photographers. There are a lot of trails accessed along the byway that will lead you into this pristine land. There's also several trails that provide the hiking novice a pleasurable and easy-going walk. In winter, cross-country ski enthusiasts will find miles of groomed trails.

If you're interested in staying overnight or a few days, the national forest has developed camping areas for you. The Douglas Fir Campground is but a few miles east of Glacier and has 30 campsites nestled under tall Douglas fir and cedar trees along the banks of the river. Further east is the Silver Fir Campground with 21 sites situated on the river. The picnic area here was built by the Civilian Conservation Corps. Both campgrounds have drinking water and comfort stations.

Local Information

Mt. Baker-Snoqualmie National Forest
21905 64th Ave. W.
Mountlake Terrace, WA 98043
Phone: 206-775-9702

Mt. Baker Foothills C of C
P.O. Box 866
Maple Falls, WA 98266
Phone: 360-599-1205

Bellingham / Whatcom C of C
1801 Roeder Ave.
Bellingham, WA 98227
Phone: 360-734-1330

Sedro - Woolley Chamber of Commerce
116 Woodworth St.
Sedro-Woolley, WA 98284
Phone: 360-855-1841

North Cascades National Park
2105 Hwy. 20
Sedro Woolley, WA 98284
Phone: 360-856-5700

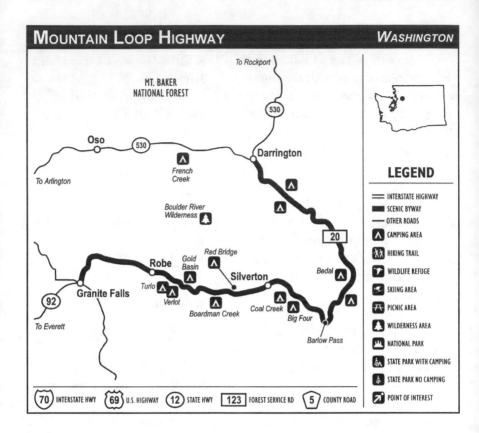

Route Location

Located in northwestern Washington, about 45 miles northeast of downtown Seattle. The byway begins in Granite Falls on Washington State Hwy. 92 and travels northeasterly across the Mt. Baker-Snoqualmie National Forest. The byway ends in Darrington at the intersection with State Hwy. 530.

Roads Traveled

The byway follows State Highway 92 and Forest Service Road 20 for a distance of about 55 miles. State Highway 92 from Granite Falls to Barlow Pass is a two-lane paved road. The next 14 miles of the byway from Barlow Pass to the confluence of Sauk and Whitechuck rivers is primarily a single-lane graveled road. From there to Darrington the byway is again a two-lane paved road. All of the roads are safe for travel by all types of vehicles.

Travel Season

The portion of the byway between Granite Falls and Silverton is usually open year-round. The rest of the by-way may be closed during the winter months because the road is not plowed.

Description

The Mountain Loop Highway takes travelers through the heart of the Mt. Baker-Snoqualmie National Forest. The byway first travels across rural countryside dotted with farmland before climbing into the dense forests of the foothills of the Cascade Range. Scenic turnouts along the route provide views of the surrounding wilderness. Flowing alongside the byway from Granite Falls to Barlow Pass is the South Fork of the Stillaguamish River. Once beyond the pass, the South Fork of the Sauk River will accompany you until it reaches its parent river near the Bedal Campground. From here on out its the Sauk River you'll see flowing beside you.

For nature trails, hiking, or horseback riding, you'll find plenty of trails along the byway to satisfy the urge to get close to nature. Many of the trails will lead to seclusion in the Boulder River Wilderness. Other trails will take you to scenic viewpoints where you can take in the beautiful mountains that surround you.

Local Information

Mt. Baker - Snoqualmie National Forest
21905 64th Ave. W.
Mountlake Terrace, WA 98043
Phone: 206-775-9702

Darrington Chamber of Commerce
P.O. Box 351
Darrington, WA 98241
Phone: 360-436-1177

Greater Lake Stevens C of C
P.O. Box 439
Lake Stevens, WA 98258
Phone: 206-334-0433

Greater Arlington C of C
P.O. Box 102
Arlington, WA 98223
Phone: 360-435-3708

Everett Area Chamber of Commerce
1710 W. Marine View Dr.
Everett, WA 98206
Phone: 206-252-5181

Rockport State Park
5051 State Rt. 20
Rockport, WA 98283
Phone: 360-853-8461

Camping areas are not in short supply along this byway. There are 94 sites at the Gold Basin Campground alone. The Verlot Campground offers 26 sites set among the trees along the river. Turlo Campground has 19 sites. Drinking water and comfort stations are provided at these three campgrounds. You'll find 18 sites along the river at the Boardman Creek Campground. There's good fishing for trout at this campground. The nearby Red Bridge Campground has 16 sites, also on the banks of the river.

Nearby Routes

Stevens Pass, page 398

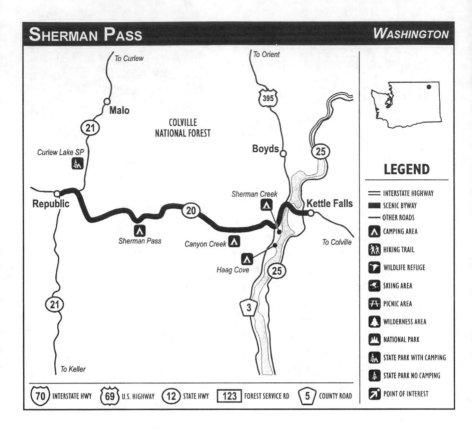

Route Location

Sherman Pass is a scenic byway approximately 80 miles northwest of Spokane in northeastern Washington. The byway crosses the Colville National Forest between the community of Republic in the west to Kettle Falls in the east on the banks of the mighty Columbia River.

Roads Traveled

The Sherman Pass byway is approximately 40 miles long following Washington State Highway 20, a two-lane pave road suitable for all types of vehicles. Thirty-five miles of this byway are officially designated a National Forest Scenic Byway.

Travel Season

Winter driving conditions may call for extra caution and delays are possible for snow removal, but otherwise the byway is normally open all year.

Description

The Sherman Pass National Forest Scenic Byway begins in Republic and takes you across the heavily forested Kettle River Range. The byway steadily climbs from Republic, crosses Sherman Pass at 5,575 feet above sea level, and then descends to Kettle Falls. Frequent turnouts are provided along the byway so you can stop and take in the beautiful scenery. The waters of O'Brien Creek will accompany you for much of the way to Sherman Pass. Once you cross the pass, Sherman Creek will guide you along the byway until its waters meet Columbia River. You're pretty much on your own after that but, not to worry, it isn't difficult finding Kettle Falls. This same route was used by Native Americans long ago as they made their way to the Columbia River for fishing purposes. The trail later became a wagon route for miners. The route is now popular with byway travelers and bicycle riders.

Local Information

Colville National Forest
765 S. Main St.
Colville, WA 99114
Phone: 509-684-3711

Republic Area Chamber of Commerce
P.O. Box 502
Republic, WA 99166
Phone: 509-775-2704

Kettle Falls Area Chamber of Commerce
265 W. 3rd St.
Kettle Falls, WA 99141
Phone: 509-738-2300

Colville Chamber of Commerce
P.O. Box 267
Colville, WA 99114
Phone: 509-684-5973

Curlew Lake State Park
974 Curlew Lake State Park Rd.
Republic, WA 99166
Phone: 509-775-3592

Wildlife observers will be pleased to find many species inhabiting the area. Mule deer and white-tailed deer can be seen, especially in the morning or evening. Other wildlife one might enjoy seeing but not want to get close to is the black bear, coyote, or mountain lion. If you stop at one of the overlooks along the byway, the many songbirds in the area would be happy to sing a tune or two for you.

If you want to take some time to explore the area a bit, there are many trails that would be pleased to provide you access. The Kettle Crest National Recreation Trail is one trail that invites the byway traveler. This trail can be accessed near the top of Sherman Pass. Other trails will take you among the lodgepole pine, subalpine fir, and Douglas fir.

There are two national forest campgrounds located directly along the byway. The Sherman Pass Campground provides nine sites and an interpretive trail. The Canyon Creek Campground has twelve sites to choose from. Other campgrounds can be found a short distance off the byway.

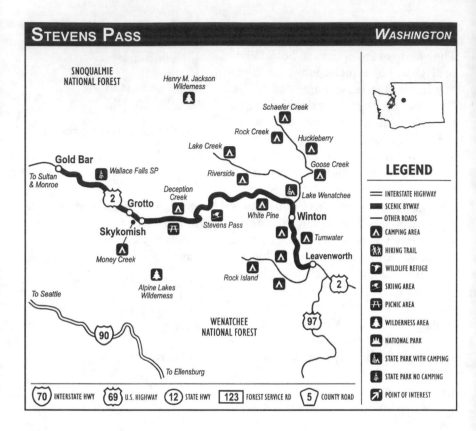

Route Location

Stevens Pass is located in west-central Washington, approximately 45 miles from downtown Seattle. The byway begins in the town of Gold Bar on U.S. Highway 2 and travels east across the Snoqualmie and Wenatchee National Forests to its end in Leavenworth.

Roads Traveled

The Stevens Pass scenic byway follows U.S. Highway 2 which is a two-lane paved road that is safe for travel by all types of vehicles. The byway is about 70 miles long and has been officially designated a National Forest Scenic Byway.

Travel Season

The entire length of the byway is usually open all year, however, winter driving conditions may dictate that drivers use extra caution, especially in the higher elevations.

Description

This drive takes travelers across the heavily forested Snoqualmie and Wenatchee National Forests as it crosses 4,061-foot Stevens Pass. The byway begins climbing the western slopes of the Cascade Mountains from Gold Bar to its climax at the pass and then descends into Leavenworth. The rushing waters of the South Fork of the Skykomish River, with its many cascading waterfalls, will guide you to the area just west of Deception Creek Campground. At that point the Tye River will take over and show you the way to Stevens Pass. The Tye River has a couple of scenic waterfalls to show off, too. Beyond the pass, Nason Creek will accompany you to State Hwy. 207, just north of Winton.

Outdoor recreational opportunities are bountiful along this byway. There are two wilderness areas for hikers, backpackers, and horseback riders. The byway's many rivers and streams provide opportunities for spending an afternoon trying to pull fish from the water. The national forest has constructed several campgrounds that provide just the right spot for pitching a tent or parking your RV. Wildlife observers can spend their time seeking the many species of wildlife inhabiting the area.

Nearby Routes

Mountain Loop Highway, page 394

Local Information

Mt. Baker-Snoqualmie National Forest
21905 64th Ave. W.
Mountlake Terrace, WA 98043
Phone: 206-775-9702

Monroe Chamber of Commerce
P.O. Box 38
Monroe, WA 98272
Phone: 360-794-5488

Sultan Chamber of Commerce
P.O. Box 46
Sultan, WA 98294
Phone: 360-793-2211

Leavenworth Chamber of Commerce
894 Hwy. 2
Leavenworth, WA 98826
Phone: 509-548-5807

Wenatchee Area Chamber of Commerce
2 S. Chelan
Wenatchee, WA 98807
Phone: 509-662-2116

Wallace Falls State Park
Ley Rd.
Gold Bar, WA 98251
Phone: 360-793-0420

Lake Wenatchee State Park
21588 A Hwy. 207
Leavenworth, WA 98826
Phone: 509-763-3101

LODGING DIRECTORY

AlpenRose Inn - Leavenworth, page 458 — Bed & Breakfast / Inns
Enzian Inn - Leavenworth, page 459 — Hotel / Motel
SkyRiver Inn - Skykomish, page 459 — Hotel / Motel

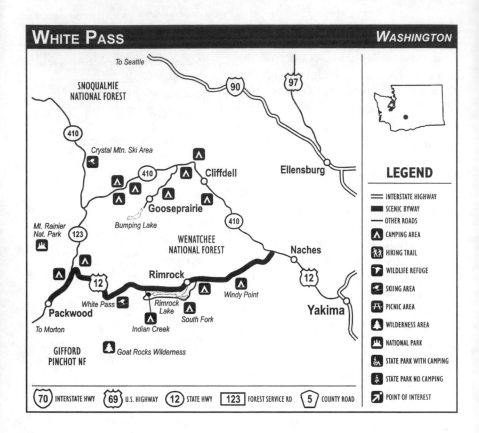

Route Location

The White Pass scenic byway is located in south-central Washington, approximately 20 miles northwest of Yakima. The byway's eastern terminus is at the junction of U.S. Highway 12 and Washington State Highway 410, about 5 miles north of Naches. The byway travels west across national forest land and ends in the town of Packwood.

Roads Traveled

The 58-mile route follows U.S. Highway 12 which is a two-lane paved road suitable for all vehicles. Fifty-five miles of this byway are officially designated a National Forest Scenic Byway.

Travel Season

U.S. Highway 12 is usually open year-round although winter driving conditions can be hazardous, especially in the higher elevations.

Description

The White Pass scenic byway takes travelers across the Gifford Pinchot and Wenatchee National Forests as it winds through a mixed conifer forest, beautiful meadows ablaze with wildflowers, and past pristine lakes and cascading waterfalls. The byway crosses 4,500 foot White Pass where the Pacific Crest National Scenic Trail may be accessed. Several scenic turnouts and overlooks provide visitors with beautiful views of the surrounding wilderness. They also provide good opportunities for spotting deer, elk, eagles, hawks, or osprey.

Rimrock Lake and the numerous other lakes along the byway provide excellent fishing and boating opportunities. The rivers that feed these lakes also offer good fishing and rafting. Campgrounds and picnic areas may also be found situated on the banks.

Near the byway's western end is the Mount Rainier National Park. Within this national park is Washington's highest point, the 14,410-foot-high Mount Rainier. This beautiful mountain peak is a dormant volcano supporting the largest glacial system in the lower 48 states. There are 27 named glaciers encompassing 35 square miles. The Wonderland Trail is a 93-mile hiking trail that completely encircles the mountain peak. To walk the entire trail takes anywhere between 10 and 14 days. Those interested in camping will find over 600 campsites in several campgrounds within the park.

Local Information

Wenatchee National Forest
301 Yakima St.
Wenatchee, WA 98807
Phone: 509-662-4335

Gifford Pinchot National Forest
P.O. Box 8944
Vancouver, WA 98668
Phone: 360-750-5000

Mt. Baker-Snoqualmie National Forest
21905 64th Ave. W.
Mountlake Terrace, WA 98043
Phone: 206-744-3200

Packwood Improvement Service
P.O. Box 253
Packwood, WA 98361
Phone: 360-494-7126

Greater Yakima Chamber of Commerce
10 N. Ninth St.
Yakima, WA 98907
Phone: 509-248-2021

Mt. Rainier National Park
Tahoma Woods, Star Route
Ashford, WA 98304
Phone: 360-569-2211

LODGING DIRECTORY

Game Ridge Motel & Lodge - Rimrock, page 461 — Resort

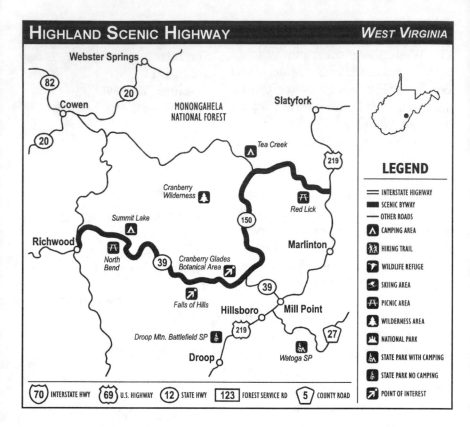

Route Location

The Highland Scenic Highway is located in eastern West Virginia, about 25 miles east of Summersville. The byway begins in Richwood and travels east across the Monongahela National Forest to the intersection with U.S. Highway 219, north of Marlinton.

Roads Traveled

The 43-mile scenic byway follows West Virginia State Highways 39 and 150. The state-maintained roads are two-lane paved roads suitable for all types of vehicles. The route has been designated a National Forest Scenic Byway as well as a National Scenic Byway by the Federal Highway Administration.

Travel Season

State Highway 39 is usually open all year but State Route 150 is not maintained for winter travel and is usually closed from early December to March.

Description

The route takes visitors through the mountainous terrain of the Allegheny Highlands and Plateau. The byway climbs over 2,000 feet from Richwood to the crest of Black Mountain standing at 4,556 feet. Your scenic journey will take you through hardwood forests of yellow poplar, beech, maples, cherry, and oak trees with wildflowers growing alongside the road. The sparkling waters of the North Fork of the Cherry River will accompany you for the first part of your trip from Richwood. Three waterfalls at Falls of Hills Creek gracefully tumble over the rock outcrops. A ¾-mile trail will lead you to these beautiful falls, including a paved, barrier-free trail to the first waterfall.

Near the intersection with State Highway 150 is the Cranberry Mountain Visitor Center. Not far from the visitor center is the Cranberry Glades Botanical Area, a National Natural Landmark. This is a 750-acre area with a ½-mile long barrier-free boardwalk among the bogs. Bogs are acidic wetlands typically found in Canada and the northern U.S. Guided tours are conducted on weekends throughout the summer. State Highway 150 travels north alongside the 35,864-acre Cranberry Wilderness. There are trailheads along this portion of the route that will lead you through the heart of this vast mountain wilderness area.

Monongahela National Forest offers two camping areas along the byway with more throughout the forest. Summit Lake Campground is situated on the shoreline of this 42-acre lake and offers 33 campsites. Fishermen will find trout in this lake and the many rivers throughout the national forest. Tea Creek Campground has 35 campsites for tents and recreational vehicles. Miles of hiking trails can also be access from here.

Local Information

Monongahela National Forest
Gauley Ranger District
P.O. Box 110
Richwood, WV 26261
Phone: 304-846-2695

Richwood Chamber of Commerce
50 Oakford Ave.
Richwood, WV 26261
Phone: 304-846-6790

Marlinton Chamber of Commerce
1010 3rd Ave.
Marlinton, WV 24954
Phone: 304-799-4048

Droop Mountain Battlefield State Park
HC64 - Box 189
Hillsboro, WV 24946
Phone: 304-653-4254

Watoga State Park
HC82 - Box 252
Marlington, WV 24954
Phone: 304-799-4087

Nearby Routes

Highlands Scenic Tour, page 388

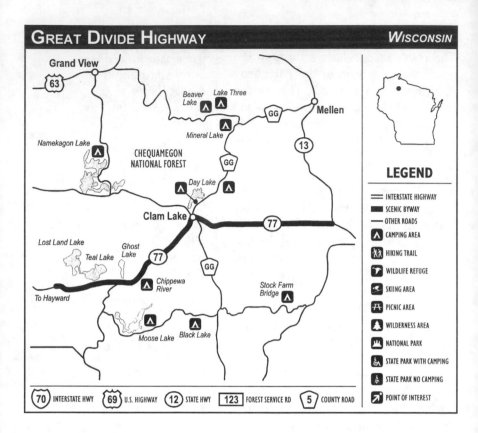

GREAT DIVIDE HIGHWAY — WISCONSIN

Route Location

The Great Divide Highway is located in northwestern Wisconsin, approximately 37 miles south of Ashland. The byway's eastern access is located at the junction of Wisconsin State Highways 13 and 77. The byway's western terminus is the entrance to the Chequamegon National Forest, approximately 20 miles east of Hayward.

Roads Traveled

The 29-mile route follows Wisconsin State Highway 77 which is a two-lane paved road suitable for all vehicles. The byway is designated a National Forest Scenic Byway.

Travel Season

State Highway 77 is maintained throughout the year, however, winter driving conditions may require drivers to use extra caution.

Description

The Great Divide Highway crosses the Chequamegon National Forest, traveling through northern hardwoods and mixed conifer. The byway also takes travelers across open meadows of wildflowers and wetlands where waterfowl congregate. The byway winds through the hills of the Penokee Range, its ridgelands forming the Great Divide that separates water flowing north to Lake Superior from water flowing south to the Mississippi River. White-tailed deer, black bear, and timber wolves inhabit the forested regions while loons, beavers, and bald eagles can be seen around the byway's many lakes. Scenic overlooks along the route provide panoramic vistas of the surrounding highlands.

Local Information

Chequamegon National Forest
1170 S. Fourth Ave.
Park Falls, WI 54552
Phone: 715-762-2461

Hayward Chamber of Commerce
P.O. Box 726
Hayward, WI 54843
Phone: 715-634-8662

Park Falls Area Chamber of Commerce
400 4th Ave. S. #8
Park Falls, WI 54552
Phone: 715-762-2703

Mellen Area Chamber of Commerce
P.O. Box 793
Mellen, WI 54546
Phone: 715-274-2330

The numerous lakes and rivers surrounding the byway make for great muskellunge, northern pike, bass, walleye, and trout fishing. Portions of the Namekagon River flowing from Namekagon Lake are part of the National Wild and Scenic River System. This river provides some Class II and III rapids for those wishing to canoe the river.

Side roads along the byway may tempt you to do some exploring. If you do, you'll be rewarded with many beautiful "hidden" lakes, rivers, and streams. You'll find campgrounds on the shores of many lakes and perfect places for pulling over and enjoying a picnic. This vast network of forest roads also makes for good mountain biking opportunities. In winter you're likely to see cross-country skiers and snowmobilers utilizing the miles of groomed trails.

There are two national forest campgrounds along the byway. Day Lake is the largest and is about one mile north of the community of Clam Lake. This campground has 66 campsites for tents and recreational vehicles. The Chippewa River camping area offers 11 sites and boat access to the river. There are no hookups at either campground.

Nearby Routes

Black River, page 185

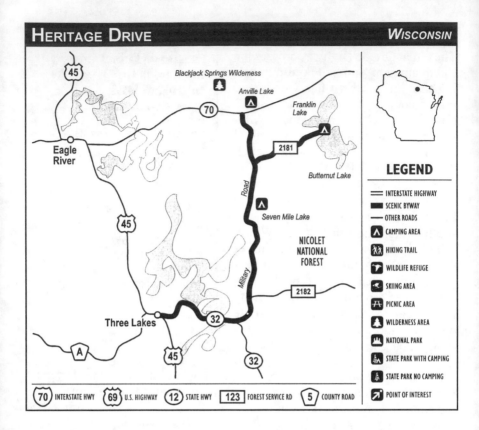

Route Location

The Heritage Drive scenic byway is located in northeastern Wisconsin, about 20 miles northeast of Rhinelander. The southwestern access is located off U.S. Highway 45 in the town of Three Lakes. The byway heads east and north to the intersection with State Highway 70. A spur road travels east to Franklin and Butternut Lakes.

Roads Traveled

The 21-mile scenic route follows Wisconsin State Highway 32 and Forest Service Roads 2178 (Military Road) and 2181 (Butternut Lake Road). The roads are narrow, two-lane paved roads suitable for all vehicles. Fifteen miles of this byway are designated a National Forest Scenic Byway.

Travel Season

The roads followed are usually open all year.

Description

The Heritage Drive crosses the Nicolet National Forest, following portions of the Lake Superior Trail used by the Menominee for trading with the Winnebago and Ojibwa Indians. By 1861 the trail was improved a bit and used as a mail route. Shortly following the trail's initial service as a mail route, the military improved the trail to a roadway transporting supplies, ammunition, and mail from fort to fort. Today the road is a scenic byway through the old-growth pine and northern hardwood forest providing travelers the opportunity for outdoor recreation.

Local Information

Nicolet National Forest
Eagle River Ranger District
P.O. Box 1809
Eagle River, WI 54521
Phone: 715-479-2827

Vilas County Chamber of Commerce
P.O. Box 369
Eagle River, WI 54521
Phone: 715-479-3649

Three Lakes Chamber of Commerce
P.O. Box 268
Three Lakes, WI 54562
Phone: 715-546-3344

In 1937 the Civilian Conservation Corps constructed eight stone buildings in the area of Franklin Lake Campground. One building has been renovated into an interpretive center where exhibits provide information on the geology and history of the area. The campground and its historic stone structures are listed on the National Register of Historic Places. Visitors will find 81 campsites suitable for tents and recreational vehicles up to 22 feet long. A nature trail and swimming area may also be found here. The lake provides good walleye and bass fishing.

Seven Mile Lake Campground sits on a bluff overlooking the lake. The campground is two miles northeast of the byway on Forest Road 2435. Campers will have 27 sites to choose from. There is boat access to the lake, a swimming area, and good musky, walleye, and bass fishing. A two-mile hiking trail leads east to encircle two wetland lakes.

Anvil Lake Campground lies just to the east of the byway's northern terminus. There are 18 campsites with picnic tables and fire rings here. Drinking water, a swimming area, and boat access are among the facilities available. Anglers will find walleye and bass inhabiting the waters of the lake.

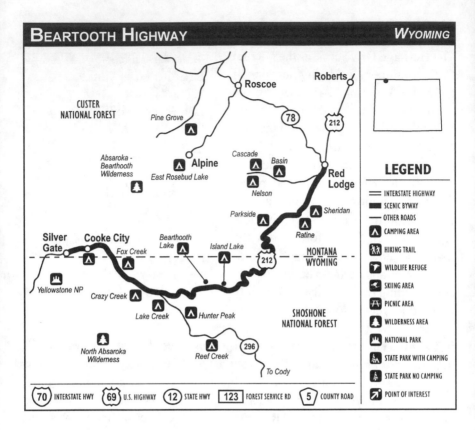

Route Location

The Beartooth Highway is located in northwestern Wyoming and southern Montana. The byway begins in Red Lodge, Montana and travels southwest, crossing into Wyoming, and ends at the entrance to Yellowstone National Park. Red Lodge, Montana is approximately 60 miles north of Cody, Wyoming.

Roads Traveled

The 68-mile byway follows U.S. Highway 212 which is a two-lane paved road suitable for all types of vehicles. The byway is designated a National Forest Scenic Byway.

Travel Season

Beartooth Highway is generally passable from late May through mid-October. Sections of the road are closed during the winter and are used as snowmobile routes.

Description

The route takes travelers on a scenic journey across the beautiful Beartooth Mountains. The byway travels through portions of Custer and Gallatin National Forests in Montana and Shoshone National Forest in Wyoming. A primitive trail was once all that connected the mining towns of Red Lodge and Cooke City until the Civilian Conservation Corps constructed a road between 1932 and 1936. Now travelers can enjoy the spectacular scenery as they climb the switchbacks of this byway to 10,947-foot Beartooth Pass. The forests consist of Engelmann spruce, Douglas fir, lodgepole pine, and aspen. The aspen leaves turn a beautiful golden color in fall, making this an even more beautiful drive.

The national forests are home to a wide variety of wildlife. Byway travelers are likely to see elk or mule deer foraging along the roadside, especially in the early morning or evening. Moose can sometimes be seen among the willows along lakes and streams. Black and grizzly bears also inhabit the area but are rarely seen. Birdwatchers will need to keep an eye on the sky for hawks, golden eagles, and prairie falcons.

Campers have nearly 200 campsites in all from which to choose and most will accommodate tents or RVs. Each campsite has a picnic table and fire ring for those nights under stars around a campfire. All of the campgrounds have drinking water and comfort stations. The lower elevation campgrounds are usually open by Memorial Day. The campgrounds higher up may not open until mid to late June, depending on snow conditions.

Local Information

Shoshone National Forest
Clarks Fork Ranger District
1002 Road 11
Powell, WY 82435
Phone: 307-754-2407

Custer National Forest
Beartooth Ranger District
Rt. 2 - Box 3420
Red Lodge, MT 59068
Phone: 406-446-2103

Red Lodge Area Chamber of Commerce
601 N. Broadway
Red Lodge, MT 59068
Phone: 406-446-1718

Gardiner Chamber of Commerce
P.O. Box 81
Gardiner, MT 59030
Phone: 406-848-7971

Cody Country Chamber of Commerce
P.O. Box 2777
Cody, WY 82414
Phone: 307-587-2777

Yellowstone National Park
P.O. Box 168
Yellowstone National Park, WY 82190
Phone: 307-344-7381

Lodging Directory

Red Lodging - Red Lodge, page 431 — Residential Lodging

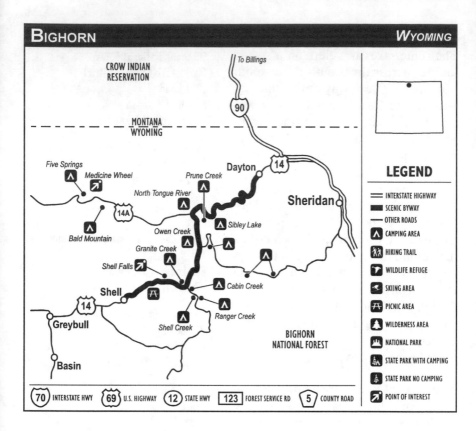

Route Location

The Bighorn scenic drive is located in north-central Wyoming, 21 miles west of Sheridan. The byway begins in Dayton off Interstate 90 and travels west across the Bighorn National Forest to end in the town of Shell. Interstate 90 travelers will want to take Exit #9 and head west to reach Dayton.

Roads Traveled

The byway is about 58 miles long and follows U.S. Highway 14 which is a two-lane paved road suitable for all vehicles. Forty miles of this byway are officially designated a National Forest Scenic Byway. Forty-seven miles are designated a Wyoming Scenic Byway.

Travel Season

U.S. Highway 14 is usually passable all year long. Temporarily closure is possible during the winter for snow removal.

Description

From Dayton, the Bighorn National
Forest Scenic Byway begins at an elevation of 3,926 feet and climbs to over
9,000 feet at Granite Pass. Between
these two points, the byway twists and
turns up switchbacks as it makes the
ascent up the Bighorn Mountains. From
Granite Pass, the byway begins its descent of nearly 5,000 feet to pass
through Shell Canyon and the byway's
end in Shell. Accompanying you for this
portion of the byway are the babbling
waters of Granite and Shell Creeks. All
along the byway, wildflowers will display their beautiful colors from spring
to autumn. Joyful songbirds will sing, telling you of the marvelous scenery
they live among. Byway travelers will pass through forests of ponderosa
pine, alpine fir, Engelmann spruce, and lodgepole pine in addition to wide
open grassy meadows and valleys.

Local Information

Bighorn National Forest
1969 S. Sheridan Ave.
Sheridan, WY 82801
Phone: 307-672-0751

Greybull Area Chamber of Commerce
330 Greybull Ave.
Greybull, WY 82426
Phone: 307-765-2100

Sheridan County Chamber of Commerce
P.O. Box 707
Sheridan, WY 82801
Phone: 307-672-2485

Wildlife observers will delight in small and large creatures inhabiting the
area. Of the smaller variety are porcupines, gophers, and beavers. Mule
deer and white-tailed deer may be seen along with elk grazing along rivers
and streams or among the grasses of open meadows. Moose, black bears,
bobcats, and coyotes also inhabit the area but are more secretive. Bighorn
sheep have been transplanted into the area and may also be spotted occasionally. Anglers may want to spend some time trying to pull rainbow, brown,
and brook trout from the forest's many rivers and streams.

Be sure to stop and view the beautiful Shell Falls. Walking trails provide
closer examination of the waterfalls. An information center located here will
provide you with some information on the area. Stay awhile and read a good
book, talk with others, or enjoy a picnic. By all means, take some pictures!

Nearby Routes

Medicine Wheel Passage, page 416 / Red Gulch - Alkali, page 420

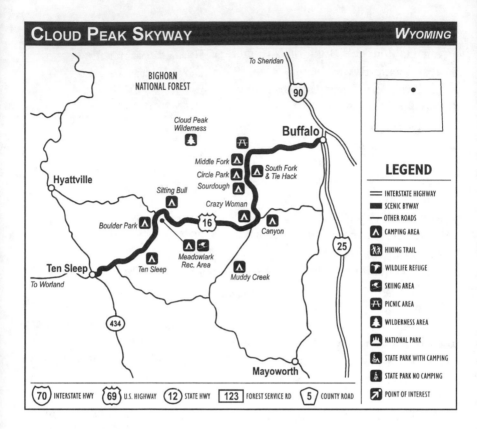

Route Location

The Cloud Peak Skyway scenic drive is located in north-central Wyoming, approximatley 35 miles south of Sheridan. The byway begins in Buffalo and travels west across the Bighorn National Forest. The western terminus of the byway is in the community of Ten Sleep.

Roads Traveled

The 67-mile route follows U.S. Highway 16 which is a two-lane paved road suitable for all vehicles. Forty-three miles of this byway are designated a National Forest Scenic Byway. Wyoming has designated 47 miles as a state scenic byway.

Travel Season

U.S. Highway 16 is usually open all year. Temporary closure is possible during winter months for snow removal.

Description

The Cloud Peak Skyway scenic drive begins at an elevation of 4,645 feet in Buffalo and heads west across the forested Bighorn Mountains. It crosses Powder River Pass at an elevation of 9,666 feet and then drops down through Ten Sleep Canyon to end in Ten Sleep at 4,206 feet. Several viewpoints provide expansive vistas into Cloud Peak Wilderness as well as the surrounding mountain scenery. Wildlife observers need to be looking for mule deer or elk among the rivers and grassy meadows. Wildflowers bloom from spring through autumn, providing a splash of color against the green of ponderosa pine.

Local Information

Bighorn National Forest
1969 S. Sheridan Ave.
Sheridan, WY 82801
Phone: 307-672-0751

Worland Area Chamber of Commerce
120 N. 10th St.
Worland, WY 82401
Phone: 307-347-3226

Buffalo Chamber of Commerce
55 N. Main St.
Buffalo, WY 82834
Phone: 307-684-5544

If you're interested in hiking, backpacking, or horseback riding, you're in the right place. To the north of this byway lies the pristine land of the vast Cloud Peak Wilderness Area. This area protects 195,000 acres of the Bighorn Mountains. Trails leading into this beautiful wilderness area can be accessed from the byway. Hikers and backpackers will find trails that will take them several days to hike.

Those less interested in hiking the back country but want to enjoy an evening around a campfire can do so at the many campgrounds found along the byway. The Meadowlark Recreation Area offers over 100 campsites in five nearby campgrounds. This is a good spot to pitch your tent or park your recreational vehicles. The lake here is popular during the summer with anglers and boaters. Middle Fork, Circle Park, South Fork, and Tie Hacks Campgrounds provide a total of 43 sites to choose from. Trailheads found here can take you into the wilderness area.

Nearby Routes

Red Gulch - Alkali, page 420

Lodging Directory

Mountain View Inn - Buffalo, page 435 — Cabin / Cottage / Guest Ranch & Campground / RV Park

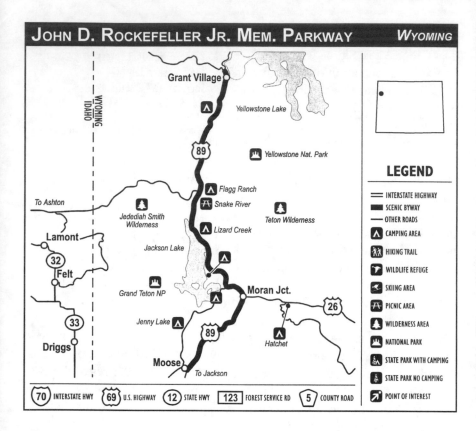

JOHN D. ROCKEFELLER JR. MEM. PARKWAY — WYOMING

Route Location

The John D. Rockefeller, Jr. Memorial Parkway is located in northwestern Wyoming. The byway travels between West Thumb in Yellowstone National Park and ends in Moose near southern boundary of Grand Teton National Park.

Roads Traveled

The 82-mile parkway follows U.S. Highway 89 which is a two-lane paved route suitable for all types of vehicles. The scenic route has been designated a National Parkway by the National Park Service. The portion of the drive from Moran Junction to Moose is also part of the Wyoming Centennial scenic byway.

Travel Season

The road north of Flagg Ranch is not plowed during the winter months, so access to Yellowstone is by snowmobile or commercial snowcoach only.

Description

The Parkway is accompanied by the scenic Snake River which empties into Jackson Lake. Cutthroat trout, brown and brook trout, mackinaw, and whitefish are abundant in the waters of the Snake River and its tributaries. Visitors along the byway may see moose feeding among the willows; elk and deer passing through the open forest; and beavers working the numerous creeks. Threatened and endangered species, such as the bald eagle and grizzly bear, find protection here.

The Parkway winds through forests of lodgepole pine, spruce, fir, and aspen. Wet meadows and willow thickets line the rivers while wildflowers and grasses cover the open hillsides during summer. Several scenic overlooks provide views of majestic Teton Range of the Rocky Mountains. A 24,000-acre parcel of land is also known as the John D. Rockefeller, Jr. Memorial Parkway. This land area connects the two national parks and was dedicated in 1972 to recognize Mr. Rockefeller's generosity in making significant contributions to several national parks across the country, including Acadia, Great Smoky Mountains, Virgin Islands, and the Blue Ridge Parkway.

There are several trails that can be accessed along the drive. Some trails are short self-guided trails while others are long, strenuous paths that will take you deep into the national parks and surrounding national forests. Wilderness areas offer the sweet silence of seclusion and two of these primitive and rugged areas can only be reached by hiking trails. Several camping areas are along this route, most offering sites for both tents and RVs. Some recreation areas also offer such amenities as restaurants, lodging, and grocery stores.

Local Information

John D. Rockefeller, Jr., Memorial Pkwy.
c/o Grand Teton National Park
P.O. Drawer 170
Moose, WY 83012
Phone: 307-733-7880

Bridger - Teton National Forest
P.O. Box 1888
Jackson, WY 83001
Phone: 307-739-5500

Yellowstone National Park
P.O. Box 168
Yellowstone Nat'l. Park, WY 82190
Phone: 307-344-7381

Jackson Hole Chamber of Commerce
P.O. Box E
Jackson, WY 83001
Phone: 307-733-3316

Nearby Routes

North Fork Highway, page 418 / Wyoming Centennial, page 428

Lodging Directory

Dornan's Spur Ranch Cabins - Moose, page 441 —— Cabin / Cottage / Guest Ranch

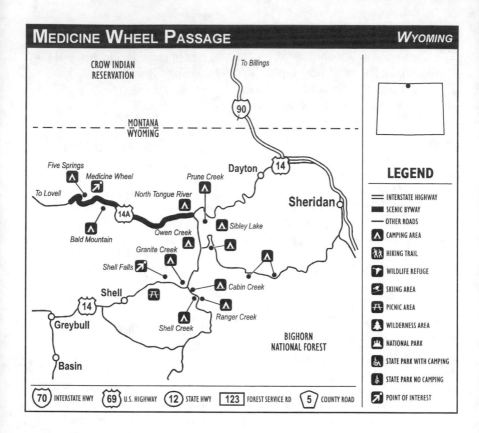

Route Location

The Medicine Wheel Passage scenic byway is located in north-central Wyoming, about 47 miles west of Sheridan. The byway begins at the Burgess Junction where U.S. Highway 14 heads south. From this point, the byway travels westerly and ends at the Bighorn National Forest boundary. Interstate 90 travelers can reach the byway by taking Exit #9 and traveling west through Dayton, which is the beginning point for the Bighorn scenic drive.

Roads Traveled

The 27-mile route follows Alternate U.S. Highway 14 which is a two-lane paved road suitable for all vehicles. The byway is designated a National Forest Scenic Byway and also a Wyoming Scenic Byway.

Travel Season

U.S. Highway 14A is usually passable from May through mid-November. Winter's blanket of snowfall closes the byway for the rest of the year.

Description

The Medicine Wheel Passage scenic byway provides an alternate route for those traveling the Bighorn scenic byway. It also provides an excuse to complete the other scenic drive and then make your way around to drive this byway. As with the sister scenic byway, the Medicine Wheel Passage takes you through the beautiful scenery known as the Bighorn Mountains. The surrounding mountains are covered with lodgepole pine, alpine fir, Engelmann spruce, and ponderosa pine.

A large parking area adjacent to the byway at Bald Mountain provides breathtaking views of the northern Bighorn Mountains. Be sure you have enough film in your camera. This area marks the center of gold mining activity during the late 1880s. To the northeast of you are the remains of Bald Mountain City, a gold mining ghost town.

Local Information

Bighorn National Forest
1969 S. Sheridan Ave.
Sheridan, WY 82801
Phone: 307-672-0751

Lovell Area Chamber of Commerce
287 E. Main
Lovell, WY 82431
Phone: 307-548-7552

Sheridan County Chamber of Commerce
P.O. Box 707
Sheridan, WY 82801
Phone: 307-672-2485

Greybull Area Chamber of Commerce
330 Greybull Ave.
Greybull, WY 82426
Phone: 307-765-2100

Not far from the Bald Mountain overlook is the Medicine Wheel National Historic Landmark. Believed to have been built by prehistoric Indians, this giant wheel is made of limestone slabs and boulders. It measures 245 feet in circumference. This wheel is recognized by Native Americans as a sacred site. The reason for its construction remains a mystery. You may want to continue exploring this area. Find Forest Service Road 11/14 near here. This road will take you to the trailhead for Bucking Mule Falls National Recreation Trail. The trail is eleven miles long but the first three will take you to a viewpoint of the thundering Bucking Mule Falls.

The camping opportunities along this stretch of U.S. Highway 14A are not as extensive as its sister byway, the Bighorn. North Tongue has eleven sites while Bald Mountain provides fifteen.

Nearby Routes

Bighorn, page 410 / Red Gulch - Alkali, page 420

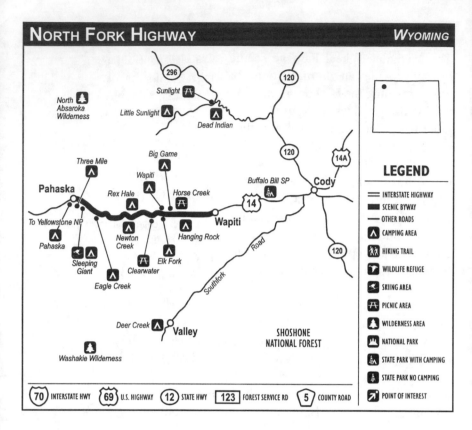

NORTH FORK HIGHWAY — *WYOMING*

LEGEND
- ═══ INTERSTATE HIGHWAY
- ▬ SCENIC BYWAY
- — OTHER ROADS
- ⛺ CAMPING AREA
- 🚶 HIKING TRAIL
- 🦌 WILDLIFE REFUGE
- ⛷ SKIING AREA
- 🍴 PICNIC AREA
- 🌲 WILDERNESS AREA
- 🏔 NATIONAL PARK
- STATE PARK WITH CAMPING
- STATE PARK NO CAMPING
- ↗ POINT OF INTEREST

(70) INTERSTATE HWY (69) U.S. HIGHWAY (12) STATE HWY [123] FOREST SERVICE RD (5) COUNTY ROAD

Route Location

This scenic drive is located in the northwestern corner of Wyoming, twenty miles west of Cody. The byway begins in Wapiti on U.S. Hwy. 14 (also U.S. 16 and U.S. 20) and travels west across the Shoshone National Forest. The byway ends in Pahaska near the entrance of Yellowstone National Park.

Roads Traveled

The North Fork Highway follows U.S. Hwy. 14 for thirty miles. The route is a two-lane paved road safe for all vehicles. Twenty-eight miles are officially designated a National Forest Scenic Byway. The byway is also known as the Buffalo Bill Cody Scenic Byway and is a Wyoming scenic drive.

Travel Season

The scenic byway is usually open all year, however, the highway continuing through Yellowstone National Park is closed from mid-November through March. It is open to snowmobilers and cross-country skiers during this time.

Description

The byway takes travelers through the beautiful Shoshone Canyon where the waters of the North Fork of the Shoshone River flow nearby. The route travels through the heart of the Shoshone National Forest and is surrounded by two wilderness areas. The canyon is a narrow valley with extremely steep slopes and vertical cliffs, giving the visitor the feeling of being embraced by the surrounding mountains.

Wildlife observers will want to be on the lookout for mule deer and elk that can sometimes be seen grazing in the meadows or along the river. Moose, bighorn sheep, black bear, and the mighty grizzly bear are also inhabitants of the area. The North Fork is believed to have one of the highest concentrations of grizzly bears in the lower 48 states.

Local Information

Shoshone National Forest
Box 2140
Cody, WY 82414
Phone: 307-527-6241

Shoshone National Forest
Wapita Ranger District
203A Yellowstone Ave.
Cody, WY 82414
Phone: 307-527-6921

Cody Country Chamber of Commerce
836 Sheridan Ave.
Cody, WY 82414
Phone: 307-587-2777

Buffalo Bill State Park
Cody, WY 82414
Phone: 307-587-9227

Yellowstone National Park
P.O. Box 168
Yellowstone National Park, WY 82190
Phone: 307-344-7381

There are numerous trailheads located along the byway that invite the traveler to explore. Many will lead into the vast wilderness areas lying to the north and south of the byway. To the north is the 350,488-acre North Absaroka Wilderness. To your south is the huge 704,529-acre Washakie Wilderness. Both of these wilderness areas provide excellent opportunities for those seeking solitude. You don't have to be a seasoned hiker or backpacker to enjoy short segments of the trails. For those that are equipped to handle the wilderness, the trails are your gateway to a wonderland of beautiful mountains and wildlife in its most natural setting. Those interested in sleeping under the stars will find a lot of campgrounds along the byway. Altogether, there are over 200 campsites. All of them but the Deer Creek Campground is situated on the banks of the river.

Nearby Routes

John D. Rockefeller Jr. Memorial Parkway, page 414

Lodging Directory

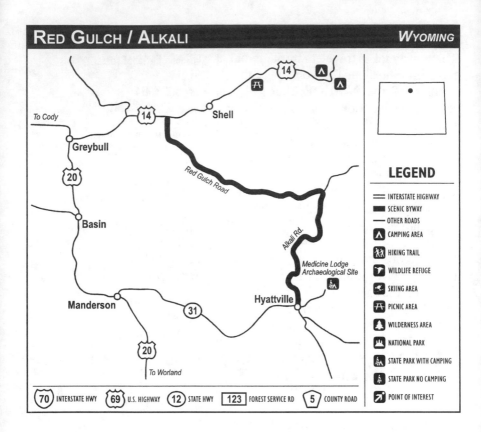

Route Location

The Red Gulch / Alkali scenic byway is located in north-central Wyoming, ten miles east of Greybull. The byway's southern terminus is in the town of Hyattville. The northern end of the byway is at the junction with U.S. Highway 14, about five miles west of Shell.

Roads Traveled

The 32-mile byway follows the Red Gulch / Alkali Road which is a combination of gravel and dirt-surfaced road. The byway requires a two-wheel drive, high-clearance vehicle to safely travel. This byway is a Type II Back Country Byway and a Wyoming Scenic Backway.

Travel Season

Visitors can usually travel the entire byway from May through October except during and after periods of rain. The road is very muddy and becomes impassable during these times.

Description

Travelers of the Red Gulch / Alkali Back Country Byway will find themselves winding through the foothills of the beautiful Bighorn Mountains. It's easy to see how the byway was named when you travel this back country route. The reddish color of the Chugwater formation is seen to the east with the Bighorn Mountains as a backdrop. The landscape is composed mostly of sagebrush that provides habitat for the sage grouse. The sage grouse will proudly display their showy plumage at dawn in early spring for those traveling that time of year. If you're traveling this byway in the fall, be on the lookout for mule deer or elk that make their way down from the higher elevations for the coming winter. You may also encounter a gold eagle or peregrine falcon soaring in the sky overhead.

As you travel along the byway you may notice stacks of stone piled upon each other. Some of these were constructed by Native Americans to mark trail routes, hunting areas, or other important features of the landscape. Others may have been constructed by sheepherders to mark bed grounds and springs or simply out of boredom.

Although there are no developed campgrounds along the byway, the Bureau of Land Management does permit dispersed camping nearly anywhere on BLM lands. It is best, however, to obtain maps from the BLM before setting up camp as there may be private property nearby. The Medicine Lodge Archaeological Site, just east of the southern end of the byway, has camping facilities. You can also see Native American petroglyphs here.

Nearby Routes

Bighorn, page 410 / Cloud Peak Skyway, page 412 / Medicine Wheel Passage, page 416

Local Information

BLM - Worland District Office
101 S. 23rd St.
Worland, WY 82401
Phone: 307-347-9871

Greybull Area Chamber of Commerce
330 Greybull Ave.
Greybull, WY 82426
Phone: 307-765-2100

Worland Area Chamber of Commerce
120 N. 10th St.
Worland, WY 82401
Phone: 307-347-3226

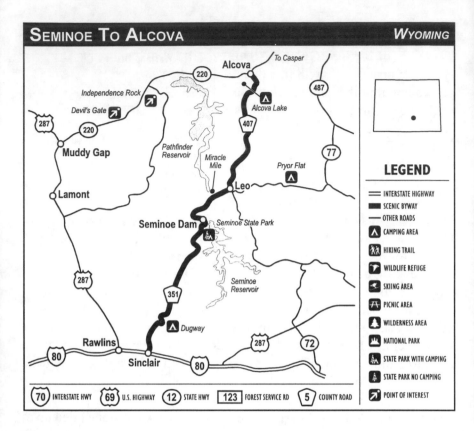

Route Location

The Seminoe To Alcova scenic drive is located in south-central Wyoming, about 32 miles southwest of Casper. The byway travels between Alcova on State Highway 220 in the north and Sinclair on Interstate 80 in the south. The byway crosses land managed by the Bureau of Land Managment.

Roads Traveled

The 64-mile route follows County Roads 351, 407, and 408. The route's gravel-surfaced roads vary from two-lane to single-lane and are suitable for most vehicles. Motorhomes and vehicles pulling trailers are not recommended on the segment from Seminoe State Park to Miracle Mile. The byway is a Type I Back Country Byway and a Wyoming Scenic Backway.

Travel Season

The byway is generally open from May through early December. The byway is closed the rest of the year.

Description

The Seminoe To Alcova Back Country Byway takes travelers across a desert landscape between the Seminoe Mountains to the west and the Shirley Mountains rising in the east. Portions of the byway travel along the banks of the North Platte River that has brought life to the Seminoe and Pathfinder Reservoirs. Byway travelers will cross the river in an area known as Miracle Mile. This stretch of the North Platte River is renowned as a blue-ribbon trout stream.

Travelers are most likely to see pronghorn antelope and mule deer grazing along the roadside. Hawks and eagles can be seen surfing the wind currents above. Elk and bighorn sheep also inhabit the area but prefer not being seen by tourists. Other wildlife preferring to keep to themselves is mountain lions, bobcats, and coyotes.

Local Information

BLM - Rawlins District Office
1300 N. 3rd St.
Rawlins, WY 82301
Phone: 307-324-7171

Rawlins - Carbon County C of C
519 W. Cedar
Rawlins, WY 82301
Phone: 800-228-3547

Casper Area Chamber of Commerce
500 N. Center St.
Casper, WY 82602
Phone: 307-234-5311

Seminoe State Park
County Road 351, Seminoe Dam Route
Sinclair, WY 82334
Phone: 307-328-0115

For those wishing to camp among the stars in the natural surroundings will find some campgrounds maintained by the BLM. The first encountered when driving south to north is the Dugway Campground. There are seven sites here with picnic tables and fire rings situated on the banks of North Platte River. A boat ramp provides access to the river. To the east of the byway is Pryor Flat Campground providing five campsites with picnic tables and fire rings.

For those seeking a more developed campground can stay at the Seminoe State Park. There are nearly 100 sites available here that can accommodate tents and recreational vehicles. Some of the sites provide hookups for RVs. Campers will also find a swimming beach and boat access to the lake.

Nearby Routes

Wyoming Centennial, page 428

LODGING DIRECTORY

Royal Inn Motel - Casper, page 455 — Hotel / Motel

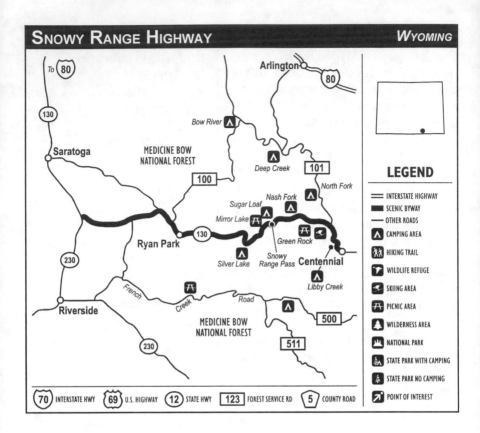

Route Location

The Snowy Range Highway is located in southern Wyoming, thirty miles west of Laramie. The byway begins in Centennial on State Highway 130 and travels west across the Medicine Bow National Forest. The byway ends at the intersection with State Highway 230.

Roads Traveled

The 40-mile scenic route follows Wyoming State Highway 130 which is a two-lane paved road suitable for all types of vehicles. Thirty miles of the byway are officially designated a National Forest Scenic Byway and a Wyoming Scenic Byway.

Travel Season

Byway travelers will find State Highway 130 open from late May through early November. Heavy winter snows close the byway the rest of the year.

Description

The Snowy Range Highway takes travelers across the Medicine Bow Mountains, also known as the Snowy Range, through forests of Engelmann Spruce, subalpine fir, and aspen. The byway climbs more than 2,000 feet from Centennial at 8,076 feet to the Snowy Range Pass, an elevation of 10,847 feet. It then descends from the pass, skirting the shores of several lakes, and ends at the national forest boundary west of Ryan Park. At the top of Snowy Range Pass is an overlook providing spectacular views of the surrounding mountains.

Local Information

Medicine Bow National Forest
2468 Jackson St.
Laramie, WY 82070
Phone: 307-745-8971

Laramie Area Chamber of Commerce
800 S. Third St.
Laramie, WY 82070
Phone: 307-745-7339

Saratoga - Platte Valley C of C
114 S. First St.
Saratoga, WY 82331
Phone: 307-326-8855

Wildflowers display beautiful colors of pink and yellow in June and July. In autumn, stands of aspen paint the mountainsides with shimmering gold. This route was originally a wagon road used in the 1800s.

During the winter months, much of the byway remains closed to automobiles but does provide access to excellent downhill and cross-country skiing. A downhill skiing area is located just five miles west of Centennial. There are over 300 miles of trails throughout the national forest, providing excellent cross-country skiing during the winter and hiking during the summer. A hiking trail at Lake Marie will lead you to the top of 12,013-foot Medicine Bow Peak. It's a three-mile hike with some steep climbs but the view from the top is worth the effort.

Visitors will find many lakes along the byway and throughout the national forest. Anglers will want to spend some time fishing for trout. Others may want to lay down a blanket and enjoy a picnic. Campgrounds can also be found on the shores of several lakes. If you're interested in pitching a tent or parking your RV, you'll find several campgrounds from which to choose. The national forest also permits dispersed camping nearly anywhere within the national forest. Check with the visitor center in Centennial for any restrictions.

LODGING DIRECTORY

Olde Depot Bed & Breakfast - Riverside, page 457 — Bed & Breakfast / Inns
Silver Moon Motel - Saratoga, page 457 — Hotel / Motel
Snowy Mountain Lodge - Centennial, page 457 — Cabin / Cottage / Guest Ranch & Resort

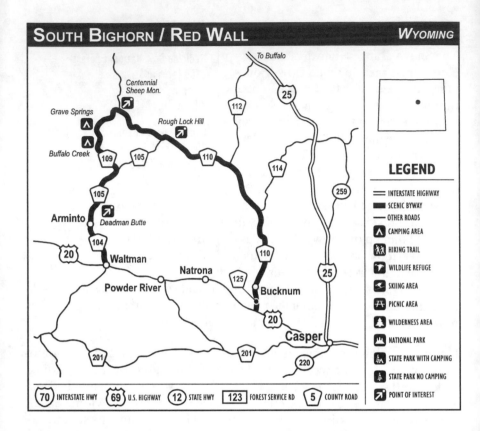

Route Location

The South Bighorn / Red Wall byway is located in central Wyoming, thirteen miles northwest of Casper. The byway forms an open loop drive traveling north of U.S. Highway 20. The western access point is in Waltman and the eastern point is the junction of U.S. 20 and County Road 125.

Roads Traveled

The 101-mile byway follows a series of Natrona County Roads that are a combination of gravel and dirt-surfaced roads. Although the roads are well maintained, a two-wheel drive, high-clearance vehicle is recommended. This scenic drive is designated a BLM Type II Back Country Byway and a Wyoming Scenic Backway.

Travel Season

The byway is generally open from May through November and then closed the rest of the year by winter's blanket of white. Portions of the roads followed may become impassable after periods of rain.

Description

The South Bighorn / Red Wall scenic drive will take visitors across the sage-covered plains northwest of Casper to the lush open pastures of the southern Bighorn Mountains. Portions of the byway follow the original path taken by early livestock pioneers. They would use the trail to move cattle and sheep to the higher mountain pastures during summer. A monument stands in recognition of these early pioneers. Elk and mule deer are likely to be seen in these high mountain pastures.

Local Information

BLM - Casper District Office
1701 East E St.
Casper, WY 82601
Phone: 307-261-7600

BLM - Platt River Resource Area
815 Connie St.
Mills, WY 82644
Phone: 307-261-5191

Casper Area Chamber of Commerce
500 N. Center St.
Casper, WY 82602
Phone: 307-234-5311

Byway travelers are also treated to scenic views of the Bighorn Mountains rising to the north. As you descend from the higher elevations, you'll be traveling alongside a portion of the Red Wall. North of here is Hole-in-the-Wall and Outlaw Cave where Butch Cassidy and the Sundance Kid once hid out. If you decide you would like to hide out also, you'll find two BLM campgrounds with several sites. Picnic tables, fire rings, and pit toilets are provided. No drinking water is available.

Roughlock Hill sits 6,200 feet above sea level and provides scenic views of the surrounding countryside. Here pioneers would lock their wagon wheels with thick branches and skid down the steep rocky slope. If you look closely, you may see the evidence left behind.

Nearby Routes

Seminoe To Alcova, page 422

LODGING DIRECTORY

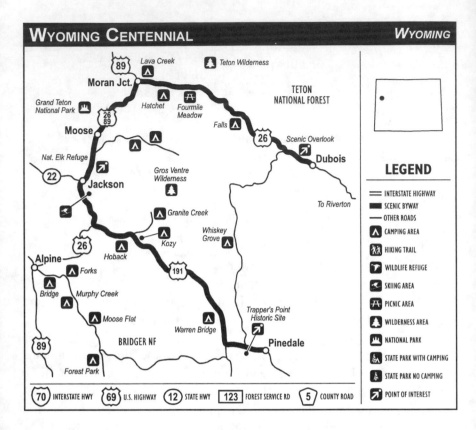

Route Location

The Wyoming Centennial scenic byway is located in northwestern Wyoming. The byway forms an open loop drive beginning in Dubois. The byway travels west to Moran Junction and then heads south through Jackson. The byway then turns southeasterly and ends in Pinedale.

Roads Traveled

The 161-mile byway follows U.S. Highways 26 and 191 which are two-lane paved roads suitable for all types of vehicles. The byway is designated a National Forest Scenic Byway. Portions of the route are also a Wyoming Scenic Byway. And yet another portion is part of the John D. Rockefeller, Jr. Memorial Parkway.

Travel Season

The roads followed usually remain open all year, however, delays may be possible during the winter months.

Description

Travelers can begin their scenic journey in Dubois and climb through the mountains to cross 9,658-foot Togwotee Pass. The view from the pass provides spectacular vistas in all directions. From this mountain pass you'll continue through the mixed conifer forest, rising and descending through meadows and mountain valleys. You'll turn south in Moran Junction and follow the path dictated by the winding Snake River. The byway will then take you through Grand Teton National Park and Jackson Hole. Continuing southeasterly you'll drive through the canyon walls of Hoback Canyon with Hoback River accompanying you. After 161 miles through beautiful mountains and valleys, the byway ends in the community of Pinedale.

Recreational opportunities abound all along this scenic drive. The huge 585,468-acre Teton Wilderness is to the north and provides unlimited exploration possibilities for the hiker, backpacker, and horseback rider. The 287,000-acre Gros Ventre Wilderness is embraced by the byway and also offers its own hiking opportunities. There are many public campgrounds situated along the banks of meandering streams and rivers or along the shore of placid mountain lakes. Some offer short nature trails taking you among wildflowers or cascading waterfalls.

Local Information

Bridger - Teton National Forest
340 North Cache
Jackson, WY 83001
Phone: 307-739-5500

Dubois Chamber of Commerce
616 W. Ramshorn
Dubois, WY 82513
Phone: 307-455-2556

Jackson Hole Chamber of Commerce
P.O. Box E
Jackson, WY 83001
Phone: 307-733-3316

Pinedale Area Chamber of Commerce
P.O. Box 176
Pinedale, WY 82941
Phone: 307-367-2242

Grand Teton National Park
P.O. Drawer 170
Moose, WY 83012
Phone: 307-733-2880

Nearby Routes

John D. Rockefeller Jr. Memorial Parkway, page 414

LODGING DIRECTORY

Dornan's Spur Ranch Cabins - Moose, page 462 — Cabin / Cottage / Guest Ranch
Elk Refuge Inn - Jackson, page 462 — Hotel / Motel
Lakeside Lodge Resort & Marina - Pinedale, page 462 — Cabin / Cottage / Guest Ranch, Camprground / RV Park & Resort
Pine Creek Ranch - Pinedale, page 462 — Cabin / Cottage / Guest Ranch
The Chambers House Bed & Breakfast - Pinedale, page 463 — Bed & Breakfast / Inns

LODGING DIRECTORY

The scenic drives covered in this book provide you with the opportunity to discover America's great outdoors and the many towns and rural communities that make up this great land of ours. This *Lodging Directory* has been included so you can take your time and explore the attractions and recreational opportunities available to you along and near the scenic byways.

With over 4,000 lodging opportunities available along or near the routes it is beyond the scope of this book to include them all. However, since it is always nice to know in advance some of the lodging opportunities available, you will find over 100 lodging establishments detailed in this section who have extended a special welcome to the byway traveler. The lodging establishments included in this directory supplied us with information and a description of their location to help you plan and enjoy your scenic byway adventure.

For easy reference, the *Lodging Directory* is arranged by scenic byway with the listings following in alphabetical order. At the end of each listing you will find a row of icons that give you a quick view of the facilities and services each offer. A list of the icons used and their description is provided on this page.

We would like to thank all the participating locations for providing you the opportunity to receive more enjoyment from the scenic drives. Please show your appreciation for their support by paying them a visit next time you are in their town.

Icons & Headings

- Wheelchair Access
- Exercise Room
- Sauna
- Swimming Pool
- Indoor Swimming Pool
- In-room Phones
- Movies / Cable
- Fireplaces
- Air Conditioning
- Restaurant
- Lounge
- Near Shopping
- Near Skiing
- Near Golf
- Near Fishing / Boating
- Near Hospital
- Near Airport
- Near Mass Transit
- Kitchen / Kitchenettes
- Pets Allowed
- Playground
- Laundry Facilities / Service
- Non-smoking Rooms
- Room Service
- Credit Cards Accepted
- Full or Continental Breakfast

Ancient Bristlecone — California, page 61

Super 8 Motel - High Sierra Lodge   Phone: 760-873-8426
1005 N. Main St.   Fax: 760-873-8060
Bishop, CA 93514

One of Bishops finest motels. Clean and comfortable rooms equipped with in-room coffee machines, free extended cable with HBO, and refrigerators. Seasonal outdoor pool and year round indoor jacuzzi. Fish cleaning & freezing facilities and BBQ area. Fantastic fishing! Walking distance to outlet mall and dining. AMEX, MC, Visa, and Discover cards accepted. Located on US Hwy. 395 at the north end of town. We appreciate your business.

Bear Lake - Caribou — Idaho, page 153

Three Sisters Motel   Phone: 208-847-2324
112 South 6th Street
Montpelier, ID 83254

Attractive motel centrally located. Very clean rooms with reasonable rates. Fridges and microwaves in most rooms. Direct dial phones in all rooms with free local calls. A gift shop, located in the lobby, features locally made gifts. Guaranteed reservations available. AAA & AARP discounts. Visa, MC, Discover, and AMEX cards accepted. Located on the corner of Highway 89 and 6th Street. Family owned and operated.

Beartooth Highway — Wyoming / Montana, page 408

Red Lodging   Phone: 406-446-1272
16½ N. Broadway   800-6-RED LODGE (800-673-3563)
P.O. Box 1477   Fax: 406-446-2327
Red Lodge, MT 59068

Red Lodging offers you the convenience, privacy and comforts of home. You'll enjoy the finest in fully furnished residential vacation lodging in the heart of Beartooth Country and Red Lodge, Montana. Beautiful Victorian homes • modern condos • creekside cabins • stone fireplaces • hot tubs • private scenic ponds • creekside fishing • antique decors • golf course access • and much more. These are special homes for special vacations in the most undiscovered resort community in the Rocky Mountains. Some homes sleep up to ten people. Personalized customer service. Single nights available during non-peak periods.

Blue Ridge Parkway — North Carolina, page 268

Chestnut Street Inn   Phone: 704-285-0705
176 E. Chestnut St.
Asheville, NC 28801

A beautifully restored c. 1905 Colonial Revival in the heart of Chestnut Hill Historic District. The Chestnut Street Inn features antique furnishings, private baths, large porches, and afternoon "tea and crumpets". In the morning you'll enjoy a sumptuous breakfast served on antique china. A short five minute walk takes you downtown for antiquing, sight-seeing, or dining. Visa • MC • Discover cards accepted.

🔲 A/C ✚ 🐾 ✅ ⛷ H ✈ 🚌 ⊘ 🍽 ☕

Lindridge House   Phone: 704-295-7343
5447 U.S. Hwy. 221 South
Blowing Rock, NC 28605

Located only one mile from the Blue Ridge Parkway offering spectacular views. Choose from small and medium size rooms or a suite, all with private baths. You'll enjoy hot coffee delivered to your door in the AM and a full family style breakfast. Amenities include: walking trails on property • 5.3 miles out of village • antique pool table • fireplace in Great Room.

🔲 ✚ 🐾 ✅ ⛷ H ⊘ 🍽 ☕

Maple Lodge   Phone: 704-295-3331
152 Sunset Drive
P.O. Box 1236
Blowing Rock, NC 28605

Located one mile off the Blue Ridge Parkway in the heart of a picturesque mountain village. The eleven guest rooms and suites feature private baths, antiques, and goose down comforters. Two parlors with stone fireplace and library. Guests are treated to a full breakfast overlooking a wildflower garden. Only a ½ block from the restaurants, shops, and galleries of Main Street. Smoke-free Inn. AAA 3-Diamond rating. All major credit cards accepted.

🔲 🔲 A/C ✚ 🐾 ✅ ⛷ H ⊘ 🍽 ☕

Oak Park Inn   Phone: 704-456-5328
314 S. Main Street   Fax: 704-456-8126
Waynesville, NC 28786

This quaint and charming renovated Inn awaits your arrival to beautiful downtown Waynesville. Oak Park Inn offers comfortable rooms with your choice of efficiency and two bedroom apartments or golf homes. All rooms have color cable TV, A/C & heat, and free rocking chairs! An easy walk to Main Street shops • boutiques • restaurants • grills • pubs • library • churches • and much more. Golf, skiing, rafting, and the Great Smoky Mountains are all nearby. Best rates in town! Our Inn and staff will have you proclaiming "I wasn't born in Waynesville but I got here as fast as I could".

☎ 🔲 A/C ✚ 🐾 ✅ ⛷ H 〰 🍽

Stone Pillar Bed & Breakfast   Phone: 704-295-4141
P.O. Box 1881   800-962-9955
144 Pine St.   Internet: http://blowingrock.com/northcarolina
Blowing Rock, NC 28605

Nestled in the beautiful mountains of western North Carolina, the Stone Pillar provides a relaxing homelike atmosphere in an historic 1920's house. The decor is a tasteful blend of heirlooms and antiques, accented by a few touches of modern. Open all year, the accommodations include six guests rooms, each with private bath. A full breakfast is created daily in the house kitchen, and served family style. Area activities and attractions include:

hiking • skiing • sight-seeing • shopping • dining • antiquing • Grandfather Mountain • the Tweetsie Railroad • or just relaxing on the front porch swing and rocking chairs. Located just off the Blue Ridge Parkway, in Blowing Rock, ½ block from Main St.

Sunset Motel   Phone: 704-884-9106
415 S. Broad St. (on US 64)
Brevard, NC 28712

A North Carolina classic motel. Clean rooms with free local calls, A/C, refrigerators, some with kitchenettes, and a refreshing cross-breeze in most rooms. AAA rated. Near the Cradle of Forestry • Brevard's renowned summer music festival • Pisgah National Forest • and trout fishing streams.

Boulder Mountain Highway — Utah, page 343

Boulder View Inn   Phone: 801-425-3800
385 West Main (Hwy. 24)   Fax: 801-425-3366
P.O. Box 750237   E-mail: cptlreef@color-country.net
Torrey, UT 84775

Boulder View Inn, located 1 mile from scenic Highway 12, welcomes travelers to a new 12 room unit with king & queen beds. Your stay includes a free continental breakfast. Guests enjoy a beautiful view of red ledges. A restaurant is located across the street. Only 4 miles from Capitol Reef National Park. Best Rates. AAA and AARP discounts. For reservations, call 24-hours a day, 800-444-3980. Visa, MC, Discover, and AMEX cards accepted.

Cactus Hill Ranch Motel   Phone: 801-425-3578
830 S. 1000 E.   800-507-2624 reservations
Teasdale, UT 84773   Fax: 801-425-3578

A beautiful location only minutes away from Boulder Mountain Highway (Hwy. 12) and Capitol Reef National Park. Available accommodations include a new 5-unit motel and one cabin on their 100 acre ranch. It's time to relax and enjoy the beauty and serenity of being "off the beaten path." Reasonable rates • free coffee • AAA & AARP discounts. Take the Teasdale exit off Hwy. 12 northwest of Grover. Located 2 miles south of Teasdale.

Cockscomb Inn & Cottage B & B   Phone: 801-425-3511
97 S. State St.   800-530-1038
P.O. Box B   Fax: 801-425-3511 (call first)
Teasdale, UT 84773

The Cockscomb Inn offers charming comfortable rooms in a turn of the century farm house in the small picturesque town of Teasdale. Guests enjoy: queen beds • private baths • spacious living room / dining room • summer patio / barbecue • and excellent full breakfasts. A fully equipped one bedroom private cottage is also available. Only minutes away from Capitol Reef National Park, Boulder Mountain (gateway to the new Grand Staircase National Monument), Thousand Lakes and Fishlake Recreation Areas. Take the Teasdale exit off Hwy. 12 northwest of Grover.

Thousand Lakes RV Park   Phone: 801-425-3500
1050 W. Hwy. 24   800-355-8995 reservations
P.O. Box 750070
Torrey, UT 84775

A beautiful location with large areas of grass and trees near Capitol Reef National
Park. Cabins, tent, and large pull-thru sites with full hook-ups. Clean showers and
restrooms • pavilion • laundry facilities • mini mart & gift shop • western dinners.
Rates: $10.50 to $16.50. AAA—Good Sam—Senior Citizen discounts. Open April 1
through October 25. Visa, MC, and Discover cards accepted.

Carson Pass Highway — California, page 71

Druid House Bed & Breakfast   Phone: 209-296-4156
13887 Druid Lane   800-267-5781
Pine Grove, CA 95665

This three story contemporary mountain retreat in the Sierra foothills offers a sweeping
view of the Sacramento Valley and Mt. Diablo. Mixing old and new, the furnishings
make the house warm and inviting. The main suite includes a private entrance, deck,
patio, bath, hot tub, pellet stove, king 4 poster, wet bar with frig & microwave, and
a small bedroom. The main floor suite includes an antique 150 year old sleigh bed,
master bath with jacuzzi tub, and a sun room. Both suites offer: cable TV & VCR,
phones, bathrobes, central air and heat, wine, beverages and snacks. Full breakfast
on weekends and expanded continental on weekdays. Close to skiing • fishing • golf •
hiking • rafting • swimming • fine restaurants & cozy cafes • historical sites • shopping • and wineries. Located one mile west of Pine Grove off upper Ridge Road on
Druid Lane.

Cascade Lakes Highway — Oregon, page 280

Shilo Inn Suites Hotel - Bend   Phone: 541-389-9600
3105 O.B. Riley Road   800-222-2244
Bend, OR 97701-7527   Fax: 541-382-4310

This full-service resort features a fine dining restaurant & lounge located along the
banks of the scenic Deschutes River. All 151 guestrooms and suites are complete
with microwave • refrigerator • coffee maker • ironing unit • and satellite TV with
premium channels. VCR and movie rentals are available to guests. Facilities include
a sauna, steam room, fitness center, and indoor/outdoor pools & spas. Amenities
include free local calls, USA Today newspaper, complimentary full breakfast buffet
and courtesy airport and Mt. Bachelor shuttle. Guests will enjoy the nearby golf
courses and shopping at the factory outlet stores.

City Of Rocks — Idaho, page 155

Best Western Burley Inn   Phone: 208-678-3501
800 North Overland Ave.   800-599-1849
Burley, ID 83318   Fax: 208-678-9532

Located near the Snake River, this Best Western offers 126 modern rooms with king and queen size beds. Amenities include: outdoor pool • volley ball • shuffle board • horseshoe pit • complimentary coffee • hot chocolate • and news paper. Convenient on-site restaurant, lounge, and convention center. Only ¼ mile south of I-84 at exit 208. For reservations please call 800-599-1849, 24 hours. AAA and senior discounts available. Visa, MC, AMEX, Discover, and Diners Club cards accepted. We appreciate your business!

Cloud Peak Skyway — Wyoming, page 412

Mountain View Inn   Phone: 307-684-2881 / 307-684-5443
585 Fort Street   E-mail: jgampetro@aol.com
Buffalo, WY 82834   Internet: www.buffalowyoming.com/mtview

Guests choose the Mountain View Inn for its authentic log cabins, quiet shaded picnic grounds and friendly Western atmosphere. Choose from individual queen bed cabins and double room family cabins, some with kitchenettes. Camping, hiking and backpacking opportunities for every level of expertise abound. Lake and stream trout fishing is excellent, while not over-crowded. Within walking distance of the museum, Buffalo's town center, the park, swimming pool, tennis courts, nature trail and golf course. RV hookups • laundry • shower facilities • and tent sites are also available.

Diamond Loop — Oregon, page 286

McCoy Creek Inn   Phone: 541-493-2131
HC 72, Box 11   Fax: 541-493-2131
Diamond, OR 97722

At the base of Steens Mountain in the heart of country rich with history lies the McCoy Creek Ranch. The turn-of-the-century home has been carefully restored and renovated to give old-fashioned ambience without giving up modern convenience. The three bedrooms in the main house as well as the bunkhouse are beautifully furnished and have private baths. Guests can enjoy the breathtaking scenery of Steens Mountain recreation area, a stroll along McCoy Creek, a relaxing soak in the hot tub, or a hike over the rim onto the gentle north face of the Steens to watch the sun set. Children are welcome at the inn.

Eastshore Drive — Nevada / California, page 226

Carson Station Hotel & Casino   Phone: 702-883-0900
900 S. Carson Street   800-501-2929
Carson City, NV 89701   Fax: 702-883-2115

The Carson Station Hotel & Casino offers travelers 92 spacious, newly remodeled hotel rooms. The full service casino with cabaret lounge treats guests to live entertainment • sports book • sports bar • restaurant • snack bar • and valet parking. Located near historical district, museums, shopping, state capitol complex, and Governor's Mansion. Only 25 minutes to Lake Tahoe and Reno. Special low-season drive-up packages. We cater to traveling golf groups. Friendly, professional staff.

Coachland RV Park
10500 Highway 89 North
Truckee, CA 96161

Phone: 916-587-3071
Fax: 916-587-6976

Coachland RV Park offers a quiet and relaxing environment on 55 acres of pines in the clean crisp air of the High Sierras. Facilities include 131 full hook-up pull through RV spaces with cable TV. On-site laundry, restrooms, and picnic tables. Historical downtown Truckee with it's fine restaurants and shops is within walking distance. Nearby attractions and activities include: golf courses • major ski resorts • Nevada casinos • excellent fishing in numerous lakes and rivers • Lake Tahoe • hiking • mountain biking • river rafting • mines and museums of "The Gold Country". Open all year. Only ¼ mile from I-80.

Lampliter Motel
4143 Cedar Avenue
South Lake Tahoe, CA 96150

Phone: 916-544-2936
Fax: 916-544-5249

A quiet location, two blocks off Highway 50, yet in the center of everything. Cozy, spotless, and individually decorated rooms complete with continental breakfast & warm hospitality. You'll want to relax in the elevated spa and enjoy the beautiful views. Guests can dine at the restaurant across the street or walk ¼ block to casino food & entertainment. Only three short blocks away from the marina, golf course and our private beach where you can swim & enjoy all water sports in the crystal waters of Lake Tahoe. Free or low cost shuttles are available to most winter and summer attractions or Reno/Tahoe airport. At Lake Tahoe, the LAMPLITER is THE PLACE to stay! AAA & AARP discounts.

Tahoe Colony Inn
3794 Montreal Road
South Lake Tahoe, CA 96157

Phone: 916-544-6481
            800-338-5552

At the Tahoe Colony Inn, a 104 unit resort, the Eldorado National Forest is your backyard — with shopping, theaters and restaurants in front. Walking distance to restaurants and casinos, only 3 blocks from Lake Tahoe. Minutes away from golf • skiing • fishing • horseback riding • shopping • and miniature golf. Free continental breakfast and shuttle service to casinos. Year round pool & spa. Discount activity coupons. AAA, AARP & Senior discounts.

Viking Motor Lodge
4083 Cedar Avenue
South Lake Tahoe, CA 96150

Phone: 916-541-5155
            800-288-4083
Fax: 916-541-5643

The 58 unit Viking Motor Lodge is conveniently located to the area's many attractions.

Only 3 blocks from Lake Tahoe and access to private beach, 1½ blocks to casino's, and 10 minutes to ski slopes. Amenities include: free local calls • cable color TV • heated pool & spa — open all year • fireplaces in some units • free continental breakfast • free parking • and meeting facilities.

Eccles Canyon — Utah, page 351

Larsen House Bed & Breakfast
298 South State St.
Mt. Pleasant, UT 84647

Phone: 801-462-9337
       800-848-5263
Fax: 801-462-3400

At the Larsen House, beautiful antiques blend with an elegant restored Victorian Mansion. Each room is tastefully decorated with its own special charm. Handsomely carved bannister • winding staircase • hand rubbed Cherrywood fireplace • and a massive stained-glass window dominates the entrance hall. Two new rooms will include whirlpool tubs and warm toasty fireplaces. For more privacy, a honeymoon cottage is available. Guest enjoy relaxing in the parlor while they sip their favorite beverage, read a good book, and admire the original hand-painted mural on the ceiling. The homemade breakfast is becoming world famous — as good as Mom used to make! Your friendly innkeepers go to great lengths to live up to their motto: "You'll feel Right at home with us".

Enchanted Circle — New Mexico, page 245

San Geronimo Lodge
1101 Witt Road
Taos, NM 87571
MAIL: 216M Paseo del Pueblo N167

Phone: 505-751-3776
       800-894-4119
Fax: 505-751-1493
E-mail: sever12893@aol.com

The San Geronimo Lodge is situated on 2½ acres with spectacular views of Taos Mountain and Kit Carson National Forest. A traditional style adobe hacienda built in 1925, the lodge has spacious common areas, high-beamed ceilings and wood floors. All rooms have handcrafted furniture, down comforters, color cable TV, private bath and telephone. Visa, MC, AMEX, and Discover cards accepted.

Terrace Towers Lodge
712 W. Main
P.O. Box 149
Red River, NM 87558

Phone: 800-695-6343
       505-754-2962
Fax: 505-754-2989
Internet: http://www.taoswebb.com/
          redriverinfo/hearts

Terrace Towers Lodge is an all-suites condominium and lodge with 1 and 2 bedroom apartments. Located in the beautiful Sangre de Cristo Mountains within the Enchanted Circle just north of Taos. Super views, quiet and convenient to shops, restaurants, fishing, skiing, and all kinds of mountain activities. Historical sites, Indian culture, southwestern art galleries and museums are just a short drive away. Enjoy Red River's special events throughout the year. Call for a free visitor's guide.

Feather River — California, page 78

Bucks Lakeshore Resort   Phone: 916-283-6900
1100 Bucks Lake Road   Fax: 916-283-6909
Bucks Lake, CA 95956

Bucks Lakeshore Resort, an alpine lodge with restaurant, offers 11 cabins (7 lakefront), RV Park & campground, and a 60-berth marina. Guests enjoy summer water sports rentals, lakeview patio dining as well as lounge with 180 degree lakeview and fireplace. Winter sports include x-country skiing, snowmobiling and snow bus to lodge. Over 100 miles of groomed snow roads start at your cabin door; northern California snow park nearby. Food, supplies, gas & on/off sale liquor are available in the Lakeshore Country Store. Wonderful low-season packages available October - December and April - May.

The Feather Bed   Phone: 916-283-0102
542 Jackson St.   800-696-8624
P.O. Box 3200
Quincy, CA 95971

The Feather Bed allows you to step back to a gracious and simpler time. Far from the crowds and urban noise —close to nature. You may choose a guest room upstairs in the main house or a private guest house, all with private baths and separate entrances. Your stay includes an abundant country breakfast in the Victorian dining room. A short walk takes you to a theatre, the County Museum, shops and restaurants. Guests can enjoy fishing, water sports, golfing, horseback riding, snowmobiling, cross country skiing, bird watching, hiking, biking, fall colors, picnicking, or just relaxing on the front porch. Located on the corner of Jackson Street and Court Street, just behind the Court House.

Flat Tops Trail — Colorado, page 118

Buford Hunting & Fishing Lodge   Phone: 970-878-4745
20474 RBC #8
Meeker, CO 81641

The Buford Lodge is located adjacent to the beautiful White River in the center of the White River National Forest offering excellent fishing and hunting. The rustic and modern housekeeping cabins, some with fireplaces or wood stoves and televisions, date back to 1908. RV sites are also available. Located on the property in an 85 year-old log building is the new Buford White River Historical Museum. The on-site grocery store, which is on the National Registry of Historic Places, is stocked with sporting goods, gifts, gas and propane. Dining is available at the nearby restaurant. The Buford Lodge will help arrange hunt/drop camps and provide guides to those interested in a real wilderness experience. Located 22 miles east of Meeker on Trappers Lake Road (County Road 8) at Buford, near milepost 20.

Forest Heritage — North Carolina, page 272

Oak Park Inn   Phone: 704-456-5328
314 S. Main Street   Fax: 704-456-8126
Waynesville, NC 28786

This quaint and charming renovated Inn awaits your arrival to beautiful downtown Waynesville. Oak Park Inn offers comfortable rooms with your choice of efficiency and two bedroom apartments or golf homes. All rooms have color cable TV, A/C & heat, and free rocking chairs! An easy walk to Main Street shops • boutiques • restaurants • grills • pubs • library • churches • and much more. Golf, skiing, rafting, and the Great Smoky Mountains are all nearby. Best rates in town! Our Inn and staff will have you proclaiming "I wasn't born in Waynesville but I got here as fast as I could".

Sunset Motel   Phone: 704-884-9106
415 S. Broad St. (on US 64)
Brevard, NC 28712

A North Carolina classic motel. Clean rooms with free local calls, A/C, refrigerators, some with kitchenettes, and a refreshing cross-breeze in most rooms. AAA rated. Near the Cradle of Forestry • Brevard's renowned summer music festival • Pisgah National Forest • and trout fishing streams.

Galice - Hellgate — Oregon, page 290
Grave Creek To Marial — Oregon, page 292

Shilo Inn - Grants Pass   Phone: 541-479-8391
1880 NW 6th Street   800-222-2244
Grants Pass, OR 97526-1038   Fax: 541-474-7344

This newly remodeled Shilo Inn is conveniently located off I-5 just two miles from city center. All 70 guestrooms feature a satellite TV with premium channels. VCR and movie rentals are available at the front desk. Facilities include an outdoor heated pool for use during the warmer seasons as well as a year-round sauna and steam room. Amenities include free local calls, USA Today newspaper, continental breakfast, and Grants Pass Airport shuttle. Meeting space is available for up to 25 people. A restaurant is located adjacent to the motel.

Hells Canyon — Oregon, page 294

Shilo Inn - Troy Wilderness Retreat   Phone: 541-828-7741
84570 Bartlett Road   800-222-2244
Enterprise, OR 97828-0085   Fax: 541-828-7891

At the Troy Wilderness Retreat you'll enjoy rustic cabins, lodge rooms and RV spaces located in the pristine Wallowa Mountains where the Wenaha River meets the Grande Ronde River. The facilities include a beautiful rustic restaurant and a country store where hunting licences and game tags can be purchased as well as basic necessities. Other facilities include a fuel service station, bath house, laundromat, game room, meat cooler, and recreation room with pool table. Your mountain vacation or hunting & fishing excursion can be an experience of a lifetime at the Shilo Inn - Troy Wilderness Retreat.

Historic Route 66 — Arizona, page 36
Hualapai Mountains — Arizona, page 38

Kingman KOA	Phone: 800-562-3991
3820 N. Roosevelt	520-757-4397
Kingman, AZ 86401	Fax: 520-757-1580

Quiet tree shaded area away from freeway noise. Large pull-thru sites, Kamping Kabins, and tent area. Swimming pool • mini golf • convenience & gift store • hot showers • game room • laundry facilities • cable TV. East bound travelers take exit 51 off I-40, Stockton Hill Road, go north ½ mile to Airway and turn right to Roosevelt. West bound travelers take exit 53 off I-40 and proceed north to Airway. Highway 93 rejoins with I-40.

Travelodge	Phone: 520-757-1188
3275 E. Andy Devine	Fax: 520-757-1010
Kingman, AZ 86401	

Travelodge offers travelers 65 beautiful rooms, queen size beds and cable TV with remote. Non-smoking rooms • heated pool • bus/RV parking • laundry facilities on premises. Only ½ block from shopping center, walking distance to restaurants, convenient store and gas. Only 4 miles to airport and ½ mile to Big Park. From I-40 take exit 53 onto Andy Devine, turn left.

Huntington Canyon — Utah, page 357

Larsen House Bed & Breakfast	Phone: 801-462-9337
298 South State St.	800-848-5263
Mt. Pleasant, UT 84647	Fax: 801-462-3400

At the Larsen House, beautiful antiques blend with an elegant restored Victorian Mansion. Each room is tastefully decorated with its own special charm. Handsomely carved bannister • winding staircase • hand rubbed Cherrywood fireplace • and a massive stained-glass window dominates the entrance hall. Two new rooms will include whirlpool tubs and warm toasty fireplaces. For more privacy, a honeymoon cottage is available. Guest enjoy relaxing in the parlor while they sip their favorite beverage, read a good book, and admire the original hand-painted mural on the ceiling. The homemade breakfast is becoming world famous — as good as Mom used to make! Your friendly innkeepers go to great lengths to live up to their motto: "You'll feel Right at home with us".

Inner Loop - Gila Cliff Dwellings — New Mexico, page 249

Holiday Motor Hotel
3420 Hwy. 180 East
Silver City, NM 88061

Phone: 505-538-3711
Fax: 505-538-3711
Internet: www.holidayhotel.com

Located within minutes of the Gila National Forest the Holiday Motor Hotel offers 80, recently renovated, modern rooms. Amenities include: cable TV • A/C • heated outdoor pool • disabled persons' rooms • no-smoking rooms • fax and copy service • banquet, meeting and convention facilities • on-premises breakfast, lunch, and fine evening dinning. Guests enjoy easy access to hiking, mountain biking, golf, tennis, and the many art galleries & museums in the area.

Silver City KOA Kampground
11824 Hwy. 180 East
Silver City, NM 88061

Phone: 505-388-3351
          800-562-7623 reservations
Fax: 505-388-0461
E-mail: sckoa@zianet.com
Internet: www.koakampgrounds.com

Camp KOA style, cook out and enjoy the great outdoors. At Silver City you can pitch your tent, stay in a Kamping Kabin®, rent their RV, or pull your rig into one of the full-service RV sites. Guests will enjoy the excellent shower and restroom facilities, laundry, TV room, playground and heated pool. Complete sight-seeing information and quality service. Open year-round. Silver City's Best Camping!

Jacinto Reyes — California, page 80

Capri Motel
1180 E. Ojai Ave.
Ojai, CA 93023

Phone: 805-646-4305
Fax: 805-646-4144

Located just across from Soule Golf Course, the Capri Motel is adjacent to tennis and golf. Each air-conditioned room has a private balcony with sliding glass doors so you can enjoy the view. Cable TV, courtesy coffee and all the amenities for the traveler. Rooms are always fresh and airy. Relax in the large adult pool while your children are playing in their pool, try the jacuzzi or simply enjoy the lawn area. AMEX, Discover, MC, and Visa cards accepted.

John D Rockefeller Jr. Memorial Parkway — Wyoming, page 414

Dornan's Spur Ranch Cabins
10 Moose St.
P.O. Box 39
Moose, WY 83012

Phone: 307-733-2522
Fax: 307-733-3544
E-mail: spur@sisna.com
Internet: http://www.sisna.com/jackson/
          dornan/spur1.htm

Dornan's Spur Ranch Cabins is located just inside Grand Teton National Park next to the

Snake River providing great views of the Teton Mountains. Accommodations include 8 one-bedroom and 4 two-bedroom housekeeping cabins with full kitchens. A grocery store, gift shop, wine shop, deli, sports shop and restaurant are all located on-site. Other services available include: scenic or whitewater float trips • sportswear and equipment shop for climbing, hiking, camping, and cross-country skiing • fishing tackle shop with guided fishing trips • rentals of mountain bikes and canoes. No pets—No TV's—No smoking.

Kancamagus Highway — New Hampshire, page 241

Kancamagus Motor Lodge	Phone: 800-346-4205
Route 112 (Kancamagus Hwy.)	603-745-3365
Lincoln, NH 03251	Fax: 603-745-6691

Located in the middle of the White Mountain region, at the start of the Kancamagus Highway with great mountain views. Close by to every imaginable activity and attraction, one could easily spend a week in this area. Modern, quiet, and spotless rooms — cable TV • A/C • phone • and in room, private steam bath. The Terrace Restaurant offers excellent and inexpensive dining. Need help? Ask for expert advice on touring the most rugged area in the northeast. AAA & Mobil good value rated. Rates from $38.00 to $64.00, double.

Three Rivers House	Phone: 603-745-2711
RR 1, Box 72	800-940-2711
S. Main St.	Fax: 603-745-2773
N. Woodstock, NH 03262	

The Three Rivers House is centrally located in the heart of the White Mountains National Forest at the western entrance of the Kancamagus Highway. Amenities include: rooms & suites • gas fireplaces • A/C • whirlpools • color cable TV • and private baths. Guests enjoy the nearby attractions, skiing, hiking, golf, and shopping. Visa, MC, Disc., & AMEX cards accepted.

Lamoille Canyon Road — Nevada, page 233

Shilo Inn - Elko	Phone: 702-738-5522
2401 Mountain City Highway	800-222-2244
Elko, NV 89801-4496	Fax: 702-738-6247

The Elko Shilo Inn is conveniently located near golf courses, convention center, gaming and equestrian center. The 70 fully equipped mini-suites provide guests with a microwave • refrigerator • wet bar • and satellite TV with premium channels. VCR and movie rentals are also available. Facilities include a 24-hour indoor pool, spa, sauna, steam room, fitness center and guest laundromat. Amenities include free local calls, USA Today newspaper, continental breakfast and airport shuttle to Harris Field/Elko Airport. Meeting space for up to 80 people is available. Several restaurants are located nearby.

Lee Vining Canyon — California, page 88

Whispering Pines
Rt. 3, Box 143
June Lake, CA 93529

Phone: 760-648-7762
        800-648-7762 (CA only)
Fax: 760-648-7589

At Whispering Pines you'll find clean comfortable rooms with scenic mountain views. All units offer kitchens and color TVs, some with VCR's and microwaves. Amenities include: indoor spa • conference room • and direct dial phones. The central location — eastern gateway to Yosemite National Park — puts you close to 4 lakes and mountain trails, only 5 minutes from June Mountain Ski Area on Hwy. 158. Cabins, A-frames and June Mountain Shuttle are also available.

Leslie Gulch - Succor Creek — Oregon, page 298

Shilo Inn - Nampa Boulevard
617 Nampa Boulevard
Nampa, ID 83687-3065

Phone: 208-466-8993
        800-222-2244
Fax: 208-465-3239

Conveniently located off I-84, this motel is one of two Shilo Inns available to travelers in the Nampa area. All 61 guestrooms feature a microwave • refrigerator • and satellite TV with premium channels. VCR and movie rentals are available to guests. Facilities include an outdoor heated pool, indoor spa, sauna, steam room and guest laundromat. Amenities include free local calls, continental breakfast, USA Today newspaper and shuttle to both Nampa & Boise Airports. Meeting space for up to 25 people is available. A restaurant is located adjacent to the motel.

Shilo Inn - Nampa Suites
1401 Shilo Drive
Nampa, ID 83687-3065

Phone: 208-465-3250
        800-222-2244
Fax: 208-465-5929

Located only 5 miles from city center, this larger of the two Shilo Inns in the Nampa area offers travelers 83 guestrooms. The mini-suites provide guests with a microwave • refrigerator • wet bar • and satellite TV with premium channels. VCR and movie rentals are also available. Facilities include a 24-hour indoor pool, spa, sauna, steam room, fitness center and guest laundromat. Amenities include free local calls, USA Today newspaper and shuttle to both Nampa and Boise Airports. Meeting space is available. O'Callahan's Restaurant & Lounge is located on premises.

Merritt Parkway — Connecticut, page 143

Roger Sherman Inn
195 Oenoke Ridge
New Canaan, CT 06840

Phone: 203-966-4541
Fax: 203-966-0503

Dating back to the mid-1700's, the beautifully refurbished Roger Shermann Inn provides guests with charming and up-to-date accommodations. The indoor and outdoor award-winning dining makes the Inn the perfect retreat in an atmosphere of light-hearted elegance. Located only two miles north of the Merritt Parkway, at exit 37.

🏨 🖵 A/C 🍴 🍽 🚻 ✓ H ✈ 🚌 🚕 ⊘ 🛍 ☕

Natchez Trace Parkway — Mississippi, page 199

Cabot Lodge - Jackson North   Phone: 601-957-0757
120 Dyess Road   800-342-2268
Ridgeland, MS 39157   Fax: 601-957-0757

Designed around a most hospitable concept, Cabot Lodge offers you such a relaxing atmosphere, you'll get the feeling you never left home. Right away you'll notice the beautiful atrium with its central fireplace, antler chandeliers, unique wooden end tables and comfortable furniture. The walls of windows lead you out into the courtyards where the gardens are meticulously maintained. All 208 attractive guest rooms offer such amenities as satellite TV, movie channels and direct dial phones. The front desk stocks a complimentary supply of travel necessities available on request. Your stay includes a generous complimentary deluxe continental breakfast and a two hour cocktail reception in the evening. Located in northeast Jackson off I-55 north, just minutes from the Natchez Trace exit.

♿ ⋆ ☎ 🖵 A/C 🚻 ✓ 🏊 H ⊘ 🛍 ☕

Fairview Inn   Phone: 888-948-1908 / 601-948-3429
734 Fairview Street   Fax: 601-948-1203
Jackson, MS 39202   E-mail: fairview@teclink.net

Colonial Revival mansion on National Register of Historic Places. Eight elegant rooms and suites all with private baths, cable TV, phones, and data ports. Full breakfast. AAA 4-Diamond. Named a "Top Inn of 1994" by Country Inns Magazine. In 1996 presented an Award of Excellence in the field of Hospitality and Fine Cuisine by Country Inns and The James Beard Foundation. AMEX, Discover, MC, and Visa cards accepted.

♿ 🏨 🖵 A/C 🚻 ✓ H 🚕 ⊘ 🛍 ☕

Nestucca River — Oregon, page 306

Sandlake Country Inn   Phone: 503-965-6745
8505 Galloway Road   Fax: 503-965-7425
Cloverdale, OR 97112

Sshhh... Sandlake Country Inn is a secret hideaway on the awesome Oregon Coast. A private, peaceful place for making memories. This 1894 shipwreck-timbered farmhouse on the Oregon Historic Registry is tucked into a bower of old roses. You'll enjoy hummingbirds, Mozart, cookies at midnight, fireplaces, whirlpools for two, honeymoon cottage, breakfast "en suite", and vintage movies. Four rooms with private baths • full breakfast • no smoking. From Beaver travel north on US 101 approximately 2 miles to Sandlake Road. Travel west on Sandlake Road to Galloway Road, 5½ miles. Turn right (west) on Galloway Road.

Shilo Inn - Newberg
501 Sitka Avenue
Newberg, OR 97132-1304

Phone: 503-537-0303
       800-222-2244
Fax: 503-537-0442

Conveniently located off highway 99 in the heart of Oregon's wine country, this Shilo Inn offers 60 mini-suites complete with microwave, refrigerator and satellite TV with premium channels. VCR and movie rentals are available to guests. Facilities include an outdoor pool for use during the warmer seasons and a year-round 24-hour indoor spa, sauna, steam room, fitness center and guest laundromat. Amenities include free local calls, continental breakfast, USA Today newspaper and McMinnville Airport shuttle. Meeting space is available for up to 50 people. A restaurant is located adjacent to the motel.

Shilo Inn - Tillamook
2515 N. Main
Tillamook, OR 97141-9216

Phone: 503-842-7971
       800-222-2244
Fax: 503-842-7960

Conveniently located on the Wilson River — the perfect retreat for the avid fishing enthusiast. Shilo Inn offers the traveler 100 guestrooms and a fine dining restaurant & lounge. The mini-suites are fully equipped with a microwave • refrigerator • wet bar • and satellite TV with premium channels. VCR and movie rentals are also available. Facilities include a 24-hour indoor pool, spa, sauna, steam room, fitness center, guest laundromat and fish cleaning room. Amenities include free local calls, USA Today newspaper and Tillamook Airport shuttle. Meeting space is available.

North Fork Highway — Wyoming, page 418

Trout Creek Inn
3656 North Fork Hwy.
Cody, WY 82414

Phone: 307-587-6288

Located right in the mountains at the western tip of the Buffalo Bill Reservoir, the Trout Creek Inn offers unparalleled beauty in every direction. As part of the Broken H Ranch (the World's original Dude Ranch), guests are treated to a wide array of recreational opportunities — fantastic trout fishing • horseback rides • swimming • windsurfing • water or ice sailing • hiking • skiing • snowmobiling • ice skating • big game and bird hunting • and much more. The plush, modern rooms include color television, queen size beds, free ice, free continental breakfast, and all the conveniences of home. Tent or vehicle camping sites, trailer-hookups, coin laundry, public bathroom and shower are also available.

North Shore Drive / Gunflint Trail — Minnesota, page 195

Cascade Lodge
HC 3, Box 445
Lutsen, MN 55612

Phone: 218-387-1112 / 800-322-9543
Fax: 218-387-1113
Internet: http://www.cascadelodgemn.com

Located in the midst of Cascade River State Park and overlooking Lake Superior offering spectacular views. Accommodation options include rooms in the main lodge, log cabins with fireplaces and a house. Some units include kitchens and whirlpools. Distinctive restaurant and gift shop. Nearby fishing, tennis, golf, and alpine skiing. Outstanding hiking, cross country skiing, and mountain bike trails begin at the lodge. The hiking trails connect to the Superior Hiking trail and the ski trails with the North Shore ski trail system. Open all year. AAA rated. Located on Hwy. 61 midway between Lutsen and Grand Marais, 100 miles NE of Duluth.

The Gunflint Trail Association   Phone: 800-338-6932
P.O. Box 205   218-387-2870
Grand Marais, MN 55604

Each season on The Gunflint Trail offers a variety of activities everyone can enjoy. The Gunflint Trail lodges, cabins, campsites, and outfitters are unique, privately owned resorts operated by families and individuals in the pioneer tradition. They have a knowledge and love of this wilderness area and an eagerness to share its beauty and recreational opportunities with you. The resorts and businesses listed below are members of The Gunflint Trail Association. These establishments along the Trail have joined together to help make your vacation here a memorable experience. You may contact the association at the address listed above for general information on the area and/or the members listed below for detailed information on their location.

Association Members:

	Cabin	Campground	Bed & Breakfast	Canoe Outfitters
Bearskin Lodge, 800-338-4170	•	•		
Borderland Lodge Resort, 800-451-1667	•			
Boundary Country Trekking, 800-322-8327	•			
Boundary Waters Adventures, 800-894-0128	•			
Clearwater Canoe Outfitters & Lodge, 800-527-0554	•			•
Golden Eagle Lodge, 800-346-2203	•	•		
Gunflint Lodge, 800-328-3325	•			
Gunflint Northwoods Outfitters, 800-362-5251	•			
Gunflint Pines Resort & Campground, 800-533-5814	•	•		
Heston's Country Store & Cabins, 800-338-7230	•			
Hungry Jack Lodge, 800-338-1566	•	•		
Hungry Jack Outfitters, 800-648-2922				•
Loon Lake Lodge, 800-552-6351	•			
Nor'Wester Lodge & Canoe Outfitters, 800-992-4FUN	•	•		•
Old Northwoods Lodge, 800-682-8264	•			
Pincushion Mountain Bed & Breakfast, 800-542-1226			•	
Rockwood Lodge & Outfitters, 800-942-2922	•			•
Sea Island Lodge Resort & Dining Room, 800-346-8906	•			
Seagull Creek Fishing Camp, 800-531-5510	•			
Seagull Outfitters, 800-346-2205				•
Spirit of the Land Island Hostel, 800-454-2922	•			
Superior Properties, 800-950-4360	•			
Superior-North Canoe Outfitters, 800-852-2008				•
Top of the Trail Outfitters, 800-869-0883				•

continued on next page

Association Members Continued

	Canoe Outfitters	Bed & Breakfast	Campground	Cabin
Trail Center, 800-972-3066				•
Trout Lake Resort, 800-258-7688				•
Tuscarora Lodge & Outfitters, 800-544-3843	•			•
Voyageur Canoe Outfitters, 800-777-7215	•		•	•
Way of the Wilderness Canoe Outfitters, 800-346-6625	•		•	•
Windigo Lodge, 800-535-4320	•	•		•

Ocoee — Tennessee, page 337

Lake Ocoee Inn & Marina   Phone: 423-338-2064
Rt. 1, Box 347   800-272-7238
Benton, TN 37307   Fax: 423-338-9514

Lake Ocoee Inn is located in the Cherokee National Forest providing beautiful views of Lake Ocoee and the surrounding mountains. Guests can choose to stay in cabins, located right on the water with a dock and kitchen facilities, or a rustic motel room located near their celebrated restaurant. At the marina you can rent a canoe, pontoon boat, fishing boat, water skis and knee boards. For those seeking a little more excitement you can take a whitewater rafting trip with Ocoee Inn Rafting. Nearby attractions and activities include: museum • trout fishing • swimming holes • hiking trails • horseback riding • and picnic areas. Located on U.S. Hwy. 64 (Ocoee Scenic Byway), east of State Hwy. 30.

Owens Valley To Death Valley — California, page 90

Super 8 Motel - High Sierra Lodge   Phone: 760-873-8426
1005 N. Main St.   Fax: 760-873-8060
Bishop, CA 93514

One of Bishops finest motels. Clean and comfortable rooms equipped with in-room coffee machines, free extended cable with HBO, and refrigerators. Seasonal outdoor pool and year round indoor jacuzzi. Fish cleaning & freezing facilities and BBQ area. Fantastic fishing! Walking distance to outlet mall and dining. AMEX, MC, Visa, and Discover cards accepted. Located on US Hwy. 395 at the north end of town. We appreciate your business.

Pacific Coast Highway — California, page 92

The Martine Inn   Phone: 408-373-3388
255 Oceanview Blvd.   800-852-5588
Pacific Grove, CA 93950   Fax: 408-373-3896

This gracious mansion, built in 1899, sits high atop the cliffs of Pacific Grove overlooking the rocky coastline of Monterey Bay. The 19 bedrooms, many with wood-burning fire-places, include a private bath, authentic antiques, and private telephone. Your stay includes a full breakfast — elegance in presentation is a part of the dining experience. Guests are invited to play pool in the game room, relax in the six-person hot tub, read in the library, sunbathe in the landscaped-enclosed courtyard or watch whales, sea otters and sailboat races from the parlor or sitting rooms. Area activities include picnics on the beach • golf • scuba diving • bicycling • tennis • historical tours • boating • and much more.

Palms To Pines — California, page 94

Casa Cody B & B Country Inn   Phone: 760-320-9346
175 S. Cahuilla Rd.   800-231-2639
Palm Springs, CA 92262   Fax: 760-325-8610

A romantic, historic hideaway nestled against the spectacular San Jacinto Mountains in the heart of Palm Springs Village. The Casa Cody — hacienda adobe style architecture Santa Fe decor — offers guests 23 single story rooms, studios, and one & two bedroom units with private patios. Kitchens and fireplaces in some units. Facilities include two pools and secluded spa. Rates: $79 - $199, summer less, all credit cards accepted. From Palm Canyon Drive (State Route 111) turn west on Tahquitz Canyon to Cahuilla Road, turn left.

Edelweiss Lodge   Phone: 909-659-2787
Pine Cove, CA 92549   E-mail: edelweis@pe.net
Mail -P.O. Box 1747
        Idyllwild, CA 92549

If you're truly looking to get away from it all, come & enjoy the Edelweiss experience. A romantic, rustic retreat located in Pine Cove, only 3 miles above Idyllwild and 1000 feet higher, the property is filled with tall Pines, Cedars, and Oak trees. The 11 individual cabins, accommodating 1 to 6 people, are fully outfitted with equipped kitchens, woodburning fireplaces, and color TV with video player. Guests enjoy the shops, restaurants and various festivities in Idyllwild and for more active pursuits—hiking, fishing, mountain biking, and rock climbing. The many activities throughout the year keep things interesting.

International Lodge   Phone: 760-346-6161
74-380 El Camino   800-874-9338 reservations
Palm Desert, CA 92260   Fax: 760-568-0563

"Best Kept Secret In The Desert" — The International Lodge offers 52 spacious, luxurious, and individually decorated condo's. Amenities include: color TV • direct dial phones • air conditioning • kitchen • private patio • two heated pools • jacuzzi hot pool • laundry room • convenient parking in front of condo • 16 person conference room and wet bar. Adults only. No pets. Open all year, 3 star rated.

Palm Springs Marquis Resort   Phone: 760-322-2121
150 S. Indian Canyon Dr.   800-223-1050
Palm Springs, CA 92262   Fax: 760-322-2380

In the heart of Palm Springs, overlooking the beautiful San Jacinto Mountains you will find this intimate and informal hotel. The resort's 265 elegant rooms and suites are decorated in contemporary California style decor. Lush garden settings make dining a special experience at the resort. Guests will enjoy two outdoor heated swimming pools with whirlpools and two championship tennis courts. Walking distance to a host of fine restaurants, shopping, art galleries, museum, and casino. Amenities include: full bath facilities • hair dryers • A/C • coffee maker • telephone • cable TV • refrigerator • radio • and private balcony or patio. If you are bringing the kids be sure to ask about the Kamp Wannakombak children's program — It's a great time for the kids while you spend some time alone.

Shilo Inn - Palm Springs Desert Resort	Phone:	760-320-7676
1875 N. Palm Canyon Drive		800-222-2244
Palm Springs, CA 92262-9213	Fax:	760-320-9543

Enjoy the spectacular San Jacinto Mountain Range from this beautiful resort hotel located near the aerial tramway. All 124 guestrooms and suites feature a microwave • refrigerator • coffee maker • satellite TV with premium channels • and much more. VCR and movie rentals are available to guests. Facilities include a spectacular courtyard with gazebo, outdoor family and adult pools & spas, steam room, sauna, fitness center and guest laundromat. Amenities include free local calls, USA Today newspaper, continental breakfast and airport shuttle. Meeting space is available for up to 60 people. Restaurants are located nearby.

Super 8 Lodge	Phone:	760-322-3757
1900 N. Palm Canyon Dr.		800-800-8000
Palm Springs, CA 92262	Fax:	760-323-5290

The Super 8 Lodge offers travelers comfort, convenience, and affordability in a resort setting. Amenities include: one 8-minute free long distance call each day of stay • electronic locks • in-room refrigerator • remote control TV with preferred channels • guest laundry • outdoor heated pool / whirlpool. Close to shopping, attractions, entertainment and gambling.

Peak To Peak — Colorado, page 132

Gold Lake Mountain Resort & Spa	Phone:	800-450-3544
3371 Gold Lake Road	Fax:	303-459-9080
Ward, CO 80481	Internet:	www.goldlake.com

At the Gold Lake Mountain Resort & Spa you'll enjoy the ambiance of our artistically restored cabins and the endless recreational opportunities provided by the Rocky Mountain wilderness. Relax in a lake side hot pool overlooking the Continental Divide or pamper yourself with a restorative treatment at the full service spa — then indulge in healthy gourmet cuisine at Alices restaurant.

Romantic RiverSong Inn   Phone: 970-586-4666
1765 Lower Broadview Rd.   Fax: 970-577-1961
Estes Park, CO 80517   E-mail: riversng@frii.com
MAIL: P.O. Box 1910   Internet: http://www.innbook.com/river.html

RiverSong, a romantic nine-room country Inn, is nestled at the end of a winding country
lane on 30 wooded acres. There are trout streams and ponds, hiking trails and tree swings.
Many of the rooms have breathtaking views of the snowcapped peaks and nearby Rocky
Mountain National Park. After a candlelight dinner prepared by their own chef, guests can
enjoy a whirlpool tub for two in front of a crackling fire. At RiverSong, you'll be lulled to
sleep by the melody of the mountain stream. Picnic backpack lunches prepared by Inns
staff. Small weddings performed by Innkeeper at the Inn or mountain top.

The Baldpate Inn, Ltd.   Phone: 970-586-KEYS
4900 S. Hwy. 7   970-586-6151
P.O. Box 4445
Estes Park, CO 80517

For a classic mountain getaway, The Baldpate Inn offers a unique bed and breakfast experience during the summer and fall. Nestled in the pine forest on the side of Twin Sisters
Mountain, near the Lily Lake Visitors Center of Rocky Mountain National Park. First
opening in 1917, the lodge is built from native hand-hewed timber and includes five massive stone fireplaces. The Inn's spacious front porch and many of the twelve guest rooms
and three cabins command a most spectacular view of the area. All rates include a delightful gourmet breakfast each morning and complimentary snacks in the evening. In January
1996 The Baldpate Inn was listed on the National Register of Historic Places. Located
seven miles south of Estes Park on Colorado route 7.

Woodlands on Fall River   Phone: 800-721-2279 / 970-586-0404
1888 Fall River Road   Fax: 970-586-3297
Estes Park, CO 80517   Internet: www.estes-park.com/woodlands

The Woodlands on Fall River offers all riverfront suites in a dramatic mountain setting.
Amenities include: separate living rooms and bedrooms • kitchens • in-room phones •
cable TV with HBO • VCRs and free video library. Large private decks and patios with
individual gas grills facing river. In-room 2 person spa tub; many suites with jetted bathtubs. Outdoor hot tub on beautifully landscaped grounds. Close to Rocky Mountain National Park. Sorry, no pets. Handicapped accessible.

Ponderosa Pine — Idaho, page 163

Shilo Inn - Boise Airport   Phone: 208-343-7662
4111 Broadway Avenue   800-222-2244
Boise, ID 83705-5302   Fax: 208-344-0318

Located only 1 mile from Boise International Airport, this Shilo Inn offers travelers 125
guestrooms & suites. All rooms feature a microwave • refrigerator • coffee maker • satellite TV with premium channels • VCP and more. Movie rentals are also available. Facili-

ties include an outdoor pool to enjoy during the warmer seasons as well as an indoor spa, sauna, steam room, fitness center and guest laundromat. Amenities include free local calls, USA Today newspaper, continental breakfast and airport shuttle. Meeting space is available for up to 50 people. A restaurant is located adjacent to the hotel.

Shilo Inn - Boise Riverside	Phone:	208-344-3521
3031 Main Street		800-222-2244
Boise, ID 83702-2048	Fax:	208-384-1217

This newly renovated Shilo Inn is located on the banks of the picturesque Boise River which harbors the Greenbelt's 25 miles of hiking and biking trails. All 112 guestrooms are complete with microwave • refrigerator • satellite TV with premium channels • and VCP. Movie rentals are available at front desk. Facilities include an indoor pool, spa, sauna, steam room, fitness center and guest laundromat. Amenities include free local calls, USA Today newspaper, continental breakfast and airport shuttle. Meeting space for up to 75 people is available. A restaurant & lounge is located adjacent to the hotel.

Torrey's Burnt Creek Inn	Phone:	888-838-2313
HC 67, Box 725		
Stanley, ID 83278		

For an enjoyable and relaxing outdoor experience, Torrey's Burnt Creek Inn offers private riverside modern log cabins with kitchenettes and RV hook-ups. On-site amenities include: laundromat • showers • restaurant • convenience store • and gift shop. Guests enjoy great fishing on the Famed River of No Return—Salmon River.

Rim Of The World — California, page 96

Shore Acres Lodge & Vacation Rentals	Phone:	909-866-8200
P.O. Box 110410		800-524-6600
Big Bear Lake, CA 92315	Fax:	909-866-1580

Year-round mountain recreation in a pristine alpine setting tucked away from traffic and big city noises. Established in 1907 as a "Gentlemen's" hunting and fishing lodge, Shore Acres Lodge & Vacation Rentals offers one of the most picturesque spots on Big Bear Lake. Accommodations include eleven classic mountain style cabins, located on 2 pine shaded, lakefront acres where the fish are really biting — two steps to Big Bear Lake or fly fish off your back porch. Guests will also enjoy the clean fresh air, singing birds and the smell of pine and manzanita. Close to shopping • restaurants • ski resorts • golf • and family fun.

Rogue Umpqua / North Umpqua River — Oregon, page 312

Budget 16 Motel	Phone:	541-673-5556
1067 NE Stephens St.		800-414-1648 reservations
Roseburg, OR 97470	Fax:	541-673-7942

One of Roseburg's most reasonable motels. Amenities include: clean rooms • outdoor pool • free cable TV • in-room phones • A/C • and complimentary coffee. Within walking distance to many restaurants. Close to shopping & area attractions. Reasonable daily and weekly rates. Located on Business Loop Hwy. 99 (Stephens Street) between exits 124 and 125 of Interstate 5. For reservations please call 800-414-1648. Visa, MC, AMEX, and Discover cards accepted.

Mountain Country RV Park   Phone: 541-498-2454
117 Elk Ridge Lane   Fax: 541-498-2454
Idleyld Park, OR 97447

Open year round, the Mountain Country RV Park offers campers spectacular scenery and an abundance of nearby recreational opportunities. Facilities include: 25 sites • full hook-ups • 20/30/50 amp • phone • laundry • restrooms • showers • video rentals • horseshoes and volleyball area. Food, gas and supplies are available next door. Area activities include world-class fly fishing and white water on the North Umpqua River, rafting, kayaking, trails, skiing, hot springs and waterfalls. Daily and weekly rates, tenters welcome. Visa, MC, Discover & AMEX credit cards accepted. Located 47 miles east of Roseburg on Hwy. 138 at milepost 47.

Saline Valley — California, page 98

Super 8 Motel - High Sierra Lodge   Phone: 760-873-8426
1005 N. Main St.   Fax: 760-873-8060
Bishop, CA 93514

One of Bishops finest motels. Clean and comfortable rooms equipped with in-room coffee machines, free extended cable with HBO, and refrigerators. Seasonal outdoor pool and year round indoor jacuzzi. Fish cleaning & freezing facilities and BBQ area. Fantastic fishing! Walking distance to outlet mall and dining. AMEX, MC, Visa, and Discover cards accepted. Located on US Hwy. 395 at the north end of town. We appreciate your business.

Salmon River — Idaho, page 165

Torrey's Burnt Creek Inn   Phone: 888-838-2313
HC 67, Box 725
Stanley, ID 83278

For an enjoyable and relaxing outdoor experience, Torrey's Burnt Creek Inn offers private riverside modern log cabins with kitchenettes and RV hook-ups. On-site amenities include: laundromat • showers • restaurant • convenience store •, and gift shop. Guests enjoy great fishing on the Famed River of No Return—Salmon River.

San Juan Skyway — Colorado, page 134

A Bed & Breakfast on Maple Street
102 S. Maple Street
P.O. Box 327
Cortez, CO 81321

Phone: 800-665-3906 / 970-565-3906
Fax: 970-565-2090
E-mail: maple@fone.net
Internet: http://subee.com/maple/home.html

A unique Rocky Mountain log and rock house in downtown Cortez. Inside you'll find a warm western Colorado welcome and a generous helping of hospitality. All rooms offer private baths, queen beds, and air conditioning — Antiques abound. Relax in the gazebo-enclosed hot tub or enjoy the beautiful flower garden. Walking distance to restaurants, shopping or Native Indian Dancing. BIG Appetite? BIG Breakfast! Smoke-free. Rates: $59.00 and up. Ask about discounts.

Anasazi Motor Inn
640 S. Broadway
Cortez, CO 81321

Phone: 970-565-3773
        800-972-6232
Fax: 970-565-1027

The Anasazi Motor Inn, with 90 units, is fully equipped to make your stay in this beautiful area an enjoyable one. Amenities include: restaurant • lounge • heated pool • spa • and conference facilities with a capacity of 300 people. AAA and AARP discounts available. Visa, MC, Discover, AMEX, and Diners Club cards welcomed.

Kelly Place
14663 Road G
Cortez, CO 81321

Phone: 970-565-3125
        800-745-4885
Fax: 970-565-3540

Kelly Place is an outdoor ed center and unique "Bed & Breakfast" near the "Trail of the Ancients", a Colorado Scenic and Historic Byway. The adobe-style lodge and cabins with kitchenettes and fireplaces are located on 100 acres, 10 miles west of Highway 160/666 in red-rock McElmo Canyon.

Purgatory Village Hotel
5 Skier Place
Durango, CO 81301

Phone: 800-693-0175 / 970-247-3397
Fax: 970-382-2248
E-mail: gmpvh@frontier.net
Internet: http://www.creativelinks.com/pvh

A deluxe lodging property located at the base of Purgatory Ski Resort. Accommodations include hotel rooms, studios with kitchenettes, and condominiums with your choice of one, two, and three bedroom units. Among the many amenities is 24 hour front desk service and daily housekeeping. You'll also enjoy a wide variety of outdoor activities. Rated by Condé Nast Traveler magazine as one of the top 40 ski lodging properties in the U.S.!

River House B & B
495 Animas View Dr.
Durango, CO 81301

Phone: 970-247-4775
        800-254-4775
Fax: 970-259-1465

The River House is a large, sprawling, southwestern home facing the Animas River. Guests dine in a large atrium filled with plants, a fountain, and eight skylights. Antiques, art, and artifacts from around the world decorate the seven bedrooms, snooker and music rooms. Enjoy a soak in the hot tub before a relaxing massage or retiring to the living room to watch a favorite video on the large screen TV, and enjoy the warmth of the fire in the beautiful stone and brass fireplace. Comfort, casualness, and fun are the themes at River House.

Riversbend Bed & Breakfast   Phone: 970-533-7353
42505 Hwy. 160   800-699-8994
Mancos, CO 81328   Internet: http://subee.com/rb/home.html

Located on the San Juan Skyway just 7 miles from Mesa Verde National Park, Riversbend provides a central location for exploring Southwestern Colorado. The two-story log inn is nestled under tall Cottonwood trees on the bank of the Mancos River. The loft-style guest rooms and entire inn are comfortably furnished with antiques and quilts reflecting the ease and simplicity of days gone by. Guests enjoy the porch swings, wooden rockers, and relaxing in the hot tub. Riversbend offers 2 common areas where guests can relax in conversation with other guests or simply enjoy a good book. Innkeepers Gaye & Jack Curran look forward to meeting you. "Where hospitality is a way of life."

Tomahawk Lodge   Phone: 970-565-8521
728 South Broadway   800-643-7705
Cortez, CO 81321   Fax: 970-564-9793

The Tomahawk Lodge welcomes travelers with 39 clean, cozy rooms. Economy rates • coffee around the clock • swimming pool • cinemax • and free local calls. Near restaurants, stores, and all major attractions.

Sandia Crest Road — New Mexico, page 255

Sandia Mountain Hostel   Phone: 505-281-4117
12234 Hwy. 14 N.
Cedar Crest, NM 87047

Sandia Mountain Hostel is a passive solar building on the Turquoise Trail only 10 miles east of Albuquerque. Located in a peaceful rural setting close to hiking, biking, climbing, and skiing. The Cibola National Forest is across the street and nearby you'll find ghost towns and ancient Indian pueblos. Dorm beds are $10.00 a night, private rooms are $25.00 per night.

Santa Fe — New Mexico, page 257

Residence Inn by Marriott   Phone: 505-988-7300
1698 Galisteo St.   Fax: 505-988-3243
Santa Fe, NM 87505

Relax in comfort at Residence Inn — the All Suite hotel. Spacious living room area with fireplace and a fully equipped kitchen. Complimentary deluxe continental breakfast and newspaper daily. Voice mail and extended stay discounts are available. Only minutes (1½ miles) from historic plaza and 18 miles to ski resort.

Sawtooth — Idaho, page 167

Torrey's Burnt Creek Inn   Phone: 888-838-2313
HC 67, Box 725
Stanley, ID 83278

For an enjoyable and relaxing outdoor experience, Torrey's Burnt Creek Inn offers private riverside modern log cabins with kitchenettes and RV hook-ups. On-site amenities include: laundromat • showers • restaurant • convenience store • and gift shop. Guests enjoy great fishing on the Famed River of No Return—Salmon River.

Seaway Trail — New York, page 263

The Vineyard Motel & Restaurant   Phone: 1-888-DUNKIRK
3929 Vineyard Drive   716-366-4400
Dunkirk, NY 14048   Fax: 716-366-3375

The Vineyard Motel offers 39 newly renovated rooms — AAA Approved — and one of western New York's finest restaurants with lounge and coffee shop. Located only 700 yards from I-90 at exit 59, tollbooth.

Seminoe To Alcova — Wyoming, page 422

Royal Inn Motel   Phone: 307-234-3501
Aries Car Rental & Western Union   Fax: 307-234-7340
440 East "A" Street
Casper, WY 82601

The Royal Inn Motel offers travelers a convenient location in the business district of downtown Casper. Located in a well lighted quiet area — accommodations include 37 rooms, 3 with kitchenettes, and an outside swimming pool. Complimentary coffee in the morning. Nearby, guests will find theaters, banks, restaurants, airport, and post office. Only 15 minutes from Casper Mountain Ski Area. Reasonable rates. All major credit cards welcome. From I-25 travel south on Centre Street, turn left on "A" Street.

Seward Highway — Alaska, page 26

The Taroka Inn Motel   Phone: 907-224-8975
235 3rd Avenue
P.O. Box 2448
Seward, AK 99664

Clean units with equipped kitchens, private bathrooms, and queen beds. Can accommodate one to nine persons. Conveniently located one block from Alaska Sealife Center. Great Rates! Please call for brochure or reservations.

Sierra Vista — California, page 100

High Sierra RV   Phone: 209-683-7662
40389 Hwy. 41
Oakhurst, CA 93644

Camp along the river in rustic mountain atmosphere with all the amenities of full hook-ups, yet within easy walking distance to shopping, restaurants, and theaters. Only 17 miles to Yosemite National Park. Facilities & Features include: hot showers • phone hook-ups • RV dump • laundry room • bathrooms • pay phone • fishing • swimming • picnic tables • cable TV hook-ups • 30 amp service • city water & sewer. Rates from $15.00 to $25.00 per night. Weekly and monthly rates available. From the junction of Hwy. 41 & 49, travel north 0.4 miles on Hwy. 41 and enter right on Golden Oak Loop at the "High Sierra RV" sign.

Shilo Inn - Oakhurst / Yosemite   Phone: 209-683-3555
40644 Highway 41   800-222-2244
Oakhurst, CA 93644-9621   Fax: 209-683-3386

Located at the Southern Gateway to Yosemite National Park, Bass Lake, and Badger Pass Ski Area, this Shilo Inn offers travelers 80 mini-suites. All rooms are complete with a microwave • refrigerator • wet bar • and satellite TV with premium channels. VCR and movie rentals are also available. Facilities include an outdoor heated pool and spa for use during the warmer seasons as well as a sauna, steam room, fitness center and guest laundromat. Amenities include free local calls, USA Today newspaper and continental breakfast. Meeting space is available. A restaurant is located adjacent to the hotel.

Silver Thread Highway — Colorado, page 137

Foothills Lodge   Phone: 719-873-5969
0035 Silver Thread Lane   800-510-3897 reservations
P.O. Box 264   Fax: 719-873-5969
South Fork, CO 81154-0264   E-mail: fhlodge@rmii.com

A relaxing—great escape! Choose from modern log cabins with aspen paneling, kitchens and woodburning fireplaces or uniquely decorated lodge apartments. Rooms with one to two bedrooms and anywhere from one queen size bed to four double beds — accommodating up to eight people. You'll enjoy hot showers, fresh towels daily, cable TV, phones, and indoor hot tub. Outdoor recreation includes hunting • skiing • snowmobiling • sightseeing • and Gold Medal fishing in the Rio Grande. Adjacent to the lodge you can enjoy a good meal at the Hungry Logger Restaurant or Croaker's Saloon. Located on Hwy. 160 (milepost 160), at the south end of town.

Smithsonian Butte — Utah, page 377

Snow Family Guest Ranch B & B   Phone: 801-635-2500
633 E. Hwy. 9   800-308-SNOW (7669)
Virgin, UT 84779   Fax: 801-635-2758

This beautiful horse ranch lies under the shadows of Zion National Park. Nine beautifully
decorated ranch-style rooms, all with private baths. Enjoy: common rooms for reading,
relaxing or watching TV; outdoor pool, spa, gazebo, and pond. Clean private atmosphere,
perfect for a peaceful get away, a true haven for the weary traveler. Western hospitality at
its finest. Your stay includes a full cooked breakfast and a light refreshment each afternoon. Close to hiking, biking, golf, and historic sites. Guided trail rides are also available.
Your hosts: Steve & Shelley Penrose. We look forward to your visit! MC • Visa • DISC •
AMEX, accepted.

Snowy Range Highway — Wyoming, page 424

Olde Depot Bed & Breakfast   Phone: 307-327-5277
201 N. 1st Street, Box 604   Fax: 307-327-5230
Riverside, WY 82325

Completely renovated train depot from the Saratoga Encampment Rail Road. Choose
from three relaxing and comfortable rooms, all with private baths. A mixture of
antique and replica furniture — 100 year old copper tub • Victorian clawfoot tub •
jacuzzi spa tub — provides a unique theme for each room. A hot tub is also available
for guests. Located in the Upper Platte River Valley between the Sierra Madre and
Snowy Range Mountains. Only 5 miles from snowmobile & cross country ski trails.
Only 100 yards to the Encampment River offering blue ribbon trout fishing.

Silver Moon Motel   Phone: 307-326-5974
412 E. Bridge St.
P.O. Box 929
Saratoga, WY 82331

A convenient location close to the main downtown area and the town's natural hot springs.
All rooms at the Silver Moon Motel provide guests with color cable TV and phones. Only
20 minutes from the beautiful mountains where you will find winter cross country and
snowmobile trails. Great fishing is only 1 block away in the North Platte River.

Snowy Mountain Lodge   Phone: 307-742-7669
P.O. Box 151   Fax: 307-742-7669
Centennial, WY 82055

Located in the Medicine Bow National Forest, nestled between two mountain streams, the
Snowy Mountain Lodge offers 15 rustic log cabins rich with 70 years of wild west history.
The cabins vary in size and can accommodate one to 16 people. The summers offer an
incredible outdoor experience with unrivaled scenery. 200 different varieties of wild flowers await your arrival as do the fish in the surrounding beaver ponds and streams. Other

summer activities include hiking, rock climbing, mountain biking, or just plain old out the car window photography. In the winter, right outside our front door is the trail head of 280 miles of groomed snowmobile trails and pristine cross country ski trails. Just 2 miles down the road is a first class down hill ski resort. Guests are invited to the main lodge to warm up with a mug of hot cocoa by the roaring fire in the big stone fireplace and savor the delicacies of fine dining in the full service restaurant. Open year-round.

South Bighorn / Red Wall — Wyoming, page 426

Royal Inn Motel
Aries Car Rental & Western Union
440 East "A" Street
Casper, WY 82601

Phone: 307-234-3501
Fax: 307-234-7340

The Royal Inn Motel offers travelers a convenient location in the business district of downtown Casper. Located in a well lighted quiet area — accommodations include 37 rooms, 3 with kitchenettes, and an outside swimming pool. Complimentary coffee in the morning. Nearby, guests will find theaters, banks, restaurants, airport, and post office. Only 15 minutes from Casper Mountain Ski Area. Reasonable rates. All major credit cards welcome. From I-25 travel south on Centre Street, turn left on "A" Street.

Spearfish Canyon — South Dakota, page 330

Days Inn
68 Main Street
Deadwood, SD 57732

Phone: 605-578-3476
             800-526-8277
Fax: 605-578-2788

Getting a good nights sleep shouldn't be something you gamble on — even in Deadwood, South Dakota! The Days Inn in Deadwood is always a sure bet if you're looking for a comfortable clean room and quiet privacy. All the rooms are newly remodeled and offer free color cable TV and free local calls. When you get an appetite the Days Inn restaurant features a $4.99 filet mignon diner, leaving enough change in your pocket to try your luck in one of the 28 slot machines.

Stevens Pass — Washington, page 398

AlpenRose Inn
500 Alpine Place
Leavenworth, WA 98826

Phone: 509-548-3000
             800-582-2474

This small European Inn offers 15 individualized decorated rooms with fireplaces, some with balconies, and jacuzzi suites. Within walking distance to Bavarian town of Leavenworth. Your stay includes a full breakfast and delicious dessert in the evening. Close to hiking, golf, and cross country skiing. Amenities include cable TV • phones • swimming pool • hot tub • and large decks. AAA ◆◆◆. Age restriction, non-smoking, and no pets.

Enzian Inn   Phone: 509-548-5269
590 Hwy. 2   800-223-8511
Leavenworth, WA 98826   Fax: 509-548-5269

One of Leavenworth's most authentic and beautiful Bavarian Inns. The 104 guest rooms
are complete with imported European furnishings and cozy down comforters. Elegant suites
with canopy bed, spa, and fireplace. You'll enjoy complimentary breakfast buffet • indoor
& outdoor pools • hot tubs • racquetball court • ping pong table • exercise room • x-country
ski equipment • and 18 hole championship putting course.

SkyRiver Inn   Phone: 360-677-2261
333 River Drive East   800-367-8194 (WA)
P.O. Box 280
Skykomish, WA 98288

For riverside lodging in the heart of the Cascades, SkyRiver Inn offers travelers a quiet,
scenic location on the Skykomish River. Guests enjoy immediate access to river across
well kept lawn, surrounded by trees and mountains. Close to whitewater rafting and Stevens
Pass skiing. Major credit cards accepted.

Tioga - Big Oak Flat — California, page 108

Marble Quarry RV Park   Phone: 209-532-9539
11551 Yankee Hill Rd.   Fax: 209-532-8631
P.O. Box 850
Columbia, CA 95310

A clean, family oriented, haven for an enjoyable camping experience — shade trees
galore. Short walking distance to historic Columbia or old quarry. Central location for
caves • museums • movies • railroad • fishing • boating • antique shopping • restaurants •
and much more.

The Groveland Hotel   Phone: 209-962-4000
18767 Main St.   Fax: 209-962-6674
P.O. Box 289   E-mail: peggy@groveland.com
Groveland, CA 95321   Internet: www.groveland.com

The Groveland Hotel provides you with a magnificent setting — from the most delightful
lodging and sumptuous dining to enjoying your favorite outdoor activities and revisiting
California's historic past. A gracious restoration with antiques, down comforters and private baths, complete with foothills hospitality. In addition to all the comforts of Grandma's
House, nearby amenities include golf • tennis • swimming • world class white-water rafting • horseback riding • fishing • and hiking. The town of Groveland offers great little
shops for browsing and antiquing. The walking tour of town will guide you through some
of the Gold Rush era's most historic areas. Only 23 miles from Yosemite.

Trail Ridge & Beaver Meadow Roads — Colorado, page 139

Romantic RiverSong Inn
1765 Lower Broadview Rd.
Estes Park, CO 80517
MAIL: P.O. Box 1910

Phone: 970-586-4666
Fax: 970-577-1961
E-mail: riversng@frii.com
Internet: http://www.innbook.com/river.html

RiverSong, a romantic nine-room country Inn, is nestled at the end of a winding country lane on 30 wooded acres. There are trout streams and ponds, hiking trails and tree swings. Many of the rooms have breathtaking views of the snowcapped peaks and nearby Rocky Mountain National Park. After a candlelight dinner prepared by their own chef, guests can enjoy a whirlpool tub for two in front of a crackling fire. At RiverSong, you'll be lulled to sleep by the melody of the mountain stream. Picnic backpack lunches prepared by Inns staff. Small weddings performed by Innkeeper at the Inn or mountain top.

The Baldpate Inn, Ltd.
4900 S. Hwy. 7
P.O. Box 4445
Estes Park, CO 80517

Phone: 970-586-KEYS
            970-586-6151

For a classic mountain getaway, The Baldpate Inn offers a unique bed and breakfast experience during the summer and fall. Nestled in the pine forest on the side of Twin Sisters Mountain, near the Lily Lake Visitors Center of Rocky Mountain National Park. First opening in 1917, the lodge is built from native hand-hewed timber and includes five massive stone fireplaces. The Inn's spacious front porch and many of the twelve guest rooms and three cabins command a most spectacular view of the area. All rates include a delightful gourmet breakfast each morning and complimentary snacks in the evening. In January 1996 The Baldpate Inn was listed on the National Register of Historic Places. Located seven miles south of Estes Park on Colorado route 7.

Victoria Cottages
P.O. Box 14
Grand Lake, CO 80447

Phone: 970-627-8027
Fax: 970-627-8027
E-mail: VictoriaCottages@juno.com

Victoria Cottages offers two romantic getaways bordering the Rocky Mountain National Park. Victoria Cottage — nestled in the pines with a view of Grand Lake has story-book charm. Victorian Elegance in a beautifully furnished, cozy two room log cottage. Guests can walk to town on the north shore of Grand Lake. Trails End — a cedar sided cabin tucked among the trees beside acres of horse pasture with a grand view of the Never Summer Mountain Range. Offers all the comforts of home in breathtaking surroundings. Both are close to horseback rides, restaurants, hiking, miniature golf and activities for the kids.

Woodlands on Fall River
1888 Fall River Road
Estes Park, CO 80517

Phone: 800-721-2279 / 970-586-0404
Fax: 970-586-3297
Internet: www.estes-park.com/woodlands

The Woodlands on Fall River offers all riverfront suites in a dramatic mountain setting.

Amenities include: separate living rooms and bedrooms • kitchens • in-room phones • cable TV with HBO • VCRs and free video library. Large private decks and patios with individual gas grills facing river. In-room 2 person spa tub; many suites with jetted bathtubs. Outdoor hot tub on beautifully landscaped grounds. Close to Rocky Mountain National Park. Sorry, no pets. Handicapped accessible.

White Mountain Scenic Highway — Arizona, page 46

Bonanza Motel   Phone: 520-367-4440
858 E. White Mtn. Blvd.
Pinetop, AZ 85935

A beautiful location surrounded by large Ponderosa Pine trees, the Bonanza Motel offers travelers spacious rooms and friendly service with reasonable rates. Your stay includes free coffee, tea and hot chocolate on weekends. Nearby outdoor recreational activities are abundant in the Sitgreaves and Apache National Forests.

White Mountain Lodge   Phone: 520-735-7568
140 Main St.   Fax: 520-735-7498
P.O. Box 143
Greer, AZ 85927

Enjoy a stay in this charming 1892 country home on the banks of the Little Colorado River in the hamlet of Greer — at 8,500 feet in the heart of Arizona's beautiful White Mountain recreation area. Remodeled in 1993-95, all rooms are individually decorated and include private baths and king or queen size beds. Full housekeeping cabins are also available. Your stay includes full breakfast with homebaked goods, and the cookie jar is always full. You can also enjoy great hiking and horseback riding.

White Pass — Washington, page 400

Game Ridge Motel & Lodge   Phone: 800-301-9354
27350 U.S. Hwy. 12   509-672-2212
Rimrock, WA 98937   Fax: 509-672-2242

Located on White Pass Highway (Hwy. 12) the *eastern gateway* to Mt. Rainier National Park and Mt. St. Helens National Volcanic Monument. Nestled on the banks of the Tieton River in the beautiful Wenatchee National Forest. Excellent hiking, climbing, hunting, stream fishing and white water rafting are just outside the motel, with lake fishing, waterskiing and windsurfing on nearby Rimrock Lake. You'll enjoy: cabins with private hot tubs • heated pool • riverside hot tub and steam room • fireside recreation room • TV's • Bar-B-Ques • horseshoes • excellent cross-country and downhill skiing • RV spaces • all facilities nearby • group, senior, and weekly rates • and friendly service.

Wyoming Centennial — Wyoming, page 428

Dornan's Spur Ranch Cabins
10 Moose St.
P.O. Box 39
Moose, WY 83012

Phone: 307-733-2522
Fax: 307-733-3544
E-mail: spur@sisna.com
Internet: http://www.sisna.com/jackson/
             dornan/spur1.htm

Dornan's Spur Ranch Cabins is located just inside Grand Teton National Park next to the Snake River providing great views of the Teton Mountains. Accommodations include 8 one-bedroom and 4 two-bedroom housekeeping cabins with full kitchens. A grocery store, gift shop, wine shop, deli, sports shop and restaurant are all located on-site. Other services available include: scenic or whitewater float trips • sportswear and equipment shop for climbing, hiking, camping, and cross-country skiing • fishing tackle shop with guided fishing trips • rentals of mountain bikes and canoes. No pets—No TV's—No smoking.

Elk Refuge Inn
1755 N. Hwy. 89
P.O. Box 2834
Jackson, WY 83001

Phone: 800-544-3582
            307-733-3582
Fax: 307-733-6531

Nestled in a scenic area 1 mile north of Jackson offering fabulous views of National Elk Refuge and Jackson Hole mountains. Accommodations include 23 modern rooms, 11 with kitchens and private balconies. Non-smoking and king rooms also available. All rooms have phones, cable TV, tub and shower. Facilities include: at door parking • winter plug-ins • horse corrals • and trailer parking. Near airport, skiing, golf courses, Teton and Yellowstone National Parks. Some pets allowed. Reasonable rates. For reservations call 800-544-3582. Your business is appreciated.

Lakeside Lodge Resort & Marina
Fremont Lake
P.O. Box 1819
Pinedale, WY 82941

Phone: 307-367-2221
Fax: 307-367-2221

Lakeside Lodge is located on Fremont Lake in the Wind River Mountains. The fifteen acre resort includes a marina, cabins, RV Park, and restaurant & lounge. The lake area offers a wide range of outdoor recreational activities for the entire family. A few of the activities guests can enjoy include: boating • fishing • skiing • hiking • wildlife observations • and golf nearby.

Pine Creek Ranch
#17 Bert Drive, Box 548
Pinedale, WY 82941

Phone: 307-367-2544
            307-367-6887

For a special retreat, the Pine Creek Ranch offers a cozy cabin, built around 1900, on the bank of Pine Creek. The cabin has been completely renovated and filled with antiques and western decor. Pine Creek Ranch offers a full kitchen, one bath, 3 bedrooms, large living area, fireplace, and peace & quiet. Abundant wildlife on property. Located just a moment from Pinedale, and a short distance from many recreational opportunities. Family rates available. Visa and MC accepted.

The Chambers House Bed & Breakfast	Phone:	800-567-2168
111 W. Magnolia St.		307-367-2168
Pinedale, WY 82941	Fax:	307-367-4209

The Chambers House is a historic log home recently renovated and decorated with a mixture of antiques and new furniture. The elegant home offers fireplaces in some rooms, private and semi-private bathrooms, sitting rooms, and a formal dining room. Located in a "real" small western town, Pinedale offers all the civilization one needs. It's the gateway to the Wind River Mountains and Bridger Teton National Forest.

Yuba Donner — California, page 114

Coachland RV Park	Phone:	916-587-3071
10500 Highway 89 North	Fax:	916-587-6976
Truckee, CA 96161		

Coachland RV Park offers a quiet and relaxing environment on 55 acres of pines in the clean crisp air of the High Sierras. Facilities include 131 full hook-up pull through RV spaces with cable TV. On-site laundry, restrooms, and picnic tables. Historical downtown Truckee with it's fine restaurants and shops is within walking distance. Nearby attractions and activities include: golf courses • major ski resorts • Nevada casinos • excellent fishing in numerous lakes and rivers • Lake Tahoe • hiking • mountain biking • river rafting • mines and museums of "The Gold Country". Open all year. Only ¼ mile from I-80.

INDEX